Strategic Environmental Assessment and Land Use Planning

Strategic Environmental Assessment and Land Use Planning

An International Evaluation

Edited by
Carys Jones, Mark Baker, Jeremy Carter, Stephen Jay,
Michael Short and Christopher Wood

EARTHSCAN

London • Sterling, VA

First published by Earthscan in the UK and USA in 2005

ISBN: 1-84407-110-3 paperback
       1-84407-109-X hardback

Typesetting by JS Typesetting Ltd, Porthcawl, Mid Glamorgan
Printed and bound in the UK by Bath Press, Bath
Cover design by Yvonne Booth

For a full list of publications please contact:

Earthscan
8–12 Camden High Street
London, NW1 0JH, UK
Tel: +44 (0)20 7387 8558
Fax: +44 (0)20 7387 8998
Email: earthinfo@earthscan.co.uk
Web: **www.earthscan.co.uk**

22883 Quicksilver Drive, Sterling, VA 20166-2012, USA

Earthscan is an imprint of James and James (Science Publishers) Ltd and publishes in association with the International Institute for Environment and Development

A catalogue record for this book is available from the British Library

Library of Congress Cataloging-in-Publication Data

Strategic environmental assessment and land use planning: an international evaluation
/ edited by Carys Jones . . . [et al.].
     p. cm.
   Includes bibliographical references and index.
   ISBN 1-84407-109-X (alk. paper) — ISBN 1-84407-110-3 (pbk. : alk. paper) 1.
Environmental impact analysis. 2. Strategic planning—Environmental aspects. 3. Land
use—Planning—Environmental aspects. 4. Environmental impact analysis—Case studies.
5. Strategic planning—Environmental aspects—Case studies. 6. Land use—Planning—
Environmental aspects—Case studies. I. Jones, Carys E., 1960–
   TD194.6.S773 2005
   333.71′4—dc22

                                                          2005015717

Contents

List of Figures, Tables and Boxes

Figures

Tables

Boxes

List of Contributors

Kulsum Ahmed is team leader of the Institutions and Governance Programme in the Environment Department of the World Bank. She has considerable experience as an operations task manager and led the team that prepared the Bank's first environment policy reform loan. This seeks to integrate environmental issues, including strategic environmental assessment (SEA), in key sectors of the Mexican economy. Email: kahmed4@worldbank.org

Elvis Au is the assistant director of the Environmental Protection Department of the Hong Kong Special Administrative Region Government. He was the President of the International Association for Impact Assessment (IAIA) in 2001. He has written numerous publications about environmental assessment (EA) in Hong Kong. Since 1993, he has been in charge of the development and application of SEA to major policies and strategies. Email: elvis_au@hk.super.net

Mark Baker is senior lecturer in planning policy and practice within the School of Environment and Development at the University of Manchester. He is a chartered town planner with previous professional planning experience in UK local and central government. His teaching and research interests focus on the operation of the UK planning system, especially regional and strategic planning and the role of SEA. Email: m.baker@manchester.ac.uk

Ronald Bass is a legal and regulatory specialist with Jones and Stokes, a Californian-based consulting firm specializing in environmental planning and natural resources management. His areas of expertise are in environmental impact assessment (EIA), land use planning and environmental law. He is the author of several books on EIA. He has also taught environmental law under the US Fulbright Scholar Programme. Email: rbass@jsanet.com

Jeremy Carter is a research associate at the School of Environment and Development, University of Manchester. His research focuses on environmental planning and management theory and practice, particularly appraisal procedures and stakeholder participation. His doctoral thesis explored the effect of appraisal procedures on the preparation of English land use plans. Email: jeremy.carter@ manchester.ac.uk

Aleg Cherp is an associate professor at the Central European University in Budapest. His research and numerous publications are focused on EIA and SEA, sustainable development and environmental history in countries in transition. He is also involved in the Swedish MiSt research programme on tools for EA in strategic decision making. Email: cherpa@ceu.hu

Jennifer Dixon is professor of planning at the University of Auckland. Her research interests include urban intensification and sustainable design, urban governance and new forms of housing, and SEA. She has written extensively on EA in New Zealand. Her current research projects focus on low-impact urban design and the management of intensive housing. Email: j.dixon@auckand.ac.nz

Bo Elling is a professor at the Department of Environment, Technology and Social Studies at Roskilde University. His research focuses on modern society, environmental planning and regulation, with particular emphases on SEA for land use planning, SEA at the policy level, and the knowledge and rationality that public participation brings to the SEA process. Email: be@ruc.dk

Thomas B. Fischer is senior lecturer in environmental planning in the Department of Civic Design, University of Liverpool. After working as a consultant and public servant on EIA in Germany from 1990 to 1995 he gained a PhD in SEA from the University of Manchester in 1999. Since then, he has researched, trained and published extensively on SEA. Email: fischer@liverpool.ac.uk

Monica L. C. Fundingsland has specialized in EA through her professional experience as a consultant and researcher within industry and academia. She is currently completing her PhD thesis on the SEA of English transport plans, with particular focus on SEA monitoring, quality control and integration into decision making, at the School of Environment and Development, University of Manchester. Email: mlc_fundingsland@yahoo.co.uk

Tuija Hilding-Rydevik is a senior researcher at the Nordic Centre for Spatial Development (Nordregio, Stockholm) and an associate professor at the Royal Institute of Technology. She has undertaken EIA and SEA research since the mid-1980s. Her main research interest is the integration of environmental perspectives in planning and programming processes (e.g. land use, regional economic development). Email: tuija.hilding-rydevik@nordregio.se

Stephen Jay is a senior lecturer in environmental management at Sheffield Hallam University. He previously taught environmental planning, EIA and SEA at the University of Manchester. He has research interests in the role of SEA within the private sector, especially privatized utilities (with a particular focus on the electricity industry). Email: s.a.jay@shu.ac.uk

Carys Jones is senior lecturer in environmental planning, School of Environment and Development, University of Manchester. She is co-director of the EIA Centre and co-editor of *Impact Assessment and Project Appraisal*. She has undertaken numerous research projects on environmental assessment and has published extensively on EIA and SEA. Email: carys.jones@manchester.ac.uk

Kin Che Lam is professor and head of the Department of Geography and Resource Management at the Chinese University of Hong Kong, and current chairman of the Advisory Council on the Environment of the Hong Kong Special Administrative Region. His teaching and research interests include EIA and SEA in Hong Kong and China. Email: kinchelam@cuhk.edu.hk

Jean-Roger Mercier is lead environmental assessment specialist at the World Bank. He has extensive private and public sector environmental assessment and management experience. He manages the Bank's safeguard policies training and capacity building programme and assists Kulsum Ahmed in analytical work on SEA. He received the IAIA Rose-Hulman Award in 2004. Email: jmercier@world bank.org

Maria Rosário Partidário is an assistant professor at the New University of Lisbon. She has extensive experience of research projects, delivering SEA training programmes, consultancy work and publishing on SEA. She is currently book review co-editor of *Impact Assessment and Project Appraisal*. She was IAIA president in 1997 and received the IAIA Individual Award for her work on SEA in 2002. Email: mp@fct.unl.pt

Francois Retief is a lecturer at the School of Environmental Sciences and Development, North West University (Potchefstroom Campus). He is currently undertaking PhD research at the University of Manchester on the quality and effectiveness of SEA within the South African context. Previously, he worked in the private sector as a town planning and environmental consultant. Email: ggffpr@puknet.puk.ac.za

Nigel Rossouw is an environmental manager with TCTA, a South African liability management body for bulk water supply development. He previously worked at the Council for Scientific and Industrial Research (CSIR), where he conducted research, consultancy and training on EA, particularly SEA. He is currently registered at Stellenbosch University for a PhD on SEA and public policy. Email: nrossouw@tcta.co.uk

Barry Sadler is an adviser on impact assessment and sustainability appraisal to a number of international organizations. He was involved in preparatory work leading to the SEA system in Canada and has been active in the field since then. He is the author of numerous EIA and SEA publications and was the recipient of the IAIA Rose-Hulman Award in 1996. Email: bsadler01@aol.com

Paul Scott is an environmental consultant with Robertson and Associates based in Dublin, Ireland. Previously with Environmental Resources Management Ireland, he was responsible for the development of a SEA methodology for plans and programmes in Ireland for the Environmental Protection Agency, advised local and central government on the requirements of the SEA Directive and has lectured widely on the implications of the SEA Directive in Ireland.
Email: paul.scott@rassociates.net

Michael Short is a chartered planner and conservation officer with professional experience in local government, the private sector and research experience in the SEA of land use plans. He is currently undertaking research on the impact of tall buildings on the built heritage for a PhD at the School of Environment and Development, University of Manchester. Email: michael.j.short@manchester.ac.uk

Gábor Szarvas is managing director of Environmental Resources Management Hungária. He is also undertaking environmental management research for a PhD at the School of Environment and Development, University of Manchester. He was an international policy fellow at the Centre for Policy Studies of the Central European University in 2003–2004. Email: Gabor.Szarvas@erm.com

Wil Thissen is professor and head of policy analysis at the Faculty of Technology, Policy and Management, Delft University of Technology. He has co-organized SEA sessions at several IAIA conferences, and edited a special issue of *Impact Assessment and Project Appraisal* on SEA. His current research concentrates on dealing with uncertainties, and on theory development at the interface of impact assessment and policy making. Email: w.a.h.thissen@tbm.tudelft.nl

Rob van der Heijden is professor in spatial planning at Radboud University, Nijmegen and part-time professor in transport and logistics at the Delft University of Technology. He is a member of the Dutch EIA Commission. His research concentrates on issues of infrastructure planning and decision making, transport innovation and urban and regional development. Email: r.vanderheijden@nsm.kun.nl

Christopher Wood is professor of environmental planning and co-director of the EIA Centre, School of Environment and Development, University of Manchester. He is co-editor of *Impact Assessment and Project Appraisal*. He has researched and taught EIA and SEA for 30 years and received the IAIA Rose-Hulman Award in 2003 'for a lifetime of excellence in promoting impact assessment'.
Email: chris.wood@manchester.ac.uk

Acknowledgements

First and foremost, we would like to thank all the contributing authors most sincerely for sharing their expertise, for submitting their drafts (mostly) on schedule and for their forebearance throughout the subsequent tortuous editing process. Without them there would be no book.

All the five editorial chapters were co-written. Jeremy Carter wrote the first draft of much of the content of Chapters 1 and 2. All the remaining chapters (4–14, 16 and 17) were co-edited. Five of the editorial team are indebted to Michael Short for his administrative contribution. He managed the convoluted editing process (and countless chapter drafts) from start to finish and kept the rest of us, and the authors, on track, earning many colourful epithets in the process.

The editors wish to thank Andries van der Walt for his dedication in providing copy-editing support (and much more) throughout the editing process. He is a lecturer in the School of Environmental Sciences and Development, North-West University, South Africa, who has been seconded to undertake a PhD on environmental assessment at the University of Manchester. We are also indebted to Juliana Smart, Technician in the School of Environment and Development, University of Manchester, for her expertise in formatting the figures used in the book.

Figure 15.1 is Crown copyright material and is reproduced with the permission of the controller of Her Majesty's Stationery Office and the Queen's Printer for Scotland.

Carys Jones, Mark Baker, Jeremy Carter, Stephen Jay, Michael Short and
Christopher Wood

List of Acronyms and Abbreviations

ACE	Advisory Council on the Environment (Hong Kong)
AEE	assessment of environmental effects
APA	Administrative Procedures Act (US)
BC	British Columbia
BLM	US Bureau of Land Management
CDC	city development concept (Hungary)
CDP	county development plan (Ireland)
CEA	country environmental analysis
CEAA	Canadian Environmental Assessment Agency
CEC	Commission of the European Communities
CEQ	Council on Environmental Quality (US)
CESD	Commissioner for Environment and Sustainable Development
CFR	Code of Federal Regulations
CPP	consultation and public participation
CSIR	Council for Scientific and Industrial Research
CTS3	Third Comprehensive Transport Study
DCP	detailed comprehensive plan
DDDA	Dublin Docks Development Authority (Ireland)
DDP	detailed development plan
DEAT	Department of Environmental Affairs and Tourism (South Africa)
DETR	Department of the Environment, Transport and the Regions (UK)
DGOTDU	Direcção-Geral do Ordenamento do Território e Desenvolvimento Urbano (Portugal)
DLA	Department of Land Affairs (South Africa)
DOE	Department of the Environment (UK)
DoEHLG	Department of the Environment, Heritage and Local Government (Ireland)
DPA	development permission area
DPL	development policy lending
DPP	detailed development plan
EA	environmental assessment/environmental appraisal (UK)
EC	European Commission
EIA	environmental impact assessment

EIS	environmental impact statement
EPA	Environmental Protection Agency (Ireland)
EPD	Environmental Protection Department
EU	European Union
FONSI	finding of no significant impact
GEF	Global Environment Facility
GIS	geographical information systems
HKSARG	Hong Kong Special Administrative Region Government
HMSO	Her Majesty's Stationery Office (UK)
IA	impact assessment
IAIA	International Association for Impact Assessment
IBRD	International Bank for Reconstruction and Development
IDA	International Development Association
IDP	integrated development planning
IDZ	industrial development zone
IEM	integrated environmental management
km	kilometre
LAP	local area plan (Ireland)
LDF	local development framework
LGA	Local Government Act (New Zealand)
LPA	local planning authority
MCP	municipal comprehensive plan
MDG	Millennium Development Goal
MEP	municipal environmental programme
MfE	Ministry for the Environment (New Zealand)
MLA	Ministry of Agriculture and Land Affairs (South Africa)
MTvSz	Magyar Természetvédők Szövetsége (Hungarian Association of Nature Conservationists)
MW	megawatt
NBI	Nile Basin Initiative
NDP	National Development Plan (Ireland)
NEMA	National Environmental Management Act (South Africa)
NEPA	National Environmental Policy Act (US)
NGO	non-governmental organization
NIMBY	not in my back yard
NIMTO	not in my term of office
NMCA	National Marine Conservation Area
NPS	National Park Service (US)
NRTEE	National Round Table on the Environment and the Economy
NSS	National Spatial Strategy (Ireland)
OD	operational directive
ODP	outline development plan
ODPM	Office of the Deputy Prime Minister (UK)
OP	operational policy
OZP	outline zoning plan (Hong Kong)
PBA	Planning and Building Act (Sweden)

PEIS	programmatic environmental impact statement
PPP	policy, plan and/or programme
PSIA	poverty and social impact analysis
RCEP	Royal Commission on Environmental Pollution (UK)
RDS2	Second Railway Development Study
REA	regional environmental assessment
REC	Regional Environmental Center for Central and Eastern Europe
RMA	Resource Management Act (New Zealand)
ROP	Operational Programme on Regional Development
RPG	regional planning guideline (Ireland)
SA	sustainability appraisal/social analysis (World Bank)
SAR	Special Administrative Region
SD	sustainable development
SDF	spatial development framework
SDI	spatial development initiative
SDZ	strategic development zone (Ireland)
SEA	strategic environmental assessment
SEIS	supplemental environmental impact statement (US)
SEMP	strategic environmental management plan (South Africa)
SI	statutory instrument
SOER	state of the environment reporting
TDS	Territorial Development Strategy (Hong Kong)
TDSR	Territorial Development Strategy Review
TEA	transboundary environmental analysis
UK	United Kingdom
UNCED	United Nations Conference on Environment and Development
UNDP	United Nations Development Programme
UNECE	United Nations Economic Commission for Europe
US	United States of America
USFLIS	US Fish and Wildlife Service
VÁTI	Hungarian Agency for Regional Development and Country Planning
VROM	Ministry of Housing, Spatial Planning and Environment
VVM	environmental impact assessment (Denmark)
WB	World Bank
WCED	World Commission on Environment and Development
WCOEEAP	West Coast Offshore Exploration Environmental Assessment Panel
WMB	Wet Milieubeheer (Environmental Management Act) (The Netherlands)
WWF	Worldwide Fund for Nature

1

Introduction

*Carys Jones, Mark Baker, Jeremy Carter, Stephen Jay,
Michael Short and Christopher Wood*

The intractability of many environmental problems, and the scarcity of meaningful solutions to them, make environmental management tools such as strategic environmental assessment (SEA), which are intended to deliver environmental improvement and raise environmental awareness, particularly important. SEA has the potential to reduce the negative and enhance the positive environmental impacts associated with the implementation of land use plans. SEA and, in many countries, land use planning, have the achievement of sustainable development as a central aim. As land use plans can encompass wide geographical areas, which, in some cases, have very large populations, the potential beneficial impacts of the SEA of land use plans are great.

    The contributors to this book examine the use of SEA in the preparation of land use plans in 13 countries and in the World Bank. This chapter commences with a brief discussion of the nature of sustainable development. It proceeds to describe the fundamentals of land use planning, in order to set the stage for the SEA of land use plans. Next are presented brief explanations of SEA itself, and of its application to land use planning. There then follows a discussion of how the use of SEA in the preparation of land use plans in different jurisdictions can be evaluated. Finally, the structure of the book is summarized.

Sustainable development

The enduring ubiquity of the term 'sustainable development' is due to the World Commission on Environment and Development (WCED) of 1987, chaired by Gro Harlem Brundtland. The most commonly cited definition of sustainable development is Brundtland's: development that 'meets the needs of the present without compromising the ability of future generations to meet their own needs'

(WCED, 1987, p43). According to this definition, sustainable development is concerned primarily with the satisfaction of human needs, but extends this concern into the future, thus setting a present duty to care for the environment.

The wording of this definition of sustainable development can be traced back to the language of the United States National Environmental Policy Act 1969 (NEPA):

> *to foster and promote the general welfare, to create and maintain conditions under which man and nature can exist in productive harmony, and fulfil the social, economic, and other requirements of present and future generations of Americans* (Section 101[a]).

NEPA was also the first environmental assessment (EA) legislation in the world (Chapter 2), so EA and sustainable development have been closely linked from the outset. The definition is linked even more recognizably to the World Conservation Strategy of 1980 (International Union for Conservation of Nature and Natural Resources, 1980). This referred to the need for development to respect the Earth's finite capacities, if it is 'to meet the needs and aspirations of future generations' (Section 1[4]).

O'Riordan and Voisey (1997) asserted that sustainable development should mean the creation of a society and an economy that can come to terms with the life-support limits of the planet. A distinction can therefore be drawn between definitions of sustainable development that are more anthropocentric (such as WCED's), promoting the satisfaction of human needs, and those such as O'Riordan and Voisey's, which are more ecocentric in that the integrity of the biosphere is considered. Moreover, approaches to fostering more sustainable forms of development range from those that are weak (business-as-usual approaches relying on technical solutions to environmental problems) to those that are strong (more radical approaches requiring fundamental societal changes).

The different approaches to sustainable development can be interpreted as reflecting different ideological systems. Baker et al (1997, p9) described a 'ladder of sustainable development' (Figure 1.1 uses their classification). Each rung on the ladder outlines a differing view of the relationship between humans and their surrounding environment, and the changes believed to be necessary to move human development on to a more sustainable course. If a government states its commitment to sustainable development, this could mean a variety of different things and, in practice, could result in a broad range of policy outcomes. Ultimately, the definition of the concept of sustainable development adopted by a government will determine, through the adoption of associated policies, the nature and extent of the management of environmental resources within that country.

The political attractiveness of the Brundtland definition stems partly from its breadth; this allows a variety of interests with a range of, sometimes conflicting, perspectives to agree in principle to the concept, if not to the detailed means of achieving sustainable development (Myerson and Rydin, 1996). Because anthropocentrism is the dominant force within national and international society, the choice of sustainable development approaches available to governments is

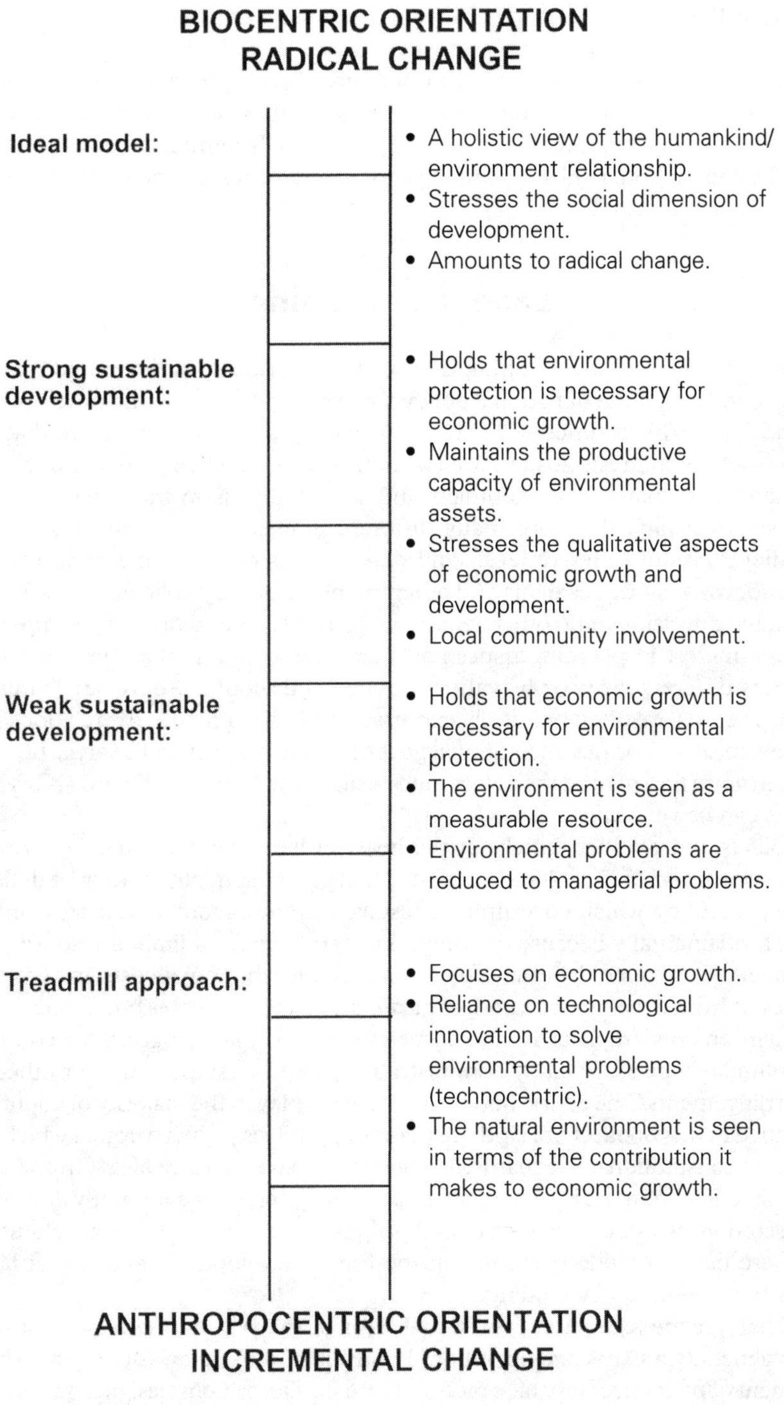

BIOCENTRIC ORIENTATION
RADICAL CHANGE

Ideal model:	• A holistic view of the humankind/ environment relationship. • Stresses the social dimension of development. • Amounts to radical change.
Strong sustainable development:	• Holds that environmental protection is necessary for economic growth. • Maintains the productive capacity of environmental assets. • Stresses the qualitative aspects of economic growth and development. • Local community involvement.
Weak sustainable development:	• Holds that economic growth is necessary for environmental protection. • The environment is seen as a measurable resource. • Environmental problems are reduced to managerial problems.
Treadmill approach:	• Focuses on economic growth. • Reliance on technological innovation to solve environmental problems (technocentric). • The natural environment is seen in terms of the contribution it makes to economic growth.

ANTHROPOCENTRIC ORIENTATION
INCREMENTAL CHANGE

Figure 1.1 *The ladder of sustainable development*

effectively limited to those at the weaker end of the spectrum. The anthropocentric understanding of the concept of sustainable development has now been incorporated into policy making by most national governments. The importance of sustainable development on the world stage is illustrated by the 2002 World Summit on Sustainable Development held in Johannesburg, where the contributions of both land use planning and SEA to its achievement were reported (United Nations, 2002).

Land use planning

The purpose of land use planning is to secure consistency and continuity in the framing and execution of national policy with respect to the use and development of land. The explicit function of the plan-making process is to ensure that the wide variety of interests at stake are taken into account when planning decisions are made, and that the development and use of land is in the general 'public interest'. In reality, there are many different interests that might be served – including those of different levels and departments of government; developers and landowners; local residents and other members of the public that are affected by planning decisions; and other agencies, organizations and pressure groups that have an interest in planning issues and outcomes – and all these interests may have very different views on how they consider land should be developed or used. These interests are often politically expressed and can influence the relationships between local authorities and national governments, between political parties and between governments and their electorates – since not-in-my-back-yard (NIMBY) groups can be very influential.

Politics and conflict thus lie at the heart of land use planning. As a result, Cullingworth and Nadin (2002) suggested that planning might usefully be defined as the process by which governments resolve disputes about land uses. Conflict arises fundamentally because of competing demands for a limited resource, for example, the use of land; because of the uneven distribution of costs and benefits that result from development; and, of particular relevance to this book, because of the environmental impacts that arise when the use of land changes. Such conflicts may ultimately be resolved by administrative procedures, the courts or other ad hoc arrangements. The courts have a major role to play in the majority of countries examined in this book where land use planning involves property rights which are subject to constitutional safeguards, or where plans have the force of law. In contrast, the United Kingdom (UK) and similar planning systems are commonly described as 'discretionary', since the policies and proposals set out in the relevant statutory plans are used to guide decisions on the future development and use of land, rather than being legally binding.

Whatever the legal or constitutional basis of the system, the control of land use is generally a two-stage operation. Firstly, a land use plan (usually a written statement of policy accompanied by diagrammatic illustrations designed to channel land use in desirable directions) is prepared. This lays down the broad pattern of land use for the whole or part of the area administered by a planning authority.

Secondly, a procedure by which permission for new development is requested and determined is employed. The responsible authority may give conditional or unconditional permission, or may refuse permission. Most new development requires some form of planning permission, which is normally granted if the proposals are in accord with the plan. A central problem for any planning system is, however, to devise a means of predicting likely future changes that may impact on the system, and to accommodate unanticipated changes (Cullingworth and Nadin, 2002). EA and other tools play an important role in attempting to meet this need.

The link between land use planning and environmental protection is well documented (Wood, 1999; Selman, 2000). Many environmental problems can be traced back to the way land is used, and the proper use of land is fundamental to working towards environmentally sustainable development (Royal Commission on Environmental Pollution (RCEP), 2002). As planning policies are instrumental in the future use of land, they are linked to potential direct and indirect environmental impacts. Healey and Shaw (1993) suggested that land use plans can influence the environment in a number of ways. These include:

- dealing with local site-related matters
- ensuring that development does not exceed ecological thresholds
- balancing the social, environmental and economic needs of new developments
- maintaining and enhancing the quality of local environments.

Moreover, it is important for land use plans to reflect an understanding of the relationship between the biosphere and human actions. The biosphere performs three anthropocentric functions: a source of resources, an assimilator of wastes, and a provider of other environmental services such as amenity and life support systems (Healey and Shaw, 1993). The planning system has the potential to influence each of these functions. Furthermore, Wood (1999) noted that, as the authorities responsible for planning help to determine the amount and location of development, they exert an important control over pollution and its distribution. Land use plans can control the location of both direct pollution sources (for example, waste incinerators) and indirect sources (such as out-of-town shopping centres), and also the siting of pollution receptors such as schools or housing estates. Planning policies can also encourage positive environmental impacts/benefits. These may include the safeguarding of greenbelt land, the promotion of energy efficient settlement patterns or the encouragement of renewable sources of energy generation.

Land use planning is therefore part of the political system through which the environment can be protected and sustainable development goals can be defined, and policies to achieve them drawn up and implemented (Owens, 1997; RCEP, 2002). Many governments actively promote the use of planning to steer society on to a more sustainable course. As Briassoulis (1999) noted, sustainable development has been declared as the ultimate planning goal, with numerous governments accepting the challenge of incorporating the concept into their planning systems. For example, Hales (2000) found that virtually every UK planning policy related document since 1992 referred, explicitly or implicitly, to the Brundtland conception of sustainable development. Indeed, land use planning has delivered many environmental successes (Wood, 1999) but the place of environmentally sustainable development in planning often owes more to rhetoric than to reality (Blowers, 1997; Evans, 1997); land use planning currently remains on the lower rungs of the ladder of sustainable development.

SEA

SEA refers to the EA of policies, plans and programmes (PPPs). The concept of SEA has evolved from the well established practice of environmental impact assessment (EIA), which has been widely accepted as a means of improving the quality of decisions about proposed projects. SEA has developed, in part, as a consequence of the emerging awareness that project EIA may occur too late in the planning process to ensure that all the alternatives and impacts relevant to sustainable development goals are adequately considered (Lee and Walsh, 1992; Wood and Djeddour, 1992). The aim of SEA is to provide decision makers and affected stakeholders with timely and relevant information on the potential environmental impacts of a PPP in order to modify the PPP to make it environmentally more sound. SEA is therefore a process that is inextricably linked to decision making (Sadler and Verheem, 1996). It facilitates the early consideration of environmental impacts, the examination of a broad array of potential alternatives, the generation of standard mitigation measures and the opportunity to address a wide range of impacts, including those that are cumulative, synergistic, indirect, long range, delayed and global.

The theoretical benefits of SEA centre on the ability of the process to help PPPs reflect sustainable development concerns. Sadler and Verheem (1996, p13) believed that 'SEA represents a promising approach to incorporating environmental and sustainability considerations into the mainstream of development policy making'. It has been suggested that, through the use of SEA, the concept of sustainable development could be incorporated as an integral part of the development of all policies and then 'trickled down' through plans to programmes, and finally to the project level (Lee and Wood, 1978; Therivel et al, 1992).

In principle, there exists a tiered[1], forward planning process, which starts with the formulation of a policy at the upper level, is followed by a plan at the second stage and by a programme at the end. A policy may thus be considered as the inspiration and guidance for action, a plan as a set of coordinated and timed objectives for implementing the policy, and a programme as a set of projects in a particular area. The tiered system can apply at the national level and also may apply at regional and local levels (Figure 1.2). It can apply to land use planning and to sectoral actions (Therivel et al, 1992; Wood and Djeddour, 1992; Therivel, 2004). In reality, however, this model oversimplifies the relationships between policies, plans, programmes and projects since, for example, a plan may contain policies (Partidário, 2000).

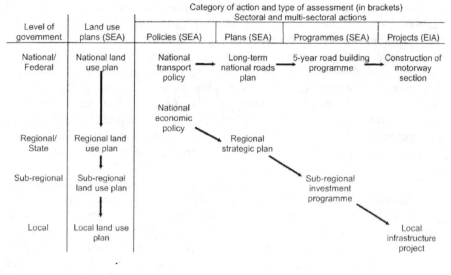

Source: Adapted from Lee and Wood (1978)

Figure 1.2 *Tiering of policy, plan, programme and project environmental assessment*

The development of SEA can be linked to the increased influence of sustainable development within policy making. The degradation of the natural environment, from the local to the global, is a facet of a growth dominated approach to business and government policy that cannot be ignored. To help to prevent this degradation, the European Commission (EC) recently agreed a directive on the assessment of plans and programmes (EC, 2001). Unsurprisingly, this 'SEA Directive' has provided a huge stimulus to thinking about SEA in Europe and beyond.

SEA and land use planning

The SEA of land use plans is intended to help predict potential environmental impacts that could occur as a result of their implementation, as part of the wider promotion of the planning system as a tool to help deliver sustainable development (Figure 1.2). Many alternative arrangements of juxtaposed land uses, and some significant synergistic and cumulative impacts, cannot be satisfactorily considered in sectoral or project environmental assessments. They can, however, be considered in the SEA of land use plans. The details of the potential environmental impacts of a plan that SEA generates can assist decision makers in taking environmental issues into account during the preparation of land use plans.

The EA of land use plans is probably the easiest to implement of all types of SEA, so it is no surprise that planning is the sector to which SEA is most commonly applied in many countries (Wood, 2002). In California, where SEA has been established for over 30 years, most SEAs have related to land use plans (Bass and Herson, 1999). The spread of SEA within planning systems across the globe indicates the extent of its acceptance and its potential effectiveness. SEA procedures can illuminate the connections between land use planning policies and environmental change, highlighting the possible environmental impacts associated with plan implementation. It is, however, important to see this diffusion in the context of the dominance of weak interpretations of sustainable development within contemporary international environmental politics. The Brundtland definition of sustainable development (WCED, 1987) enables an element of environmentalism to be added, without too much pain, to mainstream political considerations such as economic growth and social justice.

The emphasis on sustainable development has also led to the promotion of more integrated assessment procedures, especially sustainability appraisal (SA) (which has become a widespread tool in the UK). This attempts to address the impacts of PPPs on economic, social and environmental goals more comprehensively than would be possible during an environmentally focused SEA process. Various commentators have expressed support for a broader appraisal process of this kind that explores the impact of human actions on sustainable development issues (Kirkpatrick and Lee, 1997; O'Riordan, 1999). For example, the International Association for Impact Assessment (2002) suggested that SEA should address the interrelationships between biophysical, social and economic impacts, in contrast to 'traditional' SEA procedures that have tended to focus on environmental impacts. This accords with Abaza's view (1997, p27) that the separation of environmental, economic and social forms of appraisal 'has led to an artificial dichotomy between environment and development'.

Others are concerned that environmental issues may be marginalized within a broader assessment process. Owens and Cowell (2002, p52) suggested that SA's emergence might be read as 'a reassertion of economic primacy, in a pre-emptive challenge to environment led interpretations of sustainability'. The progressive widening of the scope of impacts considered within SEA (Smith and Sheate, 2001) can potentially promote weak sustainable development goals and therefore fail to discourage potentially environmentally detrimental economic growth strategies.

Evaluating the SEA of land use plans

Evaluating SEA practice is a multi faceted exercise. Thissen (2000) noted that a distinction should be made between quality and effectiveness, which relate to different aspects of SEA, when evaluating SEA practice. Quality refers to inputs such as institutional arrangements and SEA methodologies, whereas effectiveness relates to outcomes, both direct and indirect, such as the achievement of identified goals.

The consideration of the *quality* of the SEA involves focusing on inputs into the SEA process. These include factors that contribute to reaching conclusions about the possible environmental impacts of the land use plan, through the application of the SEA process. Consequently, quality related inputs into the SEA include:

- Those relating to the system supporting the process of undertaking a SEA of a land use plan. Relevant issues include legal arrangements, guidance documents and the relationship between the SEA process and sustainable development. Associated criteria therefore focus on the position of SEA within the larger land use planning system
- Those relating to the SEA procedure such as methodological elements of the SEA process (screening, scoping, consultation, public participation, etc). Such criteria therefore focus on the SEA process in relation to land use planning.

For two reasons, the consideration of the *effectiveness* of the SEA of land use plans is a more difficult task than looking at issues relating to quality:

- While there is some agreement concerning the quality of the inputs into the process, such as elements of good practice SEA methodologies, ideas of what constitutes an effective SEA of a land use plan will vary between stakeholders, who may not share common goals
- The evaluation of outcome is made difficult by the uncontrollable factors evident in every SEA. Isolating the effects of the SEA on outcomes such as improvements in environmental quality or the weight given to environmental factors in decision making is very problematic.

At present, the assessment of SEA effectiveness is largely a subjective exercise reliant on the opinions of experts and practitioners. Nevertheless, it is important to gain an indication of whether or not the SEA of land use plans is having any discernible impact on decisions about the content of the plans and consequently, on the environmental quality of the region. Thus, despite the inherent challenges involved, this book sets out to examine the effectiveness of the SEA processes. Chapter 3 presents the quality (SEA system and SEA process) criteria and the effectiveness (SEA outcome) criteria adopted.

The number of countries and organizations selected for this book was limited by length and a balance had to be struck between level of detail and breadth of coverage. It was felt that 14 SEA systems should be chosen as an appropriate compromise between these conflicting demands. The editors make no apology for the fact that European countries dominate the book. The European SEA Directive, which came into effect in July 2004, has required all the original members of the European Union (EU) and the accession countries to implement SEA requirements. Inevitably, this has been done in a number of different ways reflecting local circumstances. The UK was an obvious choice. It has been a leader in applying a form of SEA to its strong but discretionary land use planning procedures. While most other European countries have much less flexible land use planning systems, that in Ireland is similar to the UK's and it was therefore appropriate to examine the way in which SEA had been implemented in that country too.

The Netherlands was included because it is generally acknowledged to have a sophisticated system of environmental controls, including an EIA system regarded by many observers as being the most effective in Europe, and a widely admired EIA Commission. Denmark was covered because it was one of the early European leaders, applying SEA to legislative proposals. (It also has a sophisticated land use planning system.) Sweden was included because the Nordic countries have taken SEA seriously from the outset, and Sweden had made significant progress in the mandatory application of SEA within land use planning before the SEA Directive was promulgated. Germany has a strong landscape planning tradition and it was felt that examination of its SEA system would provide a valuable contrast to the other five northern European countries. The editors believed that it was essential that the book covered a southern European country and Portugal was chosen accordingly. Finally, Hungary was chosen as representative of the ten central and eastern European countries that joined the EU in 2004.

The US possesses the original EA system and, as with so much else in the environmental policy field, examination of American SEA experience offers a pointer to the future elsewhere. The Canadian federal EA system was established on an informal basis in 1973, and provided the model for The Netherlands EIA system. Canada was the first country to implement the SEA of cabinet proposals. New Zealand has a long-established EIA system and its Resource Management Act has been widely admired. Because the Resource Management Act implicitly requires the SEA of land use plans, New Zealand's integrated SEA procedure was a natural choice.

Hong Kong is a densely populated burgeoning region which has made provision for SEA within land use planning and was an obvious Asian representative. For some of its people, South Africa is a developed federal country but, for many of its population, conditions are more typical of a developing country. It has made provision for SEA within land use planning and was chosen as the African representative in the book. Finally, it was decided to include the World Bank's SEA processes as a proxy for experience within the developing world. Obviously, the treatment of the World Bank's SEA system is rather different from those of the 13 countries in the book.

The editors contacted the prospective authors, all of whom were known to them, and asked them to follow the same chapter structure and to keep to the same word limit. All the authors were sent a copy of the criteria presented in Table 3.1 to analyse their country's SEA system, SEA process and SEA outcome. They were also asked to provide an evaluation and explanatory comment in relation to each criterion in a summary table. Inevitably, particular circumstances and inclinations meant that this framework was not always followed rigidly.

The book has been deliberately subtitled 'an international evaluation' rather than 'an international comparison' because the evaluations are the individual authors' rather than the editors'. An author from another country might evaluate the SEA of land use plans there quite differently from that presented here. While the editors have endeavoured to ensure consistency between the text and the tabular evaluation of, and commentary on, each criterion in each chapter, they have not attempted to impose their own judgements. Accordingly, Table 18.1 represents the authors' evaluations rather than the editors'.

Every SEA and land use planning system is unique, and each is the product of a particular set of legal, administrative and political circumstances, so the examination of the SEA of land use plans within 13 countries and in the World Bank using the same 20 criteria designed to evaluate different aspects of SEA should achieve two objectives. The first is to enhance understanding of SEA within land use planning. The second is to encourage improvements in practice by allowing comparisons to be made with SEA in different countries. If this international evaluation leads to one practical suggestion to improve the effectiveness of the national SEA processes examined it will have been successful.

Structure of the book

The next chapter presents an overview of SEA. It describes the evolution of SEA before going on to detail the SEA process. The factors encouraging and constraining the development of SEA are then discussed in turn. Chapter 3 is concerned with the evaluation of the quality and effectiveness of SEA in land use planning. It explains the three different types of criteria employed in this book (system, process and outcome criteria) before justifying the inclusion of each of the 20 criteria adopted.

Chapters 4–17 present evaluations of the SEA of land use plans in Canada, Denmark, Germany, Hong Kong, Hungary, Ireland, The Netherlands, New Zealand, Portugal, South Africa, Sweden, the UK, the US and the World Bank. Each chapter follows a similar structure. Typically, there is a brief introduction followed by a discussion of the context in the jurisdiction concerned, usually followed by a case study. The SEA system, the SEA process and the SEA outcome are analysed before conclusions are drawn. A tabular summary of the evaluation of SEA of land use planning in the jurisdiction, utilizing symbols and notes, is presented.

Chapter 18 follows the same structure as Chapters 4–17. It presents conclusions and allows comparisons between the countries to be made on the basis of a summary table that draws together the evaluations of all 14 jurisdictions. Finally, likely future developments in the SEA of land use plans are outlined.

Note

1 The use of the word 'tiering' to describe EAs undertaken at different levels in the planning process originated in 1978 in the US (see Chapter 2)

References

Abaza, H. (1997) 'Integration of sustainability objectives in structural adjustment programmes through the use of strategic environmental assessment', in Kirkpatrick, C. and Lee, N. (eds) *Sustainable Development in a Developing World: Integrating Socio-economic Appraisal and Environmental Assessment*, Edward Elgar, Cheltenham

Baker, S., Kousis, M., Richardson, D. and Young, S. (1997) 'Introduction: the theory and practice of sustainable development in EU perspective', in Baker, S., Kousis, M., Richardson, D. and Young, S. (eds) *The Politics of Sustainable Development*, Routledge, London

Bass, R. and Herson, A. (1999) 'Environmental impact assessment of land use plans: experience under the National Environmental Policy Act and the California Environmental Quality Act', in Petts, J. (ed) *Handbook of Environmental Assessment*, Blackwell, Oxford

Blowers, A. (1997) 'Environmental planning for sustainable development', in Blowers, A. and Evans, B. (eds) *Town Planning into the 21st Century*, Routledge, London

Briassoulis, H. (1999) 'Who plans whose sustainability? Alternative roles for planners', *Journal of Environmental Planning and Management*, vol 42, pp889–902

Cullingworth, J. B. and Nadin, V. (2002) *Town and Country Planning in the UK*, 13th edition, Routledge, London

European Commission (2001) 'Directive 2001/42/EC of the European Parliament and of the Council of 27 June 2001 on the assessment of the effects of certain plans and programmes on the environment', *Official Journal of the European Communities* (21 July), vol L197, pp30–37 http://europa.eu.int/comm/environment/eia

Evans, B. (1997) 'From town planning to environmental planning', in Blowers, A. and Evans, B. (eds) *Town Planning into the 21st Century*, Routledge, London

Hales, R. (2000) 'Land use planning and the notion of sustainable development: exploring constraints and facilitation within the English planning system', *Journal of Environmental Planning and Management*, vol 43, pp99–121

Healey, P. and Shaw, T. (1993) 'Planners, plans and sustainable development', *Regional Studies*, vol 27, pp769–776

International Association for Impact Assessment (2002) *Strategic Environmental Assessment Performance Criteria*, Special Publication Series Number 1, www.iaia.org

International Union for Conservation of Nature and Natural Resources (1980) *World Conservation Strategy: Living Resource Conservation for Sustainable Development*, IUCN, Gland, Switzerland

Kirkpatrick, C. and Lee, N. (eds) (1997) *Sustainable Development in a Developing World: Integrating Socio-economic Appraisal and Environmental Assessment*, Edward Elgar, Cheltenham

Lee, N. and Walsh, F. (1992) 'Strategic environmental assessment: an overview', *Project Appraisal*, vol 7, pp126–136

Lee, N. and Wood, C. M. (1978) 'EIA – a European perspective', *Built Environment*, vol 4, pp101–110

Myerson, G. and Rydin, Y. (1996) 'Sustainable development: the implications of the global debate for land use planning', in Buckingham-Hatfield, S. and Evans, B. (eds) *Environmental Planning and Sustainability*, John Wiley, Chichester

O'Riordan, T. (1999) *Planning for Sustainable Development: a Brave New World for Emancipated Planners*, Town and Country Planning Association, London

O'Riordan, T. and Voisey, H. (1997) 'The political economy of sustainable development', *Environmental Politics*, vol 6, pp1–23

Owens, S. (1997) 'Giants in the path: planning, sustainability and environmental values', *Town Planning Review*, vol 68, pp293–304

Owens, S. and Cowell, R. (2002) *Land and Limits: Interpreting Sustainability in the Planning Process*, Routledge, London

Partidário, M. (2000) 'Elements of an SEA framework – improving the added-value of SEA', *Environmental Impact Assessment Review*, vol 20, pp647–663

Royal Commission on Environmental Pollution (2002) *Twenty-third Report: Environmental Planning*, Cm 5459, The Stationery Office, London

Sadler, B. and Verheem, R. (1996) *Strategic Environmental Assessment: Status, Challenges and Future Directions*, Publication Number 53, Ministry of Housing, Spatial Planning and the Environment, The Hague

Selman, P. (2000) *Environmental Planning*, 2nd edition, Sage, London

Smith, S. P. and Sheate, W. (2001) 'Sustainability appraisal of English regional plans: incorporating the requirements of the EU strategic environmental assessment directive', *Impact Assessment and Project Appraisal*, vol 19, pp236–276

Therivel, R. (2004) *Strategic Environmental Assessment in Action*, Earthscan, London

Therivel, R., Wilson, E., Thompson, S., Heaney, D. and Pritchard, D. (1992) *Strategic Environmental Assessment*, Earthscan, London

Thissen, W. A. H. (2000) 'Criteria for evaluation of SEA', in Partidário, M. and Clark, R. (eds) *Perspectives on Strategic Environmental Assessment*, Lewis Publishers/CRC Press, Boca Raton, FL

United Nations (2002) *Report of the World Summit on Sustainable Development*, UN, New York, www.johannesburgsummit.org

Wood, C. M. (1999) 'Environmental planning', in Cullingworth, B. J. (ed) *British Planning: 50 Years of Urban and Regional Planning*, Athlone Press, London

Wood, C. M. (2002) *Environmental Impact Assessment: a Comparative Review*, 2nd edition, Prentice Hall, Harlow

Wood, C. M. and Djeddour, M. (1992) 'Strategic environmental assessment: EA of policies, plans and programmes' *Impact Assessment Bulletin*, vol 10, pp3–22

World Commission on Environment and Development (1987) *Our Common Future*, Oxford University Press, Oxford

2

SEA: an Overview

Carys Jones, Mark Baker, Jeremy Carter, Stephen Jay,
Michael Short and Christopher Wood

Introduction

This chapter presents a more detailed explanation of the evolution and nature of SEA than was possible in Chapter 1. This provides the basis for the formulation of the process criteria for the evaluation of the SEA of land use plans outlined in Chapter 3. Firstly, the evolution of the SEA process is described. Details of Directive 2001/42/EC ('the European SEA Directive'), which has influenced land use planning SEA procedures in eight of the countries referred to in this book, are then provided. The chapter continues by discussing generic stages of the SEA process, indicating the elements that collectively constitute good practice procedures for the SEA of land use plans. Subsequently, the opportunities offered by the application of SEA during the preparation of land use plans are outlined. Factors constraining the development of SEA, and potentially jeopardizing the realization of its benefits, are then discussed.

The evolution of SEA

The earliest legislation requiring the use of SEA was, as mentioned in Chapter 1, the US National Environmental Policy Act of 1969 (NEPA). This requires the assessment of the environmental impacts of 'major federal actions significantly affecting the quality of the human environment' (Section 102[2][c]). The term 'major federal action' was subsequently defined in the Council on Environmental Quality (CEQ) Regulations to include projects and programmes, rules, regulations, plans, policies or procedures, and legislative proposals advanced by federal agencies (CEQ, 1978). SEA procedures are not distinguished from project EIA procedures in the US. The environmental impact statements (EISs) for policies, plans and programmes are called variously programmatic, regional, cumulative or generic EISs (or sometimes simply EISs) (Sigal and Webb, 1989).

CEQ indicated as early as 1972 that programmatic EISs should be prepared for federal programmes that might involve numerous actions to ensure that cumulative impacts were addressed. Such EISs were to be broad in nature and cover basic policy issues that would not have to be repeated in subsequent EISs for individual actions within a programme (Sigal and Webb, 1989). This was subsequently termed 'tiering' (CEQ, 1978). Tiering involves the preparation of an EIS to cover general issues, and particularly alternatives, in a broad policy or programme analysis. EISs at subsequent stages then incorporate the general discussions from the broader EIS by reference, while concentrating on the issues specific to the action being evaluated (Bass et al, 2001). California, which has separate EIA legislation modelled on NEPA, probably has the most established SEA system in the world and several hundred SEAs have been undertaken to date, mostly of land use plans (Bass et al, 1999).

SEA practice has received considerable impetus from a number of international organizations. The need to integrate environmental considerations with development became an accepted part of World Bank policy in 1987 when it stated that environmental issues must be addressed as part of overall policy rather than project by project (World Bank, 1987). (Subsequently, the World Bank has required regional and sectoral environmental assessments in some developing countries – Chapter 17.) The same philosophy was echoed in the Brundtland report (World Commission on Environment and Development, 1987). Two of the outputs of the 1992 Earth Summit, Agenda 21 (United Nations Conference on Environment and Development – UNCED, 1992a) and the Rio Declaration (UNCED, 1992b) provided further impetus for national governments to incorporate environmental considerations into all levels of decision making. The Rio Declaration identified the role of environmental assessment in the integration of environmental issues within policy making as a means of meeting this key institutional challenge (UNCED, 1992b, Principle 17). Similarly, the United Nations Economic Commission for Europe (UNECE) (1992) recommended the extension of EIA principles to policies, plans and programmes (PPPs).

By 2001, less than 20 countries had made formal provisions for the SEA of PPPs (Sadler, 2001b). However, this figure has now increased, with the implementation of the European SEA Directive in all the member states and with World Bank EA procedures stimulating SEA practice in developing countries (Chapter 17). In addition, the UNECE SEA protocol (UNECE, 2003) could further increase the number of countries undertaking SEA over the next decade. It is clear that SEA is currently experiencing a period of rapid growth, which will inevitably enhance the understanding of SEA theory and improve practice in the SEA of land use plans. Despite this growth, however, the development of SEA lags behind that of EIA by about 15 years.

The European SEA Directive

The European Commission (EC) has pursued the environmental assessment of PPPs since the mid-1970s because it was conscious that EIA, by its nature, inevitably occurs late in the planning process (that is, at the project level). It was during research commissioned by the EC that the name 'strategic environmental assessment' was coined:

> *The environmental assessments appropriate to policies, plans and programmes are of a more strategic nature than those applicable to individual projects and are likely to differ from them in several important respects. . .We have adopted the term 'strategic environmental assessment' (SEA) to describe this type of assessment*
>
> Wood and Djeddour (1989) p v.[1]

The preliminary first draft of the European SEA Directive was contained in the report on this research. Various drafts of the proposed directive began to appear publicly in the early 1990s.

Environmental action programmes have been an important influence on the development of environmental policy within European member states. The fifth environmental action programme (Commission of the European Communities – CEC, 1993), covering the period 1993–2000, was particularly important in this respect, as it represented a departure from previous programmes due to its anticipatory nature, and by being committed to the principle of sustainable development. The programme also promoted the need to integrate environmental issues into the development and implementation of PPPs. The European Commission (EC) noted that 'given the goal of achieving sustainable development it seems only logical, if not essential, to apply an assessment of the environmental implications to all relevant PPPs' (CEC, 1993, p70). This statement placed further emphasis on the need to develop SEA, and constituted an important policy driver encouraging European countries to develop SEA requirements.

The EC's efforts culminated in a separate directive on the assessment of plans and programmes that was formally published on 21 July 2001 (EC, 2001).[2] In some ways (for example, scoping, quality control and monitoring) it is, surprisingly, stronger than the amended European EIA Directive (CEC, 1985). The SEA Directive has the following objective:

> *to provide for a high level of protection of the environment and to contribute to the integration of environmental considerations into the preparation and adoption of plans and programmes with a view to promoting more sustainable development*
>
> EC (2001, Article 1).

The SEA Directive is based closely on the amended EIA directive. Its main features are set out in Box 2.1.

Box 2.1 Key features of European SEA Directive

- does not mention SEA by name;
- requires SEA for all land use plans establishing framework for future development consent of EIA Directive projects (Article 3 [2][a]);
- covers SEA for plans requiring assessment under Habitats Directive (Article 3 [2][b]);
- excludes minor modifications to existing plans and small area plans not having significant environmental effects (Article 3 [3]);
- recognizes the concept of tiering: member states must 'take into account the fact that the assessment will be carried out . . . at different levels of the hierarchy' (Article 4 [3]);
- establishes a scoping stage that requires authorities undertaking SEA to consult appropriate bodies on scope and detail of assessment (Article 5 [4]);
- necessitates the consideration of alternatives: 'an environmental report shall be prepared in which the likely significant effects on the environment of implementing the plan . . . and reasonable alternatives . . . are identified, described and evaluated' (Article 5 [1]);
- requires consultation and public participation: 'the draft plan . . . and the environmental report . . . shall be available to the authorities . . . and the public' (Article 6 [1]);
- demands that member states designate consultation bodies, based upon their 'specific environmental responsibilities' (Article 6 [3]);
- encourages the consideration of cumulative, synergistic and secondary impacts (Annex I [f]);
- requires an environmental report to be 'taken into account during the preparation of the plan . . . and before its adoption or submission to the legislative procedure' (Article 8);
- demands a 'statement summarising how environmental considerations have been integrated into the plan . . . and how the environmental report . . . and the results of consultations . . . have been taken into account' (Article 9 [1]);
- incorporates transboundary consultation (Article 7);
- forces member states to 'monitor the significant environmental effects of the implementation of plans . . . in order . . . to identify . . . unforeseen adverse effects, and to be able to undertake appropriate remedial action' (Article 10 [1]);
- requires member states to ensure environmental reports are of 'sufficient quality' (Article 12 [2]).

The SEA Directive affects many public institutions in the EU and encompasses many sectors other than land use planning. The Directive sets out a broad discretionary assessment framework, defining desired outputs rather than specifying particular SEA methods to be undertaken. As Risse et al (2003, p467) stated: 'the general requirements prescribed by the Directive are not restrictive and leave ample room for creativity, flexibility and adaptability to suit each member state's context.'

Consequently, the success of the implementation of the Directive depends on how each member state chooses to adopt its requirements. It is important to remember that the Directive is effectively a compromise lowest common denominator (Glasson and Gosling, 2001). It was described by Risse et al (2003) as a minimum environmental assessment framework. Nevertheless, the flexibility inherent in the Directive also allows member states to go 'beyond compliance' and to develop SEA procedures that exceed the Directive's requirements.

The SEA process

Like EIA, SEA is a process that can provide land use planners and affected stakeholders with timely and relevant information on the environmental impacts of a proposed action, thereby providing opportunities to make more environmentally sound decisions. SEAs therefore present the opportunity to improve plans from an environmental point of view, and ultimately, to work towards the achievement of sustainable development goals. Accordingly, as Sadler and Verheem (1996) noted, the SEA process is a decision aiding tool. The Canadian Environmental Assessment Agency (CEAA, 1999) indicated that SEA generally addresses a number of questions (Box 2.2) which help to clarify what the process aims to achieve.

Box 2.2 Key questions addressed by SEA

• What are the potential direct and indirect outcomes of the proposal?
• How do these outcomes interact with the environment?
• What is the scope and nature of these environmental interactions?
• Can the adverse environmental effects be mitigated?
• What is the overall potential environmental effect of the proposal after opportunities for mitigation have been incorporated?

Source: CEAA (1999, p10)

A number of different SEA procedures exist, varying in their openness, scope, intensity and duration (Verheem and Tonk, 2000). They include:

• policy SEAs – assessing policy level activities;
• sectoral SEAs – concentrating on a particular sector (e.g. transport, land use);
• sustainability-based SEAs – assessing environmental, economic and social impacts;
• regional SEAs – focusing on a particular geographical area;
• issue-based SEAs – assessing a particular impact (e.g. climate change); and

- EIA-based SEAs – following procedures derived from EIA.

Source: Noble (2000); Sadler (2001a)

SEA procedures often vary according to the circumstances under which they are applied. Consequently, this has led to confusion over whether SEA can be applied similarly in different contexts, or whether procedures should be developed specifically to suit a particular situation. Fischer and Seaton (2002) believed that SEA was, therefore, a poorly defined concept. Partidário (2000) suggested that it would be useful to perceive SEA as a family of different tools which could be used under different circumstances. Similarly, Brown and Therivel (2000, p186) stated that 'SEA should be seen as an overarching concept rather than as a unitary technique'. Although flexible SEA approaches are generally regarded as being necessary to enable the process to be tailored to the circumstances within which it is applied, there are, nevertheless, a number of particular stages that constitute elements of good practice SEA. The stages of the SEA process are outlined in Table 2.1. These provide the basis of the 'process' evaluation criteria advanced in Chapter 3.

Table 2.1 *Generic stages of the SEA process*

Generic SEA stage	Key considerations
Apply a screening process	Examine aims and objectives of plan and its overall purpose. Consider whether plan likely to have significant environmental effects. If so, SEA required
Apply a scoping process	Consider whether plan meets requirements of relevant policies, environmental protection objectives, international targets, etc. Based on objectives of plan, identify key environmental issues central to particular plan being assessed
Select SEA objectives/criteria	Develop series of SEA objectives/criteria against which performance of plan will be predicted. Targets and indicators based on these criteria can be used as basis of a strategy to monitor implementation of plan
Consideration of alternatives	Identify costs, benefits and environmental impacts of other realistic alternatives to meeting plan's objectives. Choice between alternatives ultimately a political decision
Collect baseline environmental data	Target data gathering effort on issues identified during scoping. (These may change in light of new information obtained.) Provides platform to examine predicted impacts against anticipated changes in future environment without plan
Undertake impact prediction	Using SEA objectives and criteria as a guide, identify impacts of plan policies. Predictions should be made using baseline environmental data where available. Where possible, focus on cumulative, synergistic, secondary and long-term impacts to

Table 2.1 *Generic stages of the SEA process (continued)*

Generic SEA stage	Key considerations
	increase comprehensiveness. Involves subjective and objective assessment
Undertake impact evaluation	Consider acceptability of plan and alternatives, looking at significance of predicted environmental impacts
Develop a mitigation strategy	Not explicit stage, as mitigation should be considered throughout SEA process, enabling continual refinement of plan. Nevertheless, residual impacts of chosen alternative must be addressed
Develop a monitoring strategy	Relate monitoring strategy back to environmental targets and indicators identified during scoping. Consider whether plan is achieving its objectives and if mitigation measures are working effectively. Amendments to plan may result
Prepare a report	A publicly available SEA report should be prepared to document main findings of SEA. This should include a non-technical summary
Instigate a review mechanism	Consider whether information provided by SEA and included in SEA report is sufficient for decision making. In order to maintain objectivity, some form of independent review necessary
Consultation and public participation	Not separate stage, as relevant authorities and public should be involved at various stages during SEA. External involvement important at early SEA stages (scoping and selection of objectives/criteria) and prior to plan adoption but after impact evaluation

Source: Adapted from Wood and Djeddour (1992); Sadler and Verheem (1996); Therivel and Partidário (1996); von Seht (1999); Brown and Therivel (2000).

This EIA-based SEA process is therefore similar in nature to the project EIA process, involving screening, scoping, prediction of changes from baseline parameters, mitigation of impacts, monitoring, reporting and review, consultation and public participation (UNECE, 1992). Other SEA approaches also meet the SEA principles advanced by Verheem and Tonk (2000). For example, integrated impact assessment and sustainability appraisal are objectives-led; they rely upon assessments about whether particular actions advance towards, or retreat from, sustainability objectives (Sadler, 2001a).

SEA should be a process driven by the needs of decision makers. However, Nilsson and Dalkmann (2001) noted that, because SEA processes do not always match specific decision making procedures, their influence on decision outcomes is sometimes limited. The starting point for any SEA should ideally be the decision making context into which the findings of the SEA feed (Nilsson and Dalkmann, 2001; Nitz and Brown, 2001). If the SEA process is to improve decision making it must move beyond prediction to ensuring that relevant findings are integrated into the appropriate decision making stages (Kørnøv and Thissen, 2000; Nilsson and Dalkmann, 2001; Owens et al, 2004). However, this is not always easy, given the inherent complexities of decision making procedures (see 'constraints' on p23).

SEA of land use plans: opportunities

The evolution of SEA (above) has been driven largely by a perceived need to raise the profile of environmental issues during the preparation of strategic actions within the broader context of delivering aspects of the sustainable development agenda (Brown and Therivel, 2000; Sadler, 2001a). The perceived potential of SEA in this respect stems from its proactive and strategic nature and from its capacity to integrate environmental concerns with social and economic issues during decision making.

The other widely acknowledged benefit of the SEA process is that it can streamline and strengthen project EIA practice. Whereas project EIA essentially reacts to proposed developments and their environmental impacts, the SEA process has the potential to be more proactive. SEA facilitates the earlier consideration of environmental impacts, the examination of a wider range of potential alternatives, the generation of standard mitigation measures and the opportunity to address a wider range of impacts. In addition, the SEA of land use plans has the potential to streamline the EIA process by focusing it on the most significant project issues. The original arguments advanced in favour of SEA by Wood and Djeddour (1992) are presented in Box 2.3.

When alternative arrangements of juxtaposed land uses and significant environmental impacts cannot be adequately assessed at the project level, it is often possible to assess them at the land use plan level (Therivel, 2004). Some significant synergistic and cumulative impacts cannot be satisfactorily considered in project EIA because of the effects of new activities in other sectors, or because of the cumulative effects of many activities not subject to project EIA. They can, however, be considered in the SEA of land use plans. Moreover, SEA can raise environmental awareness and understanding amongst participants and can also potentially enhance transparency and equity during the preparation of land use plans. The additional opportunities presented by the SEA of land use plans suggested since 1992 (Curran et al, 1998; Brown and Therivel, 2000; Sadler, 2001a, 2001b; Owens and Cowell, 2002; Therivel, 2004) can be summarized as follows:

- Without SEA to provide a check, political agendas motivating the preparation of land use plans may not adequately account for environmental issues
- 'There is a strong argument that planners and decision makers continue to contribute to environmental degradation, at least in part because they are inadequately informed about the current state of the environment, the pressures upon it, the consequences of their decisions and potential mitigation' (Royal Commission on Environmental Pollution, 2002, p76). SEA is designed to address this weakness

---

Box 2.3 Potential benefits of SEA

- encourages the consideration of environmental objectives during policy, plan and programme-making activities within non-environmental organizations;
- facilitates consultations between authorities on, and enhances public involvement in, evaluation of environmental aspects of policy, plan and programme formulation;
- may render some project EIAs redundant if impacts have been assessed adequately;
- may leave examination of certain impacts to project EIA;
- allows formulation of standard or generic mitigation measures for later projects;
- encourages consideration of alternatives often ignored or not feasible in project EIA;
- can help determine appropriate sites for projects subsequently subject to EIA;
- allows more effective analysis of cumulative effects of both large and small projects;
- encourages and facilitates the consideration of synergistic effects;
- allows more effective consideration of ancillary or secondary effects and activities;
- facilitates consideration of long-range and delayed impacts;
- allows analysis of the impacts of policies that may not be implemented through projects.

Source: Wood and Djeddour (1992, p7)

- SEA can generate consistency and compatibility between the aims, strategies and policies of a land use plan, highlighting potential linkages, conflicts and interactions
- SEA can improve the environmental quality of planning policies by refining their content
- By raising awareness of environmental impacts, SEA can help to ensure that decision makers acknowledge these issues during the preparation of land use plans
- Participatory SEA procedures enable a range of perspectives other than those of the planning authority to influence the content of land use plans
- SEA can inform stakeholders of the environmental impacts of strategic decisions and can also open a dialogue between stakeholder groups
- As SEA highlights how environmental issues have been taken into account during decision making, it can help to avoid delays in the implementation of land use plans by reducing the chance of costly litigation brought by affected stakeholder groups
- SEA can identify the issues to be monitored during the implementation of land use plans
- SEA can improve the green image of planning authorities.

The opportunities for the SEA of land use plans are therefore legion. The achievement of environmental goals associated with sustainable development necessitates the consideration of the environment as part of any transparent, accountable and holistic plan making system. For these reasons, the use of SEA during the preparation of land use plans is likely to continue to increase.

SEA of land use plans: constraints

SEA can deliver numerous benefits, most significantly by helping to develop land use plans that reflect sustainable development goals. However, Stinchcombe and Gibson (2001) believed that the contribution made by SEA to the delivery of sustainable development goals had been limited to date and that, despite the rhetoric, the systematic and comprehensive evaluation of the environmental impacts of plans remained rare.

The most important reason for this is the position of SEA in the political arena. Political will and support is the precondition for effective SEA (Sadler and Verheem, 1996). However, as Kørnøv (1997, p176) stated: 'in reality, policy making commonly takes place behind closed doors and involves a relatively small number of people who set the agenda and influence decisions on issues that find their way onto that agenda'. This lack of inclusiveness may be constraining the development and effective application of SEA. It means, for example, that the lack of weight given to a professional SEA in political decision making is likely to be a considerable constraint. In addition, SEA procedures may be open to political manipulation. As Stinchcombe and Gibson (2001, p367) noted: 'the assessment process itself is malleable and decision makers can manipulate it to their preferred course of action'. It cannot, therefore, be assumed that SEA reports are always unbiased, as they might, in reality, be manipulated to achieve desired political goals. It is feasible, therefore, that politically derived objectives could influence the form and function of SEAs. Such political influences over the use and undertaking of SEA are unlikely to be conducive to the realization of the potential benefits associated with SEA.

Several other factors constrain the development of SEA (Therivel et al, 1992; Sadler and Verheem, 1996; Therivel and Partidário, 1996; Curran et al, 1998; Glasson and Gosling, 2001; Wood, 2002; Owens et al, 2004; Therivel, 2004). The various constraints relating to the system within which the SEA process operates and to SEA methodologies are summarized in Box 2.4.

The political constraints central to the systemic SEA problems (Box 2.4) are probably more intractable than those relating to SEA methods (which may be easier to address in the short term). Many of the potential opportunities associated with SEA are likely to remain largely aspirational until these constraints are addressed. The effectiveness of SEA may remain limited without a 'culture shift' towards a more supportive political system. The burgeoning legal requirements for SEA in many countries should provide the stimulus to overcome some (but not all) of these constraints and allow SEA to ascend from the lower rungs of the ladder of sustainable development (Chapter 1) where it currently remains.

Box 2.4 Systemic and methodological SEA constraints

Systemic SEA constraints

- SEA operates within politically motivated decision making arena in which environmental concerns are not always paramount; political will to undertake SEA may therefore not exist
- Some plan making processes are nebulous, non-linear, complex and iterative, reducing effectiveness of rational and linear SEA techniques
- Land use plans often produced and appraised by same organization, resulting in 'poacher/gamekeeper' problems
- Public sector departments are rarely integrated, making assessing and addressing environmental impacts, which often cross institutional boundaries, problematic
- Need, at times, to maintain plan confidentiality can limit effectiveness of SEA.

Methodological SEA constraints

- Wide geographical scale, extended time horizons and broad range of alternatives inherent in assessing plans can complicate SEA
- Confusion between plan making and SEA activities often exists, hampering proper delineation of extent of SEA
- Unresolved debate over whether to incorporate social and economic issues within SEA limits development of methods
- Robust procedures for integrating SEA within plans rare, limiting its influence on decision making
- Methods for enabling tiering of assessments between different levels of decision making (eg SEA and EIA) limited
- Qualitative assessment techniques are underdeveloped
- SEA poorly equipped for handling uncertainty that characterizes many environmental systems
- Levels of consultation and public participation within SEA vary; lack of consensus on how to handle resulting representations
- Monitoring often not undertaken, reducing chance of SEA developing iteratively.

Notes

1   The first public use of this term was in a paper presented at an International Association for Impact Assessment (IAIA) conference (Wood and Djeddour, 1990) which was subsequently published in modified form in the IAIA journal (Wood and Djeddour, 1992)

2   The SEA Directive, the EIA Directive and other relevant EA documents can be accessed at: http://europa.eu.int/comm/environment/eia/

References

Bass, R. E., Herson, A. I. and Bogdan, K. M. (1999) *CEQA Deskbook: a Step-by-Step Guide on How to Comply with the California Environmental Quality Act*, 2nd edition, Solano Press, Point Arena, CA

Bass, R. E., Herson, A. I. and Bogdan, K. M. (2001) *The NEPA Book: a Step-by-Step Guide on How to Comply with the National Environmental Policy Act*, 2nd edition, Solano Press, Point Arena, CA

Brown, A. and Therivel, R. (2000) 'Principles to guide the development of strategic environmental assessment methodology', *Impact Assessment and Project Appraisal*, vol 18, pp183–189

Canadian Environmental Assessment Agency (1999) *Strategic Environmental Assessment; the 1999 Cabinet Directive on the Environmental Assessment of Policy, Plan and Program Proposals: Guidelines for Implementing the Cabinet Directive*, CEAA, Hull, Quebec

Commission of the European Communities (1985) 'Council Directive of 27 June 1985 on the assessment of the effects of certain public and private projects on the environment', *Official Journal of the European Communities*, vol L175, pp40–48, 5 July

Commission of the European Communities (1993) 'Towards Sustainability: Fifth Environmental Action Programme', *Official Journal of the European Communities*, vol C138, pp5–98, 17 May

Council on Environmental Quality (1978) 'Regulations for implementing the procedural provisions of the National Environmental Quality Act', *40 Code of Federal Regulations*, 1500–1508

Curran, J. M., Wood, C. M. and Hilton, M. (1998) 'Environmental appraisal of UK development plans: current practice and future directions', *Environment and Planning B: Planning and Design*, vol 25, pp411–433

European Commission (2001) 'Directive 2001/42/EC of the European Parliament and of the Council of 27 June 2001 on the assessment of the effects of certain plans and programmes on the environment', *Official Journal of the European Communities*, vol L197, pp30–37, 21 July

Fischer, T. and Seaton, K. (2002) 'Strategic environmental assessment: effective planning instrument or lost concept?', *Planning Practice and Research*, vol 17, pp31–44

Glasson, J. and Gosling, J. (2001) 'SEA and regional planning – overcoming the institutional constraints: some lessons from the EU', *European Environment*, vol 11, pp89–102

Kørnøv, L. (1997) 'Strategic environmental assessment: sustainability and democratization', *European Environment*, vol 7, pp175–180

Kørnøv, L. and Thissen, W. (2000) 'Rationality in decision- and policy-making: implications for strategic environmental assessment', *Impact Assessment and Project Appraisal*, vol 18, pp191–200

Nilsson, M. and Dalkmann, H. (2001) 'Decision making and strategic environmental assessment', *Journal of Environmental Assessment Policy and Management*, vol 3, pp305–329

Nitz, T. and Brown, A. (2001) 'SEA must learn how policy making works', *Journal of Environmental Assessment Policy and Management*, vol 3, pp329–343

Noble, B. (2000) 'Strategic environmental assessment: what is it? And what makes it strategic?' *Journal of Environmental Assessment Policy and Management*, vol 2, pp203–224

Owens, S. and Cowell, R. (2002) *Land and Limits: Interpreting Sustainability in the Planning Process*, Routledge, London

Owens, S., Rayner, T. and Bina, O. (2004) 'New agendas for appraisal: reflections on theory, practice, and research', *Environment and Planning A*, vol 36, pp1943–1959

Partidário, M. (2000) 'Elements of an SEA framework – improving the added-value of SEA', *Environmental Impact Assessment Review*, vol 20, pp647–663

Risse, N., Crowley, M., Vincke, P. and Waaub, J.-P. (2003) 'Implementing the European SEA Directive: the member states' margin of discretion', *Environmental Impact Assessment Review*, vol 23, pp453–470

Royal Commission on Environmental Pollution (2002) *Twenty-third Report: Environmental Planning*, Cm 5459, The Stationery Office, London

Sadler, B. (2001a) 'Strategic environmental assessment: an aide memoire to drafting a SEA protocol to the Espoo Convention', in Dusik, J. (ed) *Proceedings of International Workshop on Public Participation and Health Aspects in Strategic Environmental Assessment*, Regional Environmental Center for Central and Eastern Europe, Szentendre

Sadler, B. (2001b) 'A framework approach to strategic environmental assessment: aims, principles and elements of good practice', in Dusik, J. (ed) *Proceedings of International Workshop on Public Participation and Health Aspects in Strategic Environmental Assessment*, Regional Environmental Center for Central and Eastern Europe, Szentendre

Sadler, B. and Verheem, R. (1996) *Strategic Environmental Assessment: Status, Challenges and Future Directions*, Publication Number 53, Ministry of Housing, Spatial Planning and the Environment, The Hague

Sigal, L. L. and Webb, J. W. (1989) 'The programmatic environmental impact statement: its purpose and use', *The Environmental Professional*, vol 11, pp14–24

Stinchcombe, K. and Gibson, R. (2001) 'Strategic environmental assessment as a means of pursuing sustainability: ten advantages and ten challenges', *Journal of Environmental Assessment Policy and Management*, vol 3, pp343–373

Therivel, R. (2004) *Strategic Environmental Assessment in Action*, Earthscan, London

Therivel, R. and Partidário, M. (eds) (1996) *The Practice of Strategic Environmental Assessment*, Earthscan, London

Therivel, R., Wilson, E., Thompson, S., Heaney, D. and Pritchard, D. (1992) *Strategic Environmental Assessment*, Earthscan, London

United Nations Conference on Environment and Development (1992a) *Agenda 21*, United Nations, New York

United Nations Conference on Environment and Development (1992b) *Rio Declaration on Environment and Development: Programme of Action for Sustainable Development*, United Nations, New York

United Nations Economic Commission for Europe (1992) *Application of Environmental Impact Assessment Principles to Policies, Plans and Programmes*, Environmental Series 5, UNECE, Geneva

United Nations Economic Commission for Europe (2003) *Protocol on Strategic Environmental Assessment to the Convention on Environmental Impact Assessment in a Transboundary Context*, ECE/MP.EIA/2003/3, UNECE, Geneva, www.unece.org/env/eia/documents/protocolenglish.pdf

Verheem, R. and Tonk, J. (2000) 'Strategic environmental assessment: one concept, multiple forms', *Impact Assessment and Project Appraisal*, vol 18, pp177–182

von Seht, H. (1999) 'Requirements of a comprehensive strategic environmental assessment system', *Landscape and Urban Planning*, vol 45, pp1–14

Wood, C. M. (2002) *Environmental Impact Assessment: a Comparative Review*, 2nd edition, Prentice Hall, Harlow

Wood, C. M. and Djeddour, M. (1989) 'The environmental assessment of policies, plans and programmes', Volume 1 of Interim Report to the European Commission on

Environmental Assessment of Policies, Plans and Programmes and Preparation of a Vade Mecum, EIA Centre, University of Manchester, Manchester

Wood, C. M. and Djeddour, M. (1990) 'The environmental assessment of policies, plans and programmes', *Proceedings of 1990 Conference of the International Association for Impact Assessment*, Ecole Polytechnique Federale de Lausanne, Lausanne

Wood, C. M. and Djeddour, M. (1992) 'Strategic environmental assessment: EA of policies, plans and programmes', *Impact Assessment Bulletin*, vol 10, pp3–22

World Bank (1987) *Environment, Growth and Development*, Development Committee Paper 14, World Bank, Washington, DC

World Commission on Environment and Development (1987) *Our Common Future*, Oxford University Press, Oxford

3

Evaluating the SEA of Land Use Plans

Carys Jones, Mark Baker, Jeremy Carter, Stephen Jay,
Michael Short and Christopher Wood

Introduction

As explained in Chapter 1, evaluating SEA practice is a multifaceted exercise in which a distinction must be made between quality and effectiveness (Thissen, 2000). The former refers to determinants of quality that can be split into legal, institutional and other arrangements (system inputs) and SEA procedures and methods (process inputs). The latter relates to outputs, both direct and indirect, such as the achievement of identified goals or the contribution to best practice (outcomes). Accordingly, the judgement of the quality and effectiveness of the SEA process involves the use of different types of criteria, which can be split into three broad categories:

System criteria. These input criteria evaluate the framework within which the SEA process operates. This is effectively the supporting system guiding and shaping SEA practice in each particular country. These criteria feed in to the SEA process, and therefore relate to the quality of the supporting system. In turn, these factors are likely to influence the quality of SEA procedures and ultimately, the effectiveness of SEA of land use plans. The system criteria relate to:

- legal basis;
- integration;
- guidance;
- coverage;
- tiering;
- sustainable development.

Process criteria. The second set of input criteria evaluates the quality of SEA procedures and methods applied during the SEA of land use plans. The criteria are methodological, focusing on the different aspects of the good practice SEA process (Table 2.1). They influence the quality of the SEA process which, in turn, influences the outcome of the SEA. For example, if reasonable alternatives were considered at an early stage in the plan preparation process, the influence of the SEA on the content of the plan could potentially be increased. The process criteria relate to:

- alternatives;
- screening;
- scoping;
- prediction/evaluation;
- additional impacts;
- report preparation;
- review;
- monitoring;
- mitigation;
- consultation and public participation.

Outcome criteria. Output criteria evaluate the outcome of the SEA process. The criteria relate to the effectiveness of the SEA on decisions made about land use plans. In addition to the direct outputs of the SEA, factors influencing the future effectiveness of the SEA process and environmental quality are included in the outcome criteria:

- decision making;
- costs and benefits;
- environmental quality;
- system monitoring.

The criteria employed in this book have been developed from legislation, guidance documents, books, journal articles, workshops and interviews with practitioners. Sources include Wood and Djeddour (1992), Department of the Environment (1993), Partidário (1996), Sadler (1996, 1998), Therivel and Partidário (1996, 2000), von Seht (1999), Verheem and Tonk (2000), Fischer (2001), International Association for Impact Assessment (2002), Wood (2002) and Therivel (2004). Taken together, the criteria provide a means of gaining an indication of the quality and effectiveness of the SEA process applied to land use plan making. The 20 criteria are expressed in the form of questions designed to focus the evaluation on the central issue to which each criterion relates. Further explanation of the criteria, which are summarized in Table 3.1, follows.

System criteria

Legal basis

Until recently, SEA has developed mostly in the absence of legal provisions requiring SEA in land use planning or other strategic activities. This has allowed SEA to adapt more easily to a diverse range of strategic actions, rather than be codified into set procedures (Therivel and Partidário, 1996). It can be argued that SEA should retain maximum flexibility in order to be relevant to widely varying policy, plan and programme-making contexts (Verheem and Tonk, 2000). However, mandatory systems of SEA have a number of advantages: ensuring that strategic actions with potentially significant environmental effects do not escape assessment, helping to justify adequate resourcing of SEA, giving greater legal force to SEA findings, and so on. Moreover, legal requirements for SEA can themselves be shaped to different areas of activity, including such well-defined sectors as land use planning. It is likely, therefore, that clear legal frameworks will prove to be beneficial to SEA practice, whether providing a minimum regulatory context (Partidário, 2000), or a more prescriptive set of procedures (von Seht, 1999). As a minimum, a legal basis for the overall aims of SEA, for basic SEA requirements and standards and for the allocation of responsibilities is likely to increase effectiveness.

Integration

The fundamental aim of SEA can be described as the integration of environmental considerations into decision making processes from the earliest possible stages onwards (Sadler and Verheem, 1996). It is increasingly recognized that, for this to be achieved, the SEA process itself should be closely integrated into the preparation of the land use plan being assessed, and not be carried out as a separate exercise. SEA should be carried out concurrently, as a form of 'dialogue' with the plan, so that it is able to bring maximum influence to bear upon the plan. Integration of this kind has helped SEA to achieve its aims (Fischer, 2001), especially in the context of land use planning (Baker and Roberts, 1999; Therivel and Minas, 2002). Curran et al (1998) suggested that the benefits to be gained from assessing a land use plan from the earliest stages of preparation include: increased awareness of environmental considerations by the participants; greater levels of consultation and hence reduced levels of opposition; better comparison of alternatives; and an assurance that all potential impacts are considered. In the UK, current methodologies are being devised to enable SEA to be carried out as an integral part of plan making (Therivel, 2004).

Guidance

Given that many SEA practitioners are currently learning to utilize and develop SEA methodologies and techniques, guidance has an important role in the application and adaptation of SEA to different types of land use plan. Guidance can assist in forming the overall rationale for a SEA process and can help when carrying out more detailed aspects of SEA. It is particularly during capacity building that guidance (and associated training) is beneficial to those involved in SEA, and can accelerate the development of good practice (Therivel, 2004). This was found to be the case in the early experience of environmental assessment of development plans in the UK (Curran et al, 1998), and can continue to assist in putting SEA in place (Partidário, 1996). Guidance can be based upon regulatory requirements that are in force or upon broader, evolving, principles of SEA. It can take the form of official guidance, produced by government departments, or may be produced by practitioners, academics, agencies, etc. It is likely that land use planners will expect official guidance to provide a practical framework to enable them to carry out SEA.

Coverage

The coverage of SEA systems relates both to the range of land use plans subjected to SEA and to the range of impacts regarded as relevant. It is generally accepted that the impacts of all environmentally significant new and modified land use plans should be subject to SEA unless there is an overwhelming reason why this should not be done (for example, national security considerations). However, there may be minor modifications to land use plans which do not normally give rise to significant environmental impacts.

The definition of 'environment' in SEA has varied in different jurisdictions. The National Environmental Policy Act 1969 (NEPA) defined 'environment' to include social and economic impacts, as well as physical environmental impacts (for example, pollution, effects on ecology) (Bass et al, 2001). The coverage of later SEA systems has sometimes, but by no means always, followed the precedent set by NEPA. For example, European Directive 2001/42/EC ('the SEA Directive') (European Commission (EC), 2001) effectively eschews consideration of social and economic impacts. Whether or not SEA processes cover impacts other than those on the physical environment is probably not critical, especially as the distinction between them is often a narrow one in practice. It is, however, important that all impacts on the physical environment are encompassed by the SEA system. Thus, impacts on the various environmental media (for example, the air), on living receptors (such as people, plants) and on the built environment (buildings) should be considered (Wood, 2002).

Tiering

Since strategic actions themselves are often tiered from policy to plan to programme to project, there can therefore be tiering of their associated assessments (Chapter 1). This allows higher order policies, plans and programmes (PPPs) to set the context for actions at lower levels, including projects. A key element of tiering is to avoid duplication of issues in assessments of PPPs and projects. Therefore, once an issue has been assessed at a higher level it should not be necessary to consider it again at a lower level, other than perhaps to provide essential detail not provided in the prior assessment. For example, the SEA of a land use plan could set the terms of reference for a resulting EIA and assist its scoping. Similarly, the SEA of a land use plan might indicate either that a subsequent EIA, or the assessment of certain environmental aspects in an EIA, might not be required. Finally, the SEA can indicate mitigation measures that need to be addressed in the assessment of subsequent plans or projects (Therivel, 2004). The use of tiering should promote greater efficiency in SEA at different levels and also increase linkages between PPPs and their respective SEAs (Partidário, 1996). However, tiering between particular PPPs and projects is rarely an ordered and linear process and therefore the potential efficiencies from their assessments may not be realized in practice. Furthermore, sectors (such as waste and minerals) may often overlap, or PPPs themselves may not be distinct in terms of their terminology and content and may also overlap. It should also be borne in mind that policies and programmes often develop 'bottom up' as a result of decisions taken at lower tiers, further complicating the notion of tiering (Noble, 2000).

Sustainable development

The concept of sustainable development provides the overarching structure around which much contemporary SEA theory and practice is based (Sheate, 2001). One of the principal reasons for undertaking SEA is to help to make society's actions more sustainable (Brown and Therivel, 2000; Sadler, 2001; Stinchcombe and Gibson, 2001); to aid the achievement of what O'Riordan and Voisey (1997) have termed 'the sustainability transition'. Significantly, recent international SEA legislation, including a draft protocol on SEA (United Nations Economic Commission for Europe, 2003) and the SEA Directive (EC, 2001), have placed sustainable development at their core. If one SEA outcome is to contribute to delivering the sustainable development agenda, the concept must be incorporated as a central element of the SEA process. Sustainable development can be enshrined in SEA system legislation and guidance, and incorporated into the SEA process through the use of appropriate objectives and criteria.

Process criteria

Alternatives

Part of the original rationale for proposing a strategic level of environmental assessment was that, by the time plans for an individual project are put forward, there is little opportunity for considering alternatives to the proposal, especially of a wide ranging nature; alternatives are effectively 'foreclosed' (Lee and Walsh, 1992). SEA, on the other hand, by looking at longer-term and larger-scale plans, can give proper consideration to different ways of achieving certain aims and present a comparison of the likely environmental consequences of each option. This continues to be one of the main perceived benefits of SEA (Stinchcombe and Gibson, 2001). Indeed, Noble has defined SEA as 'the proactive assessment of alternatives' (2000, p215), suggesting that the primary aim of SEA is the choice of the preferred strategic action. It is important, therefore, that a SEA process enables the generation of a wide range of possible means of achieving a plan's objectives, and presents a comparative assessment of the most reasonable alternatives. Most probably, these will be alternative proposals *within* a land use plan, rather than alternatives *to* the plan itself. The SEA documentation should also record the justification for the choice of preferred alternatives. Overall, 'the role of SEA is to help identify more long term, sustainable alternatives; identify and assess the environmental impacts of different alternatives to help inform and support the choice of alternatives. . .; and help to document how the preferred alternative(s) was chosen' (Therivel, 2004, p110).

Screening

When considering whether SEA is required, it is necessary to look at the vision or purpose of the land use plan and its influences. Screening will therefore help to identify which plans require more consideration and thus assessment of their environmental consequences (Partidário, 1996). Not all land use plans need a SEA, and a screening stage provides a systematic approach to considering whether a particular plan warrants assessment. If there is no screening, either resources may be wasted on unnecessary SEAs or potentially severe environmental consequences may result from not undertaking a SEA (von Seht, 1999). In order to achieve consistency, an approach to screening is usually decided at the national level when establishing a SEA system (Therivel, 2004). Approaches can involve screening all plans according to specified criteria, or the use of lists, thresholds or criteria specifying broad categories of plans (for example, sectoral or regional) either to be subject to, or excluded from, SEA. Alternatively, a combination of these approaches may be applied (von Seht, 1999; Therivel, 2004). Criteria may include sensitivity of the location, nature of land uses, size and characteristics of the land use plan. Other considerations include the degree to which any plan sets a framework for subsequent projects and other activities, and the degree to which a land use plan influences other plans. The involvement of environmental and other relevant authorities, and the public as appropriate, is desirable in screening. A screening system that is clear and simple to operate will result in greater efficiency and reduced uncertainty.

Scoping

Scoping involves deciding the key issues (spatial, temporal, organizational) and the level of detail to be addressed by the SEA. The assessment can then focus on the main environmental aspects and set the framework for developing targets and indicators. Less significant issues can be disregarded, with reasons given for these decisions. A good scoping stage can enhance the efficiency and effectiveness of the assessment, and the quality of the subsequent SEA report; this is dependent on a careful choice of issues and the time available (von Seht, 1999; Therivel and

Brown, 1999). In determining what information will be needed, it is useful to be clear why information is required. (For example, baseline data may be needed to identify and address problems, to provide a basis for impact prediction and to support future monitoring.) In particular, the selection of issues should concentrate on those important for decision making in the context of the land use plan. Issues to be considered during scoping are often defined by the extant legislation, or may be identified from higher level plans (von Seht, 1999). The assessment need not aim for the level of detail of EIA, or assemble a large volume of baseline data (Therivel, 2004). Additionally, any likely procedural or technical aspects or difficulties can be considered during scoping, together with assumptions and uncertainties.

The SEA Directive specifically introduced scoping as a means of improving the quality of SEA reports (EC, 2003). Consultation of environmental authorities is important in deciding on the scope and level of information to be included in a SEA report. Public participation can be important for acceptance of the plan, but, in practice, can be problematic. The techniques involved in scoping might include literature surveys, checklists, analogy, overlay maps, public consultation and expert judgement (Therivel and Partidário, 1996). The production of a report on the scoping process and its agreed outcomes can support the consultation process and subsequent assessment.

Prediction/evaluation

Strategic actions, by their nature, have wider ranging and less predictable outcomes than individual developments. It has therefore been acknowledged, since early studies on SEA (Wood and Djeddour, 1992), that the assessment of the possible effects of strategic proposals will be characterized by a high level of uncertainty, and is not likely to be carried out as rigorously and quantitatively as the equivalent phase at project level. Nevertheless, a SEA process would be redundant without a meaningful assessment of the likely effects of strategic proposals.

Two broad approaches can be taken (Partidário, 1996; Sheate, 2001). Firstly, proposals can be assessed against empirical data to predict the likely difference that certain actions would make to a baseline environment (following the EIA model). Secondly, proposals can be tested against environmental objectives, to see whether or not they are likely to contribute to, or work against, the achievement of those objectives (more akin to the policy appraisal model). Whichever approach is taken, likely effects should be assessed against explicit environmental criteria, and should be expressed in terms of all relevant factors, such as magnitude, duration, probability, reversibility, etc. Indirect and cumulative effects resulting from multiple activities are likely to need particular attention (Therivel and Partidário, 1996). In addition, there should be an evaluation of the significance of changes likely to be brought about by the proposals, by taking into account the sensitivity of the receiving environment. A large range of techniques is available for prediction and evaluation, including modelling, overlay maps, carrying capacity and scenario analysis, expert opinion and public participation (Therivel, 2004).

Additional impacts

Secondary, cumulative and synergistic impacts have traditionally been dealt with poorly in project EIA and improving their consideration has been an important argument in the advancement of SEA (Wood and Djeddour, 1992). It is therefore unsurprising that the European SEA Directive specifies that significant effects on the environment include 'secondary, cumulative, synergistic, short, medium, and long-term, permanent and temporary, positive and negative effects' (EC, 2001, Annex I). NEPA has always required the consideration of indirect, cumulative and growth inducing effects (Bass et al, 2001). The consideration of the impacts of land use plans on global warming (a long-term effect) is becoming more common in SEA.

The EC (1999) has drawn a distinction between secondary (or indirect) impacts (for example, additional traffic arising from a major housing development), cumulative impacts (such as additional traffic arising from several minor housing developments) and impact interactions (for example, oxides of nitrogen interacting with sulphur dioxide from power stations to affect the acidity of fresh water (Council on Environmental Quality, 1997; Ross, 1998). Networks can be a valuable supplement to expert opinion in identifying indirect and cumulative impacts (EC, 1999). Checking the predicted magnitude of cumulative impacts against specific targets is an important means of evaluating these impacts in SEA (Therivel, 2004).

Report preparation

It is to be expected that any SEA process concerned with strategies that could have wide ranging consequences will involve documentation of its findings, firstly as a permanent record, and secondly as the visible 'face' of the process. This is all the more important for the SEA of publicly accountable activities, such as land use planning, where a SEA report should be available for public inspection as part of the documents associated with the planning process undergoing assessment. Von Seht (1999) argued that a SEA report should include, at least: a description of the proposed action and its main alternatives; a description of the baseline environment; the significant environmental impacts of the proposed action and alternatives; the timescale and likelihood of predicted impacts; possible mitigation measures; and comments on any assessment problems. It should be remembered, however, that the report is not an end in itself, and is subordinate to the more fundamental aim of environmental considerations being integrated into decision making (Brown and Therivel, 2000; Kørnøv and Thissen, 2000; Owens et al, 2004). The role of the SEA report is to contribute to this by making the SEA process transparent and showing the degree to which SEA has, in fact, shaped the proposed strategy. In this sense, adequate documentation can be considered as an essential part of SEA, ensuring that 'the results of the assessment are identifiable, understandable and available to all parties affected by the decision' (Verheem and Tonk, 2000, p179).

Review

Although environmental assessment procedures aim for objectivity in their approach, legitimate concerns can be raised about the outputs of any given SEA process. Questions could be asked, for example, about the scope and accuracy of assessing the effects of a proposed strategy; the adequacy of consultation; or the impartiality of those conducting the SEA. One remedy is to subject the SEA process to independent review, prior to the findings of the SEA being used in decision making. In particular, the SEA report can be scrutinized to test its sufficiency for decision making purposes. For example, von Seht (1999) recommended that the proposed plan, as already amended by the SEA process, and the final version of SEA documentation should be subject to a last round of public consultation before they are presented for decision making. Alternatively, a formal and transparent quality review mechanism could be set up, possibly involving an independent body specializing in evaluating SEA reports (Verheem and Tonk, 2000).

Monitoring

Monitoring the implementation of a plan allows linkage back to predictions made during the assessment process, and ensures that the plan achieves its objectives and that mitigation measures are implemented (Therivel and Brown, 1999). Any unexpected or underestimated negative effects can be identified. This is particularly important in SEA due to the high level of uncertainty in making predictions at the plan level (von Seht, 1999). The areas of identified uncertainty can guide any monitoring required which, in turn, can reduce the uncertainty. It is helpful if the indicators and objectives used in describing the baseline and in making predictions are also used in monitoring (Therivel, 2004). The monitoring scheme will need to be flexible as environmental impacts will rarely occur immediately after implementation of the plan and often tend to arise from consequential future actions. Monitoring thus needs to be linked to assessment tasks, decision making on the plan and plan implementation (Lee, 1998). The outputs from monitoring can provide feedback to future SEAs, which is particularly important where another SEA may need to be undertaken, for example, when a land use plan is revised at regular intervals. It is also possible to use monitoring results as an input into other assessments, such as SEAs for other plans, or EIAs for projects, and a tiering system can provide the mechanism and impetus for undertaking monitoring (Sheate et al, 2003). Resources can be used more efficiently if existing data and regimes are utilized where relevant (EC, 2003) and if the activities of various authorities and organizations can be coordinated and managed to share data (Therivel, 2004).

Mitigation

The influence of SEA on the content of land use plans stems from its ability to inject timely environmental information into the decision making process. Some of these data may take the form of mitigation measures, which highlight ways in which the potential positive and negative environmental impacts of the proposed action identified during the SEA could be enhanced or remediated. This is not an explicit SEA stage, as mitigation measures should be considered throughout the process, thus enabling the continual refinement of the plan being assessed. As Therivel and Brown (1999, p447) stated, 'the real value of SEA is as a creative tool in the design cycle in the formulation and reformulation of PPPs'. Furthermore, Partidário (2000) highlighted the role of SEA as a facilitator, describing the process as an 'aide memoire' to be considered during decision making. In order for SEA to realize this role, mitigation measures relating to improving the environmental performance of the plan must be suggested. The proposing of mitigation measures is, therefore, good practice as it increases the chances of improvements being made to the environmental performance of the plan during the political decision making process.

Consultation and public participation

Consultation and public participation within the SEA process is widely regarded as being good practice (Bedfordshire County Council and the Royal Society for the Protection of Birds, 1996; Partidário, 1996; Sadler and Verheem, 1996; Curran et al, 1998; Therivel, 2004). Public participation: 'ensures procedural integrity and provides relevant information and input to policy development' (Sadler and Verheem, 1996, p87). It is therefore important to give stakeholders the opportunity to communicate their environmental preferences and values, and to contribute to undertaking the SEA process. As stakeholders' opinions will often be in conflict with those of the plan proponent, such information enables the proponent to take these into account, thereby potentially facilitating the minimization of conflict during plan preparation. Stakeholders can also provide valuable information to improve the comprehensiveness of the impact assessment process. Moreover, consultation and pubic participation can help to generate a sense of ownership of the plan among stakeholders; can enhance stakeholders' understanding of issues including planning procedures and environmental impacts; and can increase the transparency of the plan preparation process.

Consultation and public participation do not form separate stage of the SEA process, as relevant authorities and the public should ideally be involved at various points during the SEA. In particular, external involvement (especially of the wider public) is important at early SEA stages, including scoping and the selection of objectives/criteria. Consultation and public participation are also desirable following impact evaluation, but before the plan is adopted. This would usually be during the review of the quality of the SEA process and of any documentation produced. Representations made by stakeholders should be considered during both the SEA process and plan preparation.

Outcome criteria

Decision making

It is likely that poorly informed decisions are a significant factor in the generation of many contemporary environmental problems. SEA can help to address this weakness by providing decision makers with timely and relevant information concerning the potential environmental impacts of the strategic actions that they are responsible for developing and implementing. Verheem and Tonk (2000, p177) described SEA as 'a structured proactive process to strengthen the role of environmental issues in decision making'. SEA is essentially a process driven by decision making and should influence the decisions taken during the preparation of land use plans. As Devuyst (2000, p79) stated; 'the ultimate goal of SEA is to make an optimal decision'. While the SEA process and the information it provides will not (and should not) actually make decisions, if SEA does not influence decision making about the environmental content of plans, for example, by leading to the adoption of mitigation measures, its effectiveness in plan preparation is diminished. Furthermore, it is necessary for decision makers to acknowledge how SEA influenced their actions; something that can be achieved by providing a response to the recommendations made within SEA reports.

Costs and benefits

There are numerous potential benefits associated with the application of SEA during the preparation of land use plans (Chapter 2). SEA is intended to improve the quality of decisions having environmental implications by amending the behaviour of planners, consultants, consultees, the public and the decision making authorities. Other potential benefits include raising awareness of environmental issues, generating resource savings and strengthening planning procedures. As these benefits can be difficult to identify, it is generally necessary to rely mainly on stakeholders' opinions to establish their existence. Despite their sometimes amorphous nature, it is important to ascertain SEA's potential benefits in order to provide a platform for the development of the process in the future.

Planning authorities may have to maintain or retain specialist SEA staff, or to shift personnel from other activities. Similarly, consultee organizations and the public will have to expend resources if they are to participate effectively. Closely allied to these direct costs are those of delay to planning procedures. The costs of SEA systems are difficult to distinguish from other costs incurred in the preparation of land use plans, especially where SEA is well integrated into plan making processes. However, as in the case of EIA, the additional costs attributable to SEA appear to be small; for example, Short et al (2004) reported costs of less than 3 per cent in the UK. The continued diffusion of SEA requirements around the world demonstrates the prevailing belief that SEA is an effective and efficient environmental management tool; in other words, that the benefits conferred by the SEA process outweigh the costs (Wood, 2002).

Environmental quality

The oft-repeated aim of SEA, to assist the incorporation of environmental considerations into strategic decision making, has the implicit underlying goal of protecting and improving the environment of the area affected. This is increasingly stated in terms of sustainability; SEA is seen as a means of 'moving policy . . . towards sustainable outcomes' (Brown and Therivel, 2000, p184). An important test of the effectiveness of SEA is, therefore, the difference that it makes to environmental quality 'on the ground'. This raises questions about the best approach by which SEA might achieve environmental improvement: whether SEA should have a strong advocacy role in favour of environmental protection alone; or should include economic and social objectives within its remit, and thus be better integrated into decision making (Kørnøv and Thissen, 2000). It is clear, however, that SEA must contribute 'added value' to strategic planning (Partidário, 2000), which can be most clearly demonstrated through seeing improved environmental conditions as a result of the SEA. This reinforces the need for monitoring arrangements to be established through the SEA process, by which key environmental trends can be observed, as a measure of the outcome of SEA (von Seht, 1999).

System monitoring

The principal purposes of SEA system monitoring are the evaluation of SEA system effectiveness; the amendment of SEA processes to incorporate feedback from experience and to remedy any weaknesses identified; and the diffusion of best SEA practice (Sadler, 1998). SEA system monitoring requires records to be kept of the numbers of SEA reports produced; the types of land use plans assessed; decisions reached; the numbers of plans implemented; availability of documents; and so on. The better the SEA system monitoring information available, the easier such a review will be. Ideally, all SEA reports and other SEA documents should be publicly available at one or more central locations. Collections of SEA reports provide an invaluable source of information to those engaged in preparing such documents; those responsible for reviewing them; those likely to be consulted; the public; and those undertaking research and training.

As with other elements of the SEA process, the role of consultation and participation in reviews of the SEA system is important, and the opinions of the various stakeholders in the SEA process should be sought. Experience of specific SEAs may reveal that changes need to be made in practice or in procedure within the SEA system more generally. Provision should be made for the feedback of monitoring findings, including recommendations regarding the improvement of SEA system effectiveness. Such recommendations might relate to legislation, regulations, circulars, practice advice notes, production or amendment of guidelines, training, and so on (Wood, 2002).

Conclusion

This chapter has provided an overview of the system, process and outcome criteria that have been developed to assess the quality and effectiveness of the SEA of land use plans in this book. Table 3.1 presents the evaluation criteria expressed in question form. These criteria form the basis of the evaluations of the SEA of land use plans in 13 countries, and in the World Bank, which are reported in Chapters 4–17 of this book.

Table 3.1 *Criteria for evaluating the SEA of land use plans*

System criteria	
Legal basis	Are there clear legal provisions, defining broad objectives, standards and terms of reference, to undertake the SEA of land use plans?
Integration	Is there provision for the early integration of SEA and land use plan preparation?
Guidance	Does guidance relating specifically to the SEA of land use plans exist?
Coverage	Must the significant environmental effects of all land use plans be subjected to SEA?
Tiering	Is the SEA of land use plans undertaken within a tiered system of environmental assessment?
Sustainable development	Is the concept of sustainable development integral to the SEA process?
Process criteria	
Alternatives	Does the SEA process provide for the consideration of reasonable alternatives, and must reasons for the choice of the selected alternative be outlined?
Screening	Must screening of land use plans for environmental significance take place?
Scoping	Are the boundaries of SEAs determined using scoping procedures?
Prediction/ evaluation	Are the policies within land use plans assessed against environmental criteria, and is the significance of the potential impacts evaluated?
Additional impacts	Does the SEA process explicitly require consideration of secondary, synergistic or cumulative impacts?
Report preparation	Are the SEA procedures and their main findings recorded in publicly available SEA reports?
Review	Is the information included in SEA reports subjected to a transparent review process to check that it is sufficient to inform decision making?

Table 3.1 *Criteria for evaluating the SEA of land use plans (continued)*

Monitoring	Do SEAs include monitoring strategies linked to the achievement of pre-defined objectives for land use plans?
Mitigation	Does a mitigation strategy exist to promote environmental enhancement and the reduction of potentially negative environmental effects?
Consultation and public participation	Does consultation and public participation take place within the SEA process, and are the representations recorded and acted upon?
Outcome criteria	
Decision making	Do SEAs have any discernible influence on the content of land use plans or the treatment of environmental issues during decision making?
Costs and benefits	Are the discernible environmental benefits of the SEA process perceived to outweigh its costs?
Environmental quality	Has the SEA process had any effect 'on the ground' in terms of improving the environmental quality of the area?
System monitoring	Does any form of monitoring of the SEA process take place?

References

Baker, M. and Roberts, P. (1999) *Examination of the Operation and Effectiveness of the Structure Planning Process*, Department of the Environment, Transport and the Regions, London

Bass, R. E., Herson, A. I. and Bogdan, K. M. (2001) *The NEPA Book: A Step-by-Step Guide on How to Comply with the National Environmental Policy Act*, 2nd edition, Solano Press, Point Arena, CA

Bedfordshire County Council and the Royal Society for the Protection of Birds (1996) *A Step-by-Step Guide to Environmental Appraisal*, RSPB, Sandy, Beds

Brown, A. and Therivel, R. (2000) 'Principles to guide the development of strategic environmental assessment methodology', *Impact Assessment and Project Appraisal*, vol 18, pp183–189

Council on Environmental Quality (1997) *Considering Cumulative Impacts under the National Environmental Policy Act*, CEQ, Executive Office of the President, Washington, DC

Curran, J. M., Wood, C. M. and Hilton, M. (1998) 'Environmental appraisal of UK development plans; current practice and future directions', *Environment and Planning B*, vol 25, pp411–433

Department of the Environment (1993) *Environmental Appraisal of Development Plans: a Good Practice Guide*, HMSO, London

Devuyst, D. (2000) 'Linking impact assessment and sustainable development at the local level: the introduction of sustainability assessment systems', *Sustainable Development*, vol 3, pp62–78

European Commission (1999) *Guidelines for the Assessment of Indirect and Cumulative Impacts as well as Impact Interactions*, Directorate-General XI Environment, EC, Brussels

European Commission (2001) 'Directive 2001/42/EC of the European Parliament and of the Council of 27 June 2001 on the assessment of the effects of certain plans and programmes on the environment', *Official Journal of the European Communities*, vol L197, pp30–37, 21 July

European Commission (2003) *Implementation of Directive 2001/42 on the Assessment of the Effects of Certain Plans and Programmes on the Environment*, Directorate-General XI Environment, EC, Brussels

Fischer, T. B. (2001) 'Practice of environmental assessment for transport and land-use policies, plans and programmes', *Impact Assessment and Project Appraisal*, vol 19, pp41–51

International Association for Impact Assessment (2002) *Strategic Environmental Assessment Performance Criteria*, Special Publication Series Number 1, available at www.iaia.org

Kørnøv, L. and Thissen, W. (2000) 'Rationality in decision- and policy-making: implications for strategic environmental assessment', *Impact Assessment and Project Appraisal*, vol 18, pp191–200

Lee, N. (1998) 'SEA in the European Union: some issues and proposals', in Kleinschmidt, V. and Wagner, D. (eds) *Strategic Environmental Assessment in Europe: Fourth European Workshop on Environmental Impact Assessment*, Kluwer, Dordrecht

Lee, N. and Walsh, F. (1992) 'Strategic environmental assessment: an overview', *Project Appraisal*, vol 7, pp126–136

Noble, B. (2000) 'Strategic environmental assessment: what is it? And what makes it strategic?', *Journal of Environmental Assessment Policy and Management*, vol 2, pp203–224

O'Riordan, T. and Voisey, H. (1997) 'The political economy of sustainable development', *Environmental Politics*, vol 6, pp1–23

Owens, S., Rayner, T. and Bina, O. (2004) 'New agendas for appraisal: reflections on theory, practice, and research', *Environment and Planning A*, vol 36, pp1943–1959

Partidário, M. (1996) 'Strategic environmental assessment: key issues emerging from recent practice', *Environmental Impact Assessment Review*, vol 16, pp31–55

Partidário, M. (2000) 'Elements of an SEA framework – improving the added-value of SEA', *Environmental Impact Assessment Review*, vol 20, pp647–663

Ross, W. A. (1998) 'Cumulative effects assessment: learning from Canadian case studies', *Impact Assessment and Project Appraisal*, vol 16, pp267–276

Sadler, B. (1996) *Environmental Assessment in a Changing World: Evaluating Practice to Improve Performance*, Final Report, International Study of the Effectiveness of Environmental Assessment, Canadian Environmental Assessment Agency, Ottawa

Sadler, B. (1998) 'Ex-post evaluation of the effectiveness of environmental assessment', in Porter A. L. and Fittipaldi J. J. (eds) *Environmental Methods Review: Retooling Impact Assessment for the New Century*, International Association for Impact Assessment, Fargo, ND

Sadler, B. (2001) 'A framework approach to strategic environmental assessment: aims, principles and elements of good practice', in Dusik, J. (ed) *Proceedings of International Workshop on Public Participation and Health Aspects in Strategic Environmental Assessment*, Regional Environmental Center for Central and Eastern Europe, Szentendre

Sadler, B. and Verheem, R. (1996) *Strategic Environmental Assessment: Status, Challenges and Future Directions*, Publication Number 53, Ministry of Housing, Spatial Planning and the Environment, The Hague

Sheate, W. (2001) 'The rise of strategic assessment tools', *Journal of Environmental Assessment Policy and Management*, vol 3 pp iii–x

Sheate, W. R., Dagg, S., Richardson, J., Aschemann, R., Palerm, J. and Steen, U. (2003) 'Integrating the environment into strategic decision-making: conceptualising policy SEA', *European Environment*, vol 14, pp1–18

Short, M., Jones, C., Carter, J., Baker, M. and Wood, C. M. (2004) 'Current practice in the strategic environmental assessment of development plans in England', *Regional Studies*, vol 38, pp177–190

Stinchcombe, K. and Gibson, R. (2001) 'Strategic environmental assessment as a means of pursuing sustainability: ten advantages and ten challenges', *Journal of Environmental Assessment Policy and Management*, vol 3, pp343–372

Therivel, R. (2004) *Strategic Environmental Assessment in Action*, Earthscan, London

Therivel, R. and Brown, A. L. (1999) 'Methods of strategic environmental assessment', in Petts, J. (ed) *Handbook of Environmental Impact Assessment*, Volume 1, Blackwell, Oxford

Therivel, R. and Minas, P. (2002) 'Ensuring effective sustainability appraisal', *Impact Assessment and Project Appraisal*, vol 20, pp81–91

Therivel, R. and Partidário, M. (2000) 'The future of SEA', in Partidário, M. and Clark, R. (eds) *Perspectives on Strategic Environmental Assessment*, Lewis Publishers/CRC Press, Boca Raton, FL

Therivel, R. and Partidário, M. (eds) (1996) *The Practice of Strategic Environmental Assessment*, Earthscan, London

Thissen, W. A. H. (2000) 'Criteria for evaluation of SEA', in Partidário, M. and Clark, R. (eds) *Perspectives on Strategic Environmental Assessment*, Lewis Publishers/CRC Press, Boca Raton, FL

United Nations Economic Commission for Europe (2003) *Draft Protocol on Strategic Environmental Assessment to the Convention on Environmental Impact Assessment in a Transboundary Context*, ECE/MP.EIA/2003/3, UNECE, Geneva, Switzerland

Verheem, R. and Tonk, J. (2000) 'Strategic environmental assessment: one concept, multiple forms', *Impact Assessment and Project Appraisal*, vol 18, pp177–182

von Seht, H. (1999) 'Requirements of a comprehensive strategic environmental assessment system', *Landscape and Urban Planning*, vol 45, pp1–14

Wood, C. M. (2002) *Environmental Impact Assessment: a Comparative Review*, 2nd edition Prentice Hall, Harlow

Wood, C. M. and Djeddour, M. (1992) 'Strategic environmental assessment: EA of policies, plans and programmes', *Impact Assessment Bulletin*, vol 10, pp3–22

4

Canada

Barry Sadler

Introduction

The relationship between SEA and land use planning in Canada takes a number of forms and plays out at different levels. It encompasses formal and informal approaches to SEA, although none is strictly comparable with the procedural framework laid down in the European SEA Directive or in US federal and Californian legislation (Chapters 2 and 16). Formal provision for the SEA of policy, plans and programmes (PPPs) is made primarily at the federal level, where direct jurisdiction over land and resources is restricted to protected areas, the offshore zone and the north. Major responsibility for land use planning rests with ten provinces and three territories, some of which incorporate SEA elements informally in their decision making processes.

This chapter outlines the main permutations of SEA and land use planning in Canada. Given the size of the country and the divided powers and responsibilities relating to land, resources and the environment, Canadian variants of both SEA and land use planning must be interpreted broadly. The former encompasses an extended family of SEA approaches[1], and the latter includes resource management strategies for crown lands and offshore waters that include elements of spatial allocation and environmental integration. Specific attention is given to the formal application of SEA to land use and resource planning in the federal system.

The chapter has six main sections:

1   a brief description of the main types of land and resource planning systems in Canada and their relationship to environmental assessment (EA);
2   a case study of an offshore oil and gas development SEA that represents a major departure from previous Canadian practice and procedure;
3   a critical evaluation of the federal government SEA system focusing on its institutional arrangements;

4   an evaluation of the SEA process and methodology;
5   an evaluation of the SEA outcomes so far as it can be determined;
6   conclusions and lessons for SEA practice.

Context

Land and resource planning

To understand the Canadian land use and resource planning context and the similarities to, and differences from, other countries reported in this book, it is essential to appreciate three aspects:

1   the nature of the Canadian territory and resources, which has shaped the distribution of settlement, the patterns of use and the types of plans and assessments undertaken;
2   the jurisdictional regime for land, resources and the environment, which is divided between three levels of government and amongst numerous agencies of each;
3   the correspondingly diverse systems of land use and resource planning, which vary in their aims, instruments, scales of application and relationships to EA.

Canada has an immense landmass (9.9 million km²), which is further extended by an exclusive economic zone of coastal and marine waters (3.7 million km²). At the continental scale, 15 terrestrial ecosystems (ranging in size from 200,000km² to 1.8 million km²) define the major variations in the natural landscape. These are mapped at different scales in the ecological land classification framework for Canada, which provides a baseline reference for land use and resource planning. Much information on land use change and the aggregate footprint of the major sectors of activity is also available in state of the environment reports and specialized resource inventories.

Two Canadian planning theatres with fundamentally different environmental and spatial characteristics can be demarcated:

1   *Resource and wild lands* cover the vast majority of the country and nearly all the tundra, taiga and boreal life zones, where bioclimatic conditions are harsh or extreme and population is sparse and predominantly aboriginal. Northern ecosystems are vulnerable to disruption from climate change, long-range deposition of toxic substances and the impact of resource development. There is a time-limited opportunity to preserve large tracts of relatively intact boreal-taiga temperate forest that are of global significance (Wilson, 2002; National Round Table on the Environment and the Economy (NRTEE), 2003b)
2   *The Canadian ecumene* comprises the main area of urban and rural settlement, located adjacent to the US border and extending northward as a contiguous area only in the prairie agricultural belt. Over three-quarters of the Canadian population is urban and approximately one-third is concentrated in the three

rapidly growing metropolitan regions of Toronto, Montreal and Vancouver, where land use planning, urban liveability and sustainability issues reach their highest intensity (Statistics Canada, 2001; NRTEE, 2003a).

A complex regime for land use and resource planning has evolved as a result of the jurisdictional division of powers and responsibilities in Canada. The provinces hold title to all unoccupied Crown (or public) lands and most natural resources within their boundaries and offshore waters, whereas territorial lands fall under federal control. Both levels of government also have overlapping webs of legislative power relating to these areas and the environment, which are further extended in the devolution of responsibilities from the federal to the territorial governments. In addition, a third tier of land use planning was established through early delegation of powers to urban and rural municipalities and, more recently, to native governments under comprehensive claims agreements covering areas of traditional use.

For each level of government, the 'mainstream' land and resource use planning systems can be broadly differentiated with respect to types of plans prepared, instruments used, scales of application and relationship to SEA and EIA (Table 4.1). As indicated, the federal interest and role in land and resource use planning is particularly broad and includes (after Richardson, 1989, 1995):

- direct responsibility for land use and resource planning in specified areas;
- influence on land and resource use policy exercised through environmental laws, international agreements, sustainable development strategies, etc.;
- cooperative actions to address land or resource use planning issues that do not fall exclusively within the remit of one jurisdiction, adding both to the federal reach and to the number and diversity of Canadian land use planning arrangements.

SEA

Early precedents for SEA in Canada were set well before this process was formally introduced or the term became fashionable internationally (Sadler, 1986). For example, land and resource use policy and planning issues were an integral part of several federal public inquiries and EA reviews in the 1970s and 1980s. In the case of the Mackenzie Valley Pipeline Inquiry (1974–1977), the process set the course of northern development for a generation. As a 'concept assessment', the Beaufort Sea EA panel review (1982–1984) brought into sharp focus questions about how to examine policy- and plan-level proposals (Sadler, 1990).

Formal provision for SEA was made at the federal level in 1990 through a cabinet directive. This process operates outside the regime of the Canadian Environmental Assessment Act and under its own arrangements. Recently, the Act also took on a more strategic dimension with the inclusion of a discretionary provision for regional assessment to address cumulative effects more proactively.

Table 4.1 *Canadian arrangements for land use planning*

Type and scale of approach	Key aspects and characteristics	Role of EA
Federal government Strategy oriented, broad-scale processes set direction for most areas or resources within federal jurisdiction; comprehensive land use systems in north under devolved responsibilities	Land and resource use plans for major areas of federal jurisdiction (other than north) take form of policy frameworks within which planning, management and implementation take place. Transfer of title and rights to native peoples and devolution of responsibilities to territorial governments in north have created multiple land use planning systems	EA legal regime applies only to projects (with provision for regional level assessment); separate SEA system applies to all PPP proposals including those directly affecting land use
Provincial and territorial government Resource based, regional scale approach to crown land allocation and management; processes differ by province/ territory	Provinces/territories have planning processes, systems that apply to land and resource use, development. Generally, there has been a shift from single use resource management (e.g. forest, water, wildlife) toward more integrated, strategic level approaches to sustainable land and resource use planning. These differ but emphasize: zoning to allocate land uses and intensities in relation to resource potentials; public consultation on protection of environmental values and permitted activities. Several provinces/ territories have sustainable development strategies or equivalent processes that guide land and resource planning	EA systems in place in all provinces/ territories; limited application to land or resource use plans. No separate provision for SEA but elements included (e.g. regional assessment is evident in many planning processes)
Municipal government and regional authorities Detailed land use plans at local scales (city to neighbourhood); some regional plans or growth	Enabling legislation, planning practice vary widely. Standard planning frameworks/ instruments commonly used to ensure orderly pattern of land use, development of services. Many urban plans do not integrate environmental protection or	Some EA systems in place; SEA applied to land use plans in accordance

Table 4.1 *Canadian arrangements for land use planning (continued)*

Type and scale of approach	Key aspects and characteristics	Role of EA
strategies link municipal plans to provincial policies, actions	sustainable development objectives; these issues are addressed in regional plans and, in individual cities and communities, through separate processes. Some activities are innovative and include climate change and ecological footprint offsets	with federal process (above) in National Capital Region. Informal elements recognizable in some regional plans, urban growth strategies

At the provincial level, other than possibly Quebec, no comparable systems are in place but elements of SEA are recognizable in approaches to land use and resource planning (Table 4.1). Occasionally, provincial and territorial EA processes (Doyle and Sadler, 1996) have been used to address regional land and resource issues; for example, timber harvesting in Ontario (Gibson, 1993) and salmon farming in British Columbia (BC) (Sadler, 1998a).

At the federal level, the directive was amended in 1999 in order to strengthen the SEA process and improve its role in federal decision making, and further revisions were introduced in 2004 to require the publication of SEA reports. Guidelines for Implementing the Cabinet Directive were issued in 1999, and minor revisions were made in 2004 (Canadian Environmental Assessment Agency (CEAA) 2004[2]). The Guidelines reproduce the directive, outline the responsibilities of federal departments and agencies in carrying out assessments and provide advice on good practice, including guiding principles (Box 4.1). For example, all parties should apply SEA at an early stage and integrate environmental considerations fully into policy and plan development.

SEA applies to all environmentally significant PPPs that are submitted for approval to an individual minister or to the Cabinet, which represents the highest level of governmental decision making in Canada. This process includes land and resource use plans and other proposals that have spatial implications, such as transport strategies. Such plans are not separately identified or addressed in the Guidelines. Rather, federal departments and agencies are expected to tailor the generic approach to their context and requirements. The following case study provides an example.

> ## Box 4.1 Guiding principles of SEA in Canada
>
> The Guidelines are intended to be generic (applicable in different policy settings), practical (applicable by non specialists) and systematic (based on logical, transparent analysis). Federal government departments and agencies are encouraged to tailor them to their particular circumstances.
>
> When implementing SEA, agencies should be guided by seven principles:
>
> 1 Early integration: beginning in the conceptual stages of PPP formulation;
> 2 Examine alternatives: evaluating and comparing environmental effects of options
> 3 Flexibility: agencies have discretion in determining how to conduct SEA
> 4 Self assessment: each agency is responsible for SEA process application and decision making
> 5 Appropriate level of analysis: SEA should be commensurate with the level of anticipated effect
> 6 Accountability: SEA should be part of an open and accountable decision making process
> 7 Use of existing mechanisms: to analyse effects, involve the public and report the results.
>
> *Source:* CEAA (2004) Section 2.2.1

Case study: British Columbia offshore oil and gas development

This case study lies at the leading edge of the SEA trends discussed above and promises to establish precedents with respect to SEA procedure and practice in Canada (and possibly internationally). It focuses on long-standing issues of resource use and the management of marine waters off the coast of British Columbia (BC). A federal moratorium on oil and gas development, imposed in the early 1970s, has been subject to a series of environmental studies and assessments, most recently by a BC science review panel (Strong et al, 2002[3]). In 2002, the province asked the federal government to consider lifting the moratorium, triggering a SEA of the potential impact on the marine and coastal zone in accordance with the provisions of the cabinet directive.

For the first time, an 'extended SEA' was undertaken as a federal public review (Box 4.2). This process had a number of innovative features:

Roll up assessment. The SEA attempted definitively to 'roll up' long-standing issues and uncertainties relating to the environmental justification of the moratorium. It also illustrates aspects of both continuity and innovation of approach in comparison with prior assessments, beginning with the West Coast Offshore Exploration

Environmental Assessment Panel (WCOEEAP, 1986) which was a SEA of the policy moratorium in all but name.

Policy and planning significance. The current SEA was more comprehensive in scope than its predecessor, specifically with regard to resource allocation and 'impact zoning' considerations. It referred to other (non-hydrocarbon) resources, sensitive areas identified by federal agencies and the 20km coastal exclusion zone recommended by the earlier EA panel.

Multi-track process. The SEA was undertaken as a trio of independently administered reviews, comprising the following:

- A science review undertaken by an independent expert panel in accordance with the precautionary principle. Terms of reference were to evaluate and report on information and knowledge gaps and their implications for offshore oil and gas activity, providing the necessary background for the other reviews
- Public hearings and consultation were conducted by an independent review panel to canvass views and concerns on environmental, protected area and socio economic issues relevant to the moratorium. The panel and participants were asked to have regard to resource use and management considerations consistent with the principles of Canada's Oceans Strategy[4] and to address these issues in accordance with the federal SEA Guidelines.
- First Nations engagement took place through a separate, independently facilitated dialogue to explore the issues of unique interest to coastal indigenous peoples, notably traditional use of marine resources and the potential infringement of any future decision to lift the federal moratorium. It represents a new development that draws on evolving federal First Nations consultation practice and the role of the independent facilitator had parallels with the Canadian EA Act's provisions for mediation.

Findings. The main outputs from each track were as follows:

- The expert panel enumerated the gaps to be filled prior to each phase of development if the moratorium was lifted and concluded that 'providing an adequate regulatory regime is put in place, there are no science gaps that need to be filled before lifting the moratori[um]' (Royal Society of Canada, 2004, p xix)
- The public review panel reported largely on participant inputs and opinion (which was predominantly against lifting the moratorium) and offered little comment on the substantive issues (Priddle et al, 2004). Such an interpretation represents a minimalist role for an EA panel as understood in Canada, significantly reducing its policy evaluation and advisory function
- The First Nations facilitator (Brooks, 2004) emphasized the resource use and access rights of indigenous peoples, the risk to their traditional livelihoods from offshore oil and gas development, and the need for their consent and participation in any future activities.

Box 4.2 British Columbia offshore development SEA terms of reference and scope of review

On 28 March 2003, the Minister of Natural Resources Canada announced that the federal government would undertake an 'extended SEA' of the BC Offshore Oil and Gas Moratorium as a public review that would be concluded in late 2004.

Major objectives. The purpose of the SEA was to examine the broad environmental and socio economic impacts related to offshore oil and gas development with reference to the federal moratorium in place in the Queen Charlotte Basin. Three main objectives were identified for the review:

* *to identify science gaps related to possible oil and gas activity, offshore BC (Science Review);*
* *to hear the views of the public regarding whether or not the federal moratorium should be lifted for selected areas (public hearings);*
* *to consult with First Nations to ensure that issues of unique interest to First Nations are fully explored (First Nations engagement) (p2).*

Ecosystem and geographic coverage. The review focused primarily on the Queen Charlotte Basin, which was estimated to contain the highest offshore oil and gas potential. It is a semi-enclosed marine system lying between the mainland and the Queen Charlotte Islands, with an average water depth of 100m and maximum depths of more than 400m. A number of commercially and ecologically valued species are located in the basin, including some that are identified as endangered or threatened and for which, under the Canadian Species at Risk Act, recovery plans must be prepared.

Resource use considerations. This region encompasses areas that federal agencies have deemed to be particularly sensitive and to require special attention, including:

* the 20km coastal exclusion zone recommended by the 1986 EA Panel (WCOEEAP, 1986) to minimize potential impacts on marine and nearshore environments;
* the proposed Gwaii Haanas National Marine Conservation Area (NMCA) in the southernmost Queen Charlotte Islands and selected areas on the east and south east side of Queen Charlotte Sound and Hecate Strait identified as potential candidate sites for a central coast NMCA;
* designated sponge reef complexes and the 9km no-fishing buffer zones surrounding them. Fisheries and Oceans Canada was evaluating the protection or management measures required for these areas, including their potential designation as marine protected areas, in 2002.

Source: adapted from Priddle et al (2004), Appendix A1

The federal government was considering these reports in 2005 but, with a minority federal government and a BC election looming, the prospects for lifting the moratorium in the immediate future looked remote.

SEA system: the institutional framework

As interpreted here, institutional arrangements comprise the foundations of SEA effectiveness, process elements (SEA process and methodology) represent the common denominators of effectiveness; and planning and environmental outcomes (SEA outcome and products) are the performance measures of the overall effectiveness of the SEA system or its application in specific cases (Sadler, 1998b, 2004). Canadian SEA is evaluated in Table 4.2.

Prima facie, the institutional arrangements that are currently in force meet three of the criteria fully (integration, guidance and relationship to sustainable development) and one criterion in part (coverage of proposals). Strictly defined, neither legislative nor tiering criteria are met, although the Canadian SEA system is based on a clear statement of aims and principles, and tiering occurs incidentally and variably across federal departments (Table 4.2).

A second look suggests there are differences between what is stated in guidance and what is practised, for example, with regard to integration and the linkage to sustainable development. The Guidelines provide useful advice but are short on direction and the details necessary for quality assurance and achieving integration. For example, SEA is intended to enable departments and agencies to 'implement sustainable development strategies' (CEAA, 2004, Section 2.1.1). Yet this role is mentioned rather than explained and an opportunity to tap the potential role of SEA for delivering environmentally sustainable development has been missed.

Despite recent progress, it is questionable whether the amendments to the directive (above) have had a meaningful impact on SEA practice and outcomes. In principle, the directive establishes a clear obligation on federal departments to comply with its terms. However, the language of the directive is general and permissive (for example, 'Ministers expect' SEA to be carried out), and there are no formal requirements to ensure accountability. For example, the responsibility for overseeing SEA implementation is decentralized amongst a number of participants, including the Canadian EA Agency (which provides guidance), Environment Canada (which provides expert advice) and the Commissioner for Environment and Sustainable Development (CESD) (who reviews compliance and performance). It is unclear who is responsible for quality control within this institutional framework.

There is no universal coverage of environmentally significant proposals. Apart from proposals submitted to the Cabinet and to ministers, departments and agencies are only encouraged to assess other such proposals 'when circumstances warrant' (CEAA, 2004, Section 1). There is little or no publicly available information on the number and type of proposals that are subject to SEA as part of Cabinet or ministerial decision making processes. By extension, the proportion of government land use and resource plans subject to assessment cannot be reliably estimated.

Table 4.2 *Evaluation of SEA of land use plans in Canada*

Criterion	Criterion met	Comments
	SYSTEM CRITERIA	
Legal basis	□	Provision for SEA made under non-statutory Cabinet Directive. Aims and principles stated in Guidelines; terms of reference for undertaking SEA at proponent's discretion
Integration	■	In principle, there should be early application of SEA, undertaken with social and economic analyses, to integrate environmental considerations into plan development. Practice unclear
Guidance	■	Guidelines identify SEA principles, scope, roles, responsibilities, process, procedure and provide useful general advice on good practice, leaving implementing agencies to interpret
Coverage	▲	SEA required for PPPs having potential environmental effects submitted for Cabinet or ministerial approval. Application uncertain, not comprehensive, but should cover land use plans
Tiering	□	SEA process applied separately from project EA. No formal approach to tiering, but potential linkages addressed in preliminary scan (screening)
Sustainable development	■	SEA intended to support implementation of federal departments' sustainable development strategies, but no explanation/ methodology provided
	PROCESS CRITERIA	
Alternatives	▲	Environmental considerations should be integrated into options but not necessarily common practice. No provision for considering wide range of alternatives, outlining reasons for choice
Screening	■	Major land use or resource plans potentially subject to SEA. Little evidence of how preliminary scan applied in practice
Scoping	▲	No formal scoping procedure specified but SEA should address potential effects, building on results of preliminary scan
Prediction/ evaluation	▲	Guiding policies of land use plans subject to SEA and residual potential impacts should be analysed and described. No environmental criteria specified, but Guidelines assist evaluation of significance
Additional impacts	▲	Guidelines refer to indirect, cumulative impacts; environmental effects include impacts on health, socio

Table 4.2 *Evaluation of SEA of land use plans in Canada (continued)*

Criterion	Criterion met	Comments
		economic conditions, heritage resources, aboriginal use of land and resources
Report preparation	■	Agencies required to prepare public statement of SEA findings since 2004. No guidance provided on this; few assessments under previous discretionary provisions made public
Review	☐	Inter-departmental review of submissions to Cabinet provide non-transparent checks. No formal SEA quality assurance procedure specified
Monitoring	▲	Guidelines specify monitoring but many agencies do not appear to track results
Mitigation	■	Guidelines advocate specific consideration of mitigation measures; little information on extent of application but examples of good practice exist
Consultation and public participation	▲	Public and stakeholder concerns should be identified using, inter alia, consultation; response to public representations unclear
OUTCOME CRITERIA		
Decision making	☐	Little evidence that SEA has discernible influence on content of reports or treatment of environmental issues during decision making. Some indications that early integration of SEA with plan development yields best results
Costs and benefits	■	Overall, benefits (minimizing adverse effects, etc) perceived to outweigh costs (time, resources, skills)
Environmental quality	☐	'On the ground' effects of SEA little known. Specific 'green' plans and programmes credited with helping to improve environmental quality
System monitoring	■	SEA compliance and performance audits undertaken by Commissioner of Environment and Sustainable Development. System-wide monitoring and review undertaken periodically; reports independent and authoritative

■ – Yes
▲ – Partially
☐ – No
?   – Don't know

However, it is evident that some departments and agencies perform better than others. For example, Parks Canada (2003, 2004) has:

- conducted a SEA of its corporate plan, which addresses the major environmental issues facing the national park system and the actions needed to maintain or restore ecological integrity;
- integrated SEA into the preparation of long-term management plans; and
- assessed specific development actions permitted under these plans in accordance with the legislated EIA process, providing one of the best Canadian examples of tiering.

SEA process and methodology

The Canadian SEA process is evaluated in Table 4.2. All the procedural steps are carried out in one form or another but not necessarily systematically or as discrete activities. For the most part, the evaluation criteria (Chapter 3) are met only partly or incompletely in a non statutory, flexibly implemented process. The Canadian approach to SEA promotes adaptability but, arguably, eschews the measures necessary for quality assurance. For example, no minimum procedure is specified for federal departments when developing a customized approach.

A basic premise of the SEA guidance is that there is no single best methodology. Rather, federal departments and agencies are encouraged 'to apply appropriate frameworks or techniques, and to develop approaches tailored to their particular needs and circumstances' (CEAA, 2004, Section 2.3). The Guidelines also emphasize that SEA 'should be undertaken on an iterative basis throughout the policy development process' (CEAA, 2004, Section 2.3.2) and 'linked with the ongoing economic and social analyses under way on the proposal' (CEAA, 2004, Section 2.3). A two-stage generic process is outlined, comprising a preliminary scan followed by detailed analysis, which includes certain EIA-derived steps (Figure 4.1).

The preliminary scan is a non-standardized screening procedure to address the strategic considerations associated with a proposal, including its potential environmental effects (Figure 4.1). Simple tools (such as checklists, matrices) are recommended to indicate the likelihood of potential adverse effects, identified using six criteria (CEAA, 2004, Section 2.3). This approach appears sufficient to ensure that land use and resource plans submitted to Cabinet or individual ministers are assessed. At least four, and possibly all six, of the criteria outlined in the Guidelines should automatically trigger the application of SEA; for example, because plan outcomes are likely to affect natural resources, affect the achievement of environmental quality goals or result in significant interactions with the environment. However, it is not possible to verify that this is the case since many departments do not record their activities (CESD, 2004[5]).

For proposals with potentially significant environmental effects, including cumulative impacts (CEAA, 1999), a more detailed analysis is conducted for each policy or planning option developed (Figure 4.1). In this process, scoping

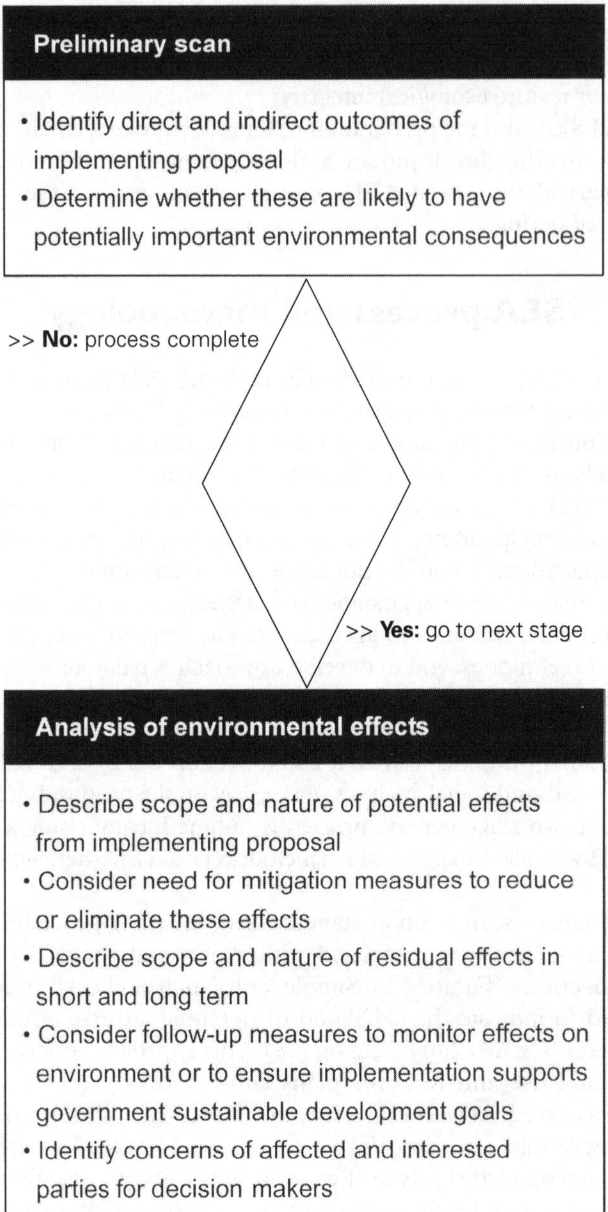

Preliminary scan

- Identify direct and indirect outcomes of implementing proposal
- Determine whether these are likely to have potentially important environmental consequences

>> **No:** process complete

>> **Yes:** go to next stage

Analysis of environmental effects

- Describe scope and nature of potential effects from implementing proposal
- Consider need for mitigation measures to reduce or eliminate these effects
- Describe scope and nature of residual effects in short and long term
- Consider follow-up measures to monitor effects on environment or to ensure implementation supports government sustainable development goals
- Identify concerns of affected and interested parties for decision makers

Source: CEAA (2004, Sections 2.3.1, 2.3.2)

Figure 4.1 *Canadian SEA process*

and prediction functions are merged together and establish the basis for subsequent phases of analysis to identify the need for mitigation measures, the scope and nature of residual effects, the requirements for follow-up, and public and stakeholder concerns. The evaluation of these four components against the criteria varies (Table 4.2). Specifically, the Canadian approach to mitigation is similar to that elsewhere; evaluation of the significance of residual effects is demanded but no explicit criteria are provided; monitoring has positive aims but little else to direct the process; and public consultation is, arguably, a much championed optional extra.

The real issue is whether these steps are carried out diligently or at all. Many federal departments and agencies cannot demonstrate that they do so and their record of process application is considered to be unsatisfactory by CESD (1998, 1999, 2004). Given these trends, it seems likely that most assessments of land use or resource plans will fall far short of the procedural and methodological criteria used in this book. However, some areas and examples of good practice can be identified, including the SEA of national park management plans, based on state of the park reports and analysis of cumulative effects (Parks Canada, 2004).

SEA outcome and products

The litmus test of SEA effectiveness lies in the results achieved in practice, measured against stated or intended aims. The extent to which the Canadian SEA system meets the outcome criteria is shown in Table 4.2. The benefits of SEA are clearly stated in guidance and are understood to outweigh the costs of process implementation. Whether these benefits are achieved in practice is another matter. In general, the contribution of SEA to decision making seems marginal at best, and any downstream improvements to environmental quality are uncertain and circumstantial rather than demonstrable.

Recently, system monitoring undertaken by CESD (1998, 1999, 2004) has brought these aspects of effectiveness into sharper focus. The most recent audit, in particular, provides a sobering picture of SEA implementation. Many departments continue to make slow and unsatisfactory progress in implementing the cabinet directive and, at best, achieve mixed results. In its fundamentals, this trend has changed little. For example, earlier studies of SEA implementation found a pattern of ad hoc compliance and inconsistent practice, attributable to a widespread lack of awareness, resources and support amongst responsible departments and agencies (CEAA, 1996).

These studies suggest that SEA is not taken seriously within the federal government and has little or no real impact on policy making and planning. For example, one factor known to maximize the contribution of SEA to decision making is early application when major alternatives are still open (Sadler, 1994). Yet there were relatively few examples of this approach in the initial phase of SEA implementation (LeBlanc and Fischer, 1996). This raises concerns about the value added to decision making and, by extension, the level of improvement of environmental quality (the main proxies of overall effectiveness of the SEA system).

These concerns were progressively highlighted in the series of CESD audits (1998, 1999, 2004).

Three conclusions regarding SEA performance stand out (CESD, 2004):

- In most cases, departments and agencies do not know how their assessments have affected the decisions made or what is likely to be the ultimate impact on the environment
- There is little assurance that 'environmental issues are assessed systematically, so that ministers and the cabinet can receive sufficient information to make informed decisions' on proposals put before them (para 4.3)
- Basic mechanisms for SEA monitoring and follow through to provide this information are not yet in place (15 years after the SEA system was first established).

The CESD audits also drew attention to important variations in SEA practice and performance across the federal government. Significantly, they noted that certain departments with development mandates, such as Industry, Natural Resources and Transport, had made better progress than departments with a stronger environmental mission, such as Agriculture and Agri-Food and Fisheries and Oceans. Some recent assessments illustrated elements of SEA good practice (CESD, 2004). These cases were not detailed but could provide material for future guidance and training activities.

Conclusion

The relationship of SEA to land use and resource planning in Canada may be characterized as asymmetrical and diverse. At the federal level, SEA is applied as a formal process to all types of higher level proposals including various land use and resource management plans initiated by government departments and agencies. At the provincial and territorial level, land use and resource planning systems incorporate more informal SEA procedures and ecosystem level tools. In these features, the Canadian scene corresponds to SEA experience internationally in encompassing a family of approaches.[1]

Following the typology proposed by Sadler (1996), the SEA system established by the federal government may be classified as an EIA-derived process with certain modifications. The approach to SEA recommended in the Guidelines incorporates features from other models, namely policy and plan appraisal (iterative analysis), integrated assessment (linked with economic and social appraisal) and sustainability assurance (implementation of sustainable development strategies). In principle, these are the main ingredients of a more inclusive paradigm (Sadler, 1999, 2002, 2004) which has different names including strategic impact assessment and integrated assessment and planning for sustainable development (United Nations Environment Programme, 2004).

In practice, the Canadian SEA system has structural and operational weaknesses that call into question its effectiveness in meeting basic procedural and environmental objectives. These limitations reflect three types of gaps:

- *Institutional gaps* within the SEA framework arise from the minimal level of the procedural requirements and from dependence on the good faith of implementing agencies. The measures for quality control in the SEA process are decentralized and insufficient to ensure full compliance or best effort. Additional procedural safeguards to improve SEA implementation, including giving the Canadian EA Agency an oversight role comparable to that it plays at the project level, and better guidance, are needed
- *Implementation gaps* relate to poor levels of compliance with the cabinet directive and the SEA Guidelines. When commitment is lacking, the flexibility in approach that is encouraged to promote adaptation of SEA to the circumstances of policy and plan making becomes a licence for superficial consideration of environmental concerns. Basic management systems are lacking and many departments and agencies cannot demonstrate that proposals have been screened or that appropriate assessments have been undertaken
- *Information gaps* underlie the limited contribution of SEA to decision making and to environmental protection. In a telling comment on SEA quality and effectiveness, CESD (2004) indicated that there is no assurance that the SEA system provides sufficient information to make informed decisions.

Yet there are positive trends and examples of SEA innovation and good practice that show what could be done within the existing framework. For example, the SEA of BC offshore oil and gas development extended the envelope of federal practice along the three tracks of science based assessment, public review and consultation with indigenous peoples. This process potentially sets a new precedent for SEA at the federal level, having procedural features that are more akin to the approach to EA panel review at the project level.

However, it may not be soon replicated: firstly because the proposal itself is relatively atypical (there are few such moratoria) and highly controversial and, secondly, because of the decision of the public review panel to report only what it heard with little comment. This singular action represents a missed opportunity to address the key policy and planning issues (whether to lift the moratorium, where development should be permitted or restricted and what type of regulatory regime should be instituted to assess and manage any future development). It may also deter others from taking the risk of innovation in SEA.

Notes

1   Dalal-Clayton and Sadler (2005) classified SEA approaches within an extended family, including formal, near equivalent and para-SEA processes which have some, but not all, of the features of SEA as formally prescribed in law or policy (see also Sadler and Verheem, 1996; Buckley, 1998; Goodland, 1998; Thissen, 2000; Marsden and Dovers, 2002). A broader schema of EA that includes ecosystem approaches, hazard and risk analysis, resource and land capability evaluation and similar planning-related instruments was delineated by Sadler (1996).
2   This document is available at: www.ceaa.gc.ca/index_e.htm

3   This document (and the other documents mentioned in this section) are available at: www.offshoreoilandgas.gov.bc.ca/reports/reports.htm
4   *Canada's Oceans Strategy* is available at: www.cos-soc.gc.ca
5   CESD documents are available at: www.oag-bvg.gc.ca/domino/cesd_cedd.nsf/html/ menu6_e.html

References

Brooks, C. A. (2004) *Rights, Risks and Respect: a First Nations Perspective on the Lifting of the Federal Moratorium on Oil and Gas Exploration in the Queen Charlotte Basin of British Columbia*, Natural Resources Canada, Ottawa

Buckley, R. (1998) 'Strategic environmental assessment', in Porter, A. and Fittipaldi, J. (eds) *Environmental Methods Review: Retooling Impact Assessment for the New Century*, International Association for Impact Assessment, Fargo, ND

Canadian Environmental Assessment Agency (1996) *Review of the Implementation of the Environmental Assessment Process for Policy and Program Proposals*, CEAA, Hull, Quebec,

Canadian Environmental Assessment Agency (1999) *Cumulative Effects Assessment: Practitioners Guide*, CEAA, Hull, Quebec

Canadian Environmental Assessment Agency (2004) *Strategic Environmental Assessment; the Cabinet Directive on the Environmental Assessment of Policy, Plan and Program Proposals: Guidelines for Implementing the Cabinet Directive*, CEAA, Hull, Quebec

Commissioner of the Environment and Sustainable Development (1998) 'Environmental assessment – a critical tool for sustainable development', *Report to the House of Commons*, Office of the Auditor General of Canada, Ottawa

Commissioner of the Environment and Sustainable Development (1999) 'Greening policies and programmes: supporting sustainable development decisions', *Report to the House of Commons*, Office of the Auditor General of Canada, Ottawa

Commissioner of the Environment and Sustainable Development (2004) 'Assessing the environmental impact of policies, plans, and programs', *Report to the House of Commons*, Office of the Auditor General of Canada, Ottawa

Dalal-Clayton, B. and Sadler, B. (2005) *Strategic Environmental Assessment: a Sourcebook and Reference Guide to International Experience*, Earthscan, London

Doyle, D. and Sadler, B. (1996) *Environmental Assessment in Canada: Frameworks, Procedures and Attributes of Effectiveness*, Canadian Environmental Assessment Agency, Ottawa

Gibson, R. (1993) 'Ontario's class assessments: lessons for policy, plan and program review', in Kennet, S. (ed) *Law and Process in Environmental Management*, Canadian Institute of Resources Law, Calgary

Goodland, R. (1998) 'Strategic environmental assessment (SEA)', in Porter, A. and Fittipaldi, J. (eds) *Environmental Methods Review: Retooling Impact Assessment for the New Century*, International Association for Impact Assessment, Fargo, ND

LeBlanc, P. and Fischer, K. (1996) 'The Canadian federal experience', in de Boer, J. J. and Sadler, B. (eds) *Environmental Assessment of Policies: Briefing Papers on Experience in Selected Countries*, Publication Number 54, Ministry of Housing, Spatial Planning and the Environment, The Hague

Marsden, S. and Dovers, S. (2002) 'Conclusions: prospects for SEA', in Marsden, S. and Dovers, S. (eds) *Strategic Environmental Assessment in Australasia*, Federation Press, Annandale, NSW

National Round Table on the Environment and the Economy (2003a) *Environmental Quality in Canadian Cities: the Federal Role*, NRTEE, Ottawa

National Round Table on the Environment and the Economy (2003b) *Securing Canada's Natural Capital: a Vision for Nature Conservation in the 21st Century*, NRTEE, Ottawa

Parks Canada (2003) 'Strategic environmental assessment' in *Parks Canada Corporate Plan*, PC, Ottawa

Parks Canada (2004) 'Amendment to the summary of environmental assessment', in *Banff National Park Management Plan*, PC, Ottawa

Priddle, R., Scott, D. and Valiela, D. (2004) *Report of the Public Review on the Government of Canada Moratorium on Offshore Oil and Gas Activities in the Queen Charlotte Region*, British Columbia, Natural Resources Canada, Ottawa

Richardson, N. (1989) *Land Use Planning and Sustainable Development in Canada*, Canadian Environmental Advisory Council, Ottawa

Richardson, N. (1995) 'Integrated approach to the planning and management of land resources', in *Canada and Agenda 21*, International Institute for Sustainable Development, Winnipeg

Royal Society of Canada (2004) *Report of the Expert Panel on Science Issues Related to Oil and Gas Activities, Offshore British Columbia*, RSC, Ottawa

Sadler, B. (1986) 'Impact assessment in transition: a framework for redeployment', in Lang, R. (ed) *Integrated Approaches to Resource Planning and Management*, University of Calgary Press, Calgary

Sadler, B. (1990) *An Evaluation of the Beaufort Sea Environmental Assessment Panel Review*, Federal Environmental Assessment Review Office, Ottawa

Sadler, B. (1994) 'Environmental assessment and development policymaking', in Goodland, R. and Edmundson, V. (eds) *Environmental Assessment and Development*, World Bank, Washington, DC

Sadler, B. (1996) *Environmental Assessment in a Changing World: Evaluating Practice to Improve Performance*, Final Report, International Study of the Effectiveness of Environmental Assessment, Canadian Environmental Assessment Agency, Ottawa

Sadler, B. (1998a) *Evaluation of the Implementation of the British Columbia Environmental Assessment Act*, Environmental Assessment Office, Victoria

Sadler, B. (1998b) 'Ex-post evaluation of the effectiveness of environmental assessment', in Porter A. L. and Fittipaldi J. J. (eds) *Environmental Methods Review: Retooling Impact Assessment for the New Century*, International Association for Impact Assessment, Fargo, ND

Sadler, B. (1999) 'A framework for environmental sustainability assessment and assurance', in Petts, J. (ed) *Handbook of Environmental Impact Assessment*, Blackwell, Oxford

Sadler, B. (2002) 'From environmental assessment to sustainability appraisal', in Billing, L., Jones, C., Sadler, B., Walmsley, J. and Wood, C. M. (eds) *Environmental Assessment Yearbook 2002*, Institute of Environmental Management and Assessment, Lincoln

Sadler, B. (2004) 'On evaluating the success of EIA and SEA', in Morrison-Saunders, A. and Arts, J. (eds) *Assessing Impact: Handbook of EIA and SEA Follow-up*, Earthscan, London

Sadler, B. and Verheem, R. (1996) *Strategic Environmental Assessment: Status, Challenges and Future Directions*, Publication Number 53, Ministry of Housing, Spatial Planning and the Environment, The Hague

Statistics Canada (2001) *A Profile of the Canadian Population: Where we Live*, 2001 Census Analysis Series, SC, Ottawa

Strong, D., Gallagher, P. and Muggeridge, D. (2002) *British Columbia Offshore Hydrocarbon Development: Report of the Scientific Review Panel*, Ministry of Energy and Mines, Victoria

Thissen, W. (2000) 'Strategic environmental assessment at a crossroads', *Impact Assessment and Project Appraisal*, vol 18, pp174–177

United Nations Environment Programme (2004) *Integrated Assessment and Planning for Sustainable Development: Guidelines for Pilot Projects*, UNEP, Geneva

West Coast Offshore Exploration Environmental Assessment Panel (1986) *Offshore Hydrocarbon Exploration: Report and Recommendations*, Ministry of Supply and Services, Ottawa

Wilson, E. (2002) *The Future of Life*, Knopf, New York

5

Denmark

Bo Elling

Introduction

In Denmark, strategic environmental assessment has been carried out in land use plan making on a limited voluntary basis since the mid-1990s but only a few regional authorities responsible for land use planning have undertaken SEAs to date. SEA was made obligatory by the implementation of the European Directive 2001/42/EC ('the SEA Directive') (European Commission (EC), 2001) in July 2004. Nevertheless, valuable lessons can be drawn from Danish experience with SEA. Danish land use planning has paid specific attention to public involvement in the planning process since the early 1970s. Consequently, focusing on how this early experience with public involvement has impacted on the quality of SEA practice and its effectiveness is a useful exercise. A second issue that will be explored is the assessment of alternatives in plan making.

First the Danish land use planning system[1] is described. Three case studies of SEA in land use planning are then presented, focusing on citizen involvement and the assessment of alternatives. Next, a review of the effectiveness of SEA in Denmark is presented, viewed from the perspective of the SEA system, the SEA process and the associated outcome. Finally, conclusions concerning SEA and land use planning in Denmark are drawn and lessons for other countries are highlighted.

Context

Land use planning has been carried out in Denmark since 1925 when urban development was first regulated. The current planning system stems from the Planning Act 1973 (and later amendments).[2] Key features of the planning system include the following:

- The Planning Act regulates land use through a tiered system of plans, each of which provides a framework for the next:
  - national planning initiatives and policy;
  - 12 general regional (county) land use plans;
  - 271 overall municipal plans;
  - local plans, prepared by the municipalities, creating the context for approvals for construction, building and land use (about 1200 prepared annually)
- The Planning Act contains rules for:
  - public participation at every planning level (including a period for the public to present ideas and proposals for the forthcoming planning process and hearings of objections to proposed plans);
  - environmental impact assessment (VVM in Danish);
  - Local Agenda 21 strategy contributions;
  - special rules for planning in coastal zones to protect coastal areas from development and installations;
  - special rules for retail trade planning to promote a diverse supply of retail shops in small and medium-sized towns
- Planning instruments operating at the national level are:
  - national planning reports;
  - national planning directives;
  - orders;
  - guidance;
  - the Minister for the Environment's right to veto regional and municipal plans
- Planning instruments at the regional level consist of planning guidelines applicable to the municipal authorities and to land use in the open countryside
- Planning instruments at the municipal level are binding local plans for specified developments.

All planning decisions may be appealed to the Nature Protection Board of Appeal, but only on points of law (Ministry of the Environment, 2002). The planning process for regional and municipal plans is summarized in Box 5.1.

Box 5.1 indicates that a notable element of regional and municipal planning in Denmark is the mandatory period for early public participation. This participation period, which lasts at least eight weeks, is intended to give the public the opportunity to influence the issues considered during the planning process through the submission of ideas and proposals. It is obligatory for planning authorities to acknowledge the submissions made by the public and other public authorities during this period. This early public participation is additional to the public participation procedures and hearings that take place after the proposed plan has been published. Individuals have the opportunity, during this 'ordinary' public participation period, to comment on how the planning authorities have dealt with the proposals they made initially and to make objections about this and other issues within the proposed plan. The public has a further opportunity to submit new proposals at this stage of the planning process.

Box 5.1 Danish planning process for regional and municipal plans

1 Prior public participation every four years:

- information on previous planning disseminated;
- regional planning: ideas and proposals solicited;
- municipal planning: a strategy for planning developed;
- deadline at least eight weeks.

2 Proposed regional or municipal plan:

- prepared in cooperation with other public authorities, citizens, non-governmental organizations, etc.

3 Proposal published:

- deadline for objections of at least eight weeks;
- proposal sent to other public authorities;
- a regional plan or municipal plan may be vetoed to uphold national interests.

4 Plan adopted:

- objections (including vetoes) and comments processed and proposed changes negotiated.

5 Final plan published:

6 Administration of plan:

- relevant planning authorities strive to implement the plan.

Source: Ministry of the Environment (2002, p5)

Since 1997, the Ministry of the Environment has recommended that municipal and regional authorities include, on a voluntary basis, a SEA report with their planning revisions. To support and encourage such efforts, the Ministry issued a proposed procedure to integrate SEA in the regional plan revision process, which takes place every fourth year (Elling, 1998). Furthermore, the Ministry issued a report on experience with SEA in the regional planning activities of North Jutland County, which were carried out between 1995 and 1998 (Elling, 1999, 2000). The Ministry of the Environment has carried out SEAs on all its national plan statements issued since 1996 (Miljø- og Energiministeriet, 1996, 2000; Miljøministeriet, 2002).

Implementation of Directive 2001/42/EC took place on 21 July 2004 as a result of the passing of an act on the environmental assessment of plans and programmes.[3]

The provisions for the conduct of SEA of plans and programmes are summarized in Box 5.2. The procedure is strictly in accordance with the requirements of the directive. However, the act gives the Minister for the Environment the right to decide whether a privately or publicly owned company must carry out a SEA on a certain plan or programme if the company is legally bound to prepare the plan or programme and is authorized to act as a public authority ('the SEA Act' Section 2.2). This provision can be important in connection with plans for the supply of electricity or gas. Furthermore, the SEA Act aims to avoid duplication of effort in two ways. Firstly, the SEA Act is overruled when other legally prescribed planning or programming activities comply with its substantive and procedural requirements (Section 8.4). This provision is particularly important in the case of land use plans prepared in accordance with the Planning Act. Secondly, existing monitoring activities must, as far as possible, be employed to fulfil the SEA Directive's requirements concerning monitoring. Finally, the broad concept of the environment specified in the Directive must always be applied, despite the fact that the legal provisions for the plan or programme may refer to a narrower concept of the environment, or may include no reference to the environment at all.

As indicated in Box 5.2, the procedure for the conduct of SEA of land use plans specified in this act is similar to that outlined in Box 5.1. The only exception relates to early public participation. The SEA Act does not prescribe a prior public participation period for the SEA, but this does not prevent the responsible authority undertaking early public participation from allowing the public to present ideas and proposals for the forthcoming plan environmental assessment.

In addition, these SEA steps follow the planning procedure for regional and municipal plans outlined in Box 5.1: the involvement of other public authorities and the public; the preparation of the environmental statement; publishing a proposal for the statement; time periods for comments and objections; adoption of the environmental statement; and publication and justification of the statement. According to the SEA Act, the environmental statement can be a separate report or it can be integrated into the document for the proposed plan or programme.

Case studies

A full-scale SEA, in accordance with the present obligatory provision for the SEA of plans and programmes, was integrated into the North Jutland Regional Development Plan for 1997–2001 and carried out as a research project in 1996–1997. Lessons learned from this case (Elling, 2000) have been widely used in the Danish land use planning system. One example concerns how planning objectives can contradict each other in environmental terms and why they must therefore be dealt with carefully in accounting for environmental impacts. Another concerns the early involvement of the public during planning activities. Moreover, the case identified the need to have clear SEA parameters, political support and appropriate institutional capacity in order to undertake the assessment process successfully. The evaluation of the likely environmental effects of the plan clearly demonstrated contradictions in environmental terms between different planning activities.

Box 5.2 Danish provisions for environmental assessment of plans and programmes

1 A public authority preparing a specified plan or programme must provide an environmental assessment of its effects (Section 3)

2 The decision on whether a plan or programme must be subject to an assessment is taken by the authority responsible for the preparation and adoption of the plan or programme (Section 4)

3 If no assessment is carried out the authority must announce this decision and the reasons for it, and whether or not it is possible to appeal against this decision (Section 4.4)

4 The environmental assessment must be carried out during the preparation of the plan or programme and before its final adoption (Section 6)

5 The environmental statement must include the likely significant impacts on the environment caused by the plan or programme and its alternatives. The statement can be a separate report or be included in the documentation for the plan or programme (Section 7). The information to be given in the statement is specified in Annex I (Section 7.2)

6 The authority must announce the proposal for the plan or programme and an environmental statement on its likely significant impacts and allow at least eight weeks for comments and objections (Section 8). If other regulations set out rules for public participation in the preparation of the plan or programme, these rules must apply to the environmental statement (Section 8.4)

7 The adoption of the final plan or programme must take into account the stated impact on the environment (Section 9) and the authority must publish a statement on how the likely impacts and comments on them have been taken into account, why the plan or programme was chosen from amongst the alternatives assessed, and how the authority will monitor significant impact on the environment (Section 9.4).

Source: SEA Act[3]

Subsequently, some sectoral regional plans have been subjected to SEA procedures on a voluntary basis. Experiments with the SEA of municipal development plans have also been carried out (Hvidtfeldt and Kørnøv, 2001).

Three SEA case studies are presented below. They relate to assessments of municipal development plans and of sectoral regional development plans.

Case study 1: Municipal plan for Hillerød

The new municipal plan for Hillerød, in North Zealand, was initiated by inviting public proposals and ideas for the plan in November 1999. The final plan was adopted by the municipal council on 25 October 2001, and the plan and the reasons for the decision, were published on 5 December 2001. The council decided to carry out a SEA of the plan, which was undertaken between April and October 2000.

The rationale for the SEA (Hillerød Kommune, 2000) was to relate the proposed Municipal Development Plan to the 1999 Municipal Environmental Plan. The proposed plan to develop 13 city areas was assessed for its impact on eight environmental objectives, which were taken from the Municipal Environmental Plan. Two major alternative actions were outlined. One was to concentrate housing and services within the city to reduce journeys within and outside the municipal area. The other alternative was to construct housing and service developments in designated development areas on the periphery of the existing urban area. The impacts of the alternatives on each environmental objective were assessed as positive, negative, neutral or not relevant. Moreover, each impact was evaluated both locally (Hillerød municipal area) and regionally (Greater Copenhagen area). The SEA affected decisions about the plan in four key ways:

1   More retail development was concentrated in the city area, thus contributing to a reduction in the number of motor vehicle-kilometres driven
2   New housing was designed to reduce the use of electricity and water and the creation of waste. Furthermore, by concentrating new housing within the city, the need for transport was reduced
3   Additional employment was concentrated around the railway station to contribute to the use of public transport and bicycles instead of private cars
4   A place for commuters to meet to share vehicles and a commuter station were established to reduce the number of drivers commuting from Hillerød to the Greater Copenhagen area.

The SEA therefore led to the negative impacts of the adopted plan being highlighted and addressed.

Case study 2: Regional groundwater plan for Vejle County

The SEA of the regional groundwater plan for Vejle County (in eastern Jutland) was carried out in 2002 as a consequence of a county decision to undertake SEA as part of the regional planning process (Vejle Amtsråd, 2002). Groundwater extraction in the county mainly takes place beneath urban areas, and is becoming increasingly problematic because of pollution from urban and other sources. Two alternative options for future ground water extraction – the 'clean-up strategy' and the 'rural strategy' – were developed and assessed separately for their major positive and negative effects on the environment. The clean-up strategy was based on the retention of existing extraction areas with pollution sources being controlled and protective mitigation measures established. The rural strategy was to extract water from forest and farming areas where the groundwater was not exposed to the same level of pollution as in urban areas.

The likely impacts on the environment from each strategy were predicted and assessed on a scale from very positive (+ +), through neutral (0), to very negative

(– –). The positive and negative effects of each strategy clearly demonstrated that assessing the environmental pros and cons did not result in a clear-cut environmental reason for choosing between the strategies. Therefore, the choice ultimately had to account for other factors such as economic considerations and a general preference to maintain a decentralized water extraction system. These factors led to the choice of the 'rural strategy'. Nevertheless, it is ironic that damage to the environment was the reason for the development of the two water extraction strategies.

Case study 3: Regional mineral extraction plan for Vejle County

A SEA of the Vejle County Regional Mineral Extraction Plan was carried out in 2003 (Vejle Amtsråd, 2003). Minerals controlled by the plan include the sand and gravel used in concrete building construction and foundations. Three different planning alternatives were selected:

1   Continued extraction from existing extraction areas.
2   The designation of minor regional extraction areas and amendments to existing practice.
3   The designation of major regional extraction areas and the restoration of existing extraction areas for recreation after the winning of minerals has ceased.

The environmental effects of six aspects of these alternatives were assessed: transportation, economy, changes in landscape, landscape dynamics, pollution suffered by local residents, and stress factors for local residents. Impacts were assessed quantitatively on a scale from -2 to $+2$. Although problematic, scores were combined and the conclusions were that alternatives 1 and 3 received a score of 0, and alternative 2 a score of -1. It was thus decided to assess the environmental impacts after available mitigation has been applied to the impacts of the three alternatives. The outcome from this assessment was that alternative 1 was preferable with a score of $+1$. This option was then chosen, indicating that the SEA influenced the planning decision.

Key features of the case studies

Each of the case studies described above exhibit notable features. The SEA of the municipal development plan for Hillerød municipality demonstrates good practice in summarizing the thematic assessment of alternatives, which made their environmental impacts apparent to decision makers, planners and the public. Moreover, this SEA affected the outcome of the plan making process. The SEAs of the regional ground water extraction plan and the regional mineral extraction plan for Vejle County also demonstrate good practice concerning the assessment of strategic alternatives during the development of plans.

SEA system

Legal basis

The legal provisions for SEA in the Danish planning system define broad objectives for the assessment using criteria for sustainable development and includes a focus on both the natural and the built environments. Standards and terms of reference for the assessment of impacts allow for qualitative assessments to be undertaken, and also for quantitative assessments to be made, where possible, on the basis of existing knowledge. The legal provisions thereby allow for a flexible and adaptive assessment in the planning process. As mentioned above, the mandatory SEA system for land use plans has drawn on the experience of voluntary SEA gained during the last ten years. All the fundamental principles of SEA have been explored previously, leading to a SEA system that is in full compliance with the principles of Directive 2004/42/EC.

Integration of SEA and plan preparation

The land use planning system provides an opportunity for the early integration of SEA into the planning process by specifying a prior public participation phase during plan preparation. This involves a public announcement about a forthcoming planning process and a request for ideas for incorporation in the planning process (which can include proposed objectives and alternatives to be assessed in the SEA). The SEA must always be carried out during the preparation of the plan and before the final plan is adopted. The responsible authority decides whether the statement on environmental impacts will be issued as a separate document or integrated within the plan documentation.

Guidance

Existing land use planning guidance for regional, municipal and local plan making includes guidance on integrating SEA in the planning process. This focuses on screening and scoping procedures, and on the involvement of the public and other authorities. Furthermore, the Ministry of the Environment has recommended that the EC guidance on the implementation of Directive 2001/42/EC (EC, 2003), which is available in Danish on the Ministry website,[4] be used. The Ministry of the Environment was expected to issue guidance on the implementation of the Environmental Assessment of Plans and Programmes Act in 2005.

Coverage

All the land use plans referred to in Article 3 of the SEA Directive are covered in the Danish legislation. In compliance with the Directive, the Danish legislation emphasizes that plans and programmes that can impact on international nature protection areas, as well as plans and programmes establishing frameworks for future projects subject to EIA, must be assessed if they are likely to cause significant impacts. All the environmental impacts listed in the SEA Directive are covered in the SEA Act.

Tiering

The SEA of land use plans is undertaken within a tiered system of environmental assessment. The SEA process for land use plans is integrated into the same planning procedures, and has similar legal provisions, as the project EIA system. Undertaking SEA is expected to create a framework for the project assessment process, although this will not make any EIAs superfluous. Danish legislation also makes policy assessment obligatory. This can result in the assessment of the land use planning legislation that creates a framework for the SEA of specific land use plans.

Sustainable development

The concept of sustainable development is integrated within the framework supporting SEA practice. In spite of the fact that the legal SEA provisions are contained in a separate act, they are closely linked to the planning act and the resulting planning activities. The overarching aim of both acts is to achieve sustainable development. Thus, a multitude of planning activities, which are all intended to promote sustainable development, create a supportive framework for undertaking the SEA of land use plans.

SEA process

Alternatives

Undertaking SEA results in a wide range of alternatives being assessed. Moreover, SEA provides reasons for the choice of alternatives, something which must be highlighted by authorities responsible for preparing land use plans. In addition, proposals for alternatives suggested during the mandatory public participation period must be taken into account by the responsible authorities. The SEA Act does not include provision for early public participation, as required by the planning act. However, the SEA Act prescribes that the provisions for public participation in the planning act must be taken into account where the SEA of regulated land use plans is undertaken. Consequently, proposals for alternatives submitted during the early public participation period must also be taken into account by the responsible authorities. However, in practice this procedure has not yet been tested, although the authorities must nevertheless take the 'do nothing' alternative into account.

Screening

All land use plans likely to cause significant environmental effects must be subjected to a SEA. Consequently, all regional development plans and all major amendments to municipal plans are assessed. Local plans need only be subject to SEA if they are likely to cause significant effects. In such cases there is no explicit screening procedure, and screening is undertaken on a case-by-case basis by the responsible authorities. When a plan establishes a framework for future project developments, the screening criteria for EIA projects[5] can be used to assess whether such future project developments are likely to cause significant environmental effects.

Scoping

The public has the opportunity to submit suggestions for the SEA of regional plans and major amendments to municipal plans, and can comment on alternatives to be assessed during the early public participation phase. The responsible authority has an obligation to take suggestions submitted by the public into account, and to make a statement about how they have done so, at the latest when the planning proposal and the draft assessment are scrutinized at the public hearing. In the case of local plans, there is no prior public participation process, and in such cases there is no public participation in scoping. The prior public participation process can thus be viewed as a specific scoping procedure in the SEA of regional and municipal land use plans.

Prediction/evaluation

Since all likely impacts on the environment are assessed during land use plan SEAs, it follows that all policies in the plan in question are assessed against relevant environmental criteria. The criteria for evaluating the significance of potential impacts are stated in Annex 2 to the SEA Act. These criteria strictly follow Annex II of Directive 2001/42/EC. The case studies outlined above are all examples of plans within which all policies were carefully assessed against relevant environmental criteria.

Additional impacts

The SEA Act explicitly requires the consideration of direct, indirect, synergistic and cumulative impacts. These must be considered in the short, medium and long term. Moreover, SEAs must address permanent and temporary positive and negative impacts (Annex 1(f) to the SEA Act).

Report preparation

The provisions for the SEA of land use plans explicitly require that the assessment procedure followed, and its main findings, are reported in a publicly available assessment report. This report can be a part of the documentation on which the plan is based, and must be made publicly available when the draft plan proposal is submitted prior to the public hearing.

Review

Reviews of the statement on environmental effects are generally not carried out. However, the ordinary (later) public participation period and the public hearing provide opportunities for the other public authorities and the public to review the assessments and propose requests for changes, where necessary. The provisions for the SEA of land use plans require proposals submitted during the public hearing to be taken into account by the responsible authorities and the outcomes to be publicly announced.

Monitoring

When a land use plan that has been subject to a SEA is adopted, the responsible authority must submit a publicly available statement on how it will monitor significant impacts caused by the plan. Furthermore, the authority must monitor the effects caused by the plan. The Minister for the Environment can issue specific rules about monitoring.

Mitigation

The SEA Act transposes the SEA Directive's requirement that the 'measures envisaged to prevent, reduce and as fully as possible offset any significant adverse effects on the environment of implementing the plan' (EC, 2001, Annex I, para g) be specified in assessment reports. The authority's publicly available statement must explain how these measures to protect the environment have been integrated into the plan.

Consultation and public participation

Consultation with other public authorities must take place at the latest during the scoping procedure for the SEA. In the case of land use plans, the involvement of the public takes place during both the early public participation and the public hearing phases. All submissions by other public authorities and the public must be recorded and such records should state how the responsible authority acted on the representations.

SEA outcome

Decision making

The SEA Act requires the responsible authority to state how the SEA findings and the comments and proposals from the public hearing were taken into account and why the adopted plan was chosen from amongst other alternatives.

In many cases, SEAs undertaken during the planning process have influenced the treatment of environmental issues during plan preparation, and even the planning process itself. This influence is likely to result from new information generated by the assessment, new lessons learned during the assessment process, or the identification of unacceptable likely impacts resulting in a change or revision in the plan. The Danish experience indicates that more changes to planning procedures and plan content result from the consideration of environmental impacts during plan preparation, than during the review phase (after the submission of the planning proposal and the environmental statement prior to the public hearing).

Costs and benefits

Interviews[6] with planning officers indicated that, in most cases, the benefits of carrying out SEA outweigh the costs. The most commonly cited benefits include:

1   Environmental protection is addressed at an early stage in the planning process.
2   Environmental factors are made more visible and consciousness about the environment develops amongst all parties.
3   Environmental protection is made more feasible during plan preparation when SEA is undertaken than when it is not.

The principal cost associated with SEA practice relates to time. However, the time expended is often minimal – for example, one day's joint work by three or four planners for the SEA of a municipal plan or a sectoral regional plan.

Environmental quality

It is too early to comment on the effect of SEA on environmental quality. In any event, it will be almost impossible to distinguish the effect of SEA from that of other environmental management provisions.

System monitoring

Until Danish implementation of Directive 2001/42/EC came into force on 21 July 2004, each new SEA involved both trying out new practice and revising recent experience, as SEA knowledge and ideas were communicated informally. There is no reason to believe that this will not continue now that SEA is mandatory. A basis for formal monitoring of the SEA system is included in Section 10.1 of the SEA Act. This makes it obligatory for the responsible authority to submit the adopted plan, the environmental statement and their proposals for monitoring the environmental impacts of the plan, to the Minister for the Environment.

Conclusion

The evaluation of the SEA of land use plans in Denmark is summarized in Table 5.1. Although the environment has been a planning issue for many years in Denmark, undertaking SEA during land use plan making has, nevertheless, been a very positive experience and a major factor promoting the integration of the environment into land use planning procedures. The explicit requirements and timetable for what must be undertaken during the SEA (which environmental factors should be assessed, at which stage in plan preparation) have contributed to significant progress in taking the environment into account during land use plan making activities. This has led to institutional learning concerning the treatment of environmental issues. Further experience points towards SEA in land use plan making improving public participation as environmental factors are motivating people to become more involved in planning decisions. Moreover, individuals have often seen their involvement in SEAs as something that could influence decisions about new developments.

Table 5.1 *Evaluation of SEA of land use plans in Denmark*

Criterion	Criteria met	Comments
		SYSTEM CRITERIA
Legal basis	■	Clear legal provisions, defining broad objectives, standards and terms of reference
Integration	■	Early integration of SEA within plan preparation procedures takes place
Guidance	▲	Informal guidance has been issued; formal guidance due to be prepared in 2004
Coverage	■	All land use plans referred to in Article 3 of European SEA Directive are covered
Tiering	■	SEA is carried out in a tiered system from policies to projects
Sustainable development	■	Sustainable development is integrated within SEA procedures
		PROCESS CRITERIA
Alternatives	■	Alternatives and reasons for choice of alternative must be outlined
Screening	■	All land use plans likely to cause significant effects must be subjected to SEA
Scoping	■	Public participation takes place in scoping regional and municipal land use plan SEAs

Table 5.1 *Evaluation of SEA of land use plans in Denmark (continued)*

Criterion	Criteria met	Comments
Prediction/ evaluation	■	All policies must be assessed against environmental criteria, and significance of impacts assessed
Additional impacts	■	All direct, indirect, secondary, synergistic or cumulative impacts must be assessed
Report preparation	■	Main findings of the SEA are reported in publicly available report
Review	■	Public authorities and public have eight weeks to submit comments on assessment report
Monitoring	▲	Monitoring must take place. Minister for the Environment can issue specific rules
Mitigation	■	Mitigation measures to prevent, reduce and offset significant environmental effects of plan implementation must be described in assessment report
Consultation and public participation	■	Consultation and public participation takes place in scoping and public hearings, and representations are recorded and acted upon
OUTCOME CRITERIA		
Decision making	■	SEAs have discernible influence on plan preparation and decision making
Costs and benefits	■	Time is major cost. Early public participation and integration, and assessment of alternatives are major benefits
Environmental quality	?	Too early to evaluate
System monitoring	▲	System monitoring takes place by informal communication

Notes: ■ – Yes
 ▲ – Partially
 ☐ – No
 ? – Don't know

If any lesson can be learned from Danish land use planning and the integration of SEA into plan preparation it is that the *prior public participation* phase clearly helps to involve the public in the planning and assessment process at an early stage. SEA practice also makes a positive contribution to the early integration of environmental considerations in the plan preparation process. Even though the three case studies did not explicitly include a prior public participation phase, this lesson is, nevertheless, valid. This is because early public participation is well-integrated in the planning process and already includes environmental considerations (this was made obligatory in 1991). Furthermore, the legal provisions for the integration of SEA in land use planning were not in place when the three case study plans were prepared. However, the successful experience with early public participation in the planning process leaves little doubt that the integration of SEA will show similarly beneficial results.

The integration of SEA into land use planning seems to facilitate the identification and description of reasonable *alternatives* during plan preparation. All three case studies included the identification of reasonable alternatives, and demonstrated that assessing alternatives helps to identify relevant environmental impacts, and therefore assists in making the choice between alternatives.

The *integration* of SEA into plan preparation, instead of carrying out SEA after a plan has been prepared, seems to be preferred by all parties, and is regarded as the only reasonable and effective way of carrying out SEA.

Finally, in each of the case studies, the assessment of environmental impacts was made by the planners responsible for the specific planning action, and not by environmental experts or individuals outside the planning authority office. This contributes to the integration of the assessment into the planning process and helps to generate clear political ownership of the assessment.

Notes

1   Local government reform was being considered in 2005. The practical impacts of abolishing the regional counties, and transferring their land use plan making and SEA duties and responsibilities to the municipal level, were being negotiated prior to the drafting of legislation.
2   The Planning Act in Denmark: Consolidated Act No 763 of 11 September 2002. English version available at www.lpa.dk/Topmenuen/Publikationer/Andre_sprog/2002/planning-act-2002.pdf
3   Act on the Environmental Assessment of Plans and Programmes: Consolidated Act No 316 of 1 May 2004
4   The Ministry of the Environment website, www.mim.dk, contains many documents in English.
5   Section 3.2, Ministry of the Environment Administrative Order No 847 of 30 September 1994
6   Information from interviews conducted with the planning officers involved in the three case studies in March 2004

References

Elling, B. (1998) *Strategic Environmental Assessment in Spatial Planning*, TemaNord, 1998: 519, Nordisk Ministerråd (Nordic Ministerial Council), København (in Danish)
Elling, B. (1999) *Strategic Environmental Assessment in Regional Land Use Planning: Evaluation of the North Jutland Project*, Miljø- og Energiministeriet, (Ministry of the Environment and Energy, Spatial Planning Department), Landsplanafdelingen, København (in Danish)

Elling B. (2000) 'Integration of strategic environmental assessment into regional spatial planning', *Impact Assessment and Project Appraisal*, vol 18, pp233–243

European Commission (2001) 'Directive 2001/42/EC of the European Parliament and of the Council of 27 June 2001 on the assessment of the effects of certain plans and programmes on the environment', *Official Journal of the European Communities*, vol L197, pp30–37, 21 July

European Commission (2003) *Implementation of Directive 2001/42 on the Assessment of the Effects of Certain Plans and Programmes on the Environment*, Directorate-General XI Environment, EC, Brussels

Hillerød Kommune (Hillerød Municipal Council) (2000) *Strategic Environmental Assessment of Hillerød Municipal Plan, 2001–2013: Report; Techniques, Town Plan and Environment*, HK, Hillerød (in Danish)

Hvidtfeldt, H. and Kørnøv, L. (2001) *Strategic Environmental Assessment of Municipal Plans II – on Sustainable Objectives in Municipal Planning*, By- og Landsplanserien, 12, Skov og Landskab (Town and National Plan Series, 12, Research Centre for Forests and Landscape), Hørsholm (in Danish)

Miljø- og Energiministeriet (Ministry of the Environment and Energy) (1996) *Strategic Environmental Assessment of the National Plan Statement 1996*, MEM, København (in Danish)

Miljø- og Energiministeriet (Ministry of the Environment and Energy) (2000) *National Planning Statement 2000: Local Identity and New Challenges*, MEM, København (in Danish)

Miljøministeriet (Ministry of the Environment) (2002) *Denmark in Balance: Proposed National Planning Statement 2002*, MM, København (in Danish)

Ministry of the Environment (2002) *Spatial Planning in Denmark*, Spatial Planning Department, ME, Copenhagen

Vejle Amtsråd (Vejle County Council) (2002) *Strategic Environmental Assessment of the Ground Water Plan*, Annex E of Volume 3 'The County Council and Ground Water' VA, Vejle (in Danish)

Vejle Amtsråd (Vejle County Council) (2003) *Proposed Regional Mineral Extraction Plan*, Amendment No 10 to the Regional Plan 2001–2013, VA, Vejle (in Danish)

6

Germany

Thomas B. Fischer

Introduction

Experience with SEA-type assessment practice in Germany is extensive, and predates formal European SEA Directive requirements in a number of fields, including land use planning (Riehl and Winkler-Kühlken, 1995; Jacoby, 2000; Fischer, 2002; Scholles et al, 2003), transport planning (Wagner, 1994; Gather, 2001; Fischer, 2003, 2004; Wende et al, 2004), energy (Kleinschmidt and Wagner, 1996) and water and waste management (Kraetzschmer, 2003).

In land use planning, prior to the coming into effect of European Directive 2001/42/EC ('the SEA Directive') on 21 July 2004 (European Commission (EC), 2001), most of the procedural aspects of SEA were reflected in plan making itself. Furthermore, many substantive SEA aspects were covered in the landscape planning system. Requirements for conducting environmental assessment at strategic levels of decision making were first introduced for legislative procedures in 1972. In 1975, 'Principles for the Environmental Assessment of Public Measures by the Federal Government' were formulated for draft governmental regulations, activities and legislation that could affect the environment. However, these were rarely applied (Cupei, 1994). There have been a number of SEA-related research projects, particularly in the land use and transport planning sectors (Kleffner and Ried, 1995; Bunge, 1998; Buschke et al, 2002; Fischer, 2002).

This chapter describes and evaluates SEA type practice in land use planning at a time of transition. While SEA had become a formal requirement in spatial and land use planning through the 'Act to Accommodate EU Requirements in Federal Construction Act'[1] ('the SEA Act') the main German Framework SEA Act was only ratified in May 2005. There were, however, no indications that post-SEA Directive practice in land use planning was changing significantly, compared with the practice described in this chapter, which predates legal requirements.

As practice varies considerably between different *Länder* (states), the focus of this chapter is on the state of Brandenburg, which had previously been identified as an example of good SEA practice (Fischer, 2002). Land use planning and the consideration of environmental aspects is first described in this chapter. The SEA system and procedural and substantive process aspects are then reviewed. SEA outcomes in Brandenburg land use planning are then evaluated. A case study of a landscape plan (SEA) for the municipality of Nauen is presented. Finally, the SEA situation is summarized and conclusions are drawn.

Context

This section sets the context for the remainder of the chapter. The land use planning system in the Federal Republic of Germany is explained in terms of levels of decision making, principles and responsibilities. This is followed by a description of the consideration of environmental aspects in land use planning.

Land use planning system

There are four main levels of public decision making in land use planning. These match the levels of the democratically elected bodies in the Federal Republic of Germany, that is, the federal, state (*Land*), county (*Kreis*) and local levels. In addition, regions are formed by cooperating counties and unitary cities. There is neither a top-down nor a bottom-up approach to land use decision making. Instead, the so called 'counter current principle' is applied, according to which land use decisions at all administrative levels need to take the policies, plans and programmes (PPPs) prepared at other levels into account. Furthermore, there is institutional backing for the subsidiarity principle in planning. Different administrative bodies at the various levels of decision making need to cooperate fully and to coordinate their activities. As decision making is supposed to be 'administration consensus based' (Fischer, 2002), all bodies normally participate in important administrative decisions. Direct public participation takes place in project authorizations. Furthermore, the public is also involved in PPP preparation at the local level.

Principles of land use planning are defined through federal spatial orientation and action frameworks, taking the spatial development objectives of the states into account. While official spatial planning documentation is prepared at state, regional, and county levels, preparatory land use plans (sometimes called zoning plans) and legally binding master plans (sometimes called building schemes or development plans) are prepared at the local level.

Land use planning in Germany is supposed to be coordinated closely with planning in other sectors. In reality, however, split responsibilities (e.g. for federal, state, county and community transport infrastructure networks), and the wide range of different planning instruments, make the system highly complex. Effective coordination between different administrative levels and authorities is therefore difficult to achieve.

The consideration of environmental aspects

Environmental aspects in land use planning are considered mainly through the landscape planning system, which serves to foster the precautionary principle and sustainable development. Landscape programmes are prepared at the state level, landscape framework plans are prepared at regional and county levels, landscape plans are prepared at the city and community level, and open space master plans are prepared at the neighbourhood level. Table 6.1 shows the German land use plans and programmes with their corresponding landscape plans and programmes. The two-tier system of local land use plans and master plans is at the heart of the land use planning system. While land use plans are binding for authorities, master plans are legally binding for everyone.

Originally, landscape plans and programmes mainly served as state of the environment reports, proactively setting objectives for environmentally sustainable land use. However, in the mid-1990s certain states, including Brandenburg, started to deal explicitly with the potential impacts of the changes and developments put forward in local land use plans. Thus, they effectively became SEA reports.

Table 6.1 *Land use and landscape planning instruments in Germany*

Planning level	Land use planning	Landscape planning	Scale of maps
State *(Land)*	State spatial development plan *(Landesentwicklungs-plan/-programme)*	Landscape programme *(Landschaftsprogramm)*	1:200,000–1:500,000
Region	Regional plan *(regionales Raumordnungskonzept)*	Landscape framework plan *(Landschafts-rahmenplan)*	1:25,000–1:100,000
County *(Kreis)* (informal)	County development plan *(Kreisentwicklungsplan)*		
Community, city	Land use plan *(Flächennutzungsplan,* Section 1 Federal Construction Act – BauGB)	Landscape plan *(Landschaftsplan).* In some states, e.g. Brandenburg, these include SEA	1:5000–1:10,000
City district (informal)	e.g. city district plan *(Bereichsentwicklungs plan)*		circa 1:3000
Neighbourhood	Master plan *(Bebauungsplan,* Section 1 BauGB)	Open space master plan *(Grünordnungsplan)*	1:1000–1:2500

Source: Fischer (2002, adapted from Bundesumweltministerium für Umwelt, 1993)

Fischer (2002) suggested that landscape plans were potentially meeting the requirements of the European SEA Directive to the greatest extent of all statutory and formally applied assessments of land use plans in Europe. This was mainly due to the way in which baseline data were collected and presented, environmental objectives were set, professional consultation and participation were conducted, impacts were appraised and potential mitigation and compensation measures were specified (below). In addition, assessment experience had also grown at the regional level and the SEA Directive's requirements were being partially met in regional plan making (Siemoneit and Fischer, 2002; Jacoby et al, 2003; Schmidt et al, 2003).

In addition to landscape plan and programme making practice, more than 200 local communities in Germany introduced environmental assessment (EA) into local land use plan making between 1975 and the mid-1990s (Hodek and Kleinschmidt, 1998). The focus was usually on possible projects arising from land use plans. The SEA Directive's requirement to consider environmental impacts at the local land use planning level was thus being fulfilled. Furthermore, there were several SEA trial runs for local land use plans during the mid-1990s, including, for example, those for the municipalities of Saarbrücken (Kleffner and Ried, 1995), Kaiserslautern and Landau/Pfalz (Jacoby, 1996) and Erlangen (Bunge, 1998). Whilst there had been various suggestions that landscape plans and programmes themselves should be subject to SEA, it is now widely accepted that this would mean a SEA of a SEA, leading to further complexity in land use plan making. The resulting assessment system would have been ineffective (Heidtmann, 2003).

SEA system

This section discusses pre-SEA legislation practice in land use planning in Germany. As there are substantial differences between the different states, the focus is on Brandenburg, a state that has used landscape plans as SEAs for assessing the environmental impacts of land use plans. The legal basis for current and future requirements is described. This is followed by an explanation of SEA integration and guidance. Current SEA coverage and tiering practice are explained. Finally, the extent to which sustainable development is considered in land use planning and assessment frameworks is explored.

Legal basis

There are statutory requirements for the preparation of landscape plans and programmes, following the Federal Environmental Protection Act and state-specific regulations, such as the Brandenburg Land Environmental Protection Act. Landscape plans and programmes covered many important SEA elements even before the European SEA Directive came into force, as is demonstrated by the Nauen case study (below). The preparation procedures for regional and local land use plans are regulated by the Federal Construction Law Act other state legislation. Through the 1998 Federal Construction and Spatial Planning Act, nature protection became an integral part of the Federal Construction Act. In 1994 the regulations on land use and landscape planning[2] required local landscape plans to consider the potential impacts of local land use plans in Brandenburg. In mid-2004, there were about 430 landscape plans in Brandenburg, including around 100 that were still in preparation (Jordan, 2004).

Legislation adapting the Federal Construction Act to provide for the SEA of land use plans became operative in July 2004[1] but debate about the content of a formal (post-directive) SEA system for other types of plans and programmes, which had commenced earlier, continued (Wille, 2003). Draft SEA legislation was prepared in 2003 which implemented SEA in a similar manner to project EIA and integrated the legal requirements for SEA, EIA and assessments prepared under the European Habitats directive.[2] Following further discussion and consultation, the federal framework SEA act was ratified in May 2005. It will be implemented through supplementary amendments to existing sectoral legislation at federal or state levels.

Integration

While local land use and landscape plan (SEA) making procedures are supposed to be integrated, in reality this has not always been the case. In fact, there have been instances where the landscape plan was prepared only after the land use plan was finalized. In addition, landscape plans sometimes cover geographical areas for which several land use plans are prepared, making integration more difficult. There is still a lack of proper integration of regional plans and regional landscape framework plans. However, regional plans themselves consider alternatives and impacts to some extent. While local and regional landscape plans and programmes are supposed to define overall environmental and sustainability objectives, in the state of Brandenburg, local landscape plans (SEAs) also consider the possible environmental and landscape impacts of land use plans. Furthermore, regional plans themselves consider certain impacts (for example, the extraction of raw materials).

Guidance

Even before general formal framework SEA requirements came into force, a range of guidance documents is available to assessors, including both formal and informal guidance. In Brandenburg, regional plans are prepared according to the 'procedural guidelines'. Local land use plans and landscape plans are prepared following the regulations on land use and landscape planning.[3] Informal federal guidance is also available, for example, from the Federal Environment Agency (Bunzel and Hinzen, 2000; see also Prinz, 1999). In a general sense, the Federal Construction Act provides detailed guidance for land use plan making. Most importantly, in the context of SEA, this establishes that all public and private concerns need to be weighed and balanced in a just manner.

Coverage and tiering

It is a requirement that impact assessment is conducted for local land use plans, and, to some extent, regional plans, in Brandenburg. Furthermore, the need to conduct EA for project oriented local master plans derives from the implementation of the EIA Directive.

Effective assessment tiering in German land use plan making practice is not fully developed and it is clear that it would be difficult to achieve. This is mainly due to the rather complex relationships between the different instruments within the current planning system. As the SEA Directive does not formulate any requirements for policy SEA, spatial policy plans at the state level are not likely to be covered by formal SEA. Therefore, many decisions on basic alternatives and objectives continue to be made without assessing their impacts and without wide participation. The SEA Directive is, of course, unable to solve problems connected with an over-complicated planning system (Fischer, 2002).

Sustainable development

The concept of sustainable development has, to some extent, been integrated with spatial and land use planning in Germany for several decades. Socioeconomic and environmental aspects have always been evaluated in good planning practice in Germany. However, only since 1998 has there been a need to consider sustainable development in all spatial/land use planning decisions as a result of the requirements of the Federal Act for Spatial Planning and of the Federal Construction Act. While environmental impacts of local land use plans are appraised in landscape plans, socioeconomic impacts remain largely unassessed. Instead, economic and social aspects are usually reflected in underlying planning objectives. An informal federal sustainable development strategy was in place by 1994 and a formal strategy by 2002 (Bundesregierung, 2002), but these do not appear to have had any discernible impact on spatial/land use planning. In Brandenburg, the landscape programme covers important aspects of environmentally sustainable development but there is no proper sustainable development strategy in place. The impact of Local Agenda 21 on land use plan making has been very small (Fischer, 1999; Oels, 2000).

SEA process

This section deals with the different procedural aspects and stages of pre-SEA legislation practice in land use planning in Brandenburg. The consideration of substantive aspects is discussed first. This is followed by a discussion of the extent to which core procedural SEA stages are covered at regional and local levels prior to the transposition of the SEA Directive. Finally, the impacts included in German SEA practice are considered.

Substantive aspects

The alternatives considered vary according to the administrative level of application, increasing with a decreasing level of detail (Figure 6.1). While the number of possible alternatives to be considered at the state level is potentially high, it is comparatively low at the local level. The level of detail, on the other hand, is high in local planning and low in state planning.

At the state level, many fundamental policy decisions are made without any real assessment of their effects. These include the designation of towns within a hierarchy (based on the quality and quantity of services provided) in the state of Brandenburg and the number and size of development areas. Regional planning implements state policies and focuses on proposed development areas, as well as energy issues, raw materials and tourism. Regional plans assess the environmental impacts of different development options in an integrated way.

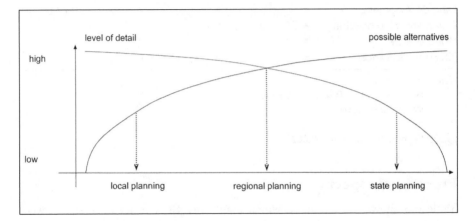

Source: Siemoneit and Fischer (2002)

Figure 6.1 *Detail and alternatives at different planning levels in Germany*

At the local level in Brandenburg, there is an indirect (but quite proactive) means of considering site alternatives and development projects. Development is allowed only in those areas that the landscape plans (SEAs) identify as not being sensitive. However, no documentation is prepared that clearly sets out whether (or which) alternatives are considered during the assessment process. Potential compensation is considered at both regional and local levels, based on the German Environmental Protection Act Intervention Rule. This requires compensation for any significant impacts that cannot be mitigated.

Table 6.2 summarizes the four main topics considered in the Lausitz-Spreewald regional integrated plan/SEA. These included environmental protection targets, mitigation measures and the assessment of alternatives. While mitigation measures were fully considered for all four topics, implementing the requirements of the federal Intervention Rule, environmental protection objectives were only partly considered. The failure to make reference to international or national targets was a particular shortcoming. A full evaluation of alternatives took place for the extraction of raw materials. Furthermore, there were only a few shortcomings regarding the consideration of land development alternatives and of alternative sites for wind energy generation. However, tourism/recreation alternatives were only partially evaluated.

Table 6.2 *Topics considered in the integrated Lausitz-Spreewald (Germany) regional plan/SEA*

Regional planning topics	Do nothing alternative	Environmental protection	Mitigation measures targets	Assessment of alternatives
Land development	✗	⇔	✓	(✓)
Raw material extraction	✗	⇔	✓	✓
Wind energy	✗	⇔	✓	(✓)
Tourism/recreation	✗	⇔	✓	⇔

Notes: ✓ = yes
      (✓) = yes, but a few shortcomings
      ⇔ = only partly
      ✗ = no

Source: Siemoneit and Fischer (2002)

Procedural aspects

Table 6.3 shows the extent to which eight core SEA procedural stages were undertaken in regional plan, local land use plan and landscape plan making in Germany prior to the transposition of the SEA Directive. Screening, scoping, prediction/evaluation, report preparation, review, monitoring, consultation and public participation are all formal requirements of the SEA Directive.

Most SEA stages were carried out. However, scoping, the prediction/evaluation of impacts and monitoring were only partly undertaken in regional plans. Furthermore, there was no public participation. All the stages were undertaken during the preparation of local land use plans apart from impact prediction/ evaluation. This, however, was undertaken through the landscape plans (SEAs). While most procedural stages were discharged fully, monitoring and public participation were undertaken only indirectly through the underlying local land use plans.

Impacts included in SEAs

Before formal SEA requirements came into force, informal SEAs (landscape plans) considered impacts on soil, water, climatic factors, fauna, flora and landscape.

Table 6.3 *Main SEA stages covered in land use planning in Brandenburg,*
Germany

	Regional plans	*Local land use plans*	*Landscape plans*
Screening	✓	✓	✓
Scoping	⇔	✓	✓
Prediction/evaluation	⇔	✗	✓
Report preparation	✓	✓	✓
Review	✓	✓	✓
Monitoring	⇔	✓	⇔
Consultation	✓	✓	✓
Public participation	✗	✓	⇔

Notes: ✓ = yes
⇔ = partly
✗ = no

The consideration of non-environmental impacts mainly took place as explicitly or implicitly stated assumptions. These included population growth, economic development, housing, public service and, usually, social development objectives. Additional aspects covered under the SEA Directive include biodiversity (covered to some extent under flora and fauna), population, human health, material assets and cultural heritage. The way in which secondary, synergistic and cumulative impacts are considered remains unclear.

SEA outcome

SEA outcomes include the impact of SEA on decision making, perceived costs and benefits, and whether SEA results in an improvement of environmental quality. The focus of this section is on the landscape plans (SEAs) for local land use plans. Impacts on the plan making process and costs are difficult to establish as impact assessment is conducted in a partially integrated manner.

Decision making

Pre-legislation SEAs for local land use plans are regarded as having a discernible impact on the treatment of environmental issues. In the case of the Nauen land use plan (below), the SEA ensured that no development was assigned to those areas identified as being sensitive. In earlier research on 14 landscape plans in Brandenburg (Fischer, 2002), 12 of the authorities interviewed averred that assessments were either reasonably or very influential. None said the SEA was not influential. The extent to which a landscape plan was thought to be influential was correlated with its perceived quality. Those authorities that stated that their SEAs were of good quality also said that they were influential.

Costs and benefits

The time involved in preparing SEAs depends on a number of factors. These include:

- the existence of a previous SEA;
- the size of the geographical area covered;
- existing databases;
- sensitivity of the natural environment;
- the existence of nature conservation or landscape strategies/policies/plans/ programmes;
- the stage that preparation of the underlying land use plan(s) has reached;
- the proposed developments.

On average, the preparation of a SEA takes up to two person years. Generally speaking, while SEAs are perceived by many authorities as a necessary evil, benefits are acknowledged to result from their application. SEAs clearly lead to more systematic and effective consideration of environmental issues in local land use plans (Fischer, 2002).

Environmental quality

There is no landscape plan monitoring that would allow a connection to be made between the assessment and an observed improvement or deterioration of the environmental quality of an area. The landscape planning (SEA) system has two main aims:

- to protect areas of high natural and landscape value;
- to conserve and improve parts of the landscape.

This is achieved firstly by keeping certain areas free from development. Secondly, SEAs formulate overall aims and targets for the conservation of the natural environment that are considered in the local land use plan and in any development activities. Thirdly, landscape plans consider the mitigation and compensation measures required by the federal Intervention Rule for the anticipated impacts of future developments that cannot be mitigated. In all three respects, SEAs for local land use plans lead to an improvement of the environmental quality in the relevant areas.

Monitoring

SEAs are subject to external review by the lower environment authorities or, in the case of unitary municipalities, the State Environment Agency. The Agency and the lower environmental authorities hold regular meetings (about four times a year) to ensure that landscape plans are of high overall quality. Furthermore, review also takes place through consultation (directly) and participation (indirectly through the local land use plans). The Brandenburg State Environment Agency possesses an inventory of all SEAs. Monitoring of the environmental quality of an area is undertaken indirectly through the preparation of annual environmental quality reports, usually at the state level (see, for example, Landesumweltamt, 2003). While every municipality is required to conduct spatial/land use monitoring based on the local land use plan, some fall short of this requirement.

Case study: Nauen landscape plan

This section describes the landscape plan (SEA) for the local land use plan of the municipality of Nauen in Brandenburg (Gemeinde Nauen, 2000). As explained earlier, landscape plans in Brandenburg have been equivalent to SEAs since the mid-1990s. The Nauen SEA can be considered to be an example of good practice (Buschke et al, 2002).

Nauen is located approximately 15km west of Berlin and has 11,000 inhabitants. Figure 6.2 shows the geographical location of Nauen in the state of Brandenburg. The core development area around Berlin, of which Nauen is part, and selected types of formally promoted development centres that form part of a hierarchy of towns in the state of Brandenburg are also shown. Due to its good railway connection with Berlin, it has been designated as a municipality that may accommodate substantial population growth. The preparatory land use plan for Nauen anticipated population growth of 50 per cent.

Table 6.4 shows how the SEA for the Nauen land use plan compared with 25 key requirements of the SEA Directive. The analysis is summarized in terms of four main themes.

Overall, the SEA met most requirements, either fully or in part. The only aspect that was entirely lacking was a non-technical summary. Tiering with other levels and sectors was fairly well developed. However, there was also some duplication, caused mainly by an over-complicated land use planning system. While communication and consultation were reasonably well developed, public participation was formally conducted only for the local land use plan. However, the general public was also able to consult the landscape plan.

The various requirements of the SEA Directive were covered to a large extent. However, there was no obvious consideration of international or national environmental/sustainability objectives and targets. Furthermore, while proposed developments in the land use plan were only brought forward in those areas identified in the landscape plan as not being sensitive, the alternatives considered during the SEA were not presented.

In the Nauen SEA, potential mitigation and compensation measures were given full consideration, as required by the Federal Environmental Protection Act Intervention Rule. While some general spatial/ land use monitoring took place, the landscape plan was monitored only indirectly through local land use plan monitoring.

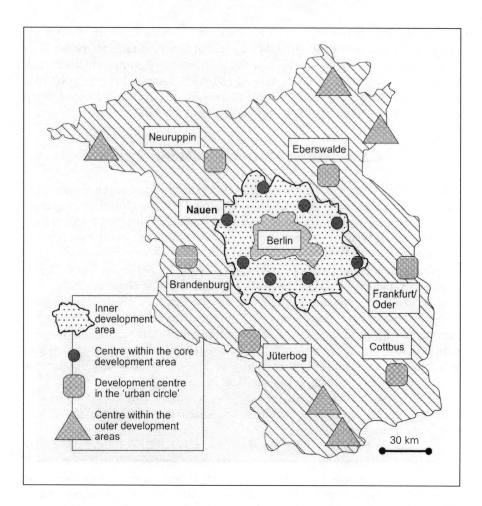

Source: based on Ministerium für Umwelt, Naturschutz und Raumordnung (1995)

Figure 6.2 *Location of Nauen in the Land Brandenburg, Germany*

Conclusion

SEA practice in the Federal Republic of Germany pre-dated SEA Directive implementation and formalized SEA was able to build upon the important role played by the landscape planning system. While the wheel does not need to be reinvented in the post-SEA Directive era, certain elements of existing practice need to be improved, particularly in terms of:

• the identification and assessment of all impacts including those on health, material and cultural assets, population and biodiversity;
• the consideration of international, European and national environmental goals and objectives;

Table 6.4 *Nauen landscape plan and SEA Directive requirements in Germany*

	Requirement met
TIERING – VERTICAL AND HORIZONTAL	●
Is the assessment focusing on those issues appropriate to the hierarchical level of the plan?	✓
Is the assessment being carried out as part of a wider procedure to avoid duplication within a tiered system of decision making?	⇔
Have existing monitoring arrangements been checked and utilized to avoid unnecessary duplication?	✓
COMMUNICATION, CONSULTATION & PARTICIPATION	●
Is there public consultation/participation?	⇔
Is there expert consultation?	✓
Have relevant environmental authorities been involved in determining the scope of the appraisal?	✓
Did the consultees receive a draft version of the plan and an accompanying environmental report (ER)/ plan section on assessment?	✓
Is it clear how the opinions collected during consultation influenced the preparation of the plan?	⇔
Has adequate consideration been given to publication and advertisement of the plan once formally adopted?	✓
SUBSTANTIVE – REPORT AND ALTERNATIVES	◉
Is there a separate ER?	✓
Does the ER/assessment section outline the relationship with other plans/programmes?	⇔
Does the ER/assessment section include baseline data for the state of the environment?	✓
Does the ER/assessment section include the environmental characteristics of areas likely to be significantly affected?	✓
Is there information on existing environmental problems and on areas of particular environmental importance?	✓
Have reasonable alternatives been identified, described and evaluated?	⇔
Does the ER/assessment section outline the reasons for selecting alternatives?	⇔
Does the ER/assessment section consider environmental protection objectives?	⇔
Does the ER/assessment section consider the significant effects on the environment?	✓
Does the ER/assessment section include information on mitigation?	✓
Does the ER/assessment section include a description of how the assessment was undertaken?	⇔
Is there a description of measures concerning monitoring?	⇔

Table 6.4 *Nauen landscape plan and SEA Directive requirements in Germany (continued)*

	Requirement met
Is there a non-technical summary of the ER/assessment section?	✗
MONITORING	O
Are the significant environmental effects arising from the implementation of the plan monitored?	⇔
Are the measures envisaged within the monitoring process included within the ER/assessment section?	⇔
Does monitoring include the identification of progress towards the plan and SEA objectives?	⇔

Notes: Extent to which SEA requirements are met:
✓ = yes, fully (scores 2)
⇔ = partly (scores 1)
✗ = no (scores 0)
● = 83 per cent
⊙ = 69 per cent
O = 50 per cent
Source: adapted from Fischer (2003)

- the explicit consideration of alternatives;
- the preparation of a separate report for regional plans and of a non-technical summary for local land use plan SEAs;
- full public participation;
- monitoring.

Table 6.5 summarizes the German SEA of land use plans prior to the implementation of the SEA Directive. It also evaluates the prospective post-legislation situation. Problems with the formal SEA of land use plans include an over-complicated planning system that makes proper coordination and tiering difficult, if not impossible. Furthermore, due to the fact that policies are not covered by the SEA Directive, strategic plans prepared at the state level do not include an assessment of their environmental impacts. This means that important strategic decisions will continue to be made without assessing their impacts and without sufficiently wide participation.

Acknowledgement

The author wishes to thank Ronald Jordan of the Landesumweltamt Brandenburg (Land Environment Agency) for his detailed and useful comments on a draft of this chapter.

Table 6.5 *Evaluation of SEA of land use plans in Germany*

Criterion	Criterion met pre-SEA Directive	Criterion met post-SEA Directive	Comments
		SYSTEM CRITERIA	
Legal basis	▲	■	SEA formalized through revision of Federal Construction Act (20 July 2004) and through federal framework SEA Act (not yet ratified)
Integration	▲	■	Federal Construction Act adapted to improve integration
Guidance	▲	▲	Both formal and informal guidance exists; somewhat fragmented
Coverage	▲	■	Legal requirements to prepare landscape plans existed previously
Tiering	▲	▲	Tiered landscape planning system previously in place; over-complicated planning system is a deterrent
Sustainable development	▲	▲	Previous legislation required consideration of sustainable development; no discernible impact from sustainable development strategies or Local Agenda 21 documents
		PROCESS CRITERIA	
Alternatives	▲	■	Plan alternatives now fully considered; fundamental policy alternatives remain unaddressed
Screening	■	■	Based on clear thresholds
Scoping	■	■	Perceived as being of fundamental importance
Prediction/evaluation	■	■	Includes mitigation and compensation requirements
Additional impacts	□	▲	Unclear
Report preparation	■	■	Considered to be core of SEA
Review	▲	▲	No independent review body
Monitoring	▲	■	Monitoring undertaken indirectly through land use plans
Mitigation	▲	■	Previously undertaken indirectly through choice of minimum impact development sites

Table 6.5 *Evaluation of SEA of land use plans in Germany (continued)*

Criterion	Criterion met pre-SEA Directive	Criterion met post-SEA Directive	Comments
Consultation and public participation	▲	■	Considered to be at core of SEA
OUTCOME CRITERIA			
Decision making	■	■	Post-SEA Directive practice expected to achieve, at least, standard of pre-Directive practice
Costs and benefits	■	■	As above
Environmental quality	▲	▲	As above
System monitoring	▲	▲	As above

Notes: ■ – Yes
  ▲ – Partially
  □ – No
  ? – Don't know

Notes

1   Act to Accommodate EU Requirements in Federal Construction Act, Berlin, Bundesministerium für Verkehr, Bau- und Wohnungswesen (German Federal Ministry for Transport, Construction and Housing), 20 July 2004 (in German)
2   Gesetzentwurf der Bundesregierung (Bill of the German Federal Government) (2003) Draft Bill to Implement the SEA Directive [SUP-Act], 29 July 2003, Berlin (in German)
3   Gemeinsamer Erlaß des Ministeriums für Umwelt, Naturschutz und Raumordnung und des Ministeriums für Stadtentwicklung, Wohnen und Verkehr vom 24.10.1994 – Bauleitplanung und Landschaftsplanung (Joint Decree of the Ministry for the Environment, Nature Protection and Spatial Organization and the Ministry for City Development, Housing and Transport of 24.10.1994 – Construction Planning and Landscape Planning), Official Journal for Brandenburg of 6.12.1994), last amended 29 April 1997 (Official Journal for Brandenburg of 23 May 1997) (in German)

References

Bundesministerium für Umwelt, Naturschutz und Reaktorsicherheit (German Federal Ministry for the Environment, Nature Protection and Nuclear Safety) (1993) *Landscape Planning*, BUNR, Bonn
Bundesregierung (German Federal Government) (2002) *National Strategy for Sustainable Development*, www.bundesregierung.de (in German)
Bunge, T. (1998) 'SEA in land use planning: the Erlangen case study', in Kleinschmidt, V. and Wagner, D. (eds) *SEA in Europe: Fourth European Workshop on EIA*, Kluwer, Dordrecht

Bunzel, A. and Hinzen, A. (2000) *Guide to Environmental Protection in Construction Planning*, Federal Environment Agency, Erich Schmidt Verlag, Berlin (in German)

Buschke, M., Derwick, B., Faust, S., Finger, A., Flatow, D., Funke, J., Hudy, S., Köller, J., Krsynowski, A., Lermen, A., Reinsch, N., Stein, M., Sommer, S., Träger, N., Unsöld, D. and Walter, U. (2002) *Can the Landscape Plan be a Suitable Plan SEA? – the Example of the Municipality of Nauen*, Study Project 2001/2002, Institute for Landscape and Environmental Planning, Technical University of Berlin, Berlin (in German)

Cupei, J. (1994) 'History and development of EIA in the Federal Republic of Germany', in Kleinschmidt, V. (ed) *EIA Primer for Authorities, Consultants and Stakeholders: Basics, Procedures and Implementation*, 2nd edition, Dortmunder Vertrieb für Bau- und planungs-literatur, Dortmund (in German)

European Commission (2001) 'Directive 2001/42/EC of the European Parliament and of the Council of 27 June 2001 on the assessment of the effects of certain plans and programmes on the environment', *Official Journal of the European Communities*, vol L197, pp30–37, 21 July

Fischer, T. B. (1999) 'The consideration of sustainability aspects within transport infrastructure-related policies, plans and programmes', *Journal of Environmental Planning and Management*, vol 42, pp189–219

Fischer, T. B. (2002) *Strategic Environmental Assessment in Transport and Land Use Planning*, Earthscan, London

Fischer, T. B. (2003) 'Sustainability appraisal of the Oldham UDP – a critical evaluation of a positively perceived process', *UVP-Report*, vol 17, pp29–33 (in German)

Fischer, T. B. (2004) 'Transport policy making and SEA in Liverpool, Amsterdam and Berlin – 1997 and 2002', *Environmental Impact Assessment Review*, vol 24, pp319–336

Gather, M. (2001) 'Experiences with SEA of transport plans in Germany', *UVP-Report*, vol 15, pp138–143 (in German)

Gemeinde Nauen (Municipality of Nauen) (2000) *Statutory Land Use Plan – Draft*, Nauen, GN (in German)

Heidtmann, E. (2003) 'The future relationship of landscape planning and SEA', *UVP-Report*, vol 17, pp70–84 (in German)

Hodek, J. and Kleinschmidt, V. (1998) 'Strategic environmental impact assessment in Germany with a focus on the state of Brandenburg', in Kleinschmidt, V. and Wagner, D. (eds) *SEA in Europe*, Kluwer, Dordrecht

Jacoby, C. (1996) 'Methodological approaches to SEA in land-use planning', *Journal of Applied Environmental Research*, vol 7, pp168–184 (in German)

Jacoby, C. (2000) *Strategic Environmental Assessment in Spatial Planning: Instruments, Methods and Legal Basis for the Evaluation of Spatial Alternatives in Town and Regional Planning*, Erich Schmidt Verlag, Berlin (in German)

Jacoby, C., Kraetzschmer, D. and Kreja, R. (2003) 'Environmental assessment for regional plans – interim results of practical tests', *UVP-Report*, vol 17, pp68–73 (in German)

Jordan, R., Brandenburg State Environment Authority (2004) Oral communication, June

Kleffner, U. and Ried, W. M. (1995) 'Programme SEA in statutory land use planning by the Saarbrücken Regional Authority', Paper to *Saarbrücken Regional Authority Congress*, 30–31 March, Stadtverband Saarbrücken (City Regional Association of Saarbrücken), Saarbrücken (in German)

Kleinschmidt, V. and Wagner, D. (1996) 'Wind farms in the Soest district', in Therivel, R. and Partidário, M. (eds) *The Practice of Strategic Environmental Assessment*, Earthscan, London

Kraetzschmer, D. (2003) 'Environmental assessment for waste and water management plans and programmes', *UVP-Report*, vol 17, pp64–67 (in German)

Landesumweltamt (Land Environment Agency) (2003) *Environmental Data for Brandenburg*, LUA, Potsdam (in German)

Ministerium für Umwelt, Naturschutz und Raumordnung (Ministry for the Environment, Environmental Protection and Spatial Organization) (1995) *Brandenburg Land Development Plan: Order of Central Places*, MUNR, Potsdam (in German)

Oels, A. (2000) '"Let's get together and feel alright!" a critical evaluation of Agenda 21 processes in England and Germany', in Heinelt, H. and Mühlich, E. (eds) *Local Agenda 21: Processes, Explanatory Approaches, Concepts and Results*, Leske und Budrich, Opladen (in German)

Prinz, D. (1999) *Town Construction Volume 1: Design*, 7th edition, Kohlhammer, Stuttgart (in German)

Riehl, C. and Winkler-Kühlken, B. (1995) *Environmental Impact Assessment in Area Master Planning: Practical Problems and Suggested Solutions*, Institute for Town Research and Structural Policy, Berlin

Schmidt, C., Gather, M., Knoll, C. and Müntz, S. (2003) 'Testing an SEA methodology for regional planning', *UVP-Report*, vol 17, pp74–75 (in German)

Scholles, F., van Haaren, C., Myrzik, A., Ott, S., Wilke, T., Winkelbrandt, A. and Wulfert, K. (2003) 'SEA and landscape planning', *UVP-Report*, vol 17, pp76–82 (in German)

Siemoneit, D. and Fischer, T. B. (2002) 'SEA – the example of the Lausitz-Spreewald Regional Plan in Brandenburg', *UVP-Report*, vol 16, pp253–258 (in German)

Wagner, D. (1994) 'Strategic environmental assessment for transport planning in Germany', in Commission of the European Communities *Third EU Workshop on Environmental Impact Assessment in Delphi*, Directorate-General XI Environment, European Commission, Brussels

Wende, W., Hanusch, M., Gassner, E., Guennewig, D., Koeppel, J., Lambrecht, H., Langenheld, A., Peters, W. and Roethke-Habeck, P. (2004). 'Requirements of the SEA Directive and the German Federal Transport Infrastructure Plan', *European Environment*, vol 14, pp105–122.

Wille, V. (2003) 'Plan SEA as a new instrument of environmental law', *ARL – Academy for Spatial Research and Land Planning Newsletter*, vol 2, p9 (in German)

7

Hong Kong

Elvis Au and Kin Che Lam[1]

Introduction

In the last few decades, the economic growth of Hong Kong has been phenomenal, turning a small fishing village into a modern metropolis. Hong Kong has several notable characteristics that influence land use planning practice in the city. Most significantly, the scarcity of land, and the associated high concentration of activities in the space available, give rise to different types of land use conflicts, with development in Hong Kong being characterized by high-rise and high-density patterns.

Moreover, a unique set of environmental problems exists in the city, partly due to the hilly landscape, which creates a number of small watersheds and air sheds with limited dispersal capacity. With a potential increase of population from 6.4 million in 1996 to about 8.1 million in 2011, the associated land use conflicts and environmental stresses are likely to be amplified.

In response to these challenges, the government has been looking for ways to harmonize the conflicts between development and the environment. An important part of this effort is the emphasis placed on the application of SEA during the planning of development strategies.

Context

Hong Kong has a three-tier planning system (Figure 7.1) that comprises development strategies at the territorial and at the sub-regional levels, and various types of statutory and administrative plans at the district/local level (Planning Department, 2000). The territorial development strategy (TDS) provides a planning framework which integrates, and to some extent balances, the consideration of land use, environment and transport. The TDS is intended to facilitate the preparation of sub-regional development strategies and district plans

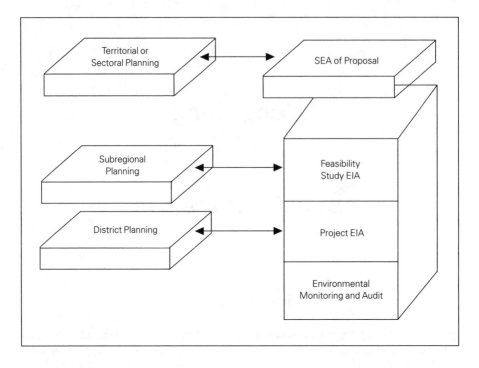

Source: Au (1998, 2000)

Figure 7.1 *Planning hierarchy and SEA in Hong Kong*

and integrates public policies on major land and infrastructure development. Moreover, the TDS is designed to increase the emphasis on large-scale, long-term redevelopment strategies and cross-boundary cooperation.

Subregional development strategies are prepared in order to translate the TDS into more specific planning objectives and initiatives for all five subregions of Hong Kong. They stand between the TDS and local district plans, and therefore provide a framework for the preparation of more specific and detailed statutory district plan and work programmes. District/local plans consist of two types of statutory plan prepared under the provisions of the Town Planning Ordinance. These are outline zoning plans (OZPs) and development permission area plans (DPAs). Two types of administrative plans also exist; outline development plans (ODPs) and layout plans. OZPs highlight proposed land uses and cover residential, commercial, industrial, open space, institutional, green belt and conservation areas. The major road systems serving individual planning schemes are also defined within these plans.

Since the early 1990s, environmental assessment (EA) has been integrated with the spatial planning process in Hong Kong (Au, 2000). This has been particularly noticeable during the preparation of the TDS and associated development plans. SEA has been undertaken during spatial planning processes in Hong Kong largely as a result of the publication of a government circular in 1988 that related to the environmental review of major development projects. This covered new town developments as well as all major projects. Since then, major development plans have been subject to SEA and more than a dozen major SEAs of plans or new town developments have been carried out. Examples of SEAs include theTseung Kwan O NewTown and the North Lantau Development new towns (Environmental Protection Department (EPD), 2002). Major SEAs for the strategic growth areas in NorthWest NewTerritories and North East New Territories are currently being carried out. Unlike project EAs, these SEAs have:

- assessed, at an early stage in the planning process, environmental issues to aid planning decision making;
- examined a range of possible alternatives;
- evaluated the likely cumulative environmental implications of the proposals and plans.

Hong Kong's experience of SEA has covered a wide range of sectors, including strategic growth areas, territorial land use planning, transportation strategies and policies, and strategic power generation technology proposals and siting options (Au, 1999; EPD, 2004).Table 7.1 presents examples of SEAs of major development strategies.

A strong link between SEA and the general planning hierarchy (Figure 7.1) has been developed within Hong Kong's framework of environmental planning standards and guidelines (Hong Kong SpecialAdministrative Region Government (HKSARG), 1990). These standards and guidelines provide assistance for planners, architects and engineers during the planning and design of major developments (Au, 1998). SEA has therefore become an important tool in guiding the planning process at territorial, strategic and subregional levels.The planning standards and guidelines have also facilitated the systematic integration of environmental factors and cumulative environmental concerns during the planning process (Au, 2000).

Case study: Hong Kong Territorial Development Strategy Review

The Territorial Development Strategy Review (TDSR) (HKSARG, 1995) was a comprehensive review of the land use development strategy for the territory and involved the first application of formal SEA in Hong Kong.The review commenced in 1992, with the SEA being completed in December 1995.The Advisory Council on the Environment (ACE), which comprises representatives from industry, professional bodies, academia and green groups, was consulted about the SEA report in July 1996. The SEA analysed the environmental implications of more than 20 alternative development options which outlined different rates and extents of economic and regional development.The findings of the SEA led to a number

Table 7.1 *Examples of Hong Kong SEAs*

Study	Key sectors involved	Scale	Dimension of environmental issues	Strategic environmental concerns and foci
TERRITORIAL LAND USE PLANNING				
Territorial Development Strategy Review	Territorial land use and transportation	Territory wide	Territorial and district	Potential environmental implications and acceptability of various development options
TRANSPORTATION STRATEGIES				
Third Comprehensive Transport Study	Transportation	Territory wide	Territorial, district and local	Environmental implications of different transport modes, policies and major developments
Second Railway Development Study	Transportation, fuel consumption and land use	Territory wide	Territorial, district and local	Potential environmental implications of railway development options
Electronic Road Pricing Study	Road transport, economic and charging technology	Territory wide	Territorial, district and local	Environmental performance and potential benefits of various charging schemes
1800MW Power Station	Power supply, local land use, fuel supply, power generation and technology	1800MW power generation capacity	Global, regional, territorial, district and local	Potential environmental implications and acceptability of various fuels, technologies and site options

Source: Au (1999, 2002)

of environmentally damaging options being discarded or significantly modified during different stages of the review. Examples of these modifications included the deletion of potentially damaging development options planned for the east and south of Hong Kong – areas that are to be preserved for nature conservation, amenity and recreation.

Three fundamental sustainability principles were developed during the SEA that formed the basis of the TDSR assessment framework:

- *Connection Principle.* This emphasized the building of connections, or bridges, between sustainability concerns and concepts, development approaches and policy guidelines being used in Hong Kong
- *Integration Principle.* This promoted the greatest possible integration of the SEA with other economic and planning approaches to encourage holistic strategy formulation
- *Pragmatic Principle.* This addressed complex, multisectoral, multimedia and multidisciplinary issues with the aim of developing pragmatic, realistic and workable planning approaches.

Guided by these principles, an analytical assessment framework was formulated. The framework was underpinned by three central themes, namely natural capital, environmental carrying capacity and tiered sustainability issues (Au, 2002). Each of these themes is now addressed in turn.

Natural capital

Natural capital is the stock of assets including soil, the atmosphere, flora, fauna, water, and wetlands that provides a flow of environmental goods or services. These assets can be renewable or non-renewable, marketed or non-marketed. The concept of natural capital stock has been applied to territorial land use planning in Hong Kong in order to view the linkages between land uses and various environmental attributes from a strategic perspective. The concept, as applied to territorial land use planning studies, is illustrated in Figure 7.2.

Hong Kong is a city state that has no major natural resources of its own except for a unique natural harbour and some diverse ecosystems. It relies on food, water and other natural resources from mainland China and other parts of the world. The concept of natural capital, as applied in Hong Kong, has been broken down into natural, man-made and ecological components. The natural component refers to the self-purification processes that help to maintain the state of the environment and the health of the local people. The man-made environmental infrastructure includes sewerage, sewage treatment facilities and landfills, which help to alleviate the burdens exerted on the natural processes that assimilate human waste products. Hong Kong's ecological assets provide essential functions or services locally (for example, leisure and recreation) and internationally (such as Ramsar sites). These three components of natural capital are used to help prescribe, predict and define:

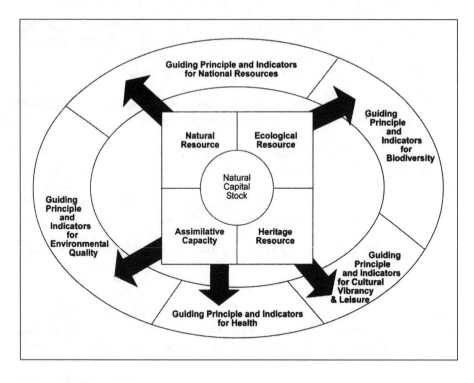

Source: HKSARG (2000b)

Figure 7.2 *Elements of natural capital stock in Hong Kong*

- the assimilative capacity of key local air sheds to take in air pollutants;
- the assimilative capacity of the harbour and of the main tidal currents and key water basins within and outside Hong Kong to absorb waterborne pollutants;
- the assimilative capacities of regional air sheds and of the Pearl River in mainland China;
- internationally important wetlands in the region such as the Ramsar site for migratory birds in Mai Po;
- important land conservation areas and marine conservation areas that are essential for the education, amenity and recreation of 6.4 million people.

During the SEA of the TDSR, qualitative, quantitative and semi-quantitative methods were used to identify critical, natural self-purification processes and to assess their carrying capacities. Spatial mapping techniques were deployed to identify all key land and marine conservation areas and sites of special scientific interest. This approach helped to avoid inappropriate development and provided a means of evaluating, in a qualitative fashion, the extent of the potential loss of ecological assets arising from the implementation of the TDSR.

Environmental carrying capacity

Environmental carrying capacity and associated thresholds are central to the concept of environmental sustainability, and have become essential considerations in territorial land use planning in Hong Kong. Examples of parameters that have been adopted to assess environmental carrying capacity and thresholds are shown in Table 7.2. These have enabled proposed development thresholds and strategies to be tested against environmental carrying capacities and the cost implications of mitigation or avoidance measures to be incorporated into strategy formulation.

Table 7.2 *Analysis of environmental carrying capacity in Hong Kong*

Environmental carrying capacity	Examples of methods of analysis
Air quality carrying capacities to accommodate industrial and traffic emissions	Air quality modelling to define carrying capacities for individual air sheds and to develop appropriate policy responses
Noise climate resulting from road traffic and industrial activities	Forecasting major changes in noise levels due to development strategies and estimating the cost of mitigation
Carrying capacities of water bodies and sewerage and sewage treatment facilities	Forecasting increases in pollution loads in different waterbodies, estimating extent to which statutory water quality objectives will be exceeded, assessing degree of overloading of sewerage and sewage treatment facilities and identifying associated cost implications
Carrying capacities of strategic landfills and waste transfer facilities	Assessing the extent of overloading of existing and committed landfills and waste transfer facilities, and identifying policy and cost implications

Source: Au (2002)

Apart from land use, the environmental sustainability implications of land use plans on other sectoral issues need to be examined. SEAs may therefore include analyses of the environmental impacts (air, water, waste, noise, ecology) of key sectors such as transportation, port-related activities and industrial and commercial activities.

Tiered sustainability issues

Tiers of issues related to sustainability goals were developed for the TDSR SEA, enabling different types and levels of government responses to be formulated. Examples of such tiers of sustainability issues are given in Table 7.3 and Figure 7.3.

Table 7.3 *Tiers of sustainability issues and types of responses in Hong Kong*

Levels of issues	Critical environmental sustainability issues	Examples of evaluation methods and types of responses
Local sustainability issues	Environmental carrying capacities and thresholds at local levels (air, water, noise, hazards, waste, sewage), effects on local terrestrial, marine ecological assets	Performance measures applied to options evaluation. *Responses:* strategy modification, investment, technological fixes, policy changes
Regional sustainability issues	Demand for, and supply of, food, energy, water and resources in Pearl River Delta, deterioration in air and water quality in Pearl River Delta	Qualitative evaluation of regional sustainability implications of the entire strategy. *Responses:* cross-border environmental cooperation
Compliance with Agenda 21 components	Greenhouse gases, biodiversity, ecological footprint, energy conservation and population	Based on findings of quantitative and qualitative assessments, evaluation of entire strategy against key components of Agenda 21. *Responses:* policy changes, investment, technology, international environmental cooperation

Source: Dubin and Au (1997); Au (2002)

SEA system

The Hong Kong EIA Ordinance, which came into force in April 1998, required EA to be conducted for major development plans of more than 20 hectares or involving more than 100,000 people. Previously, in 1992, a governor's policy initiative had required SEA for all policy proposals with significant environmental implications submitted to the executive council (EPD, 2004, Section 7). The TDSR case study falls under this administrative requirement. It demonstrates that SEA can be successfully applied even if there is no legislative requirement to undertake SEA during the preparation of strategies and policies. The application of SEA to major policies and strategies relies first on the actions of authorities who must be convinced of the merits of undertaking such an assessment and then engage the relevant parties in the process. This ensures not only the participation of concerned government departments and bureaux but also their early involvement in the assessment process. The requirement has fostered a strong link between SEA and

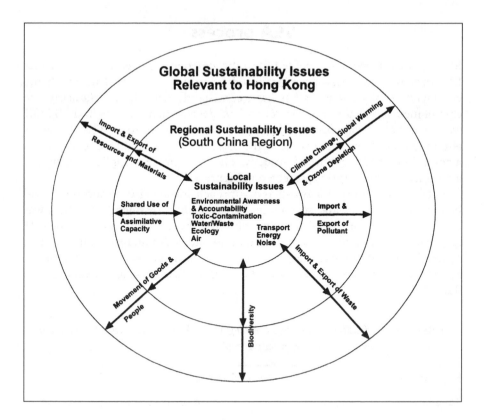

Global Sustainability Issues
Relevant to Hong Kong

Regional Sustainability Issues
(South China Region)

Local
Sustainability Issues

Environmental Awareness
& Accountability
Toxic-Contamination
Water/Waste
Ecology
Air

Transport
Energy
Noise

Import & Export of
Resources and Materials

Climate Change, Global Warming
& Ozone Depletion

Shared Use of
Assimilative
Capacity

Import &
Export of
Pollutant

Movement of Goods &
People

Import & Export of Waste

Biodiversity

Source: Ho and Au (1997)

Figure 7.3 *Relevance of environmental sustainability issues to Hong Kong*

the planning system. Moreover, a clear framework of environmental planning standards and guidelines has been developed which provides assistance for planners, architects and engineers undertaking SEA during the planning of major developments.

Without legislative backing, there is a danger that SEAs of strategies or policies can potentially lose their focus. In Hong Kong, this problem has been addressed by requiring a carefully prepared study brief for each SEA, which is issued by the EPD. The brief defines the scope of, and approach to, the SEA and sets out the terms of reference and other relevant guidance to assist those undertaking the SEA. In the process of preparing the study brief, the EPD conducts a systematic scoping of key issues for proponents to consider when undertaking the SEA. The EPD also chairs an inter-departmental environmental study management group to guide the SEA process and review its findings. The involvement of the EPD throughout the SEA process helps proponents to identify, and focus on, key sustainability issues. SEAs are also guided by adherence to the three sustainability principles and the three central themes that emerged during the TDSR SEA.

SEA process

SEA in Hong Kong has benefited from the experience gained from the project EIA process which has been practised since the 1980s and in which the consideration of alternatives has been consistently emphasized. Similarly, the environmental benefits and costs of various development options in the TDSR were thoroughly examined and compared. Discussion of these TDSR options also raised questions about some of the basic population and economic growth assumptions made within the strategy. The SEA process applied during the assessment of the TDSR is presented in Figure 7.4.

The SEA employed a two-tiered approach involving both top-down and bottom-up initiatives, and sectoral and component assessments. A matrix was used to link environmental carrying capacity, the ability to meet Agenda 21 responsibilities and other issues, including public health and survival concerns. Macro-level study to assess environmental sustainability was also undertaken. Several difficulties were experienced during this SEA. These are summarized in Table 7.4.

Table 7.4 *Difficulties encountered during Hong Kong Territorial Development Strategy Review SEA*

Key difficulties	Solutions
Time/budget constraints	Reliance on existing available data and studies
Full quantification not possible	'Best estimate' approach
Support from proponents/departments not continuous	Focus on common goal and on value added to public; process simplified

Source: Dubin and Au (1997)

SEAs sometimes fail to focus on the most critical issues concerning a particular strategy or area. They can be either too broad in their attempts to deal with many issues/options or too shallow in their level of analysis. This has been partly resolved in Hong Kong by adopting the natural capital approach, through which key environmental attributes and strategic environmental constraints are identified during the environmental baseline study conducted as part of the SEA. The sustainability, precautionary and avoidance principles are applied to the formulation of assessment criteria and the generation of development options during this baseline study stage of the SEA.

The unique high-rise and high-density development patterns in Hong Kong reduce the utility of conventional assessment methodologies developed elsewhere. Consequently, a number of assessment techniques and methods specifically fitted to the purpose of Hong Kong SEA have been developed, for example, the widespread application of the environmental guidelines in the Hong Kong Planning Standards and Guidelines (HKSARG, 1990).

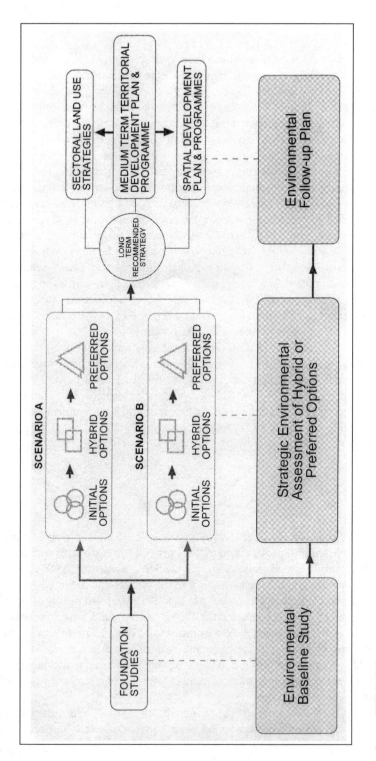

Source: EPD (2004)

Figure 7.4 *Hong Kong Territorial Development Strategy Review SEA and land use planning processes*

Consultation on the findings of a SEA with the general public and ACE represents an important step in the SEA process in Hong Kong. The major findings of the SEA are summarized for consultation with the relevant stakeholders before final decisions concerning the action being assessed are made. These consultation procedures have brought significant benefits. For example, comments received during the first stage of the public consultation process have helped to identify key sustainability issues, sharpen the scope of the study and redefine the evaluation framework. Consultation has also flagged up key issues for the attention of relevant government departments or bureaux.

A number of processes are commonly undertaken as part of Hong Kong SEA. Alternative strategies are evaluated against environmental 'bottom lines' based on the concept of environmental carrying capacities, so that appropriate strategies can be identified to enable negative implications on environmental sustainability to be minimized or avoided. Whenever sustainability issues are identified, cross-sectoral and cumulative impact analyses are also undertaken. Moreover, the appraisal of sectoral issues helps to establish linkages and causal relationships between different policies and can also identify necessary modifications to policies or institutional structures. The evaluation of the cumulative implications of development strategies against key sustainability indicators also helps to identify necessary policy adjustments and planning responses.

Hong Kong has devised a strategic environmental monitoring and review framework to track policy and planning decisions. One of the key ingredients of success in Hong Kong is that the findings of the SEA must be presented in an understandable and usable form for decision makers to consider the impact of future development strategies on environmental and sustainability issues. This helps to provide decision makers with a better knowledge of the implications of the proposal and to initiate follow-up studies or actions to address any outstanding sustainability issues.

SEA outcome

The case of Hong Kong's TDSR demonstrates that SEA can trigger beneficial government actions and policy changes. This process usually begins with a scoping of possible government responses to impacts identified during the SEA, followed by the development of adaptive management techniques and action plans to tackle major outstanding sustainability issues predicted to arise from the implementation of the proposal. This process enabled the TDSR SEA to yield considerable benefits to decision makers, the public, the environment and others. The first major benefit was consensus building on the need for action on sustainability issues. The systematic SEA approach resulted in the acceptance by decision makers and some key stakeholders of the need to act on some major local and regional sustainability issues before it was too late.

Secondly, the SEA improved the sustainability of the TDSR and enabled key natural habitats to be protected against major environmental damage. Thirdly, although it is not possible for the analysis of sustainability impacts to lead to immediate solutions to all major outstanding issues, the SEA produced an agenda for the actions necessary to address these issues.

The SEA successfully brought the potential adverse impacts on environmental quality of implementing the TDSR, and consequently the urgent need for action to deal with these issues, to the attention of the general public and decision makers. Further, the SEA led to a number of follow-up actions being instigated. Firstly, it prompted the initiation of a major government study on sustainable development in Hong Kong, *Sustainable Development for the 21st Century*, which was completed in 2001 (HKSARG, 2001). Secondly, it led to the compilation of an environmental baseline report,[2] which provided a comprehensive review of current development pressures and environmental conditions in Hong Kong. This baseline report has provided a platform to evaluate the environmental sustainability impacts of future policies or strategic proposals in the area.

The TDSR SEA not only raised some critical issues underpinning sustainable development in Hong Kong, but also laid the framework for a number of other SEAs. Recognizing that transportation is a key to delivering sustainable development goals, two strategic transportation studies were conducted by the Hong Kong Government, each of which contained a SEA component. The first and most notable was the Third Comprehensive Transport Study (CTS3), which identified, reviewed and recommended the transportation policies and associated major developments required to meet the anticipated growth in demand for transport by 2016 (HKSARG, 1999). The accompanying SEA evaluated the potential environmental implications of various strategic options, identified environmental constraints and opportunities, and set out a series of actions to be addressed in the future. The findings of the SEA were presented to ACE and to the Legislative Council and led to a much greater awareness of the long-term environmental implications of various development options concerning transportation provision.

The TDSR also led to a further SEA which concerned transportation and rail development; the Second Railway Development Study (RDS2). RDS2 was intended to identify railway development options and railway management and operation improvements, with inputs from CTS3, to meet projected transport demand and improve the efficiency of the railway network by 2016. The SEA commenced in March 1998 and evaluated the potential environmental implications of various railway network options and individual links (HKSARG, 2000a). It covered strategic environmental issues such as the potential environmental advantages arising from a modal shift from road to rail and addressed the indirect environmental implications of the proposal on environmentally sensitive areas. The SEA also identified the environmentally preferred option and established the environmental acceptability of other options.

Prompted by the TDSR SEA, the SEAs undertaken during CTS3 and RDS2 underscored the need to:

- integrate land use, transport and environmental planning;
- minimize the need for travel;

- control vehicle emissions and aim for air quality standards that prevent damage to human health;
- increase the number of people and amount of freight transported by less environmentally sensitive modes;
- increase investment in public transport, especially passenger railways, to alleviate air pollution;
- restrict private car ownership;
- Include external costs (for example, the loss of land and maintenance costs associated with mitigation measures) in cost comparisons undertaken between transport options.

Conclusion

The application of SEA in Hong Kong has proved to be worthwhile. A SEA manual, based on experience of SEA in Hong Kong, was published in 2004 (EPD, 2004). The need for the careful planning of the SEA, so that relevant concepts can be understood by policy makers and other professionals working on the assessment, is apparent – good intentions do not necessarily bring about good results unless they can be understood by all those involved. It is also apparent that much more effort needs to be directed to building connections between sustainability concerns and existing decision making processes. Any rigorous analysis of sustainability issues is likely to require huge amounts of data, some of which it may not be possible to gather during the time frame of the SEA. Also, data gathering tools may not be well established. A pragmatic approach is therefore needed to identify the best available workable methods for carrying out SEAs.

Suitable spatial tiers of sustainability issues and associated government responses, and equivalent tiers of SEA and EIA to help to achieve different sustainable development goals, are needed. It is a fallacy that a single SEA can resolve every complex sustainability issue. It must also be remembered that, like EIA, any SEA or sustainability analysis is doomed to become a paper exercise unless there is an equally rigorous strategic environmental follow-up and audit mechanism.

Several key lessons can be drawn from experience of SEA in Hong Kong:

Process design. It is apparent that SEA has to be tailored to suit different types of policy strategy, decision making and political system. Nonetheless, the most essential components of a SEA include processes to:

- assess critically the environmental implications of different policy or strategy alternatives and options;
- scope the types and levels of decision inputs that are appropriate to each policy or strategy decision;
- involve relevant stakeholders in some form of meaningful, structured and informed debate concerning critical strategic environmental issues.

Process management. Since strategy development and policy making, unlike projects, involve many policy bureaux, ministries and departments, suitable technical oversight is necessary to ensure the success of the process. This can ensure that the objectivity of the assessment process is maintained, without other policy making parameters having undue influence. Moreover, in order to be effective, SEA must also be integrated with the mainstream policy making process.

Stakeholder involvement and public participation. Compared with project EIA, this is easier said than done because many policies and strategies are highly sensitive and controversial. In addition, late public consultation undermines the credibility of the process and can result in a lack of focus during the SEA, whereas consultation too early in the process can lead to broad discussion with little meaningful information and few options being available for consideration. Ideally, the participation process needs to be split into meaningful stages, each having different purposes, and to be based on varying types and levels of assessment information and findings.

The TDSR SEA not only provided succinct information on the environmental implications of various development and land use options but also highlighted the need for: a sustainable transport strategy; integrated policy development with neighbouring regions; long-term monitoring of environmental impacts; and the need to undertake SEA at the conceptual stage of strategy development. The need for a sustainable transport strategy arose from the recognition that land use and transport planning are intricately linked and therefore need to be considered holistically to minimize the need to travel, reduce the cost of noise mitigation measures and encourage environmentally friendly modes of transport. At the same time, the TDSR made decision makers aware that the environmental sustainability of Hong Kong is increasingly being determined by global and regional economics, transboundary environmental problems and global environmental issues. The status of SEA in Hong Kong is summarized in Table 7.5.

To bridge the gap between local and regional environmental sustainability, due consideration needs to be given to regional cooperation and to other critical issues identified during SEAs. The Hong Kong experience also affirms the need for monitoring to assess the effectiveness of various measures designed to mitigate negative impacts identified during the SEA. The key challenge for the future is to develop appropriate procedures and methods to assess the environmental implications of major policies at a conceptual stage with a view to building early consensus on appropriate policy responses to major sustainability issues.

Notes

1   The views expressed in this chapter are those of the authors and do not necessarily represent the views of their employers or their organizations
2   Details of the environmental baseline report are available at: www.epd.gov.hk/epd/english/environmentinhk/eia_planning/sea/baseline.html

Table 7.5 *Evaluation of SEA of land use plans in Hong Kong*

Criterion	Criterion met	Comments
		SYSTEM CRITERIA
Legal basis	▲	EIA Ordinance requires environmental assessment to be conducted for development plans for more than 20ha or 100,000 people. For strategies or policies, requirement imposed through governor's initiative
Integration	■	SEA closely linked to territorial, strategic and sub regional planning
Guidance	■	For each SEA, Environmental Protection Department issues detailed study brief setting out issues including scope, assessment approach. Past SEA reports, examples and interim SEA manual published
Coverage	▲	All major issues related to environmental sustainability covered
Tiering	■	Process allows for tiering, facilitating more in depth study of critical issues
Sustainable development	■	Hong Kong SEA focused on sustainability
		PROCESS CRITERIA
Alternatives	■	All reasonable and practicable options must be considered and preferred option justified
Screening	■	Developments larger than 20ha or involving more than 100,000 people must undergo SEA
Scoping	■	All issues which have a bearing on sustainable development concerns must be assessed
Prediction/evaluation	■	Methodologies stipulated in the EIA Ordinance Technical Memorandum or deemed fit for particular SEA utilized
Additional impacts	▲	Cumulative impacts must be addressed. No provision yet for secondary or socioeconomic impacts
Report preparation	■	SEAs recorded in reports available for public inspection on government website
Review	■	Advisory Council for Environment (ACE) reviews and endorses SEA report
Monitoring	■	Mechanisms must be set up to monitor effects of development and to follow up SEA recommendations
Mitigation	■	All known unacceptable impacts must be mitigated

Table 7.5 *Evaluation of SEA of land use plans in Hong Kong (continued)*

Criterion	Criterion met	Comments
Consultation and public participation	■	Consultation with ACE, reports available for public inspection on government website
OUTCOME CRITERIA		
Decision making	■	SEAs have often had significant influence on planning decisions, development of strategies and policies
Costs and benefits	▲	Benefits of SEA perceived to outweigh costs when dealing with major policies, strategies or plans that have significant environmental implications
Environmental quality	▲	SEA has helped to safeguard Hong Kong's environmental quality and injected environmental considerations into other policy areas such as transportation
System monitoring	▲	Some monitoring of SEA system exists but more needs to be done

Notes: ■ – Yes
　　▲ – Partially
　　□ – No
　　? – Don't know

References

Au, E. W. K. (1998) 'Status and progress of environmental assessment in Hong Kong: facing the challenges in the 21st century', *Journal of Impact Assessment and Project Appraisal*, vol 16, pp162–166

Au, E. W. K. (1999) 'The implementation of EIA and strategic environmental assessment in Hong Kong', in *Proceedings of the China Mainland and Hong Kong Symposium on Regional Environmental Impact Assessment*, Open University of Hong Kong, Hong Kong

Au, E. W. K. (2000) 'Environmental planning and impact assessment of major development projects in Hong Kong', in Wong, W. S. and Chan, E. (eds) *Building Hong Kong – Environmental Considerations*, Hong Kong University Press, Hong Kong

Au, E. W. K. (2002) 'International trend of strategic environmental assessment and the evolution of strategic environmental assessment development in Hong Kong', in *Proceedings of the Conference on Reshaping Environmental Assessment Tools for Sustainability, Chinese University of Hong Kong and Nankai University*, Hong Kong

Dubin, B. I. and Au, E. W. K. (1997) 'Application of strategic environmental assessment principles in developing a sustainable long-term physical planning framework', in *Proceedings of the Conference on Sustainability in the 21st Century – the Challenge for Asian Cities, Pollution in the Metropolitan and Urban Environment*, POLMET '97, Hong Kong Institution of Engineers, Hong Kong

Environmental Protection Department (2002) *Examples of Strategic Environmental Assessment (SEA) in Hong Kong*, www.epd.gov.hk/epd/english/environmentinhk/eia_planning/sea/ebook1.html

Environmental Protection Department (2004) *Hong Kong Strategic Environmental Assessment (SEA) Manual*, www.epd.gov.hk/epd/english/environmentinhk/eia_planning/sea/hksea_manual.html

Ho, S.C. and Au, E.W. K. (1997) 'In search of a path towards environmental sustainability in a city like Hong Kong', in *Proceedings of the Conference on Sustainability in the 21st Century – the Challenge for Asian Cities, Pollution in the Metropolitan and Urban Environment, POLMET '97*, Hong Kong Institution of Engineers, Hong Kong

Hong Kong Special Administrative Region Government (1990) 'Environmental Guidelines for Planning in Hong Kong', *Hong Kong Planning Standards and Guidelines*, Chapter 9, HKSARG, Hong Kong

Hong Kong Special Administrative Region Government (1995) *Strategic Environmental Assessment of the Preferred Options, Territorial Development Strategy Review*, www.epd.gov.hk/epd/english/environmentinhk/eia_planning/sea/territorial_dept.html

Hong Kong Special Administrative Region Government (1999) *Strategic Environmental Assessment Technical Report, Third Comprehensive Transport Study*, www.epd.gov.hk/epd/english/environmentinhk/eia_planning/sea/third_comp.html

Hong Kong Special Administrative Region Government (2000a) *Final Strategic Environmental Assessment Report, the Second Railway Development Study*, www.epd.gov.hk/epd/english/environmentinhk/eia_planning/sea/second_railway.html

Hong Kong Special Administrative Region Government (2000b) *Sustainable Development for the 21st Century: Environmental Baseline Study Reports*, www.epd.gov.hk/epd/english/environmentinhk/eia_planning/sea/baseline.html

Hong Kong Special Administrative Region Government (2001) *Sustainable Development for the 21st Century*, www.info.gov.hk/planning/p_study/comp_s/susdev/ex_summary/final_eng/index.htm

Planning Department (2000), *Town Planning – Hong Kong: the Facts*, Hong Kong Special Administrative Region Government, Hong Kong

8

Hungary

Aleg Cherp and Gábor Szarvas

Introduction

Hungary is a central European country with a population of over 10 million people and an area of 93,036km². It is located in the Carpathian Basin, primarily on the alluvial plains of the Danube and Tisza. For over 40 years following World War II, Hungary had a centrally planned economy and a one-party political system strongly influenced by the Soviet Union. During this period, some heavy industry (for example, chemicals and metals) was developed in addition to the traditionally strong agricultural and manufacturing sectors. As a result of the political and economic reforms in the 1990s, a consolidated free-market democracy has been established. During the same period, laws and institutions in Hungary have been transformed to enable its accession to the European Union (EU) in May 2004.

Administratively, the country is divided into 19 counties and the metropolitan (capital) area of Budapest. Together, Budapest and cities with over 10,000 inhabitants account for about 60 per cent of the population. The second administrative tier is made up of 3,157 municipalities, comprising 23 districts of the capital, 22 cities with county rights, 199 towns and 2,913 villages. All these 3,177 counties and municipalities have certain rights and responsibilities in relation to land use planning and, potentially, SEA.

Context

The Regional Development and Spatial Planning Act of 1996[1] regulates the organization and responsibilities of local governments and quasi-governmental organizations in the field of regional development. This Act introduced a new system of regional development and spatial planning, composed of three different types of plan, applicable to all levels of administration (see Box 8.1). Two types of plan, referred to as the *development concept* and the *development programme,* are of a strategic nature and are intended to guide the (economic) development of an area. The development concept has to be prepared before the development programme and guides the preparation of the latter. The third type of plan, referred to as the *spatial plan* or *land use plan,* is of a regulatory nature; it establishes binding rules and procedures for land use, building and construction in an area.

Box 8.1 Development and spatial plans in Hungary

The *development concept* defines the development objectives of an area (county, city, and so on) and the priorities for development programmes. It also provides guidance to the various bodies concerned with sectoral and spatial planning and regional development.

When the development concept has been prepared, a *development programme* is drawn up consisting of strategic and operational sections. The strategic section identifies short- and medium-term tasks, and the responsibilities for their implementation in line with the priorities established in the development concept. The operational sector is divided into sub-programmes and partial programmes, and contains operational and scheduling details as well as financial plans. It also specifies the methods of, and the bodies responsible for, implementation.

The *spatial plan* determines the long-term spatial (physical) structure of a region. It provides for the utilization and protection of regional features and resources, for environmental protection, for the location of infrastructure networks, for the disposition of land uses and for the legal enforcement of compliance with the plan.

Source: Regional Development and Spatial Planning Act 1996 (Article 5)

The creation of development concepts and programmes is mandatory at the national, regional and county levels. In addition, several municipalities can set up municipal associations to prepare development concepts at the micro-regional level. The appropriate councils formally approve these concepts and programmes. The drafting of spatial plans is mandatory at the national, county and municipal levels, and they are approved by the national and county assemblies, and the municipal councils of representatives, respectively (Table 8.1).

The structure, content and format of the development and spatial plans are regulated by a Ministry for Environment and Regional Policy decree.[2] In particular, it requires that the economic, social and environmental consequences of the implementation of each type of plan are assessed and reported. In addition, public consultation on draft plans is required by a further decree which regulates the coordination and adoption of regional development concepts, programmes and plans.[3]

Table 8.1 *Administration of development and spatial plans in Hungary*

Administrative level	Development concept and programme		Spatial (land use) plan	
	Preparation	Approval by	Preparation	Approval by
National	Mandatory	Parliament	Mandatory	Parliament
Regional	Mandatory	Regional Development Council	–	–
County	Mandatory	County Development Council	Mandatory	County Assembly
Micro-region	Optional	Micro-regional Development Council	–	–
Municipality	Optional	Council of Representatives	Mandatory	Council of Representatives

Source: adapted from Körmendy (2002)

In 2000, the Hungarian Agency for Regional Development and Country Planning (VÁTI) undertook a study of the state of implementation of Hungarian regional development policies and laws (VÁTI, 2001). The researchers analysed the regional development concepts and programmes prepared at the county and micro-regional levels following the enactment of the 1996 Regional Development Act. The report identified 217 municipal associations that had prepared concepts and programmes, in addition to the ones at county levels. Only about 5 per cent of the settlements in Hungary chose not to take part in micro-regional cooperation through municipal associations. The report stated that, in terms of sectoral focus, about half the development plans targeted agrarian and rural development, and environmental protection. Environmental objectives were common at the county level, whereas rural development programmes were central at micro-regional level.

Environmental issues can be considered in local planning, as well as in spatial and development planning, through the unique system of municipal environmental programmes (MEPs) introduced by the framework Environment Act 1995.[4] The Environment Act contains a statutory obligation for local governments to prepare MEPs, but provides only a limited degree of guidance and does not set a specific deadline for their adoption. Guidelines on preparing MEPs have subsequently been developed, the most widely known issued by the Ministry of Environment (ÖKO Rt, 1998; see also Független Ökológiai Központ, 1997; Flachner and F. Nagy, 1998; and Markowitz, 2000 for less widely disseminated guidance).

However, it was only in the larger towns that local authorities prepared their MEPs before 2000. The preparation of MEPs has been eligible for funding from the Central Environmental Fund since 2001, and this has provided a major motivation for local government to become involved. Moreover, local environmental development projects became eligible for funding in 2002 only on condition that local authorities had prepared an MEP and that the projects were in line with the objectives of the MEP.

In summary, several types of land use and development plans are prepared at all administrative levels in Hungary. The relevant planning laws provide general requirements for incorporating environmental considerations into these plans and for consulting the public during their preparation. Although some of these requirements are reflected in practice, it is clear that integrating consideration of the environment fully in planning processes can only be achieved by introducing more systematic tools such as SEA.

The SEA of land use plans only became a specific legislative requirement in Hungary in 2005, although very general provisions for the SEA of national policies had already been established in Articles 43 and 44 of the Environment Act 1995, which required such policies to be accompanied by a description of their environmental effects. This requirement was not used in practice, except in the case of the SEA of the Regional Operational Programme of the National Development Plan, which is the only practical application of full-scale SEA in Hungary to date.

The transposition of the European Union Directive 2001/42/EC ('the SEA Directive') (European Commission, 2001) was achieved in Hungary through the adoption of amendments to the Environment Act in 2004[7] and of a Government Decree on the environmental assessment of certain plans and programmes in 2005.[8]

Case studies

SEA of the Regional Operational Programme of the National Development Plan

As part of its accession to the EU, Hungary prepared a National Development Plan (NDP). This was a condition of future support from European Structural Funds and the European Cohesion Fund. The NDP was prepared in accordance with Council Regulation (EC) No 1260/1999 (European Commission, 1999) laying down general provisions on the use of Structural Funds. It consisted of a general strategy together with five operational programmes.

The preparation of the NDP started in early 2001, the situation analyses were prepared by mid-2002, and most programming elements were drafted during the second half of 2002. The process was completed by an intensive round of public consultation and an ex ante evaluation of the draft NDP. Altogether, 3000 opinions were submitted on those parts of the plan that were subject to public debate (Magyar Természetvédők Szövetsége (MTvSz), 2003). The final version of the NDP was approved and submitted to the EC by the Hungarian Government in March 2003, while the operational programmes were submitted in September 2003.

In response to a suggestion from the Regional Environmental Center for Central and Eastern Europe (REC), a decision was made in early 2002 to undertake a SEA of one of the five operational programmes as a pilot exercise. The Operational Programme on Regional Development (ROP) was consequently selected, and the Ministry of Environment and Water, the Hungarian Institute for Regional Development and VÁTI, together with REC, commissioned a consultancy team to undertake the SEA in April 2002.

The SEA was undertaken in two phases. The initial period involved extensive consultations between the planners preparing the programme and the SEA consultants, and led to the drafting of the ROP itself. The second phase consisted of a more structured assessment of the draft ROP.

According to a major regional umbrella non-governmental organization (NGO) (Central and Eastern European Working Group for the Enhancement of Biodiversity, 2003), about 20 NGOs expressed their views on the ROP. The SEA report was submitted in August 2003. The report, which was around 120 pages in length, concluded that the ROP did not give rise to major risks of environmental degradation, except for the tourism development proposals. These were considered to pose a relatively high risk at the local level.

The SEA team attempted to follow the objectives-led approach to SEA:

The SEA team ... intended to appraise this document against formal environmental objectives established by the National Programme for the Protection of the Environment, the National Nature Conservation Plan, the National Environmental Health Action Programme, the National Regional Development Concept and the National Agro-Environmental Programme. Close scrutiny of these guiding documents, however, revealed that the various plans, including those for the environment, had no common approach and were rooted in different assumptions. The SEA team had to select between the goals and objectives of various programmes to ensure consistency in their evaluation framework. They finally selected a set of 32 quantitative environmental policy objectives for the state of the environment and various impact factors. In addition, they decided to establish a set of general sustainability criteria that reflected three main objectives of the National Development Plan for Hungary (that is, objectives serving social, economic and environmental development) and anchored principles of sustainable regional development planning. These sustainability criteria were suggested as a design requirement in the elaboration of all sectoral operational programmes, which were being developed in parallel with the Regional Operational Programme

Dusik and Sadler (2004, p95).

As a result of initial consultation, the ROP was improved significantly in terms of better integration of environmental issues. However, to a certain extent, this 'greening' process led to the 'greying' of other operational programmes (MTvSz, 2003). For example, the SEA consultants argued strongly that the development of regional airports would be detrimental to the local environment. As a result, this proposal was removed from the ROP. However, it was consequently incorporated into the Operational Programme on Economic Development, also prepared under the NDP.[5]

The evaluation of this pilot SEA (MTvSz, 2003) also revealed significant differences in the level of involvement in, and attitude towards, the SEA amongst the various stakeholders. The SEA consultants generally cooperated constructively with the technical team of the programming authority. However, cooperation with strategic decision makers was limited and the SEA consultants had no information about, let alone effect on, the main target setting process for the ROP.

A major problem encountered by the SEA consultants was that their work was limited to the ROP. Although both the strategic part of the NDP and the individual Operational Programme were subject to ex ante evaluations, these and the SEA were not formally linked. Furthermore, the integration of SEA into the decision making (planning) process was incomplete. The SEA report was prepared as a stand-alone study, and was referenced only briefly in the ROP itself. Nevertheless, the project was of major significance in the development of SEA in Hungary, as it was the first formal environmental assessment carried out at the policy level. In addition to developing and testing a methodology, it gained significant publicity and involved a large number of NGOs.

Environmental assessment of Debrecen City Plan

Debrecen, with 210,000 inhabitants, is the second largest city in Hungary, and is situated in the east of the country. In compliance with the requirements of the Development and Protection of the Built Environment Act 1997,[6] Debrecen Council decided to revise its land use planning framework in 1998 in order to integrate the 62 land use plans developed at different times for specific parts of the city.

These city-wide planning processes were prepared by two private consulting companies, selected by tender. Their outputs included:

- a *city development concept* (CDC) that outlined the desired nature of future development, the aspirations and vision of the community and the priorities for local development and land use planning;
- a *land use plan* that identified the possible uses of land in accordance with the CDC – the land use plan was also presented as a map;
- a *building code and a regulatory plan* that provided the legal background for the implementation of the CDC and land use plan by making local rules for land use and construction, and regulations to protect both the built and natural environment.

The environmental assessment of the Debrecen City Plan can be considered to be an informal SEA conducted within the framework of the 1996 Regional Development Act and subsequent regulations requiring analysis of the socio-economic and environmental consequences of the implementation of development and spatial plans. It is typical of other environmental analyses conducted within the planning system in Hungary.

The planning and environmental analysis process proceeded as follows:

Phase 1:   The detailed planning methodology, which included the environmental analysis, was approved by the Debrecen Environmental and City Development Committee in December 1998

Phase 2:   The collection of data and analysis of baseline conditions was completed in March 1999

Phase 3:   A situation report on the identification of opportunities and problems related to land use was submitted to the local council and approved in November 1999

Phase 4:   The CDC was drafted and debated in public fora in which local inhabitants and citizens' groups participated. The final version was adopted by the local council in April 2000

Phase 5:   The land use plan was drafted in June 2000. Building, environmental and water management authorities reviewed the document and submitted their suggestions for modifications. In early 2001, public meetings were held to gain additional input from the local community. In March 2003, the final version was submitted to the local council and adopted

Phase 6:   The working version of the Debrecen Building Code and Regulatory Plan was prepared in December 2001. The documents were reviewed by the relevant authorities and the modified version was submitted to the local council in September 2002

Phase 7:   The implementation of the plan started in December 2002 with the setting up of a reformed land use information system.

This planning process therefore proceeded through a well defined system of stages incorporating both analytical and participatory elements. However, although environmental issues were addressed, no systematic SEA process was conducted. In particular, neither the process nor the outcome of the environmental analysis were separately discussed with the public or the authorities. Nevertheless, the Debrecen City Plan case demonstrates that a good basis for the introduction of a formal SEA system, integrated with land use planning, exists in Hungary.

SEA system

The legal requirements for SEA of land use plans in Hungary were general and non-specific before the SEA decree was adopted in 2005. Every land use (or development) plan must include an assessment of its socioeconomic and environmental impacts (above). However, no specific methodology for incorporating the findings of this assessment was prescribed. In particular, the previous regulations did not provide for the integration of environmental assessments into spatial plans at an early stage in their preparation. Moreover, the extent to which this requirement was implemented in practice is not clear, since no systematic research has been conducted and most Hungarian local governments (except for counties and major cities) only started to prepare their first plans in 2003.

The requirement for integrating SEA into the planning process has been strengthened by the amendments to the Environment Act, which require that SEA be conducted in parallel with the drafting of plans. In addition, the SEA decree stipulates that the SEA report must describe the interaction between the SEA and the planning process, and any modifications made to the plan as a result of SEA, thus promoting the integration of SEA and plan making. Moreover, the decree requires that, while SEA must be undertaken by an independent expert, the means of cooperation and coordination between the SEA expert/team and the proponent must be specified.

The coverage of the SEA of land use plans is an important issue in Hungary. The 1997 regulations require 'environmental assessment' to be undertaken, irrespective of the environmental significance, nature or scale of the spatial plans. This may, however, represent a problem since the large number of mainly small local authorities in Hungary (above) means that it may not be feasible (or desirable) to conduct SEAs of all the thousands of land use plans that are being prepared.

The SEA decree requires SEA for those categories of plans and programmes that are subject to mandatory SEA according to the SEA Directive. It also stipulates that SEA be conducted for all types of regional development and spatial plans prepared in Hungary (Table 8.1) that may have significant environmental effects, for the NDP and its operational programmes, for waste management and transport plans at all levels, and for certain forestry, agricultural, water management and other plans and programmes.

If a plan does not fall into a category that requires mandatory SEA but may, nevertheless, have significant environmental implications, the proponent can consult the environmental authority on the need for SEA. After receiving a brief description of the plan, the environmental authority should provide its opinion on the potential environmental significance of the proposed plan within 30 days. If the proponent decides not to follow the authority's recommendation that a SEA be conducted, a written justification must be prepared and be made publicly available.

The fact that the existing provisions for the environmental assessment of spatial plans are part of the planning, rather than the environmental, regulations probably explains the lack of tiering in the system. There are no mandatory requirements to connect project level EIAs to the environmental assessments of the relevant spatial plans in either the existing or the forthcoming regulations. The concept of sustainable development is not explicitly used in either the previous or the new decrees (regulations), or in practice.

In addition to legal requirements, several SEA guidance documents have recently been issued in Hungary. In 2003, VÁTI issued a 145-page publication on the methodological issues of socioeconomic and environmental impact assessments of regional development programmes (VÁTI, 2003). This contained an overview of international experience of impact assessment (IA), including European regional policy IA provisions, IA requirements in respect of European Structural Funds support programmes, IA models, examples of IA practice and both European and Hungarian EIA and SEA regulations. In addition, it presented two case studies of project-level EIAs: the description (but not the assessment) of the socioeconomic and environmental impacts described in the spatial plan for Borsod-Abaúj-Zemplén County; and the SEA report for the ROP of the NDP.

A 62-page SEA guidance document was published in 2003 by MTvSz. This included a description and brief evaluation of the methodology used for the SEA of the ROP of the NPD, an abbreviated translation of guidelines for the SEA of land use plans in the Czech Republic, and Hungarian translations of the SEA Directive and of the 2003 Kiev SEA Protocol (United Nations Economic Commission for Europe (UNECE), 2003).

SEA process

Before detailed legal provisions for SEA were adopted in 2005, many of the elements of the conventional SEA process were either absent or are implemented on an ad hoc basis. Thus, planning documents usually outlined alternative land uses but these were not assessed against environmental criteria. The criteria employed for choosing between alternatives were usually economic, social or environmental, but the three criteria were not integrated. The policies and their potential impacts were typically assessed against national norms and standards for noise levels and for air, water and soil pollution. Some impacts were modelled (for example, that of changes to the road system) but the majority were only tentatively estimated or acknowledged as being likely to occur. There was no requirement to prepare separate publicly available SEA reports. Rather, SEA findings were reflected in the plans themselves.

Most of the key SEA process elements required by the SEA Directive have now been introduced in the new SEA regulations. In particular, the amendments to the Environment Act require that: an environmental report be prepared as a result of SEA; the environmental authority be consulted on the intended content of this report (scoping); and the draft plan and its environmental report be made public and sent to the environmental authorities for comment. Consultation with neighbouring counties must take place if transboundary effects are expected, and the results of all these and other consultations must be taken into account in the plan.

After finalizing the plan, the relevant authorities, the general public and the affected country (in the case of transboundary impacts) must be informed, inter alia, about how the outcomes of the consultation and environmental assessment were incorporated in the final decision and how monitoring will be conducted.

Annex 4 to the decree on SEA specifies the coverage of the SEA. It is an extended version of Article 5 and Annex I of the SEA Directive. In particular, the SEA report should reflect the SEA process, including its relation to planning, relevant environmental and other objectives, the recommendations made during the planning process, the outcomes of public participation, and the sources of data and information employed. Furthermore, the SEA report should contain a description of the plan and its relation to other plans and, in accordance with the SEA Directive, a description of significant environmental impacts on air, water, land, biodiversity, the cultural heritage, ecological systems, health, population, and so on.

The decree requires any transboundary impacts and indirect impacts to be described. A section of the decree explains the concept of indirect impacts such as potential environmental conflicts, environmentally significant changes in lifestyle, effects on environmental awareness and the use of local resources and of renewable energy. There is, however, no direct mention of cumulative impacts. According to the draft decree, the proponent has to consider several alternatives to the draft plan and provide justification for the selection of the preferred alternative. The decree's requirements for monitoring and mitigation of environmental impacts are identical to those in the SEA Directive (Article 10 and Annex I).

The previous 'informal' practice of SEA and the pilot SEA point to certain challenges and opportunities which are likely to arise after now that the decree has been adopted. In particular, the experience of the SEA of the ROP of the NDP indicates the potential value of NGO involvement.

SEA outcome

It is too early to judge SEA outcomes in Hungary, since systematic SEA regulations were only introduced in 2005. The discussion in this section is consequently primarily based on SEA experience in other Central European countries, on experience of the application of project-level EIA and spatial planning in Hungary, and on insights from conducting the pilot SEA of the ROP of the NDP (above).

Dusik and Sadler (2004) argued that the effectiveness of the SEA systems of land use plans in Central and Eastern Europe (particularly in Bulgaria, the Czech Republic, Poland and Slovakia) largely depended upon the extent to which they were integrated with their respective planning processes. SEA systems that were integrated with the planning procedures generally performed better than those in which SEAs were conducted as separate processes. It therefore appears that the main challenge for the Hungarian SEA system is to achieve proper integration with the land use planning system (which already has its own system of environmental analyses in place). Such integration is arguably most important in meeting at least two of the four effectiveness criteria for SEA outcomes:

- decision making – through ensuring that the content of plans is actually influenced by SEA findings;
- costs and benefits – through ensuring that planning processes are supported rather than disrupted by the application of SEA.

The fulfilment of the latter criterion also depends significantly upon the coverage of SEA provisions and on the screening process. The detailed debate about the SEA decree primarily focused on the best solution for screening in an attempt to ensure that the benefits of SEA exceeded its costs. The remaining two criteria for SEA outcomes – environmental quality and system monitoring – are also likely to be met in Hungary, given its successful track record of implementing and monitoring the outcomes of project level EIA procedures.

Conclusion

Hungary has a well-developed spatial and development planning system that requires the preparation of land use and other plans at different administrative levels. Formal requirements for the SEA of land use plans were introduced in 2005. The current planning regulations require assessment of the environmental consequences of land use plans, but very few such assessments have been conducted. In addition, although no systematic evaluation of these has been undertaken, it is known that most fall far short of SEA procedural and methodological best practice. In general, the concept of SEA is not familiar in Hungary since SEAs of other types of policies, plans and programmes (PPPs) are not legally required either.

There are, however, significant opportunities for introducing an effective SEA system in Hungary. The first such opportunity was the transposition of the SEA Directive into national law and the accession of Hungary to the 2003 UNECE Protocol on SEA. The process of implementing SEA policies is being led by the Ministry of Environment, which is one of the most experienced in EIA in Central Europe. As the lessons of the pilot application of SEA to the ROP of the NDP demonstrate, the SEA actors and stakeholders in Hungary have sufficient capacity to undertake SEA and integrate it into planning processes. Emerging guidance on SEA, the ability of environmental authorities to monitor and critically evaluate the system (as evidenced in several studies of the effectiveness of project level EIA), and the participation of SEA professionals in international networks, should further strengthen this capacity in the future.

At the same time, the challenges to the introduction of an effective SEA system in Hungary should also be acknowledged. One of them is the very large number of local authorities obliged to prepare land use plans. Clearly, not all these plans should be made subject to SEA, otherwise there is a danger of repeating the Estonian experience, where the requirement to undertake SEA of all land use plans had to be repealed after three years of unsuccessfully trying to cover the whole range of planning documents (Peterson, 2004). Another related problem is that the SEA procedure specified in the decree is the same for land use plans as for a wide variety of other planning and policy documents. It is yet to be seen whether such a 'one-size-fits-all' approach will be conducive to the effective integration of SEA in widely different planning and decision-making processes in Hungary.

In summary, as shown in Table 8.2, the strength of the land use planning system and the opportunities for integrating effective SEA provisions into it are likely to ensure that an effective SEA system is established in Hungary.

Notes

1   Act No. XXI of 1996 on regional development and spatial planning (*1996.* évi XXI. törvény a területfejlesztésről és a területrendezésről)
2   Government Decree No. 18/1998 (June 25) on the requirements for the content of regional development concepts, programmes and spatial plans (18/1998. (VI. 25) KTM

Table 8.2 *Evaluation of SEA of land use plans in Hungary*

Criterion	Criterion met previously	Criterion met in SEA regulations	Comments
		SYSTEM CRITERIA	
Legal basis	☐	■	SEA regulations (decree) provide basis for SEA system
Integration	☐	▲	SEA regulations require SEA to be conducted in land use plan making with explanation of how SEA findings used
Guidance	▲	▲	Several guidance documents issued in 1990s only partially address SEA of land use plans
Coverage	■	■	SEA regulations cover impacts defined in SEA Directive
Tiering	☐	☐	SEA regulations do not explicitly link SEA to project level EIAs (project level EIAs can be indirectly influenced by plan SEAs)
Sustainable development	☐	☐	Concept of sustainable development not explicitly mentioned or operationalized in SEA regulations
		PROCESS CRITERIA	
Alternatives	▲	■	Current planning regulations require consideration of plan alternatives. Draft SEA regulations require comparison of environmental aspects of alternatives
Screening	☐	■	SEA regulations provide for environmental screening of land use plans.
Scoping	☐	■	SEA regulations define issues to be covered. Environmental authorities should be consulted on scope of SEA reports
Prediction/evaluation	▲	■	SEA regulations require prediction of various environmental impacts
Additional impacts	☐	▲	Indirect impacts (but not cumulative impacts) explicitly mentioned in SEA regulations

Table 8.2 *Evaluation of SEA of land use plans in Hungary (continued)*

Criterion	Criterion met previously	Criterion met in SEA regulations	Comments
Report preparation	▲	■	Draft plans currently publicly available. SEA regulations require separate SEA report
Review	□	■	SEA report must be submitted to environmental authorities who should express opinion on adequacy
Monitoring	□	■	SEA regulations prescribe monitoring arrangements
Mitigation	▲	■	SEA regulations require description of measures to reduce or eliminate significant negative environmental impacts
Consultation and public participation	▲	■	Provisions exist for public discussion of land use plans. Range of specific SEA participation provisions included in SEA regulations
OUTCOME CRITERIA			
Decision making	▲	?	Not yet possible to judge outcome. SEA might facilitate more systematic incorporation of various stakeholder concerns into land use planning
Costs and benefits	▲	?	Not yet possible to judge outcome. Protracted debate reflects perception of some that SEA costs may outweigh benefits
Environmental quality	?	?	Not yet possible to judge outcome, but likely SEA will have some positive environmental effects
System monitoring	□	?	Not yet possible to judge outcome, but likely implementation of SEA will be closely monitored

Notes: ■ – Yes; ▲ – Partially; □ – No; ? – Don't know

rendelet a területfejlesztési koncepciók, programok és a területrendezési tervek tartalmi követelményeiről)

3   Government Decree No. 184/1996 (December 11) on the procedure for approving and consulting on development concepts and programmes, as well as spatial plans (184/1996. (XII. 11) Korm. rendelet a területfejlesztési koncepciók és programok, valamint a területrendezési tervek egyeztetésének és elfogadásának rendjéről)

4   Act No. LIII of 1995 on the general rules for the protection of the environment (1995. évi LIII. Törvény a környezet védelmének általános szabályairól)

5   Pálvölgyi, T., Managing Director, Env-in-Cent Kft. (2004) Interview, 30 January

6   Act No LXXVIII of 1997 on the development and protection of the built environment (1997. évi LXXVIII. törvény az épített környezet alakításáról és védelméről)

7   By Act No LXXVI of 2004

8   Government Decree No 2/2005 (January 11) on the environmental assessment of certain plans and programmes (2/2005. (I. 11) Korm. rendelet egyes tervek, illetve programok környezeti vizsgálatáról)

References

Central and Eastern European Working Group for the Enhancement of Biodiversity (CEEWEB) (2003) *Safeguarding Biodiversity in National Development Plans – Hungarian Report*, Central and Eastern European Working Group for the Enhancement of Biodiversity www.ceeweb.org/a0ceeweb/digital_library/NDP.pdf

Dusik, J. and Sadler, B. (2004) 'Reforming strategic environmental assessment systems: lessons from Central and Eastern Europe', *Impact Assessment and Project Appraisal*, vol 22, pp89–97

European Commission (1999) 'Council Regulation (EC) No 1260/1999 of 21 June 1999 laying down general provisions on the Structural Funds', *Official Journal of the European Communities*, vol L161, pp1–42, 26 July

European Commission (2001) 'Directive 2001/42/EC of the European Parliament and of the Council of 27 June 2001 on the assessment of the effects of certain plans and programmes on the environment', *Official Journal of the European Communities*, vol L197, pp30–37, 21 July

Flachner, Z. F. and Nagy, Z. (eds) (1998) *Guide for the Preparation of Environmental Programmes*, Magyar Természetvédők Szövetsége, Budapest (in Hungarian)

Független Ökológiai Központ (FÖK) (1997) *Community Environmental Action Plan*, Center for Environmental Studies, Budapest (in Hungarian)

Körmendy, J. (2002) *The Structure of the Spatial Planning System in the Republic of Hungary* Hungarian Agency for Regional Development and Country Planning (in Hungarian) www.terport.hu/owa/vati/showdoc?url=/doctar/vati/egysegek/nemzetkozi/referencia/magyar.rtf

Magyar Természetvédők Szövetsége (Hungarian Association of Nature Conservationists) (2003) *Strategic Environmental Assessment*, Pálvölgyi, T., Tombácz, E., Dusík, J., Rosecky, D. and Vyhnalek, V. (edited by Dönsz, T., Mayer, Z. and Ponicsán, P.), MTvSz, Budapest (in Hungarian)

Markowitz, P. (2000) *Guide to Implementing Local Environmental Action Programs in Central and Eastern Europe*, Institute for Sustainable Communities, Montpelier, VT, and the Regional Environmental Center for Central and Eastern Europe, Budapest

ÖKO Rt (1998) *Guide for the Preparation of Environmental Programmes*, Phare[Q2] Project No. HU 9402-01-01-L4, EUROPROJEKT GmbH, Budapest (in Hungarian)

Peterson, K. (2004) 'The role and value of SEA in Estonia: stakeholders' perspective', *Impact Assessment and Project Appraisal*, vol 22, pp159–165

United Nations Economic Commission for Europe (2003) *Protocol on Strategic Environmental Assessment to the Convention on Environmental Impact Assessment in a Transboundary Context* ECE/MP.EIA/2003/3, UNECE, Geneva

VÁTI (Hungarian Agency for Regional Development and Country Planning) (2001) *Report of the Government of the Republic of Hungary on Spatial Processes, on the Implementation of Spatial Development Policy and the National Regional Development Concept*, VÁTI, Budapest (in Hungarian)

VÁTI (Hungarian Agency for Regional Development and Country Planning) (2003) *Methodological Questions of the Socio-economic and Environmental Impact Assessments associated with Regional Development Programmes*, VÁTI, Budapest (in Hungarian)

9

Ireland

Paul Scott

Introduction

This chapter presents an analysis of strategic environmental assessment as practised to date in the Republic of Ireland, and describes the effectiveness and quality of the SEA process as it is increasingly applied across the country. The chapter examines the historical and administrative context within which European Directive 2001/42/EC ('the SEA Directive') (European Commission (EC), 2001a) is being implemented, and analyses the framework that has been provided by central and local government to facilitate compliance with the SEA Directive's requirements.

While the formal SEA of land use plans in Ireland is in its infancy, Irish experience is an important piece in the jigsaw of the implementation of a framework directive across 25 countries. Not only does it provide a good example of how the challenges of SEA are being overcome as they are faced, it also clearly demonstrates the need for the institutional support and strong administrative systems that are crucial prerequisites to the effective application of SEA procedures. Finally, the example of Irish SEA highlights the importance of analysing the historical context in which the directive is to operate as this may explain the effectiveness of the system, process and outcome in practice.

Context

While there have never been any formal procedures to integrate environmental issues with the preparation of Irish land use plans, there is a clear hierarchy of strategic plans and programmes. If SEA procedures were fully integrated in this hierarchy, this would allow the integration of environmental safeguards at the national level to be cascaded down to the regional, county and local levels. The existing structure of plans and programmes in Ireland is therefore very conducive, at least in principle, to delivering the aims of SEA.

Ireland's land use planning system is regulated by the Planning and Development Act 2000[1] ('the Planning Act'). The Planning and Development (Strategic Environmental Assessment) Regulations 2004[2] implemented the Planning Act with respect to the environmental assessment (EA) of specific land use plans. Another set of regulations[3] extends the same requirements for SEA to other sectors, for example, regional waste management plans), in line with the SEA Directive. At present, these are the only requirements for the EA of plans and programmes in Ireland.

The 2000 Planning Act requires the preparation of several strategic development plans that may be interpreted as a hierarchy, each providing a context for the plan beneath it. The hierarchy of land use plans and programmes is shown in Table 9.1.

Table 9.1 *Land use planning in Ireland*

Plan	Description	Assessment
National Development Plan (NDP)	Aims to secure sustainable economic and social development while striking correct balance between protecting and preserving environment, promoting economic and employment growth, improving competitiveness and addressing social exclusion. Includes commitment to prepare and implement National Spatial Strategy	Did not undergo a full SEA during preparation but contains analysis of environmental situation in Ireland. Was subject of pilot eco-audit. Environmental Coordinating Committee monitored and oversaw implementation of plan from environmental perspective
National Spatial Strategy (NSS)	20 year planning framework for all parts of Republic. Published in 2002. Aims to achieve better balance of social, economic and physical development across Ireland, supported by more effective land use planning. Provides strategic link between NDP and lower levels of development planning	Did not undergo formal SEA or eco-audit. Underwent 'proofing' against numerous sustainability and quality of life indicators. NSS policy that use of SEA will ensure environmental issues are integrated into implementation of NSS
Regional planning guidelines (RPGs)	Prepared for eight regional authorities in Ireland to implement NSS. These deliver NSS at regional level but do not set site specific provisions for	Various types of objective-led SEAs undertaken for these RPGs, as required by the Planning Act

Table 9.1 *Land use planning in Ireland (continued)*

Plan	Description	Assessment
	development opportunities and restrictions	
County development plans (CDPs)	CDPs include policies for land use and development control within counties and provide site zonings for land use types. A new CDP must be prepared for each county every six years, within a two year timetable	Reviewed against strategic environmental objectives as form of SEA with varying degrees of effectiveness. Planning Act requires each CDP to include statement of likely significant effects of implementing plan. Initially undertaken in 2001–2004 in the absence of any guidelines, so early examples of UK environmental appraisals used as templates
Strategic development zones (SDZs)	SDZs promote development opportunities, urban regeneration and generally fast track approval and completion of development for social and economic reasons	Controlled by planning schemes (Planning requires environmental Act assessment). A few planning schemes have been proposed, to meet increasing housing requirements in parts of Dublin's commuter belt. Assessment is more in keeping with project EIA than SEA (level of detail addressed is often site specific)
Local area plans (LAPs)	Produced by county councils for areas (principally small towns) that may undergo an intensive development phase	Planning Act requires LAPs to include statement of likely significant environmental effects of implementing plan. Usually implemented to date in an objectives-led fashion without recourse to environmental data to support judgements

A strong feature of the Irish land use planning system is the clear hierarchy of land use plans and programmes that can feasibly undergo SEA. The extent to which this will happen, and the effectiveness of the outcomes, are primarily influenced by the position taken by central government. In order to understand fully the government approach to EA, it is important to appreciate the historical context of impact assessment in Ireland. While much has been written on the advanced EA systems in some member states, little attention has been paid to the history of EA in Ireland, which has delivered equally important lessons on establishing such regimes.

The first formal requirement in Ireland for the production of environmental impact studies was embodied in the Local Government (Planning and Development) Act 1976. The range of projects to which the requirement applied was extremely limited, particularly when compared with the later European EIA directive. After the implementation of the EIA directive, the establishment of the Environmental Protection Agency (EPA) in 1993 contributed to an improvement in the quality of project EIA reports and the development of EIA expertise in Ireland. Due to its access to greater technical expertise, EPA became responsible for preparing guidelines (EPA, 2002, 2003) to support EIA studies and the preparation of Irish EIA reports.

The controversial nature of most developments that require an EIA, coupled with an increasing level of environmental awareness amongst the Irish public, leads to the majority of projects involving EIA being subject to appeals from third parties and hence being approved or refused by the Planning Appeals Board (*An Bord Pleanála*) either as appeal cases or as public sector development proposals. Third party appeals frequently focus on the perceived inadequacy of the EIA process, including the unsatisfactory consideration of strategic and project alternatives, and the lack of consideration of wider cumulative impacts. In addition, appeals are often made on the basis that the proposed development runs contrary to the strategic plan for the area or sector concerned. In the light of the preponderance of strategic considerations that give rise to appeals, the application of techniques to assess the strategic level implications for the environment is seen by planning and environmental professionals as a means of addressing these inadequacies at an earlier stage. This, of course, is the raison d'être for practising SEA.

However, Irish SEA practitioners and local authorities are under no illusions about the limitations of SEA. It is acknowledged that SEA in itself will not address site specific concerns regarding the siting and operation of controversial developments (such as landfill sites, waste incinerators, motorways and so on). More detailed objections based upon NIMBY (not in my back yard) or even NIMTO (not in my term of office, which allegedly applies to some members of local government) have their rightful place in the democratic decision making process for such developments.

Prior to the 2004 regulations, several authorities undertook non-statutory assessments of a range of land use plans, for example, heritage appraisals (which were based upon the UK environmental appraisal procedures). The heritage appraisal process was designed for application to development plans and was successfully piloted on the Draft County Donegal Development Plan 1998 (Heritage Council, 2000). The appraisal process was closer to meeting the requirements of the SEA Directive than the eco-audits undertaken within government departments on European Union-funded operational programmes, but lacked specific public participation and documentation requirements. Interestingly, the heritage appraisal guidelines include advice on the monitoring of impacts during the implementation of the plan – an important, and particularly challenging, element of the SEA Directive's requirements. SEA is now generally regarded as having superseded the heritage appraisal process.

Despite the lack of formal regulations requiring SEA, several county authorities undertook SEAs that were heavily reliant upon the impact matrix approach. Anecdotal evidence suggests that these were undertaken as a tentative foray into SEA, but that they had little effect on the plan under assessment. Examples of SEAs of CDPs using the matrix approach include those undertaken by Cork County Council and Galway County Council.[4]

Case study: Dublin Docklands Master Plan SEA

There are few examples of formal and comprehensive SEAs in Ireland that took place prior to the SEA regulations being adopted in 2004. There are several cases of impact matrices being published within CDPs, but these were neither comprehensive nor influential. However, in 2002, in anticipation of the implementation of the SEA Directive, the Department of the Environment, Heritage and Local Government (DoEHLG) asked the Dublin Docklands Development Authority (DDDA) to undertake a pilot SEA of the review of the 1997 Dublin Docklands Master Plan (DDDA, 2003). This was the first formal SEA undertaken in Ireland and was, therefore, a significant event in the history of Irish SEA practice. It thus forms a useful example showing how Irish practitioners are addressing the directive's challenging procedural requirements (Box 9.1).

SEA system

Legal basis

In Ireland, the legal requirements for strategic assessment of environmental effects exist in the form of the Planning and Development Act 2000 and the 2004 regulations. The regulations adhere to the requirements of the SEA Directive while ensuring that the SEA timetable is compatible with that for the preparation of land use plans. Specifically, the regulations endeavour to ensure that consultation of environmental authorities designated as SEA consultees does not add to the number of existing parties already consulted during plan preparation. In addition, authorities do not want SEA to add significantly to the opportunities for the planning process to be challenged by third parties. It is, however, questionable whether third parties will appreciate this loophole in the plan preparation process, since the 2004 regulations give little access to the general public to the SEA process prior to the plan being drafted.

Integration

Irish land use plans follow procedures and a timetable established by the 2000 act. Land use plans are drafted by local planning authorities (or regional

Box 9.1 Dublin Docklands Master Plan Review SEA

Context

- The Dublin Docklands Area Master Plan Review outlines a strategy for 'the sustainable social and economic regeneration of the area, with improvements to the physical area being a vital ingredient' (DDDA, 2003, p iv). Under the Dublin Docklands Development Authority Act 1997, the master plan must be reviewed after five years. DDDA is a statutory body established by DoEHLG responsible for the delivery of the regeneration of the Dublin docklands
- The review represented an updating of the 1997 master plan.

SEA practitioners

- The SEA was undertaken during the review of the 1997 master plan in 2002–2003 by an external consultant who worked closely with those preparing the draft plan
- The methodology applied was influenced by several factors, notably the formal procedural and information requirements of the SEA Directive and the UK experience of the environmental appraisal of development plans.

Scoping

- The master plan review was assessed for compatibility with other plans and guidance documents at national, regional and local level, to ensure consistency
- Various government bodies and NGOs were consulted in order to determine their opinion on the scope of the SEA process
- The results of a separate consultation exercise specifically on the master plan review were also analysed. Sustainability criteria were subsequently prepared on the basis of these consultations.

Collection of baseline information

- Baseline data were collected on the topics listed in the SEA Directive – that is, biodiversity, population, human health and so on
- It was found necessary to combine some indicators in order to avoid unnecessary duplication. Human health was not considered separately as a topic in itself but arose under a variety of other topic headings – population, water, air and so on
- The SEA also addressed the anticipated changes to the baseline environment in the absence of the implementation of the master plan review
- Wherever possible, all the baseline data were derived from existing environmental data.

Consideration of alternatives

- The SEA process addressed two very strategic options. These were the do nothing option (not to implement the plan) and the option of not reviewing the 1997 master plan
- The lack of any additional alternatives indicated the difficulty that the SEA practitioners encountered in generating additional options. It was felt, however, that more alternatives could have been generated and assessed if the SEA had been undertaken of a plan that was being prepared 'from scratch' rather than of a review of an existing plan.

Assessment of impacts against sustainability criteria

- An impact matrix formed the basis of the assessment and the means of presenting the results in the SEA report. It was reported that completing the matrices 'led to a refinement and refocusing of the objectives and policies of the Master Plan Review' (DDDA, 2003, pvii)
- The objectives and policies of the master plan were assessed against a set of sustainability criteria – strategic objectives that were prepared during the scoping stage.

Preparation of mitigation and monitoring measures

- This was undertaken by the inclusion of extra policies, refinement of other policies and clarification of policies
- The proposed monitoring measures (to take place during the implementation of the plan) included a commitment to publish an annual monitoring report and to cooperate with other agencies in collecting and reporting on changes to the environment. No specific monitoring programmes were proposed.

Source: DDDA (2003)

development boards in the case of RPGs) and undergo a period of statutory consultation prior to revision and adoption. The SEA process is being fully integrated into the plan preparation process, and the regulations and guidance fully support this approach. As mentioned above, government representatives were under considerable pressure to ensure that the SEA process would not add to the administrative burden already experienced by local planners.

One aspect of the Irish land use planning process that the SEA Directive and regulations may fail to address is the potential for judgements made in the SEA process to be overridden by political influences immediately prior to adoption of the plan. In Ireland, elected members of a local council may wish certain changes to be made to the draft land use plan (for example, re-zoning of specific areas of land) at the final stages of its preparation. If these amendments are not assessed for their potential environmental impacts, then the SEA process could become a paper exercise and fail to influence the plan. However, the 2004 regulations not only integrate SEA into the preparation of development plans, but also into any material alterations or variations to the plan. This should limit unchecked post-adoption changes to development plans. Any such changes must be screened for significant environmental effects, ie whether a formal SEA needs to be undertaken.

Guidance

The first guidance on SEA that reflected the requirements of the SEA Directive was on SEA methodologies for plans and programmes (Environmental Resources Management Ireland (ERM), 2003). While this guidance applied to all types of SEA, the document underpinned the 2004 regulations. It also influenced the subsequent preparation of central government guidelines, which have the specific purpose of instructing regional authorities and planning authorities how to undertake SEA for land use plans. The land use planning guidelines were published in November 2004 (DoEHLG, 2004).

Coverage

The two sets of Irish SEA regulations fully implement the Directive's requirements for SEA to apply both to specific sectors and to other plans and programmes that may have significant effects on the environment. The types of land use plans and programmes that will require SEA are, starting at the most strategic level, RPGs, followed by CDPs, LAPs and planning schemes that apply to SPZs. For development plans and LAPs there will be a degree of case-by-case screening if the population served by the plan is less than 10,000 people, or if it might affect a Natura 2000 designated site. This rule is likely to be challenged in the courts, particularly where there are seasonal changes in population in the west of Ireland and other holiday towns that may temporarily push small towns above the screening threshold.

Tiering

One of the key strengths of the Irish land use planning system is the clear hierarchy of plans that allows the transposition of national spatial planning policy to the regional level (via RPGs) and hence to the county and local levels. However, the absence of formal SEA at the most strategic levels (the NDP and the NSS) means that the most important decisions regarding national spatial planning are not subject to the structured appraisal that SEA provides. Anecdotally, one planner recently pointed out that it would take the best part of 20 years before all the levels of the Irish planning system experience SEA (Anon, 2004).

Sustainable development

While the Irish government recognizes that sustainability appraisal is superseding traditional environment-driven appraisal in other countries such as the UK, the approach in Ireland is to focus initially on environmental issues. The 2004 SEA regulations do not use sustainability or sustainable development as a key principle, but briefly acknowledge the concept. One of the screening criteria is to determine whether the plan is able to integrate environmental considerations 'with a view to promoting sustainable development' (Schedule 2A[1]). The environmental impacts of development will thus remain the focus for Irish SEAs until more experience has been acquired.

SEA process

Alternatives

Experience of dealing with alternatives in SEAs undertaken to date in Ireland suggests a lack of understanding of how to address alternatives in a comprehensive manner. This is not uncommon and has been seen in the development of most SEA systems. However, the confusion may be exacerbated by guidance published by the European Commission (EC) (2003) which conflicts with the experience of Irish SEA practitioners. While the European guidance suggests assessing a range of reasonable alternatives to an equal level of detail and then identifying the preferred alternative, Irish experience suggests a more pragmatic approach. Several county level SEAs identified alternatives at an early stage and screened out those having potential environmental impacts. In such cases, only the preferred environmental option was assessed in detail and carried through the SEA process. This approach is faster and less likely to cause delays during plan preparation but is less in keeping with a SEA process that encourages all alternatives to be explored fully until the best environmental option emerges. The 2004 regulations require the SEA report to include a description of the reasons for choosing the alternatives, but do not expand upon this basic requirement. The SEA guidelines for land use plans contain more advice on the types of alternatives that should be considered and state that the options considered must be set in the context of the planning hierarchy and the level at which the plan sits.

Screening

The 2004 regulations and the SEA guidelines for land use plans indicate that all RPGs and planning schemes for SPZs require SEA, suggesting that systematic screening is not required for these types of plan. All other development plans and LAPs are screened for SEA applicability if they serve a population of less than 10,000 people. If the authority decides that the plans serving a population below this threshold will not have significant environmental effects, the process stops and the authority issues a public notice to this effect. If environmental effects are likely, the authority must invite submissions from a range of specified environmental bodies on the need for a SEA.

Scoping

In Ireland, scoping is a formal stage in all land use plan SEAs. After deciding that the plan requires SEA, the local authority must request the environmental authorities to submit any observations on the scope or level of detail of the assessment. According to the 2004 SEA regulations, the consultees have four weeks to provide a response (three weeks for a variation to a development plan). However, it is questionable whether consultees will do more than simply request compliance with the relevant regulations or guidelines. The first time the environmental authorities were formally requested to provide inputs to the scoping stage was during the Dublin Docklands SEA. The breadth of the topics covered by the SEA Directive meant that it was a considerable task to identify the government departments that should become the designated environmental authorities.

The SEA guidelines suggest that the scoping stage can be integrated into the initial public consultations that take place during development plan preparation. They also suggest that the scoping stage should follow the publication of a scoping issues paper that will help to flag up the key issues to be addressed in the SEA (DoEHLG, 2004).

Prediction/evaluation

The nature of the prediction and evaluation of environmental impacts is not set out in the Irish SEA regulations. Nevertheless, the list of SEA report requirements (Schedule 2B) emphasizes the importance of reporting on environmental objectives, standards and conventions, and how these aspects have been taken into account in the plan. The SEA guidelines for land use plans include a list of environmental protection objectives based on international 'policy documents, strategies, guidelines, directives, conventions' and advises that 'objectives should be adapted to local circumstances as necessary' (DoEHLG, 2004, p29).

Much of the Irish SEA experience has been based upon the early UK environmental appraisal system, and practitioners have adopted many of its tools. Impact matrices were used in almost all pre-2004 Irish SEA reports and, while they can be useful tools to check progress through the appraisal process, they are not effective at presenting the outputs of the process or at evaluating the impacts themselves. Nevertheless, this over-reliance on matrices has been carried through into the advice given in the guidelines.

Additional impacts

The consideration of secondary, synergistic or cumulative impacts has not been addressed to any comprehensive extent in either project or strategic EAs in Ireland. The SEA guidelines for land use plans make reference to the ability of SEA to address cumulative impacts but there is no specific advice as to the best way to undertake this.

Report preparation

The findings from SEA, to date, have usually been integrated within plans (or as appendices) but there is increasing encouragement to publish a separate report. The tendency to integrate the SEA report into a plan reflects the brevity of the SEA and the tendency simply to include the impact matrices with little or no explanatory text. The SEA guidelines (DoEHLG, 2004, p22) offer support to the preparation of a SEA report:

> *The preparation of, and consultation on, the report will be a learning curve for all concerned; despite the resources and time which will be required, it has the potential to bring considerable added value to the plan making process.*

Review

Currently, there is no system for formal review of SEA reports, nor is there any system to handle deficiencies. The SEA regulations do not require review, but the guidelines suggest two approaches to ensure that the documentation is of 'sufficient quality':

> *Authorities could take into account a checklist in a recent EPA Report on SEA methodology [ERM, 2003] for reviewing the adequacy of the SEA process in general and the Environmental Report in particular. Where SEA consultants are employed, the consultants should ideally (i) have undergone a qualification in SEA recognized by a member state of the European Economic Area . . . and (ii) have a track record in SEA relating to land use planning*

> DoEHLG (2004, p40).

The checklist referred to was developed as part of an overall SEA methodology and was based upon the format of the EC environmental impact statement review checklist (EC, 2001b), with adaptations to reflect the SEA process. Its use is proposed to determine performance during the SEA process, as well as the quality of the documented output.

Monitoring and mitigation

The 2004 regulations require monitoring to take place in accordance with the SEA Directive. The results of monitoring have to be recorded and presented in a manager's report for development plan SEAs. There is no reporting requirement for the monitoring of other types of land use plans. EPA publishes frequent reports on the water and air quality measurements recorded by a monitoring network covering the country. Most of the key environmental variables are presented in state of the environment reports every four years, and in annual air, water and waste reports.

The SEA guidelines for land use plans highlight the purpose of monitoring as a means of detecting unforeseen impacts, and of improving the SEA process when a plan is revised. The guidelines also highlight how monitoring may be cost effective: by using existing monitoring results; by sharing the data collected with other authorities; and by using indicators and criteria to determine the most significant parameters that require monitoring.

Mitigation in SEA in Ireland has not been helped by the fact that most of the first SEAs were retrospective in nature and could not influence the plan or programme being assessed. More recent examples (for example, Dublin Docklands) have proved to be more practical for mitigation purposes, and they have led to the rewording, expanding or clarifying policies.

Consultation and public participation

SEA experience in Ireland suggests that meaningful consultations are limited by the lack of awareness by NGOs, environmental authorities and other government departments of the aims of SEA (ERM, 2003). However, the stages at which the authority consults, and makes information available to the public, are clearly set out in the 2004 SEA regulations. Environmental authorities must be consulted when:

* carrying out case-by-case screening of plans;
* deciding on the scope of the SEA;
* dealing with potential transboundary impacts.

They are also notified of the outcomes from the SEA process via a formal statement. The public are given formal notice of events at several stages, specifically:

* when a plan is screened out of requiring SEA;
* during transboundary consultations;
* when the draft plan and SEA report are published – this being the only stage at which the public can forward submissions on the SEA report;
* when the plan is adopted.

SEA outcome

Although other SEA systems around the world have witnessed the evolution of SEA principles and practice, and have been able to record the SEA life cycle from assessment to implementation, the Irish SEA system is still at an early stage of development. While there is evidence of SEAs taking place, there is a lack of sufficient practical experience on decision-making, recognizing costs and benefits, and of environmental quality and SEA system monitoring in Ireland.

Discernible outcomes of SEA are still rarely found in Irish SEA reports or in the plan being assessed. SEA practitioners have reported a greater understanding of the plan or recognition of how the plan interacts with other policies but rarely has SEA created any significant changes in how environmental protection objectives are treated during plan preparation.

Similarly, it is too early to make an informed judgement on improvements to environmental quality as a result of SEA. The key to success is allowing the SEA to set terms of reference for subsequent EIAs of development proposals so that such proposals may be dealt with more efficiently.

Conclusion

Ireland's land use planning system is structured according to a clear hierarchy, from the national strategic plans at the higher levels, through regional and county administrative levels, to LAPs. The SEA process is integrated into the regional level and downwards. The absence of SEA at the highest levels of planning (for example, the NDP and the NSS) was a significant deficiency at the time of their preparation, although the National Hazardous Waste Plan will be subject to a SEA when it is reviewed in 2006, as will other strategic plans.

SEA has been required by law for a selected range of land use plans since the SEA Directive and Irish regulations came into force in July 2004. A set of planning guidelines adopted in December 2004 supports the SEA regulations (DoEHLG, 2004). In addition, best practice methodological guidance on SEA (ERM, 2003) was published by EPA in 2003. These three sources (regulations, guidance and methodology) will underpin the development of SEA practice in Ireland. A summary of the extent to which the current Irish SEA system appears to meet system, process and output criteria is presented in Table 9.2.

A few SEA-type studies of CDPs have been completed to date in Ireland. While these do not resemble the SEA reports that would be required under the SEA regulations, they represent Ireland's first attempts to integrate environmental issues fully into development plans. The SEA of the Dublin Docklands Master Plan Review was the first SEA undertaken in Ireland that aimed to meet the requirements of the directive. It also helped to highlight some of the key challenges that will be faced when the first formalized SEAs are undertaken:

- screening sub-threshold plans for SEA and ensuring that environmental authorities contribute effectively to the process;
- scoping the SEA process and the report, and ensuring that environmental authorities and the public contribute effectively to the process;
- defining, agreeing upon and using environmental objectives, targets and indicators for the purposes of SEA benchmarks and clarifying the scope of monitoring;
- understanding the relationships between different environmental plans and the plan being assessed;

Table 9.2 *Evaluation of SEA of land use plans in Ireland*

Criterion	Criterion met	Comments
	SYSTEM CRITERIA	
Legal basis	■	SEA formalized through two sets of regulations in 2004
Integration	■	SEA of land use plans fully integrated with plan preparation and consultation processes
Guidance	▲	Formal methodological guidance published in 2003. Guidance on SEA of land use plans published in 2004
Coverage	■	SEA generally applies to all land use plans but some smaller LAPs may not require SEA
Tiering	■	Tiered land use planning system exists and, encouragingly, SEA can be applied at all levels apart from the national spatial planning level
Sustainable development	▲	Role of SEA in promoting sustainable development recognized but SEA system limited to addressing physical environmental issues
	PROCESS CRITERIA	
Alternatives	■	Plan alternatives must be considered although confusion exists as to detail in which each alternative should be examined
Screening	■	Undertaken using population based and significance criteria for smaller LAPs
Scoping	■	Formal stage involving consultation with environmental authorities
Prediction/evaluation	■	Required by legislation, and guidance recommends use of environmental protection objectives
Additional impacts	▲	Little guidance on how to address these impacts
Report preparation	■	Required by legislation, and seen as having potential to bring added value to plan making
Review	▲	No independent body for review exists and local authorities expected to enforce their own quality standards
Monitoring	■	Required under Irish SEA regulations but reliance upon existing environmental monitoring regimes likely
Mitigation	■	Likely to take place by rewording, expanding or clarifying policies in plans
Consultation and public participation	■	Consultation takes place as part of land use plan preparation process and SEA consultation integrates with this

Table 9.2 *Evaluation of SEA of land use plans in Ireland (continued)*

Criterion	Criterion met	Comments
	OUTCOME CRITERIA	
Decision making	?	Very few formal SEAs undertaken to date, and little evidence of influence on decision making
Costs and benefits	?	No evidence of costs or benefits yet
Environmental quality	?	No evidence of effects on environmental quality
System monitoring	?	No mechanisms in place to enable this

Notes: ■ – Yes
▲ – Partially
□ – No
? – Don't know

- ensuring that government departments and authorities communicate effectively with each other;
- ensuring that SEAs influence EIAs by setting the terms of reference for EIAs or by providing clear guidance on development preferences.

These challenges will hopefully be overcome as more SEAs are undertaken in the future.

Notes

1   The text of the act, and of all the other Irish central government documents referenced, can be viewed at: www.environ.ie/DOEI/DOEIPol.nsf/wvNavView/Planning?OpenDocument&Lang=#25
2   Planning and Development (Strategic Environmental Assessment) Regulations 2004 (SI No 436 of 2004)
3   European Communities (Environmental Assessment of Certain Plans and Programmes) Regulations 2004 (SI No 435 of 2004)
4   www.corkcoco.com/cccmm/publicts/DevPlan/volume1/chapter11, /www.galway.ie/planning/developmentplan/environment/assess.doc

References

Anon (2004) Anonymous contributor, *Seminar on Strategic Environmental Assessment*, 19 May, Tullamore, Environmental Protection Agency, Wexford

Department of the Environment, Heritage and Local Government (2004) *Implementation of SEA Directive (2001/42/EC): Assessment of the Effects of Certain Plans/Programmes on the Environment, Guidelines for Regional Authorities and Planning Authorities*, Government Publications Office, Dublin

Dublin Docklands Development Authority (2003) *Strategic Environmental Assessment of the Draft Master Plan*, DDDA, Dublin

Environmental Protection Agency (2002) *Guidelines on the Information to be contained in Environmental Impact Statements*, EPA, Wexford

Environmental Protection Agency (2003) *Advice Notes on Current Practice (in the Preparation of Environmental Impact Statements)*, EPA, Wexford

Environmental Resources Management Ireland (2003) *Development of Strategic Environmental Assessment Methodologies for Plans and Programmes in Ireland*, EPA, Wexford

European Commission (2001a) 'Directive 2001/42/EC of the European Parliament and of the Council of 27 June 2001 on the assessment of the effects of certain plans and programmes on the environment', *Official Journal of the European Communities*, vol L197, pp30–37, 21 July

European Commission (2001b) *Guidance on EIA: EIS Review*, Office for Official Publications of the European Communities, Luxembourg, http://europa.eu.int/comm/environment/eia/eia-guidelines/g-review-full-text.pdf

European Commission (2003) *Implementation of Directive 2001/42 on the Assessment of the Effects of Certain Plans and Programmes on the Environment*, Directorate-General XI Environment, EC, Brussels

Heritage Council (2000) *Heritage Appraisal of Development Plans*, An Chomhairle Oidhreachta/HC, Kilkenny

10

The Netherlands

Wil Thissen and Rob van der Heijden

Introduction

Both land use planning and concern for environmental issues have a long tradition in The Netherlands. Significant parts of the country – essentially parts of the lower deltas of the Rhine, Meuse and Scheldt rivers – are below sea level. Collective efforts to manage water and reclaim land from the swamps had to be organized and managed almost from the start of human settlement. Industrial development and ever increasing population density have led to strong pressures on, and competition for, land. Industrialization and population density also led to an early sensitivity to environmental issues. For example, in the early 1970s, when the Club of Rome's *Limits to Growth* was published (Meadows et al, 1972), politicians as well as the general public were receptive to its notion of the limits to nature's carrying capacity. Concerns about environmental degradation were also the basis for the early adoption and implementation of legislation requiring environmental impact assessment at the project level. Internationally, The Netherlands has been one of the forerunners in implementing legislation and building up experience in this field.

This chapter outlines the situation in The Netherlands with respect to strategic environmental assessment within the context of land use planning. It focuses on the process of implementation of European Directive 2001/42/EC ('the SEA Directive') (European Commission (EC), 2001). Because the SEA Directive has not yet been transposed into Dutch law, it is not possible to evaluate formal SEA system practice in The Netherlands, nor to report on experience with its processes and outcomes. The following discussion therefore relates primarily to the regulations currently proposed by the national government.

The framework of land use planning in The Netherlands is presented first in this chapter. The role of EIA at the project level is then addressed. Next, a brief case study of a voluntary SEA of a spatial development plan is outlined. This is followed by a description of the Dutch proposals for the implementation of the SEA Directive. Some preliminary observations are drawn from a limited set of exploratory pilot studies in which a SEA-like approach was adopted. Finally, conclusions are drawn.

Context

The planning system in The Netherlands is based on the Spatial Planning Act 1965 and the accompanying (regularly updated) Decree of the Minister of Spatial Planning, Housing and Environmental Protection. Before 1965, there was a tradition of local regulation of the rapid urban expansion taking place between the end of the 19th century and World War II. This regulation focused on building activities at the municipal level: housing, the provision of sanitary and transport infrastructure, and an active land supply role. The growing tradition of land use planning resulted in the 1965 act. Although the Spatial Planning Act has been subject to minor changes since 1965, it still constitutes the basic framework for Dutch land use planning practice.

The Spatial Planning Act builds upon the concept of vertical coordination between the three major layers of government: the national (state), the provincial and the municipal levels. Basically, the spatial plan prepared at a higher administrative level for a larger-scale area sets the framework for detailed decisions regarding local areas. Coordination, based on formal and informal consultation, is intended to avoid conflicts between the actual development of a certain area and the intended development agreed at the higher level. Instruments for adapting plans prepared at a lower level to comply with spatial plans at a higher level are included in the Spatial Planning Act but, in practice, these are rarely used. However, there is no hierarchy in the sense that a higher level authority specifies the details of land use at the local level.

The principle of vertical coordination based on consultation is consistent with The Netherlands being a decentralized unitary state (Newman and Thornley, 1996; Needham, 2004). Each level of government has independent legislative and administrative powers under the overall supervision of the central state and formulates its own regulations and plans as long as they do not conflict with those prepared at a higher level. Consequently, in general, much effort is put into actively finding consensus about difficult matters. This has made a major contribution to the acceptance of certain principles for land use planning (such as preserving the 'green heart' of the Randstad area) and to the continuity of Dutch land use planning since the early 1960s.

The Spatial Planning Act requires a statement of national planning policy to be prepared by central government about every ten years. The first policy document on spatial planning was published in 1960, and the fifth was published in 2004 (Ministry of Housing, Spatial Planning and Environment (VROM) et al, 2004). These statements are subject to public consultation and approval by parliament. The Infrastructure Alignment Act 1994 made key decisions regarding transport infrastructure projects of national importance obligatory for lower level land use plans. Moreover, some key decisions are now made under the special regulatory regimes applying in certain sensitive areas, such as the Wadden Sea.

At the provincial level, the Spatial Planning Act requires the preparation of a regional plan covering the whole, or major parts, of a provincial area. These plans, which should be updated about every ten years, are subject to public consultation and approved by the provincial representatives. The physical, economic and environmental proposals of different sectoral bodies are integrated in policy strategies and transformed into land use development proposals in the regional plans. These plans provide the framework for the approval of municipal plans and are indicative rather than legally binding. Provincial authorities can either accept or reject municipal plans, but they can only give detailed directions to municipalities in extreme situations. Moreover, the provincial plan serves as a framework for regional sectoral policy plans, for example, plans for water, transport or landscape protection.

At the municipal level, two kinds of plans are provided for in the Spatial Planning Act – the municipal structure plan and the detailed land use plan. The non-obligatory structure plan provides a long-term vision of the development of the municipal territory and serves as a means of communication with the local population.

The municipal land use plan is the most important planning instrument. It is the only plan that legally binds citizens, organizations and public bodies, thereby creating legal certainty for individuals concerning their interests, particularly their property rights. Moreover, the detailed land use plan is the basis of a system of permits for changing land uses, building activities, the avoidance of environmental nuisance and the protection of historic sites. The land use plan shows the designated land uses that are permitted in various locations.

Municipal authorities are obliged to produce plans for built-up areas. In many cases, this has resulted in a blanket of plans for small areas covering the territory of an authority. An opportunity for public consultation is provided prior to the final decision on the content of the plan. The procedure for requesting and granting permits provides the basis for compensating others for possible loss of property value. Permit decisions are subject to an appeal procedure at various levels up to the Council of State, a national independent court.

The system of spatial plans is intended to guide spatial development. In most areas, these plans work in a relatively passive way. However, they allow for special projects aimed at more active land use change. Such projects might have significant spatial and environmental impacts and, since legislation was passed in 1987, have often required an EIA. In the context of this procedure, the independent EIA Commission provides terms of reference for the EIA and publishes evaluations of the quality of the resulting report (Wood, 2002).

The project-focused EIA procedure has become a well-established approach since the 1980s and has a significant impact on decision making. This is due to the formalized EIA procedures that have been developed in The Netherlands, including provisions for public consultation. EIA reports appear to play a significant role in appeal procedures up to the level of the Council of State. In contrast, there is no tradition of SEA of the plans prepared under the Spatial Planning Act or of related strategic policy documents. In anticipation of the SEA Directive, informal and voluntary SEAs were undertaken on an experimental basis.. A few of these initiatives were in the field of land use planning and one of these is described in the next section.

Case study: spatial strategy plan for North Holland–south

The south of the Province of North Holland constitutes the northern part of the Randstad, which has almost two million inhabitants, and faces a number of complex development issues. These include the growth of Amsterdam, the growth of Schiphol National Airport, the economic restructuring of the North Sea Channel harbour and industrial area, and the perceived need to build about 150,000 new houses by 2020.

The strategic planning procedure started with a report published in the spring of 2001 that included a description of the area and the challenges faced. The aim was to develop a strategic view of the area as the first step in the preparation of a regional spatial plan, the central objective of which was to maintain and strengthen the function of the area as an economic driving force. Five alternative development concepts were presented. The provincial government voluntarily decided to prepare a SEA report, following the project-oriented EIA procedure. The EIA Commission appointed an independent working party of experts, who published their guidance on the aspects to be studied in August 2001. The SEA report was published in April 2002 together with the draft spatial plan. A wide-ranging consultation phase followed. The EIA Commission working party evaluated the documents and the comments arising from consultation, and published its opinion in July 2002 stating that the SEA report gave sufficient information to make a decision on the main lines of future development. However, it also observed that certain decisions with anticipated significant environmental impacts had yet to be made.

The EIA Commission struggled with two issues: the construction of alternative development concepts; and the question of how to evaluate the strategic information presented. With respect to the first issue, the EIA Commission observed that the alternative strategic development concepts were only partially linked to the central objective. The development concepts and the impacts assessed were largely based on traditional housing, transport and business area considerations. Since economic, social and water management sub-goals were not explicitly translated into alternative spatial developments, the policy dilemmas were insufficiently clarified.

The second issue, the evaluation framework, was related to the first. A clear specification of strategic policy dilemmas supports the development of a strategic evaluation framework. The discussion between the EIA Commission working party and the authorities did not result in a search for new alternative strategic concepts. Instead, an attempt was made to transfer the available impact information for the more traditional impact categories (water, ecology, landscape and archaeology, transport, the urban environment, the living environment and the economy) into a quantitative score for each category for a set of eight basic policy alternatives:

- accommodate housing needs selectively or accommodate all needs;
- offer opportunities for all economic development or accept basic restrictions on economic development;
- actively invest in better living quality or preserve present quality;
- develop a new landscape identity or stimulate more uniformity in landscape;
- actively stimulate more biodiversity or protect existing biodiversity;
- integrate regional living and labour zones to reduce mobility needs or stimulate spatial segregation to improve living quality;
- create flexibility for accommodating unforeseen developments or take significant risks due to inflexibility regarding unforeseen developments;
- limit vulnerability due to future financial uncertainties or increase vulnerability due to high financial risks.

Although the relative positioning of the development alternatives in this evaluation framework appeared to be difficult and was subject to debate, the attempt to specify them was appreciated by the EIA Commission working party as a step forward in the strategic assessment approach. Overall, the SEA was judged to be useful by the provincial government (Verheem, 2003b). The consultation of the general public did not result in significant feedback because the debate was at too general a level. Unfortunately, the SEA took about a year, which appeared to be too long for those preparing the formal regional spatial plan. This time period did not match the formal procedure for developing the new regional plan and explains the lack of willingness to develop new alternatives. An emphasis on broad qualitative assessments instead of a focus on selective quantitative impact assessments (which take time, can never be complete and require decisions on details) would have reduced some of the pressure on time.

SEA system

Introduction

The Dutch authorities are lagging behind in the implementation of various European regulations (Versteegh, 2004), including the SEA Directive, which should have been implemented by 24 July 2004. The proposed SEA regulations were submitted to parliament in 2004 but formal implementation was not expected until the second half of 2005.

There are two major reasons for this delay. Firstly, the governing coalition elected in 2002 has a more conservative orientation than the previous government, with stronger anti-regulation and pro-market preferences and a reduced emphasis on environmental issues. Secondly, in preparing for the implementation of the SEA Directive, a long and time consuming dispute took place about the desirability of having stricter procedures for situations in which plans or programmes would affect areas considered to be ecologically valuable, or that were covered by the European Habitats Directive.

The main Dutch law regarding environmental protection is the 'Wet Milieubeheer' 1994 (WMB, or Environmental Management Act). The current government regulations, based on that law, and that have been in effect since 1994 require EIAs for projects of a specific type and size. Responsibility for implementing the requirements rests with the competent authority. A key ingredient in the EIA process is the requirement for approval of the terms of reference of the EIA and for evaluation of the EIA report by the EIA Commission, an independent entity sponsored by the government. Depending on the type of project, a committee of independent experts is assembled by the EIA Commission to perform these tasks. The independent EIA Commission's guidance is published and there are many examples where it has influenced decision making processes significantly. The government proposes to implement the SEA Directive by grafting it on to both the WMB and the existing EIA regulations. The aim is a single regulatory framework, which covers both project EIA and plan/programme SEA requirements.

The proposed procedures for implementing the SEA Directive show some differences from the project-oriented EIA procedures in The Netherlands (de Groot et al, 2003; de Haas et al, 2004). While the project-oriented approach requires the proponent to prepare an inception memorandum explaining the aims of the project and presenting a first scan of alternative options which is subject to public consultation, this is not required for SEA. Further, no independent and public evaluation of the quality of the assessment report is required for SEA. A third difference from the project-oriented approach is that the specification of the environmentally preferable alternative is not obligatory. Similarities with the present project-EIA procedure include:

- the obligatory consultation of certain authorities;
- a report describing the proposed initiative, its environmental impacts, and so on;
- public consultation;
- decision making taking all the available information into account;
- monitoring.

Summary of proposals

The Dutch government proposes, as a principle, to implement the SEA Directive to the letter. That is, it will implement the minimum regulatory provisions necessary to satisfy the requirements of the Directive but will not enact any additional specific national policy elements. While this may be surprising for a nation that has built a reputation of being a forerunner in environmental legislation, it reflects the current political climate. Key elements of the proposed regulations include the following:

- A requirement for those preparing plans and programmes designated in the SEA Directive to include a SEA in the preparation process. This will be required for (a) all those plans or programmes setting the framework for decisions on the siting of projects for which an EIA is required, including most land use plans, and (b) plans that have significant impacts on areas protected by the European Habitats or Birds directives

- Responsibility for implementing the SEA requirements will rest with the competent authority. In spatial planning, the competent authority will generally be the same government body that prepares the plan. In The Netherlands, therefore, the national authorities, the provinces and the local municipalities will have a key role in the SEA process
- A provision to prevent duplication with project EIAs if the same impacts have already been covered at the plan or programme level. Assessments at different levels need to be complementary and cumulative, and this requires a reconsideration of the full body of rules governing all environmental assessments, including the existing EIA regulations (below).

The new SEA provisions may lead to requirements different from those under existing EIA regulations. The distinction between a plan or programme, on the one hand and a project, on the other hand, becomes more important. In the past, plans containing elements or projects for which an EIA was required were subject to the EIA regulations. Under the new regulations, such plans will be subject to the (less stringent) requirements for SEA, with specific projects remaining subject to the EIA regime.

Specific regulations with respect to plans and programmes affecting areas covered by the Habitats Directive, and other specific nationally designated areas of ecological importance (the so-called Ecologische Hoofdstructuur), have been a key exception to the current government's principle of strict implementation, and the subject of heated debate between different government agencies. Plans affecting these areas might have particularly significant impacts and therefore should be subject to a particularly thorough assessment.

The proposed regulations now contain a provision that SEAs of plans potentially affecting European habitats and other areas of ecological importance will be evaluated independently by the EIA Commission. In contrast to the EIA regulations, which are exclusive in the sense that they specify a limited list of the types of projects for which an EIA is required, the SEA regulations are inclusive in that SEA may apply to all kinds of activities affecting the environment in European habitats and other areas of ecological importance. It is left to the competent authority to decide whether or not this is the case.

Although the desirability of assessing social and economic impacts on a comparable basis to environmental impacts, and thereby addressing sustainable development, is referred to in the document explaining the formal legislative proposal, it does not include any requirement to assess these impacts.

SEA process

Given the relationship between the existing EIA procedures and the proposed SEA procedures in The Netherlands (for example, van Eck, 2004), a process has been started to streamline and simplify the existing EIA regulations in parallel with the process of formal implementation of the SEA Directive. This is part of the government's overall desire to reduce the amount and complexity of regulations, and also part of the attempt to develop a more unified approach to environmental assessment. The general guidelines for the content of environmental assessment reports are therefore identical for SEA and EIA. However, the proposed unified set of rules clearly reflects the need for a more flexible approach, enabling broader and more qualitative assessments to be made at the strategic level, and requiring more specific and quantitative analyses at the project level.

For example, the competent authority is required to consult other relevant authorities about the terms of reference of the SEA, but there is no requirement for an assessment of the terms of reference by an independent body like the EIA Commission at the initiation stage. However, there is a formal requirement to publicize the procedure that will be followed at the start of a planning process, similar to the EIA process. The proposed SEA regulations also include a requirement to explain why the alternatives considered were selected. However, it is not necessary to include either the environmentally preferable alternative or a broad set of alternatives. Possible mitigation measures for undesirable environmental impacts, however, should be considered.

To date, no specific requirements have been formulated regarding procedures for scoping, prediction or evaluation of impacts, other than those specified by the SEA Directive. The government has, however, taken the initiative of developing guidance to support the authorities who will be responsible for application of the SEA Directive and has published a brief document outlining requirements for the interim period between the SEA Directive coming into effect and the national legislation becoming operative (VROM, 2004b). This indicates that the SEA report will be a separate document that will be published in conjunction with the proposed land use plan as the basis for public consultation. It is suggested that there should be a clear link with other preparatory documents so that social and economic impacts can be compared with environmental impacts within a unified framework. There is no formal requirement in this respect, however. In cases in which there is also a requirement for an assessment according to the Habitats Directive, both assessments need to be identified as separate entities, for example, by being presented in separate chapters of the report.

The competent authority has the option of including an independent evaluation of the SEA report in the procedure but there is no requirement to do so. This is a significant difference from the EIA procedure, in which the EIA Commission performs this important role. However, SEAs for plans that potentially affect European habitats and other areas of ecological importance must be evaluated independently by the EIA Commission.

The existing public consultation in Dutch spatial planning prior to the decision being made will be extended to include the SEA report. The proposed legislation also includes a requirement to indicate explicitly, in the final decision document, how the information on environmental impacts has been taken into account.

Finally, there will be a requirement to include monitoring following implementation of the plan. The guidance recognizes that a plan may often not in itself have environmental impacts, but that these may occur only as a consequence of projects realized within the framework of the plan. In such cases, the monitoring requirement relates to the impacts of these projects rather than to those of the plan.

There has been a recent surge in the number of expert publications on the implementation of the SEA Directive (see, for example, van der Wel et al, 2004). In addition to the case study (above), a few other pilot studies have been documented (see, for example, Verheem, 2003a) and several more are in progress. An interesting pilot study related to the future development of the Scheldt Estuary may be one of the first truly transboundary Dutch SEA pilots (Zanting et al, 2004). A number of process-related observations can be made on the basis of these pilot studies:

- With new technology (such as geographical information systems (GIS)) it is possible to collect and process impressive amounts of data within a limited time frame. There is a tendency, however, to collect data that are too detailed and to perform too many in-depth quantitative analyses of them
- A cornerstone of the SEA process is the development of an adequate evaluation framework. The evaluation framework guides the separation of relevant information from irrelevant information, thereby helping to focus on the key differences between alternatives
- There is no need to describe differences between alternatives in great detail if the differences and their orders of magnitude are evident. Rather, the focus should be on key conceptual differences between alternatives
- Interaction with key stakeholders from the start can help to select the right issues and to create an atmosphere of transparency and openness. Further interaction at key milestones in the SEA process will help to build acceptance and support for the findings of the assessment
- Timing is a key factor. The assessment should be started early in the process in order to reduce pressure on the study and to create more freedom to discuss its implications
- It pays to build on earlier experiences. In one of the pilot studies (the spatial plan for the West Netherlands (Verheem, 2003a)) a process similar to the mandatory EIA process, of which there is substantial experience, was followed successfully.

SEA outcome

As indicated earlier, it is too early to provide any conclusive evidence regarding the impact of SEA on land use plan decision making in The Netherlands. However, the first indications from the limited number of pilot studies undertaken are positive.

It is estimated that about 100 plans per year will be subject to the SEA regulations in The Netherlands, most of them at the municipal level and, to a lesser extent, at the provincial level (de Haas et al, 2004). While it is very difficult to assess the additional costs resulting from the implementation of the SEA Directive in The Netherlands, a rough estimate is that they may be of the order of €600,000 per year (VROM, 2004a). This estimate is based on the assumption that attention is already paid to the environmental impacts of plans in most existing planning practice and that additional requirements as a result of the SEA Directive will therefore be limited. Provinces and municipalities will be compensated for these additional costs. This additional cost estimate appears to be rather low since economic motives are dominant in current spatial planning practice and systematic attention to environmental aspects is generally limited to the projects for which an EIA is required.

Conclusion

Experience with the application of SEA in land use planning in The Netherlands is limited to date. The Netherlands has a long planning tradition, with land use plans at the national, provincial and municipal levels. The largest numbers of plans are prepared at the municipal or local level and, while attention is often paid to environmental issues in local planning processes (if only because authorities are forced to do so by non-governmental organizations and local action groups), this does not appear to be done in a systematic way, and varies greatly across the range of plans, municipalities and provinces (see Fischer, 1999, 2002). Now that the prevailing political climate lays more emphasis on economic development, this situation is unlikely to change in favour of the environment. Conclusions must therefore be based on a limited number of pilot studies, and on the formal proposal to implement the SEA Directive.

Firstly, promulgating the formal regulations required to implement the SEA Directive is a non-trivial task. While, on the one hand, the SEA regulations need to be attuned to the EIA regulations (to prevent duplication), on the other hand, they need to be flexible enough to accommodate different planning situations and to enable integration with existing planning procedures to occur. Modification and adaptation of existing EIA legislation seems inevitable. As indicated in Table 10.1, and closely following the SEA Directive, The Netherlands has opted to give a significant degree of freedom regarding the formal quality control requirements to the competent authorities. However, local authorities are uncertain about how to cope with this freedom and are asking for a clearer framework. Moreover, they fear that SEA might result in claims for property value loss. Consequently, local authorities will initially follow a very cautious strategy and the extent to which this will lead to a serious assessment of the environmental impacts of strategic spatial plans remains to be seen.

Secondly, to provide additional protection to areas considered to have particular ecological value, additional requirements for independent quality control by the present EIA Commission are being proposed. Land use plans and projects affecting areas covered by the Habitats or Birds directives are already subject to public and independent evaluation by the EIA Commission. However, plans affecting Dutch areas of ecological importance have now been added to this category. This reflects

Table 10.1 *Evaluation of SEA of land use plans in The Netherlands*

Criterion	Criterion met	Comments
	SYSTEM CRITERIA	
Legal basis	■	Implements European SEA Directive in 'strict' (minimal) way, from 2005
Integration	▲	System open to integration; integration suggested but not required
Guidance	▲	Guidance documents in preparation
Coverage	■	All plans providing framework for projects subject to EIA; plans influencing areas protected by Habitats and Birds directives and other ecologically important areas
Tiering	▲	Generally recommended; land use planning system is itself tiered
Sustainable development	☐	SD not emphasized, suggestions to seek integrated approaches implicitly hint at SD
	PROCESS CRITERIA	
Alternatives	▲	No requirement to consider environmentally preferable alternative; left to judgement of competent authority
Screening	■	Proposed regulation specifies plans needing SEA; some decisions left to competent authority
Scoping	?	Not in formal requirements; probably in guidelines being developed
Prediction/evaluation	■	Required; reality remains to be seen
Additional impacts	■	Required; reality remains to be seen
Report preparation	■	Required
Review	▲	Left to competent authority to decide, except in Habitats and Birds directives/ ecologically important areas
Monitoring	■	General requirement; sometimes to be shifted to project level
Mitigation	▲	Inclusion suggested
Consultation and public participation	■	Required; whether decision makers will act on results cannot yet be determined
	OUTCOME CRITERIA	
Decision making	?	Will become clear only after years of implementation; pilot study results show positive signs

Table 10.1 *Evaluation of SEA of land use plans in The Netherlands (continued)*

Criterion	Criterion met	Comments
Costs and benefits	▲	Rough (but optimistic) estimate of costs; no statements about whether costs outweighed by benefits
Environmental quality	?	Will be clear only in 5–10 years
System monitoring	■	Introduction of SEA system triggered evaluation of EIA system; formal SEA proposal requires evaluation 2 years after implementation

Notes: ■ – Yes
    ▲ – Partially
    □ – No
    ? – Don't know

governmental awareness of the importance of the independence of the assessing body. Thus, a direct relationship between the initiating body (including municipal authorities) and the assessors is regarded as more undesirable than, for example, the EIA Commission being funded by the government.

Third, experience with pilot SEA studies so far seems to confirm the importance of:

- adequate timing with respect both to starting the study early in the process and to reporting before the decision is made;
- adequate consideration of the design and inclusion of an adequate spectrum of alternatives; the alternatives should include all the key issues, not just two or three obvious ones;
- broad, qualitative assessment across alternatives and types of impacts, rather than focusing on quantitative and more detailed assessments of selected impacts.

References

de Groot, I., van Eck, P. and Jurakic, E. (2003) 'Cold feet for SEA not justified', *Kenmerken*, vol 10(6), pp4–7 (in Dutch)

de Haas, L., Berkenbosch, R. and van der Wiel, K. (2004) 'SEA: scope, procedure, substance', *Kenmerken*, vol 11(3), pp14–19 (in Dutch)

European Commission (2001) 'Directive 2001/42/EC of the European Parliament and of the Council of 27 June 2001 on the assessment of the effects of certain plans and programmes on the environment', *Official Journal of the European Communities*, vol L197, pp30–37, 21 July

Fischer, T. B. (1999) 'Benefits from SEA application – a comparative review of North West England, Noord-Holland and EVR Brandenburg-Berlin', *Environmental Impact Assessment Review*, vol 19, pp143–173

Fischer, T. B. (2002) *Strategic Environmental Assessment in Transport and Land Use Planning*, Earthscan, London

Meadows, D. H., Meadows, D. L., Randers, J. and Behrens, W. W. III (1972), *Limits to Growth*, Potomac Associates, New York

Ministries of Housing, Spatial Planning and Environment, of Agriculture, Nature Management and Fisheries, of Transport, Public Works and Water Management, and of Economic Affairs (2004) *Nota Ruimte: Policy Memorandum on Land Use in The Netherlands*, VROM, The Hague (in Dutch)

Ministry of Housing, Spatial Planning and Environment (2004a) *Explanatory Statement Accompanying the Bill to Change the Environmental Protection Law*, VROM, The Hague, 28 September (in Dutch)

Ministry of Housing, Spatial Planning and Environment (2004b) *Strategic Environmental Assessment: Implementation of European Directive 2001/42/EC on Strategic Environmental Assessment*, VROM, The Hague (in Dutch)

Needham, B. (2004) *The New Dutch Spatial Planning Act*, Working Paper 2004/2, Governance and Places Research Group, Nijmegen School of Management, Radboud University, Nijmegen

Newman, P. and Thornley, A. (1996) *Urban Planning in Europe: International Competition, National Systems and Planning Projects*, Routledge, London

van der Wel, K., Weijers, P. and Berkenbosch, R. (2004) 'Getting to work with strategic environmental assessment', *Kenmerken*, vol 11(5), pp14–17 (in Dutch)

van Eck, M. (2004) 'Requirements for environmental impact assessment of land use plans', *Kenmerken*, vol 11(2), pp18–20 (in Dutch)

Verheem, R. (2003a) 'National spatial plan for the West of The Netherlands', in Hayashi, K., Sadler, B., Dusik, J., Tomlinson, P. and Verheem, R., *Effective SEA System and Case Studies*, Ministry of Environment, Government of Japan, and Mitsubishi Research Institute, Tokyo

Verheem, R. (2003b) 'SEA of the North Holland-South Spatial Strategy Plan', in Hayashi, K., Sadler, B., Dusik, J., Tomlinson, P. and Verheem, R., *Effective SEA System and Case Studies*, Ministry of Environment, Government of Japan and Mitsubishi Research Institute, Tokyo

Versteegh, K. (2004) 'Netherlands slow with European legislation', *Rotterdam NRC/Handelsblad*, 26 June (in Dutch)

Wood, C. M. (2002) *Environmental Impact Assessment: a Comparative Review*, 2nd edition, Prentice Hall, Harlow (2nd edition)

Zanting, H. A., Weijers, P. and van Essen, E. (2004) 'Strategic environmental assessment for the Scheldt Estuary', *Kenmerken*, vol 11(5), pp4–7 (in Dutch)

11

New Zealand

Jennifer Dixon

Introduction

The New Zealand approach to SEA is intertwined with the statutory framework for land use planning and its practice. In this respect, SEA is not formally prescribed as a mandatory requirement within the Resource Management Act 1991 (RMA), the key planning statute that guides the management of most of New Zealand's natural and physical resources. When the Resource Management Act was drafted in the late 1980s, principles and elements of environmental assessment (EA) were deliberately woven into the statute to focus on achieving the beneficial outcomes of project and policy EA rather than enshrining it in legislation (Fookes, 2000). However, as this chapter will demonstrate, features of SEA are easily discernible within both legislation and practice.

Despite this lack of prescription, it is possible to identify several variants of SEA in plan making and practice. These include those embedded in statutory requirements for plan making under the act, statutory and non-statutory planning activities that take place under the Local Government Act (LGA) 2002 and, to a much lesser extent, in strategies, reports or inquiries at central government level (Dixon, 2002). More recently, the revised LGA has become an influential instrument in shaping planning practice and its potential for SEA needs to be considered alongside that of the RMA and of the plans produced by local government.

This chapter provides a summary overview of where SEA sits in the context of land use planning both within and outside New Zealand's statutory planning system. It then presents a case study of the Christchurch City Plan that highlights the informal and loose style of SEA that is emerging in New Zealand as a consequence of a relatively integrated approach to planning. The case typifies an iterative response to planning that is unlikely to be formally concluded for a number of years, given the playing out of legal processes in respect of the completion of the City Plan. However, it shows the adoption of a methodological approach that has remained intact, despite some political setbacks along the way. This case study provides the basis of the remainder of the chapter. Given that the case study is still in progress and it is too soon to discern outcomes, the text of the chapter focuses on the system criteria (Chapter 3) and some of the process criteria and does not address outcomes. However, the performance of the New Zealand SEA system is evaluated against each of the effectiveness criteria in Table 11.1.

Context

Since 1991, with the passing of the RMA, New Zealand has had an effects-based land use planning system that is largely devolved from central government. At the national level, the RMA[1] is the main statute under which planning policies are formulated by regional and local government. Implementation of the act rests largely in the hands of local (74 district and city council) and regional (12 regional and four unitary council) authorities. The assessment of environmental effects forms the cornerstone of the act, the purpose of which is 'the promotion of sustainable management of physical and natural resources' (Section 5(1)). The RMA establishes broad principles within which councils are free to develop their own approach to sustainable management on the basis of avoiding or mitigating adverse environmental effects. This has led to the development of the current effects-based planning system, with an emphasis on the management of environmental effects rather than on the prescription of activities (as was the case under the previous town and country planning regime).

Regional councils are responsible for activities such as managing water, soil, air and coasts, mitigating natural hazards and hazardous wastes, managing contaminant discharges and land transport planning. District and city councils are responsible for district planning, noise control, hazard mitigation and land subdivision, along with a wide range of other regulatory and discretionary functions.

The RMA provides a hierarchy of plans where lower level plans 'shall not be inconsistent with' higher level plans (Sections 62(3), 67(2) and 75(2)). This includes provision for national and regional policy statements, which set a statutory framework within which regional and district plans are prepared. While the act requires the preparation of a coastal policy statement, other national policy statements can be developed at the discretion of central government. To date, only the coastal policy statement has been prepared. The government has recently announced a suite of measures designed to improve the RMA, including strengthening the integration of planning documents at the district and regional levels, sharpening the role of the Environment Court (the judicial body that hears appeals in respect of council decisions and other environmental matters) and facilitating the preparation of more national policy statements (Benson-Pope, 2004). The development of national policy statements will fill a major policy gap that has been widely regarded as impeding implementation of the RMA (Ericksen et al, 2001; Parliamentary Commissioner for the Environment, 2001) and should be helpful in assisting the forthcoming round of second-generation plans.

Regional councils are required to prepare regional policy statements that provide an overview of resource management issues in their region. In turn, these govern the administration of resource consents covering land, water, air and coastal management. Regional plans, with the exception of regional coastal plans, are not mandatory but can be prepared on topics considered appropriate by regional councils. District plans, a mandatory requirement for district and city councils, deal with land use planning, noise and subdivision controls.

The act provides for both project and policy-based EA. However, project based EA, termed assessment of environmental effects (AEE), has had a much stronger profile than SEA, as it is a mandatory requirement. At the policy level, efforts have focused mainly on the development and analysis of policies through the implementation of Section 32 of the act, which advocates a duty to consider alternatives, assess benefits and costs, and so on, in the preparation of regional policy statements, regional and district plans. Section 32 requires a systematic approach to policy development and plan preparation resulting in a policy assessment of the environmental effects of policies and plans (Fookes, 2000). In particular, it requires the consideration of alternatives, which has not previously been a strong feature of EIA or of planning practice in New Zealand (Morgan, 1998; Wood, 2002).

Another feature of importance to SEA is the inclusion of Section 35 on monitoring in the RMA which requires local government to monitor not only consent compliance but also policy outcomes and the state of the environment. An amendment to the act in 2003 strengthened provisions for policy analysis and monitoring by requiring councils formally to prepare reports under Section 32 and to publish the results of monitoring under Section 35 on a regular basis. Other provisions of the act relevant to the practice of SEA include emphasis on wide opportunities for consultation in the plan-making process, including that with Maori, and mediation. Some of these features are likely to be changed in the forthcoming amendments to the act noted above (Benson-Pope, 2004).

The development of an integrated approach inevitably means that there are some gaps in what SEA advocates might argue comprises an ideal SEA system. Given the integrated nature of EA and statutory planning, it is sometimes hard to distinguish between both sets of practices. For example, there is no specific requirement to prepare a sustainability appraisal report as part of the plan-making process, other than to show how the requirements of Section 32 have been met.

Furthermore, there is no provision for an independent review of the SEA process. While decisions of councils can be contested in the Environment Court, the criteria used by the court are, of course, determined by the provisions of the act, which are, in turn, derived from its 'Purpose and Principles' (Part 2).

Finally – and most importantly – it is significant to note that neither the phrase 'SEA' nor any variant of the term, nor the word 'planning', appears in the act. There is, therefore, no explicit requirement to undertake SEA, as such. Thus, the mandate for SEA within the act is limited at best.

It is vital to look beyond the RMA when considering SEA. While the goal of the RMA is the promotion of sustainable management, in theory it forms only a part of a national agenda for sustainable development, along with other government statutes and policies (Ministry for the Environment [MfE], 1994). Significant new legislative and policy initiatives have taken place since the RMA was enacted in 1991. At the national level, the Labour government's programme of action reflects its commitment to a range of actions for promoting sustainable development (Department of the Prime Minister and Cabinet, 2003). At the local level, the advent of the LGA places planning at the centre of local government activities. New long-term council community plans are intended to become the key strategic planning documents within councils. The extent to which linkages under this statute are made with plans prepared under the RMA will be critical for policy integration and SEA practice. While this is not formally required by either the LGA or the RMA, special legislation makes it a requirement in the Auckland region.

An intuitive assessment of SEA practice in the local government context suggests the mixed picture that could be expected as a consequence of a loose and uncertain mandate for SEA. The implementation of the RMA over the last decade has proved to be problematic for a number of reasons and the quality of plan making under the RMA has been shown to be generally poor (Ericksen et al, 2001, 2004).

Perhaps more significantly, however, there has been no strong advocacy of SEA by MfE or by the planning profession. SEA, as a specific activity, is not promoted by the planning profession or by other environmental professionals (apart from the small impact assessment community). This was confirmed in a series of interviews undertaken with key practitioners, who revealed a poor understanding of the term SEA and its key principles, yet a familiarity with many of its ideas (Davies, 2002).

At a broader level, it is much more difficult to assess the extent to which SEA is being applied to the raft of planning documents being prepared, sometimes initially outside the scope of the RMA, such as growth strategies, structure plans and asset management plans. However, while processes that take place under the LGA can be somewhat less formal and not be subject to the same degree of legal recourse, there is evidence that SEA principles are being implemented.

A particularly significant example of where SEA processes and methods have been applied, as opposed to the more limited policy assessments under the RMA, is in the development of the *Auckland Regional Growth Strategy 2050* (Auckland Regional Growth Forum, 1999). The Auckland region is New Zealand's largest conurbation, and has grown rapidly over the last few decades to 1.3 million people, with the prospect of the population doubling in 50 years. There are pressing environmental and social problems created by increasing urban sprawl. While the strategy was not developed with explicit reference to SEA, nor necessarily underpinned by a strong commitment to sustainability, analysis reveals a strong fit with SEA principles and methods (Fookes, 2002). What is also encouraging is that this strategy has not been driven by legislation but developed collaboratively by the seven district and city councils and the regional council as a strategic solution to some major urban problems. It is now being embedded in regional and district plans through statutory processes and by the implementation of non-statutory plans.

In summary, the institutional context and planning domain for SEA is often more implicit than explicit, and more ad hoc than might be expected given the integrated nature of the RMA. Consequently, what can be determined as the practice of SEA is diffuse and highly variable, yet the opportunities to embrace SEA more firmly in practice have probably never been more promising. There is a discernible shift away from the neo-liberal agenda of the 1990s, with its focus on effects-based environmental management, towards a more strategic approach to planning that embraces economic, environmental and social concerns (Dixon, 2003).

Case study: South West Christchurch

The proposed urbanization of land on the fringe of Christchurch City has been selected as an example of the informal and iterative approach to SEA undertaken by local government. It exemplifies an increasing trend in land use practice whereby detailed planning of greenfield or peri-urban areas is undertaken in consultation with communities, prior to any engagement in the statutory planning process. The practice of preparing structure or area plans outside the district planning process has been a direct response to the effects-based nature of the planning system, with its focus on managing effects rather than prescribing land use patterns.

The Halswell-Wigram Urban Expansion Investigation took place in response to submissions made to the proposed Christchurch City Plan in the late 1990s. The results are now under further review as the work on the site has been broadened into a major area study covering South West Christchurch, the outcome of which will assist the council in providing a framework for the integrated use, development and protection of natural resources (Christchurch City Council, 2003). The South West Area Plan, which is still in preparation, will lead to the development of more detailed structure plans, as necessary, together with changes which will be made to the city plan through the formal statutory processes.

The case shows how SEA principles can be incorporated within a planning framework to identify preferred land use patterns, taking account of sustainable development principles. In this sense, it is an example of the integration of SEA and planning. The work for the Halswell-Wigram study was undertaken by Christchurch City staff (Briggs and Thomson, 1999) in a series of teams focusing on topics such as transport, land drainage, the natural environment and Maori perspectives. The purpose was to show how the principles of sustainable development, broader than those of sustainable management as prescribed in the RMA and new urbanism, could be translated practically within a market-led context.

The area involved 350 hectares at Halswell-Wigram on the southern fringe of Christchurch City. The land had some major physical constraints, including its location in the upper catchment of a flood-prone river. However, studies had identified some major opportunities for developing a sustainable, compact urban area with good connections to the central city and other employment areas. A process was identified to assess the environmental capacity of the area. The first two stages involved the collection and analysis of baseline material that examined both the constraints and the development potential of the study area. The third stage assessed environmental capacity and opportunities for sustainable development by identifying critical, transferable and negotiable constraints. The study proceeded to identify parts of the area that had a development priority, were free of constraints or hazards, could be serviced by existing infrastructure, and took account of local community identity. Key design principles were developed and applied (Briggs and Thomson, 1999).

The findings of the study were reported back to the city council as part of the city plan hearings process in 1999. The council officers proposed to rezone the land but wanted development to be undertaken in accordance with a comprehensive plan for the area. Under strong pressure from developers and persuasive evidence from legal and expert witnesses, the council agreed to rezone part of the area to enable development to proceed (Thomson, 2004). By 2001, however, it had become evident that a broader approach was needed, particularly given the need to provide more residential land to accommodate increasing demand in the city's fastest growing area, and to rethink the approach to stormwater disposal, a critical issue in the southwestern part of the city.

In 2003, the council undertook to prepare an area plan for South West Christchurch, covering 8400 hectares, although staff initially focused on half of the area. The purpose of this exercise was to take a 30-year view, to incorporate local community aspirations on 'if further development occurs in this area, what needs to be done?', and to ensure the best possible integration of competing land uses to avoid adverse effects on the environment. Several technical studies have been undertaken with a view to testing options and adopting a preference for guiding overall development. It was intended that a draft area plan would be completed in 2006 which would, in turn, inform the development of more detailed plans. The principles of a liveable environment, competitiveness (including cost efficient services and a friendly regulatory environment for business) and global sustainability, which underpinned the Halswell-Wigram study, have been incorporated and extended in this much broader study (Christchurch City Council, 2003).

SEA system

As already noted, the SEA system in the New Zealand context is both informal and formal. This case study in Christchurch City represents both elements. The approach is increasingly typical of those taken by councils faced with managing rapid urban growth where there is a need to make major changes to the statutory land use plan (district or city plan) and other council plans. In Christchurch, rapid urban growth began during the early 1990s. At the same time, the city plan was undergoing the formal statutory processes of notification, hearings and submissions, but the planners had not anticipated the increasing rates of growth. Thus, there was a need to undertake some additional work that would later inform the statutory plan-making processes.

One of the aims of the work undertaken by the council is to ensure that the statutory requirements of the RMA can be met when changes to the city plan are notified and formal documentation is required – that is, when a Section 32 report is prepared. Thus, there is a minimalist *legal basis* and statutory test to be met at a later time. However, good practice has also ensured that a more substantive analysis is carried out than that prescribed in the legislation. In this respect, the approach taken has also ensured that the work undertaken will inform statutory plan preparation which should ensure that the council's obligations under the LGA are satisfied. It reflects, therefore, an *integrated* approach to planning in that SEA is not identifiable as a separate process and that SEA principles are not discernible as such, but are incorporated within the land use planning process.

Guidance on undertaking SEA in New Zealand has been limited. The MfE, the government agency charged with overseeing the RMA, has issued two publications on preparing Section 32 reports (MfE, 1993, 2000). Neither document contains specific reference to terms such as SEA or policy environmental assessment. However, a considerable volume of guidance material has been published on plan making generally. The 'quality planning' website,[2] a recent innovation managed by MfE, provides further guidance for planners, consistent with the content of the published documentation, and gives examples of best practice and council contacts. In Christchurch, council staff developed their own methodology for the Halswell-Wigram study, adapted from a UK publication *Sustainable Settlements* (Barton et al, 1995). Since then, council staff have developed a detailed internal protocol to guide the preparation of area plans which includes key principles, outcomes and forms of consultation, as well as covering aspects of content, evaluation and project management (Christchurch City Council, 2003). It is this protocol that is guiding the development of the South West Area Plan.

The only *coverage* requirement for an assessment of potential environmental effects of policies is the need for a Section 32 report to be prepared to accompany plans or plan changes notified under the RMA. However, the principles and methodology associated with SEA underpinned the work carried out in the Halswell-Wigram investigations and those that are now underway in the preparation of the area plan. Their inclusion, and the methodological approach adopted by council staff, suggest a considerable degree of innovation and adaptation of some traditional tools used by land use planners, along with a strong emphasis on environmental assessment and analysis.

What is significant from a SEA perspective is that there is a particular form of local *tiering* emerging. The tiering reflects a partial hierarchy of purpose that informs policy making and implementation to meet a range of council functions and requirements, moving from the strategic overview to more detailed land use planning and implementation as required. While the area plan sits effectively above a raft of specific-purpose or functional plans, these plans will be developed sequentially and inform several dimensions of the development process in a complementary, rather than hierarchical way, assisting integration (above) across the council.

It is pertinent that this form of tiering is developing within the broader framework of tiering under the RMA. This local response can be viewed as, in part, informing policy development in the city plan, which, in turn, sits within the formal or statutory hierarchy of national and regional policy statements and plans developed under the RMA. On the one hand, a consequence is the production of a number of different types of statutory and non-statutory plans that can potentially add various layers of council requirements and guidelines to an already complicated land use policy arena.

Furthermore, the proliferation of terms such as 'structure plans' and 'neighbourhood plans' being used in slightly different ways around the country can be confusing for the wider professional and development communities. On the other hand, these documents may well add considerable clarity and justification for more targeted intervention in a market-led context where the council wishes to be proactive in shaping the long-term development of the city.

The area plan is seen as providing a long-term framework for the preparation of more detailed structure plans, design guides and other forms of statutory and non-statutory guidance (Christchurch City Council, 2003). The area plans have a limited role under the RMA but will have effect through changes to the city plan and the production of Section 32 reports. Structure plans will provide financial information and design guidance. Development plans will have the same purpose as the structure plans, but will be incorporated in the city plan to assist implementation at a detailed site level. The form of tiering occurring thus cuts across statutes (in this case the RMA and the LGA) but demonstrates an attempt to integrate various requirements in a series of documents that are linked both horizontally and vertically.

Finally, the documentation clearly notes that principles of *sustainable development* underpin the planning approach. While a narrower definition of sustainable management exists under the RMA, a feature of the Halswell-Wigram study was to go beyond the legislative requirements and provide an opportunity for the council to set urban growth in the context of a liveable environment, sustaining natural resources and global sustainability (Briggs and Thomson, 1999). This is being pursued similarly in the development of the much larger South West Area Plan. The planning approach is underpinned by an understanding of ecological systems, significant in Christchurch where surface water and groundwater are critical features of city life and well-being.

The extent of citizen support for the process and underlying principles is yet to be tested. It is often assumed by council practitioners that there is a good fit between the views of a council with those of its residents on concepts of sustainability. However, the application of the sustainability paradigm to cities can be problematic from a social science perspective (Perkins and Thorns, 1999; Thorns, 2002). While there is unquestionably a strong focus in this case on environmental sustainability, the social dimension will need specific attention and strengthening as a critical element of sustainable development.

SEA process

Several principles that are representative of good SEA practice can be observed in the range and type of plans and the processes put in place by council staff to develop them. The principles referred to here will be found across several types of plans, both statutory and non-statutory, reflecting current New Zealand practice. For example, *screening* and *scoping* will take place in all the plans (see Table 11.1) and especially in the area plan and the city plan, given their particular functions. It is useful to reiterate that, apart from the city plan that will be amended much later in the planning process, the initial documents prepared for South West Christchurch are non-statutory. Furthermore, there is, in effect, no independent *review* process. The only formal appraisal, other than legal reviews undertaken by the Environment Court, is that recorded in the Section 32 *reports* prepared by councils.

Table 11.1 *Evaluation of SEA of land use plans in New Zealand*

Criterion	Criterion met	Comments
		SYSTEM CRITERIA
Legal basis	▲	SEA provided for on limited basis in Resource Management Act (RMA); occurring increasingly informally in planning practice
Integration	■	SEA is provided for in RMA plan preparation process; integration with other non-statutory and Local Government Act (LGA) plans occurring in practice
Guidance	▲	Limited for Section 32 reports; more extensive for plan making generally
Coverage	▲	Legal requirements to prepare environmental assessments of policies (Section 32 reports)
Tiering	■	Formally in RMA; informally in respect of other non-statutory local government plans (such as structure plans)
Sustainable development	▲	RMA provides for sustainable management of natural and physical resources; LGA promotes a sustainable development approach by local authorities
		PROCESS CRITERIA
Alternatives	■	Policy alternatives in RMA plans have to be considered; also carried out in other non-statutory local government plans

Table 11.1 *Evaluation of SEA of land use plans in New Zealand (continued)*

Criterion	Criterion met	Comments
Screening	▲	RMA plans required to identify and address environmental issues so screening process takes place in plan preparation
Scoping	▲	As screening
Prediction/ evaluation	▲	Occurs within plan making but not formally required; dependent on internal council practices
Additional impacts	▲	RMA requires consideration but not done well in practice
Report preparation	▲	No independent appraisal report is required, other than Section 32 report prepared by council staff
Review	▲	No independent body for reviews, unless matter is taken on appeal to Environment Court
Monitoring	■	Monitoring of policies required explicitly by the RMA and unsystematically included in plans. Reporting on community outcomes in long term council community plans now required by LGA
Mitigation	▲	Occurs in implementation of plans via resource consent process
Consultation and public participation	■	Strong emphasis on consultation and public participation in RMA and LGA plans
		OUTCOME CRITERIA
Decision making	▲	Difficult to discern extent of influence given wide number of parties and other factors involved in decision-making process
Costs and benefits	?	Diffuse nature and mix of formal and informal practices makes it difficult to discern costs and benefits of SEA generally; but benefits likely to be perceived as outweighing costs in specific cases
Environmental quality	?	Many factors influence whether plans and their appraisals result in improved environmental quality so very difficult to determine; would have to be assessed on case-by-case basis
System monitoring	▲	In respect of formal RMA plans and LGA long-term council community plans only

Notes: ■ – Yes
▲ – Partially
□ – No
? – Don't know

It is too soon to determine in any systematic way the effectiveness of the plans and processes being put in place, as it will be decades before the South West Christchurch area is fully developed. Much can happen between concept and implementation, as occurred in the Halswell-Wigram area (above). However, the inclusion of these principles suggests that formal documentation, such as changes to the city plan and the Section 32 reports that will be produced and tested later in the statutory planning process, should be well informed and technically robust.

Looking ahead, formal *monitoring* of policies in the city plan relevant to South West Christchurch will be undertaken as required by the RMA. A second, much broader form of monitoring will also take place under the LGA. This requires that the council reports on the achievement of identified community outcomes in the long term council community plan at least once every three years. *Mitigation* of the environmental effects of development in the South West area will occur through the resource consent process under the ambit of the city plan.

Three aspects of SEA are worthy of specific attention. The first is the focus on *alternatives*. As already noted, performance against this criterion has always been a weak feature of the New Zealand approach to EA. However, both the area and structure plans have a strong focus on the consideration of options. For example, the purpose of the area plan is to generate land use options, opportunities and constraints, and implications for physical and community infrastructure.

The initial investigations are being carried out in four phases. Phase 1 comprises technical studies which inform the development of three documents in Phase 2, an integrated catchment management plan, a 'greenprint' and a statement of issues. A greenprint is defined as the minimum area needed to be kept free from development in order to protect important natural, cultural, spiritual and heritage values (Christchurch City Council, 2003). It will identify non-negotiable areas for development and other constraints, and assist in generating land use options. The greenprint is a further development of the methodological approach used in the Halswell-Wigram study.

Phase 3 reviews and analyses the investigations and studies with a view to producing the area plan, which will present a preferred land use option, in Phase 4. Similarly, the structure plans developed as part of implementation will be derived by testing the alternative concepts arising out of the preferred land use option identified in the area plan. Structure plans in this context will show physical features such as roads, reserves, other land use features, surface water management requirements and cost share information for stakeholders.

The strong focus on consideration of options should reduce the prospects for market driven traditional approaches to infrastructure provision and open up possibilities for the implementation of low-impact design solutions. The council is known nationally, for example, for the innovative work it has undertaken in riparian restoration and stream naturalization (Christchurch City Council, 1999). In addition, the South West study forms one of several case studies in a major research programme on the implementation of low impact design and development techniques (Eason et al, in press).

The second aspect is the strong emphasis on environmental *evaluation* in several of the key phases of preparation, particularly Phase 3. This has already been noted in respect of the production of a greenprint which will outline the areas within SouthWest Christchurch where development cannot occur, and where it can occur under appropriate conditions. The subsequent structure and development plans will provide more detailed guidance on how physical development might take place, constraints, opportunities, and so on. The various technical studies underway in Phase 1 will provide an important baseline for the overall evaluation.

While consideration of *additional impacts* is formally required by the RMA, they do not generally receive much explicit attention in plan preparation. However, this emphasis on evaluation should enable a more systematic assessment of cumulative effects to occur than is usually the case in New Zealand planning practice.

The third aspect is that of *consultation and public participation.* There are likely to be two key points where the wider community is given opportunities to influence development. First, informal consultation will be undertaken during the development of the area plan and, second, there will be statutory opportunities when changes are notified to the city plan. A consultation plan will be developed which draws on the council's draft 'consultation kit', along with a preliminary list of stakeholders. The kit outlines tasks and probing questions for staff undertaking consultation which are designed to clarify objectives, process, feedback, resourcing needs and evaluation at the end of the process. In addition, a separate process will be undertaken with the local iwi (tribe), Ngai Tahu.

A key challenge for the council will be to maintain the active engagement of its various communities over a long period of time, as experience shows that there is a constant turnover of participants (both citizens and council staff) during consultation undertaken in processes of this nature. Inevitably, consultation processes will also contain a strong component of education as citizens both inform and are informed throughout the period of development. Long-term commitment to the principles underpinning the area plan by both the council and its many communities will be critical for its successful implementation.

Conclusion

The case study suggests some substantive developments in SEA practice in New Zealand that have emerged in the context of both national institutional arrangements and local planning innovations. Firstly, the nature of the land use planning that is being undertaken is more detailed and prescriptive than that envisaged by those promoting the RMA in its early years, when government-led rhetoric demanded minimum intervention on the part of local councils. Yet, secondly, it can be regarded as a systematic response to the need for comprehensive assessment and evaluation to meet the requirements of an effects-based planning mandate and of associated critical legal tests. Thirdly, the methodological approach developed through the tiering of specific-purpose plans represents an innovative integration of traditional land use planning and SEA.

While the adoption of the Halswell-Wigram study findings in the Christchurch city plan was compromised significantly by the political process, the experience of undertaking the study was used to underpin and extend the establishment of the process driving the formulation of the South West Christchurch Area Plan. In this sense it represents the implementation of an approach developed conceptually over a period of several years. In shaping the methodology, the planners took on board key principles of sustainable development and ecological issues (particularly those of surface water management) which needed to be managed differently than in the past, as well as traditional land use planning methods.

The result is an example of the systematic application of methods that focus on the achievement of environmental, economic and social outcomes in an integrated way, albeit with a stronger focus on environmental and economic dimensions than social ones. In particular, it is akin to the appraisal process used widely in the UK, from which it was developed (Briggs and Thomson, 1999). However, 'appraisal' is used differently in the New Zealand context where the methodology has been incorporated at the 'front end' of the planning process, rather than carried out as a separate and independent activity.

A risk is that the planning approach could be jeopardized by inadequate consultation and council down-sizing in the implementation phase. The short-term nature of the political process where councillors are elected on a three-year election cycle, and the inevitable tensions that arise between developers, communities and councils in respect of major land use change, remain potential obstacles. However, as a systematic process, it represents a significant development in planning practice that is likely to serve as a benchmark for other similar projects. Not unexpectedly, given the integrated nature of land use planning, SEA does not have a high profile as such. Rather, it informs the strategic approach and mix of methods being used by council staff as they initiate a major programme of land use change.

Finally, in an international context, the Christchurch case shows that a particular set of local planning instruments can be adapted for SEA through good practice and perseverance. While, at face value, it can be difficult readily to discern SEA as a specific activity, evaluation against system and process criteria has shown SEA principles to be important elements underpinning the city's approach to long-term planning in this area. Most importantly, the case has shown that practitioners do not have to rely on legislation to embrace the principles and methods of SEA. What has emerged in Christchurch is a response to local problems influenced by principles in the national planning mandates of the RMA and the LGA, which is also attempting to move well beyond statutory imperatives and grapple with how to put in place a process that will significantly influence land use change over a long period. What can be observed is the development of an integrated approach that incorporates both SEA and land use planning, and should result in a strengthening of both activities. This is characteristic of New Zealand practice (Table 11.1). In the long term, it may be difficult to distinguish the boundaries of SEA and land use planning but, in the short term, SEA appears to be making a difference at the front end of this process.

Notes

1   The Resource Management Act, and other useful documents, can be consulted at www.mfe.govt.nz
2   www.qualityplanning.org.nz

References

Auckland Regional Growth Forum (1999) *A Vision for Managing Growth in the Auckland Region: Auckland Regional Growth Strategy, 2050*, Auckland Regional Growth Forum, Auckland Regional Council, Auckland

Barton, H., Davis, G. and Guise, R. (1995) *Sustainable Settlements: a Guide for Planners, Designers and Developers*, Local Government Management Board, Luton, and University of the West of England, Bristol

Benson-Pope, the Hon. D., Associate Minister for the Environment (2004) 'Improving the Resource Management Act 1991, Cabinet Paper CAB Min (04) 30/10, 13 September, Ministry for the Environment, Wellington

Briggs, L. and Thomson, I. (1999) "Market Forces" or *"The Truman Show"*: which way do we go?', Paper to *New Zealand Planning Institute Conference*, 27–30 April, Hastings

Christchurch City Council (1999) *Waterways and Wetlands Natural Asset Management Strategy, Volume 1*, Christchurch City Council, Christchurch

Christchurch City Council (2003) *Area Planning Protocol*, Internal document, Christchurch City Development Group, Christchurch City Council, Christchurch

Davies, T. (2002) 'Strategic environmental assessment: a decade after the Resource Management Act 1991: a progress report on a study of the perception and integration of SEA in New Zealand', Paper to *International Association for Impact Assessment Conference, The Hague*, IAIA, Fargo, ND

Department of the Prime Minister and Cabinet (2003) *Sustainable Development for New Zealand: Programme of Action*, DPMC, Wellington

Dixon, J. (2002) 'All at SEA?: Strategic environmental assessment in New Zealand', in Marsden, S. and Dovers, S. (eds) *SEA in Australasia*, Federation Press, Annandale, NSW

Dixon, J. (2003) 'Planning in New Zealand: legacy of ambivalence and prospects for repositioning', *Planning Theory and Practice*, vol 4, pp348–353

Eason, C., Dixon, J. and van Roon, M. (in press) 'A transdisciplinary research approach providing a platform for improved urban design, quality of life and biodiverse urban ecosystems', in McDonnell, M., Breuste, J. and Hahs, A. K. (eds) *The Ecology of Cities and Towns: a Comparative Approach*, Cambridge University Press, Cambridge

Ericksen, N., Berke, P., Crawford, J. and Dixon, J. (2001) *Resource Management, Plan Quality and Governance, a Report to Government*, International Global Change Institute, University of Waikato, Hamilton

Ericksen, N., Berke, P., Crawford, J. and Dixon, J. (2004) *Plan-making for Sustainability: the New Zealand Experience*, Ashgate, Aldershot

Fookes, T. (2000) 'Environmental assessment under the RM Act', in Memon, A. and Perkins, H. (eds) *Environmental Planning and Management in New Zealand*, Dunmore Press, Palmerston North

Fookes, T. (2002) *Auckland's Regional Growth Strategy 2050: an Application of Strategic Environmental Assessment*, Working Paper, Department of Planning, University of Auckland, Auckland

Ministry for the Environment (1993) *Section 32: a Guide to Good Practice*, MfE, Wellington

Ministry for the Environment (1994) *Environment 2010 Strategy: a Statement of the Government's Strategy for the Environment*, MfE, Wellington

Ministry for the Environment (2000) *What are the Options? a Guide to using Section 32 of the Resource Management Act*, MfE, Wellington

Morgan, R. K. (1998) *Environmental Impact Assessment: a Methodological Perspective*, Kluwer, Dordrecht

Parliamentary Commissioner for the Environment (2001) *Sustainable Development and New Zealand's Environmental Management Performance: an Interim Summary Based on the Findings of the Parliamentary Commissioner for the Environment's Reports Between 1992 and 2001*, Office of the Parliamentary Commissioner for the Environment, Wellington

Perkins, H. and Thorns, D. (1999) 'Urban sustainability – the basis for renewed urban planning and management project?', Paper to *Royal Society of New Zealand, New Zealand National Commission for UNESCO and Parliamentary Commissioner for the Environment Workshop on Urban Sustainability in New Zealand, October 1998*, Wellington

Thomson, I., Area Development and Planning Team Leader, Planning Strategy Unit, Christchurch City Council (2004), personal communication, 23 March

Thorns, D. C. (2002) *The Transformation of Cities: Urban Theory and Urban Life*, Palgrave Macmillan, Basingstoke

Wood, C. M. (2002) *Environmental Impact Assessment: a Comparative Review*, 2nd edition, Prentice Hall, Harlow

12

Portugal

Maria Rosário Partidário

Introduction

Strategic environmental assessment is still an emerging practice in Portugal. Resistance to its adoption and difficulties with implementation relate more to the characteristics of development decisions, and to the existing institutional context, than to the social and political acceptance of the concept of SEA.

Most development processes in Portugal are driven by project decisions. Policy making is still highly diffuse and non-systematic (and mostly undocumented). Planning at the sectoral level (where documented) lacks specific objectives and drivers and, consequently, effective application. Land use plans are mainly spatial plans, prepared at regional, municipal and urban scales, that specify restrictions and conditions on investments in the relevant areas, rather than indicating locations for development. The largest group of spatial plans consists of urban design plans which have a strongly project-orientated nature. In brief, difficulties with the implementation of SEA in Portugal exist because of a weak strategic planning and decision making culture in which development decisions are essentially taken from a pragmatic project-centred perspective.

There is, however, another reason for the difficulty in fostering SEA in Portugal: the insufficient emphasis given to the integration of environmental issues in sectoral decision making both at the project level and, especially, at the early stages of the policy making and planning processes leading to development. Environmental policy is still operating as a barrier, rather than as an incentive that adds to the value of development actions and processes. In particular, the environmental impact assessment of projects and current nature conservation policy have been responsible for many of the difficulties experienced by the development sectors in their limited attempts to engage in more environmentally benign practices. These difficulties have generated negative attitudes towards further environmental policy initiatives, which are regarded as additional burdens.

Debate about the transposition of Directive 2001/42/EC ('the SEA Directive') (European Commission (EC), 2001) in Portugal, prior to its coming into effect on 21 July 2004, demonstrated both enthusiasm and concern. Enthusiasm was based on recognition of the potential of SEA to add value to those decision processes that involve EIA, since EIA processes can be improved if they are preceded by an earlier assessment that provides a broader contextual framework for project EIA. Concern arose because of a lack of definition of how SEA would operate and how it would link to, and influence, project EIA. Neither the national government nor the environmental authorities, particularly the EIA authority, had specified the nature of the broad system for impact assessment that would bring together SEA and EIA by mid-2005. Other sectoral authorities appeared to be awaiting further instructions because responsibility for SEA at higher levels of government decision making remained undefined.

Given this situation, it is not surprising that current SEA practice is basically non-existent. Only a handful of SEAs have been undertaken in Portugal and there was neither any public involvement nor any review by public authorities in these assessments. Most of these SEAs were either environmental baseline studies that formed part of planning design proposals, or involved the assessment of very large projects in which the project perspective was maintained only at the cost of correspondingly large and complex studies. It should be noted, on the other hand, that what is sometimes called SEA in other countries, namely the assessment of site or other project alternatives, has been carried out in Portugal under the project EIA requirements since 2000, with practice dating back to the mid-1990s.

In these circumstances, it would be misleading to present details and case studies of the very limited practical application of SEA in Portugal. Rather, this chapter analyses the context for the application of SEA to land use planning in Portugal and the challenges facing its future development. It also addresses the steps that have already been initiated in relation to formal guidance for land use planning and SEA, and concludes by commenting on the policy and institutional context for the implementation of SEA in Portugal.

Context

The Portuguese Land Use Planning Act 1998[1] ('the Land Use Planning Act') provides the basis for land use planning and urban development policy in Portugal. It defines policy objectives, key land use planning principles[2] and the land use planning system (termed the 'territorial management system'). The land use planning system is a hierarchical structure with national, regional and municipal levels. Four types of planning instrument are defined: those of a strategic nature; sectoral policies having spatial definition; those of a special nature; and those of a planning and regulatory nature.

The Land Use Planning Act regulations[3] established the requirements for the different plans prepared under the land use planning system. They describe the concept and general objectives of the different plans; the institutional responsibilities for formulating the plans; the contents of the plans; the institutional

Table 12.1 *Types and characteristics of statutorily defined land use plans in Portugal*

Type of plan	Purpose	Scale
Sectoral plan	Programmatic plan of sectoral policies with spatial implications	National/regional
Special plan	Protection of natural resources	National/regional
Regional land use plan	Strategic direction for regional planning based on territorial model, on regional transport and services networks and on framework for municipal plans	Regional
Inter-municipal plan	Non-binding, strategic plan agreed between different territorial areas	Sub-regional/ municipal
Master municipal plan	Based on local development strategy, sets spatial structure and classification of land use	Municipal
Urban development plan	Organization of urban space of parts of municipal area	Municipal
Urban design plan	Detailed use of any part of municipal area	Municipal

Source: Land Use Planning Act Regulations[3]

consultation and review processes prior to plan approval; the requirements for public involvement; and the mechanism for approval of the plans. Table 12.1 summarizes the purpose and the scale of each type of Portuguese land use plan.

Existing regulations do not stipulate the technical methodology for land use plan preparation, nor is there any formal guidance about suggested planning methodologies in Portugal. There are no regulations relating to processes and procedures for plan monitoring, quality control or follow-up of plan implementation. The process of plan formulation prior to submission to the formal approval procedures is therefore not standardized. It is consequently not surprising that current planning practice complies with the planning regulations on approval requirements and procedures, but does not employ uniform planning methodologies. The methodological approach adopted is determined mainly by the planning background and practical experience of the planning team working for the authority responsible for plan preparation. Crucially, the methodology adopted (for example, objective-led, problem-solving, programmatic agenda for prioritized projects, and so on) will affect the way SEA engages with planning practice.

For example, the capacity for systematic integration of SEA findings into plan formulation, which is crucial to the success of SEA, varies with the type of planning methodology adopted. Effective integration requires flexibility in planning, clearness about the issues of concern, early participation and consideration of issues, and a willingness to accept alternative views and to reject previous conceptions or stereotypes. Strategic planning, given its nature, would normally encourage such flexibility. In these circumstances, SEA can support planning decisions by providing information on key issues relevant to the decision, suggesting options and discussing alternatives that will help in choosing the most desirable planning options.

Unfortunately, more traditional forms of rational planning often inhibit flexibility during plan preparation. In these circumstances, the capacity of SEA to influence the planning process is limited to the assessment of significant effects, and to the proposing of measures to minimize negative impacts that might have been avoided altogether if there had been an opportunity to think more flexibly during the planning process.

Instruments of a strategic nature are defined at national, regional and local levels. The National Programme for Land Use Planning Policy is currently being developed to establish a national framework for land use planning. Although a few regional land use plans have been prepared under previous legal powers of a prescriptive nature, the new generation of regional plans is expected to have a more strategic focus. Inter-municipal plans are an innovation of the Land Use Planning Act 1998 and, to date, none has been prepared.

Regional and inter-municipal plans will fall under the scope of the SEA Directive (EC, 2001) if (as they inevitably will) these land use plans provide the context for subsequent projects. SEA will eventually play a potentially crucial role in this type of planning by improving the overall quality of plans and helping to integrate environmental concerns within the land use planning framework. Paradoxically, the application of the SEA Directive to the National Programme for Land Use Planning Policy is still unclear, largely because of uncertainty about whether it should be designated as a policy or as a programme.

Sectoral plans are new to the land use planning system and, in general, because of their spatial expression and capacity to induce development, the SEA Directive will also apply to them. Sectoral plans identify development scenarios for different governmental sectors, such as transport and communications, energy and mineral resources, education and training, culture, health, housing, tourism, agriculture, commerce and industry, forestry and the environment. They establish options and objectives for sectoral policy and actions to implement these objectives. They also express sectoral policy in spatial form, and describe its interactions with other sectoral and land use plans. To date, few sectoral plans have been prepared. The roads, energy, forestry, tourism, water resources and infrastructure sectors provide the main examples of sectoral plans that are either completed or currently in preparation.

Special plans have the specific purpose of regulating the protection and enhancement of natural resources and include plans for designated natural protection areas, areas within 500 metres of the coast, and within 500 metres of reservoirs. Previously, the plans for these three types of area, known as environmental plans, were all made under separate regulations. However, in 1998, the Land Use Planning Act brought these plans together in a special group because their principal purpose was environmental protection – as opposed to all the other sectoral, regional and municipal plans, the purpose of which was principally development. Despite their significant role in relation to land use change, the environmental nature of special plans makes it unclear whether they will trigger the national legislation to implement the SEA Directive in Portugal, as the directive does not specify the environment as a sector.

Instruments of a planning and regulatory nature are defined only at the municipal level and include municipal master plans, urban development plans and urban design plans. This broad category of detailed municipal plans is the most numerous, representing about 96 per cent of the land use plans prepared in Portugal[4] (Partidário et al, 2004). This also means that local authorities lead the regional and national authorities in the preparation of land use plans in Portugal.

Master plans are expected to be quite different from other municipal urban plans. Master plans establish the municipal strategy and development framework, while urban development and urban design plans have a more operational focus, providing a context for project design. This difference is important from a SEA perspective. For example, a plan that forms the basis for project design is quite amenable to an EIA-based SEA methodology (the type of SEA that follows a similar methodology to that used for project EIA) (Sadler and Verheem, 1996; Partidário, 2004. However, municipal master plans, which engage with municipal strategy, create opportunities for a more flexible approach to SEA.

The first generation of municipal master plans was developed between 1990 (when regulations for municipal plans were adopted in Portugal) and 1995. Table 12.2 illustrates the rate of approval of municipal plans over the last 13 years (Partidário et al, 2004). Table 12.2 demonstrates that, because it is a legal requirement that master plans be reviewed within a ten-year period, the SEA

Table 12.2 *Number of Portuguese municipal plans approved, 1990–2003*

Year	Master plan	Urban development plan	Urban design plan	Total
1990	1	3	19	23
1991	1	13	37	51
1992	4	24	109	137
1993	22	8	45	75
1994	84	8	37	129
1995	103	5	36	144
1996	8	5	49	62
1997	23	16	58	97
1998	5	13	34	52
1999	10	9	48	67
2000	10	8	30	48
2001	2	8	29	39
2002	6	5	27	38
2003	4	10	23	37
Total	283	135	581	999

Source: Partidário et al (2004)

Directive will affect the preparation of the new generation of municipal master plans about to start the review process.

As indicated in the introduction, there are as yet no examples of formal SEAs of land use plans in Portugal. In the absence of legislation, guidance for the SEA of land use plans was developed by the national authority for land use planning and formally adopted in late 2003. Just before 21 July 2004, when national legislation should have been adopted to comply with the directive, a proposal for a decree on SEA was released for limited consultation. It basically reproduced the requirements of the SEA Directive but, although it proposed the current EIA national authority as the SEA authority, it made no reference to the role or involvement of other sectoral authorities, except for the purpose of institutional consultation. It included the same list of sectors as the directive, but excluded urban development and design plans. There was no linkage to EIA procedures or to other sectoral decision-making and planning procedures.

Even though there is still no formal legislation regarding the SEA of land use plans, or any other form of SEA, responsibilities regarding the promotion and development of SEA have been allocated to the agencies of the ministry responsible for land use planning and the environment. These include the Institute of the Environment, which is the EIA national authority; the Directorate-General for Land Use Planning and Urban Development (Direcção-Geral do Ordenamento do Território e Desenvolvimento Urbano (DGOTDU)), which is the national authority for land use planning; and the various regional commissions for development coordination that administer national environmental and land use planning responsibilities at regional level. The way responsibilities are defined is, however, not explicit, and this is creating confusion about precise SEA responsibilities in Portugal.

Apart from research and training, the only significant Portuguese SEA initiative to date has been the preparation of the *Guidance for Strategic Impact Assessment in Land Use Planning* (DGOTDU, 2003). The following sections explain the context for this guidance and explore the assumptions that led to the choice of SEA model adopted. Pilot SEA applications are currently being carried out by planning teams involved in the review of municipal plans and in the preparation of regional plans.

Case study: national guidance on SEA methodology

Because no sufficiently documented case study of SEA practice in Portugal exists, this section describes the SEA methodology included in the national guidance. The Portuguese guidance on the SEA of land use plans is one of several European examples of guidance on SEA that EU member states have prepared following the promulgation of the SEA Directive (Therivel et al, 2004).

In 2000, DGOTDU commissioned a research team at the New University of Lisbon to develop a methodological approach and associated guidance for the strategic impact assessment of land use plans in Portugal (Partidário, 2002). Official guidance, based on this research, was produced and formally launched in 2003 by the Secretary of State for Land Use Planning (DGOTDU, 2003).

The term 'strategic impact assessment' (strategic IA) was adopted to ensure that a wide range of environmental, social and economic impacts of land use planning and development was included. Planners believed that the name of the methodology should reflect their concern that the use of the term 'environment' would undermine this wider perspective. This does not mean, however, that the environment is not crucial in this approach but rather that a solely environmental focus, isolated from integrated impact and/or sustainable development goals, was felt to be insufficient.

Strategic IA is defined in the guidance as 'a decision support tool with application to strategic decisions, and should be conceived as a systematic approach to the identification, analysis and assessment of impacts, anticipating and facilitating strategic decision-making' (DGOTDU, 2003, p19). Strategic IA is therefore a decision-centred approach that is derived from the concept of SEA being driven by the decision-making process to which it applies, in this case the land use planning process. The terms strategic IA and SEA are thus used interchangeably in this chapter.

The strategic IA methodology was conceived primarily for use by planning teams whose job is to define, formulate and design spatial plans. It was also intended to be useful to planning teams with responsibility for overseeing the effective implementation of spatial plans. It was therefore intended to be used during the planning process as part of the conception, preparation, discussion, approval, implementation and review of spatial plans in Portugal. The guidance is based on a simplified planning process, represented by the inner dark arrows in Figure 12.1. This enables the linkage of the strategic IA methodology to fundamental planning functions, and activities to be understood irrespective of the planning methodology used, or of the scale and level of detail of the plan.

The methodology for strategic IA has two main objectives:

1   To improve the planning process, and the quality of plans, in relation to all relevant spatial parameters, thereby contributing to global sustainability.
2   To ensure compliance with the technical requirements of Directive 2001/42/ EC in the context of the Portuguese legal and institutional framework and administrative procedures.

The strategic IA methodology is designed to be integrated with the planning methodology (that is, to be accommodated in the sequence of planning activities and functions that are normally part of the process of plan making). Only through this close relationship of planning and impact assessment methodologies can strategic IA be effective in assisting the integration of environmental, social and economic concerns in plan preparation and implementation, and thus contribute to sustainable planning.

Figure 12.1 outlines the various components of the strategic IA methodology. It commences with the simplified planning process (the inner ring of black arrows) structured in four phases – analysis of context, scenarios, choice and follow-up – that run through the key cultural, analytical and political components of the planning process. The strategic IA activities are then integrated with the planning

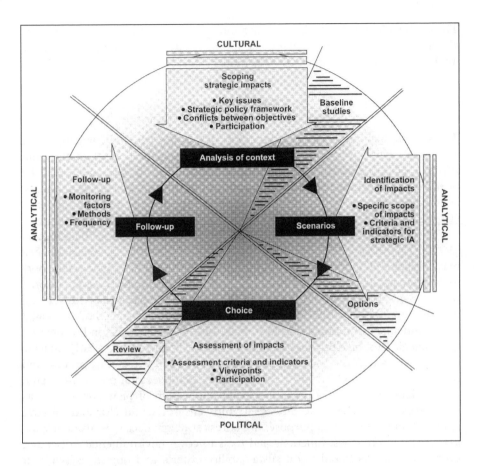

Source: DGOTDU (2003)

Figure 12.1 *The Portuguese strategic impact assessment methodology*

process at four corresponding stages: scoping; identification of impacts; assessment of impacts; and follow-up. Four aspects of the methodology should be noted:

1 Baseline studies are considered to be part of the planning process. Those involved in undertaking such studies should take the issues and priorities identified during the scoping stage of the strategic IA as their starting point
2 Alternatives are a critical component of strategic IA and relate closely to the scenario planning stage and to the consideration of planning options
3 Public participation is a key activity that brings planning and strategic IA objectives together. It must therefore be carried out simultaneously for planning and for strategic IA
4 Follow-up is another stage where planning and strategic IA share common objectives. Professional activities should therefore be undertaken jointly or in close collaboration (DGOTDU, 2003).

The methodology requires the planning and strategic IA tasks and activities to be closely connected. The following sections provide further details about the methodology and the underlying SEA model.

SEA system

The institutional and legal procedures for SEA in Portugal are currently being established. However, previous discussions between sectoral representatives and EIA and planning practitioners concluded that the impact assessment and the planning procedures, while closely connected, should be kept separate. Accordingly, as indicated above, the strategic IA methodology described in the guidance (DGOTDU, 2003) was designed to relate very closely to planning procedures.

The guidance applies to land use plans defined in the Land Use Planning Act 1998 and in the regulations, including regional, special, inter-municipal, municipal master plans and the strategic component of urban master plans. It does not apply to the National Programme for Land Use Planning Policy (which was considered to be a policy) or to sectoral plans, for which responsibility rests with sectoral institutions and not with DGOTDU. Because the guidance is methodological, it does not define institutional responsibilities for undertaking SEA in Portugal.

Strategic IA should be proactive and, as its name implies, have a clearly strategic nature. Strategic IA is expected to act as a facilitator of the planning process and not as an obstacle to it. It must consider all relevant sectoral policy areas and, where plans are part of a hierarchy, avoid duplication of plan assessments as required by the SEA Directive. Strategic IA must ensure a sound, clear and objective approach in relation to its purpose: to address strategic decisions, using impact assessment approaches, functions and tools to cover environmental, social and economic impacts based upon sustainability criteria and objectives (without limiting assessment to environmental issues). The broad coverage of the assessment should be consistent with the scale and scope of the strategic decision to which it applies.

SEA process

The guidance on strategic IA methodology describes four stages of strategic IA activity closely coordinated with the planning process. In this decision-centred SEA approach, the strategic IA process is driven by the logical sequence of the planning process. The formal delineation of a SEA procedure is not dealt with in the guidance, since (as mentioned above) the statutory definition of SEA had not been agreed when it was written.[5]

The guidance suggests alternative approaches to conducting the strategic IA. It indicates that the land use planning team may include professionals with expertise in environmental issues and impact assessment who will be responsible for carrying out the strategic IA and preparing the relevant reports. Alternatively, it suggests that the strategic IA and the land use planning teams may act separately to ensure that greater independence and clear responsibility for each activity are achieved. The management of the strategic IA and the planning teams may therefore be joint or separate. However independent the teams are, they may operate under the same management team if that proves to be convenient from an institutional perspective. In the case of the full separation of teams and management roles, the guidance recommends that the respective team leaders should cooperate closely.

As required by the SEA Directive, the final strategic IA report should be separate from the planning report. However, the guidance suggests that a report should be issued at each of the four stages of the SEA methodology to provide information at key stages of the planning process. These reports should be timely and be able to influence the planning process but not be too long or too complex. Consequently, the timing of the strategic IA process must be in accordance with that of the land use planning process.

When they are delineated, the procedural requirements for applying strategic IA to the planning process, as specified in the planning regulations, should be kept to a minimum. The review of quality in strategic IA, a requirement of the SEA Directive, must be integrated with the assessment of the land use planning proposals to avoid bureaucratic overload. However, it is essential that an independent third party authority be involved in the quality review. Public participation in both the strategic IA and the land use planning processes must be simultaneous. The role of the environmental authorities must be well defined, since their collaboration with the land use planning authorities is indispensable. The participation of all the sectoral authorities with direct responsibility and/or institutional interest in the process must also be ensured, as required by the SEA Directive.

SEA outcome

The intention is that the outcome of strategic IA will influence planning decisions and improve the quality of land use plans in general. This should reduce the costs involved in the process of producing, reviewing and approving the final plans, while generating overall sustainable development benefits.

It is difficult to judge the extent to which these objectives will be achieved prior to SEA becoming routine. However, an indication of the willingness of institutions to adopt particular approaches to SEA can be gained from the views expressed at an inter-sectoral forum held in Portugal on models of SEA to support the implementation of the SEA Directive. The participants emphasized the expected benefits of SEA with respect both to land use and to sectoral decision making. SEA was seen as an instrument that forces the consideration of strategic issues before committing proposed developments to particular areas. In particular, SEA was seen as playing a key role in improving the consideration of ecological and social issues during the preparation of land use plans.

In addition, the roles of SEA in improving the conditions for carrying out the EIA of development projects, and in improving the preparation and development of land use plans that currently give very little consideration to environmental and social issues, were emphasized. Key features of SEA that were regarded as crucial in improving planning practice included:

- the consideration of planning alternatives;
- the assessment of alternatives against a wider range of parameters;
- earlier public participation;
- the justification of the planning options adopted;
- effective monitoring of plan implementation and review/consideration of unexpected or uncertain impacts.

Conclusion

The absence of formal requirements for SEA, and of SEA practice, has prevented a thorough assessment of the Portuguese SEA system, process and outcome. The content of this chapter has, therefore, necessarily been limited to the contextual issues associated with the implementation of SEA in Portugal. Table 12.3 summarizes the Portuguese SEA situation by anticipating how Directive 2001/42/EC might be implemented.

Table 12.3 *Evaluation of SEA of land use plans in Portugal*

Criterion	Criterion met	Comments
		SYSTEM CRITERIA
Legal basis	☐	Formal national legal provisions not yet adopted
Integration	▲	Land use planning system has potential to provide for early integration of SEA in plan preparation, as recommended in existing guidance
Guidance	■	Formal guidance issued but no evidence of application yet available
Coverage	■	Regional, special, sectoral, inter-municipal and municipal master plans covered by existing guidance
Tiering	?	When in place, expected that SEA system will link to EIA system
Sustainable development	?	Even though SEA system not in place, expected it will form part of National Sustainable Development Strategy framework
		PROCESS CRITERIA
Alternatives	▲	Should be at least partially met, since required by SEA Directive
Screening	▲	Should be at least partially met, since required by SEA Directive

Table 12.3 *Evaluation of SEA of land use plans in Portugal (continued)*

Criterion	Criterion met	Comments
Scoping	▲	Scoping is key major activity during early stages of SEA process in strategic IA methodology
Prediction/evaluation	▲	Prediction and evaluation expected to take place along with scenarios and options discussion in planning in strategic IA methodology
Additional impacts	▲	Should be at least partially met, since required by SEA Directive
Report preparation	▲	Should be at least partially met, since required by SEA Directive
Review	▲	Should be at least partially met since required by SEA Directive and recommended in current guidance
Monitoring	▲	Should be at least partially met, since required by SEA Directive and recommended in current guidance
Mitigation	?	Issue still to be defined but should be at least partially met, since required by Directive
Consultation and public participation	▲	Should be at least partially met, since required by SEA Directive and recommended in current guidance
	OUTCOME CRITERIA	
Decision making	?	No system yet in place
Costs and benefits	?	No system yet in place
Environmental quality	?	No system yet in place
System monitoring	▲	Should be at least partially met since required by SEA Directive and recommended in current guidance

Notes: ■ – Yes
  ▲ – Partially
  □ – No
  ? – Don't know

The variety of planning practices existing in Portugal, and the resistance of planners to following standardized methodological processes, is likely to create difficulties both in the adaptation of planning procedures to SEA requirements and in the adoption of the methodology for the SEA of land use plans outlined in the published guidance (DGOTDU, 2003). The key conclusions from the inter-sectoral forum on the EIA of plans and programmes provide a useful summary of the main concerns about the implementation of Directive 2001/42/EC in Portugal. These were that a Portuguese SEA system should:

- consider all the dimensions of sustainable development – environmental, social and economic – in an integrated way;
- follow a planning culture of a strategic, not a project orientated, nature;
- ensure that the public participate in ways appropriate to the consideration of strategic issues;
- ensure that the assessment is independent by using third party reviewers with the necessary expertise in strategic decision processes;
- result from cross-sectoral interaction to define assessment processes and issues of concern that are appropriate to different sectors and decision levels;
- ensure that SEA is operationalized by avoiding conflicts of interest between development sectors;
- be assisted by institutional capacity building within the different sectors involved in SEA to implement changes in institutional paradigms;
- be based on a clarification of the relationship between SEA and project EIA, particularly with respect to its duration, scope and focus;
- avoid repeating the mistakes and difficulties associated with the implementation of EIA in Portugal;
- be implemented under the leadership of a national authority that delivers the independence and inter-disciplinarity necessary for effective implementation, notwithstanding the number of sectors covered by the SEA Directive.

Notes

1 Portuguese Land Use Planning Act 1998 (Law 48/98 of 11 August 1998)
2 Including sustainability, economy, coordination, sovereignty, equity, participation, responsibility, public–private partnerships and legal safety
3 Land Use Planning Act Regulations (Decree 380/99 of 22 September 1999)
4 These figures are derived from a review of the type and number of plans and programmes likely to require SEA under the requirements of Directive 2001/42/EC (Partidário et al, 2004)
5 'Process' and 'procedure' are different in the guidance. Process consists of a series of actions that constitute the strategic IA methodology. Procedure relates to the formal institutional requirements (which are not yet in place). In the Portuguese guidance, the decision-centred SEA process is closely coordinated with the land use planning process, while the SEA and the land use planning procedures are assumed to be clearly differentiated

References

Direcção-Geral do Ordenamento do Território e Desenvolvimento Urbano (2003) *Guia para Avaliação Estratégica de Impactes em Ordenamento do Território*, Ministério das Cidades, Ordenamento do Território e Ambiente – Direcção-Geral do Ordenamento do Território e Desenvolvimento Urbano, Lisboa (An English translation, *Guidance for Strategic Impact Assessment in Portugal*, will be available on CD-ROM from DGOTDU)

European Commission (2001) 'Directive 2001/42/EC of the European Parliament and of the Council of 27 June 2001 on the assessment of the effects of certain plans and programmes on the environment', *Official Journal of the European Communities*, vol L197, pp30–37, 21 July

Partidário, M. R. (2002) *Proposta para um Guia sobre a Metodologia de Avaliação Estratégica de Impactes de Planos de Ordenamento do Território em Portugal*, Relatório de projecto não publicado, Faculdade de Ciências e Tecnologia – Universidade Nova de Lisboa, Lisboa (An English version entitled *Strategic Impact Assessment for Spatial Planning – Methodological Guidance for Application in Portugal* is available on CD-ROM from the author.)

Partidário, M. R. (2004) 'La valutazione di strategie per uno sviluppo urbano ed ambientale sostenibile' (Evaluation of strategies for urban and rural sustainable development), in Girard, L. F. and Nijkamp, P. (eds) *Energia, Belezza, Partecipazione: la Sfida della Sostenibilità: Valutazioni Integrate tra Conservazione e Sviluppo*, Franco Angeli, Milano (in Italian)

Partidário, M. R., Coelho, M. J. and Augusto, B. (2004) 'Analysis of the potential scope for the implementation of Directive 2001/42/CE in Portugal', *Proceedings of the Workshop on Models for Environmental Impact Assessment of Plans and Programmes in Portugal*, Annex I, Associação Portuguesa de Avaliação de Impactes, Lisboa (in Portuguese)

Sadler, B. and Verheem, R. (1996) *Strategic Environmental Assessment: Status, Challenges and Future Directions*, Publication Number 53, Ministry of Housing, Spatial Planning and the Environment, The Hague

Therivel, R., Caratti P., Partidário, M. R., Theodorsdóttir, A. H. and Tyldesley, D. (2004) 'Writing strategic environmental assessment guidance', *Impact Assessment and Project Appraisal*, vol 22, pp259–270

13

South Africa

Nigel Rossouw and Francois Retief

Introduction

Since the arrival of European settlers in 1652, segregation and unequal development has characterized South African society. Segregationist policies resulted in black South Africans being dispossessed from their land and moved into overcrowded and impoverished reserves, homelands and townships. From the 1940s, systematic and radical forms of segregationist policies emerged, which became known as apartheid. These racially based land policies were a cause of landlessness amongst black people. Dispossession and forced removal resulted not only in the physical separation of people along racial lines, but extreme land shortages and insecurity of tenure (Lahiff, 2001, 2003). It also resulted in inefficient urban and rural land use patterns and a fragmented system of land administration (Aliber and Mokoena, 2003).

Apartheid acts and policies codified the distribution of South Africa's natural resource wealth along racial lines (Reed, 2003) and resulted in different standards of municipal services for the racially separated areas (Hanekom et al, 1987; Khan, 2002). Since 1923, black people were kept out of, or removed from, white urban areas through the use of pass laws. Until the 1990s, it was government policy that black people should not own land. Consequently, the majority of the population was squeezed into the urban townships and black homeland areas. This resulted in poverty and extreme pressure on the land (Department of Land Affairs (DLA), 1997). The backlog caused by these restrictions has created a pressing need for access to urban land. Because of the premium on land close to city centres, the poor are forced to live in informal settlements in peri-urban areas. In most of these informal settlements, tenure is insecure (DLA, 1999).

Apartheid planning was integrally linked to the concept of blueprint or master planning as the favoured planning approach. Planning was mainly focused on physical planning and land use control to promote the spatial ordering of land. The manipulation of the physical environment to foster orderly, racially separate and unequal development was the prime objective of plan making (Ministry of

Agriculture and Land Affairs (MLA), 2001). Public participation in planning under apartheid was limited, mainly providing the opportunity to raise issues after draft plans had been prepared. After 1994, planning became a central function for strategic decision making at all spheres of government, rather than being a sectoral function of spatial planning departments. This change is contributing to institutional transformation, and is encouraging accountability and transparency in decision making and more participative forms of governance. Planning in South Africa has thus shifted from traditional forms of land use control to normative forms of planning.

During the apartheid era, environmental input into planning was not prescribed and therefore received minimal attention. South Africa's history of environmental assessment practice dates back to the 1970s. Initially, environmental assessment was conducted largely separately from planning procedures. The first legislated environmental impact assessment (EIA) requirement came into effect in 1997 but it excluded provision for SEA (Wood, 2002). EIA continued to be poorly linked to planning. Acknowledgement of EIA's lack of integration with planning procedures, alongside the recognition of other limitations of the process, led to the emergence of SEA in South Africa during the 1990s. This chapter outlines the nature of SEA practice in South Africa and describes how the process is being applied to contribute to the resolution of planning and development challenges.

Context

Elections in 1994 marked South Africa's peaceful transition to democracy and ushered in a new era of accountability in policy making systems. Because land use issues in South Africa are closely tied with addressing historical injustices, key issues that the planning system seeks to address include:

- the need for equitable distribution of land ownership;
- the provision of services to communities in an environmentally sustainable manner;
- the provision of a healthy environment for all citizens;
- security of tenure;
- a system of management that supports sustainable land use patterns (DLA, 1997, 1999; MLA, 2001).

The planning system in South Africa encompasses land reform, spatial planning and municipal planning. Economic programmes and the environmental assessment policy system also have distinct implications for the planning system. Because planning policy and practice prior to 1994 led to racial segregation, it is not surprising that most of South Africa's planning policies have a spatial component that aims to promote spatial integration and the equitable distribution of natural resources.

Land reform

The aims and objectives of South Africa's land policies and legislation include redressing the racial imbalance in landholding and improving the livelihoods of the poor (Lahiff, 2001). They also include dealing with the past injustices of land dispossession, contributing towards poverty eradication and promoting economic growth (Booysen and Erasmus, 1998). The White Paper on South African Land Policy (DLA, 1997) emphasizes the links between land use, poverty and environmental degradation. It stresses the need to incorporate environmental issues into project planning. The focus of the land policy is the land reform programme, which has three components: land redistribution; land restitution; and land tenure reform. Land redistribution aims to provide the disadvantaged in urban and rural areas with access to land for residential and agricultural purposes. Land restitution involves returning land or compensating people from whom land was forcibly removed after 1913. Land tenure aims to bring everyone occupying land under a unitary legal system of landholding to provide for secure land tenure (DLA, 1997).

DLA has recognized that land resources need to be utilized sustainably so that inequality and poverty are reduced (Turner, 2001). Implementation of land reform projects in South Africa initially resulted in unintended negative impacts on the natural resource base. Because of these initial negative experiences, DLA acknowledged that land reform cannot be sustainable without proactively taking account of environmental constraints. Administrative policy and guideline documents for the integration of environmental tools into the land reform and land development programme were therefore prepared (DLA, 2001a, b). The policy and the guidelines are based on the principle that land reform and sustainable livelihoods are dependent on integrated planning of natural resources.

Spatial planning and land use management

The national policy on spatial planning (MLA, 2001), reflected in the Land Use Bill,[1] is intended to provide a uniform, effective and efficient framework for spatial planning and land use management in urban and rural areas. The intention of this policy is to rationalize the plethora of planning laws inherited from the apartheid era into one national system to achieve the objective of sustainable land use. The policy specifies that each province and municipality must compile a spatial development framework (SDF) which should have a SEA component. SDFs show desired patterns of land use, directions of growth, urban edges, special development areas and conservation areas. The policy also requires that every municipality must have a land use management system in place, which should include a scheme recording the rights and restrictions applicable to land in the municipal area.

Municipal planning

The Municipal Systems Act[2] establishes a framework for community participation in planning and specifies that municipal services must be environmentally sustainable. It has a number of obligations for environmental management, which must be accommodated in the institutional framework developed by the local government authority. These include:

- striving to ensure that municipal services are provided to the local community in a financially and environmentally sustainable manner;
- promoting a safe and healthy environment in the municipality.

The Municipal Systems Act also requires local government to engage in a new form of planning, termed integrated development planning (IDP). The central aims of IDP are to provide a holistic, integrated and participatory strategic plan guiding the work of the municipality (Department of Provincial and Local Government and German Agency for Technical Co-operation, 2001). The Municipal Planning Regulations[3] state that the SDF, which forms an integral part of a municipality's IDP must 'contain a strategic assessment of the environmental impact of the spatial development framework' (Section 4(f)). The guidelines for IDP implementation mention the need to consider environmental issues, but provide no guidance on how environmental issues should be addressed. The Department of Environmental Affairs and Tourism (DEAT) recognized this need and published guidelines describing methods for integrating environmental sustainability issues into the local planning process (DEAT, 2002).

Spatial economic programmes

The Department of Trade and Industry is promoting two key economic programmes, which have defined geographical impacts, spatial development initiatives (SDIs) and industrial development zones (IDZs). The aim of IDZs is to consolidate manufacturing industries for export. Examples are the Coega IDZ near Port Elizabeth and the West Bank IDZ in East London. Both these IDZs have been subject to SEA. SDIs aim to leverage investment for job creation, infrastructure development and socioeconomic regeneration. An example of a SDI is the Maputo Development Corridor, which links the Gauteng and Mpumalanga Provinces with Mozambique. A SEA was undertaken during the preparation of this SDI, and one of its key outputs was a strategic environmental management plan (SEMP).

Environmental assessment

The National Environmental Management Act (NEMA)[4] is a framework law, providing overarching principles that apply to all state activities. NEMA provides for the development of cooperative governance structures and for integrated environmental management (IEM) and EIA procedures. The term IEM indicates an approach that integrates environmental considerations into all stages of the planning and development cycle for policies, programmes, plans and projects (Sowman et al, 1995). NEMA provides a legal framework for IEM, which was introduced in 1989 as a voluntary measure and included application to policies and plans. It was originally intended that IEM and planning procedures would be integrated but separate processes and decision making procedures were subsequently developed. When the statutory 1997 EIA requirements excluded policies and plans, the opportunity to integrate environmental issues into all the stages of the policy, planning and project cycle was lost.

SEA system

At present, there is no codified SEA legislation within South Africa. The SEA system, however, is supported by planning policy (MLA, 2001), by the Municipal Planning Regulations and by the Land Use Bill that require SEA to be undertaken as part of the process of developing SDFs, and by guidelines (DEAT, 2000). According to Wiseman (2000), SEA has emerged in South Africa because of three key issues:

1   the widespread recognition of the limitations of project-specific EIA;
2   the lack of integration of environmental tools and issues into planning;
3   the new approaches to planning, which recognized environmental sustainability as the fundamental basis for planning.

Whereas the policy on spatial planning (MLA, 2001), the Land Use Bill and the Municipal Planning Regulations advocate the use of SEA, none defines how SEA should be applied. The NEMA Amendment Act 2004[5] makes provision for the promulgation of SEA regulations (not activated by mid-2005) but NEMA does not provide sufficient detail to guide SEA application. Generic guidance for SEA in South Africa is provided by guidelines published by the Department of Environmental Affairs and Tourism (DEAT, 2000). The DEAT guidance is not part of either the environmental policy or the legal systems, and is unfortunately not being actively promoted. The Department of Water Affairs and Forestry (2001) has also produced SEA guidance for managing water use in catchments.

The SEA guidance states that the purpose of SEA is to promote biophysical, social and economic sustainability through the incorporation of environmental issues at an early stage of plan and programme preparation. The SEA approach described in the guidance is based on three key concepts, namely that SEA is context specific, sustainability-led and integrative (DEAT, 2000). Since spatial development frameworks form an integral part of IDPs and other strategic plans prepared to satisfy sectoral legislation, the requirement to undertake SEA during the preparation of provincial and municipal SDFs could have far reaching implications. SEA may thus be given the opportunity to influence strategic decisions within a wide range of sectors. Despite the lack of clear guidance, SEA practice in South Africa has increased steadily since the early 1990s. SEA practice has tended to be varied, flexible and responsive to the different decision making contexts in which it is applied (Table 13.1). Despite the provision for the process in planning policy and legislation, most SEAs have been undertaken voluntarily.

Table 13.1 *Examples of SEAs linked to South African planning system*

SEA case studies	Purpose of SEA
SEAs applied to municipal planning (i.e. integrated development planning)	
Empangeni Transitional Local Council (2001)	To provide an environmental information base, guidelines for decision making and a system to streamline EIA
uMhlathuze Municipality (2002)	To develop an environmental management framework for decision making and ensure that environmental issues were integrated into IDP process
Richards Bay Transitional Local Council (2000)	To provide environmental information for strategic planning and decision making for future industrial development
SEAs applied to spatial planning	
Northern Metropolitan Council (1997)	To inform a strategic planning framework to ensure that environmentally sensitive areas were protected and areas unsuitable for development were identified
Cato Manor Draft Structure Plan (1998)	To assess biophysical impacts of structure plan. In practice, it identified costs and benefits which might result from development in area and informed design of open space system
North West Province Spatial Development Framework (2003)	To integrate the concept of sustainability into plan making, set limits of acceptable change and identify environmental opportunities. In practice, it also facilitated improvement of EIA practice
SEAs applied to infrastructure programmes	
Klipgat A Tenure Upgrading Project (2002)	To develop a strategic environmental management plan for township establishment and associated infrastructure and to streamline EIA decision making processes
Itsoseng Redevelopment Programme (2002)	To address environmental issues early in programme formulation and to implement SEA as part of settlement programme
Kgalagadi Cross Border Municipality (2002)	To incorporate environmental issues early in plan and programme formulation as part of rural redevelopment
SEAs applied to economic programmes having a defined spatial area of application	
Coega Industrial Development Zone	To ensure that environmental issues were addressed early in planning stages of IDZ. In practice, SEA assessed opportunities and constraints for development. Principles and detailed guidelines were proposed to facilitate ongoing management and review of development

Table 13.1 *Examples of SEAs linked to the South African planning system (continued)*

SEA case studies	Purpose of SEA
	proposals. A spatial framework for development was also proposed
East London Industrial Development Zone	To ensure that environmental issues were addressed early in planning stages of IDZ. In practice, SEA formed part of feasibility studies and assessed opportunities and constraints for development. A strategic environmental management plan was prepared to facilitate ongoing management and review of development proposals
Maputo Development Corridor	To prepare a strategic environmental management plan to guide management of future development. In practice, SEA incorporated environmental and social objectives into economic policy and investment decisions

SEA process

South Africa does not implement SEA according to a standard, legally prescribed, process. The South African SEA guidance (DEAT, 2000) does, however, recommend that the SEA principles and processes should be tailored for specific contexts to ensure their relevance and viability when undertaking SEA. Flexibility is the key message. Despite the document not forming part of the formal policy system, it has shaped the processes of a number of SEAs at plan and programme level (Rossouw et al, 2000; Retief, 2003).

Retief et al (2004) undertook a preliminary review of SEAs conducted in South Africa between 1996 and 2003, and identified a total of 50 studies (see Figure 13.1). Only studies specifically called SEAs were considered. The number of SEAs conducted is surprising, especially considering the voluntary nature of SEA in South Africa. It is evident that SEA is well established, and practice is expected to increase dramatically when government institutions stabilize and start responding to the SEA provisions in the planning legislation. This potential increase in SEA practice in the wake of legislative reforms will necessitate the development of effective screening mechanisms and the promotion of integrative approaches rather than a reliance on more resource intensive EIA-based approaches to SEA.

Retief et al (2004) categorized SEA according to whether it was undertaken at policy, plan or programme (PPP) level, but this was not as simple as it seems. SEAs were found which were not specifically linked to decision-making processes at the PPP level. Only 64 per cent of the case studies (32) could be classified in the traditional manner as being PPP SEAs. Of these, the large majority were plan SEAs (27). Significantly, very few SEAs were formally integrated with PPP decision-making processes. Rather, they were undertaken in a parallel process to inform decision making at a later stage in the PPP preparation process. Few

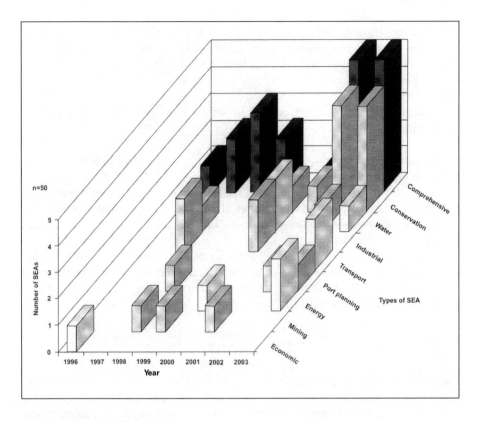

Source: Retief et al (2004)

Figure 13.1 *The nature of SEA practice in South Africa, 1996–2003*

examples existed where tiering arrangements between SEA and EIA were specified in the SEA report.

The SEAs not directly linked to decision-making processes appeared to fill a void between policy requirements and project level implementation. They effectively provided a strategic basis for project decision making.

The main SEA approach adopted was to assess the capacity and status of the resource base (Retief et al, 2004). In many cases, the SEAs functioned as a process that used various tools and techniques – for example, limits of acceptable change, sustainability criteria, environmental indicators and opportunities and constraints analysis) to establish a decision making framework that aimed to identify what strategic choices to pursue and what the trade-offs between certain decisions would be.

Examples of SEA practice at all tiers exist, but only one policy level assessment was identified for the period under consideration. The classification of SEA types presented in Figure 13.1 (adapted from Therivel and Partidário, 1996; Annandale et al 2001) used two broad categories, namely 'sectoral' and 'comprehensive'. Sectoral SEAs are those where the focus of the assessment was on water, conservation, mining, industrial, transport, economic development, and so on. Comprehensive SEAs are those where all activities in a defined area are considered, and where the outputs of the SEA will help to guide future development. Of the total sample, sectoral case studies constituted 62 per cent, while 38 per cent were comprehensive.

Some of the key findings from this preliminary review of the SEA processes utilized in South Africa included:

- Scoping relied on public participation as a means for stakeholders to identify strategic issues
- In certain cases, the SEAs did not include separate participation processes but linked into, or used the outcomes of, the IDP participation process
- State of the environment reporting (SOER) was used to gather and present environmental data
- SEAs developed a sustainability framework that consisted of sustainability objectives, criteria and indicators, against which assessments could be calibrated
- A number of SEAs focused on the preparation of a SEMP for ongoing management and monitoring.

Case studies

Planning policies require that SEAs be conducted for SDFs, while the IDP guidelines recommend that environmental issues be integrated into the planning policy process. Despite these formal provisions, no example could be found where a SEA was triggered because of the specific requirements of planning policy. However, there are examples of planning processes that contain elements and characteristics of SEA, but which were not called SEAs. Distinct SEA processes did not form part of these planning processes.

However, it could be argued that good planning practice would not require SEA, because it already achieves what SEA sets out to do. The case study of the Lower Breede River (see Box 13.1) provides an example of an integrative approach to planning in Western Cape Province, where economic, social, biophysical and heritage resources and issues were analysed holistically, and the findings used as the basis for developing a SDF. In other cases, SEA has been applied to planning procedures and can be recognized as a distinct process with defined outputs, as in the case study of the uMhlathuze Municipality (see Box 13.2). In these cases, SEA seems to have been triggered where planning was weak or where specific environmental issues needed to be addressed.

The two case studies were not selected to make a comparative analysis of their processes. Rather, the case studies were chosen to illustrate the point that SEA should be tailored to fit the context to which it is being applied. A SEA process, or elements of SEA procedures, should fit into locally defined approaches for planning and decision making. The issue is not whether one approach is better than another, but whether the approach responds to locally defined needs and processes. Debate should not solely focus on process, but rather on whether a framework for sustainable development was provided. The main goal of SEA should be adding value to decision making, but the type and manner of the approach can differ.

Integrative planning approach with elements of SEA

This case study illustrates a planning process in which SEA elements can be recognized. For example, the planning process was integrative (it considered the full range of environmental issues in conjunction with social and economic factors) and participative (wide public participation was initiated).

The process included a strong focus on environmentally sustainable development. This involved determining the capacity and status of the natural resource base. This information formed the basis for a development strategy and spatial implementation plan. The environmental issues identified formed an integral part of the plans for the social and economic development and management of the region.

Box 13.1 Lower Breede River (South Africa) Sub-regional Spatial Development Framework

Purpose of study

Because of increasing development pressure and the lack of a spatial plan, a process for the development of a sub-regional SDF was initiated. The primary objective of the SDF was to manage the type, location and quality of future growth so that it contributed to sustainable development goals. It would also be used to inform land use management policy and to clarify the sub-region's needs and associated implementation priorities.

Process

The study team included a firm of town and regional planners working in association with environmental consultants to prepare the SDF. The process of determining a vision, goals, and development and management objectives was participative. Wide public participation was initiated early in the planning process, and formed an integral part of the study. An integrated planning process was used to prepare the SDF. This process comprised three main phases:

Phase 1: obtaining a development perspective of the sub-region through the process of:

* defining the scope and purpose of the study;
* defining the spatial boundaries of the study;
* considering the broader policy and planning context;

- collecting, analysing and evaluating relevant information on the socioeconomic environment, heritage resources, the natural environment and institutional context.

Phase 2: formulating a development strategy by deciding on a vision, goals and objectives for development and management of the sub-region by:

- determining optimum spatial development and management zones;
- formulating policies and strategies by which the goals and objectives could be realized, covering land use policies, agricultural land use, ecological conservation, tourism development, bulk services infrastructure and community facilities.

Phase 3: preparing an implementation plan, by:

- considering spatial implications for core urban area and river corridor management zones;
- considering institutional and financial implications;
- prioritizing actions, linked to the development of budgets;
- recommending monitoring and feedback to allow re-evaluation of priorities.

Main lessons learned

- The process was interdisciplinary and proactive, which allowed a full spectrum of environmental issues to be identified and considered
- There was extensive participation in the planning process, which increased accountability and the legitimacy of results
- Proposals arising from the study were clearly linked to an implementation strategy to facilitate successful implementation
- Recommendations were made for future actions and periodic reviews, which ensured overall quality control.

Source: Urban Dynamics and deVilliers Brownlie Associates (2001)

Distinct SEA process applied to planning procedures

Box 13.2 describes the SEA process applied to the planning process of a municipality located in the KwaZulu-Natal Province of South Africa. A concerted effort was made to integrate SEA requirements into the administrative planning procedures. Although separate environmental documents were produced as part of the process, they were prepared to address particular needs prioritized by the municipality. Even though the SEA and planning process were integrated, institutional arrangements for environmental management were developed as a distinct and separate municipal function.

Box 13.2 SEA for uMhlathuze Municipality, South Africa

Purpose of study

The purpose of the study was to develop an environmental management framework to assist environmental decision making. The SEA also ensured that environmental sustainability issues were integrated into the IDP process.

Process

The uMhlathuze SEA was conducted as part of the municipal IDP process. The SEA consultants worked closely with the planning consultants. The principal outputs of the SEA were:

IDP Phase 1: analysis

- status quo analysis and preparation of SOER;
- identification of key environmental and development issues.

IDP Phase 2: strategies

- formulation of a vision for the municipality;
- development of criteria for selecting indicators.

IDP Phase 3: projects

- development of biophysical and socioeconomic indicators for the ongoing planning, assessment and management of activities in the municipality;
- preparation of a SEMP, which provided a synthesis of the environmental opportunities and constraints to development, and a framework for environmental decision making. The SEMP included: an environmental management policy, an environmental management strategy, indicators, environmental management cooperation agreements, environmental education and environmental management and assessment tools for environmental decision making.

Main lessons learned

- In order for the SEA process to be efficient, and for the outcomes of the SEA to be implemented, it needs to be integrated within the planning process
- When SEA is applied early in the process and is intimately linked to planning, environmental issues are more easily integrated into the formulation of visions, objectives, programmes and implementation plans for the municipality.

Source: Council for Scientific and Industrial Research (2002)

SEA outcome

To date, the outcomes of SEA practice in South Africa have not been evaluated. It is therefore difficult to determine the influence that SEA has had on decision making. Similarly, post-SEA follow-up and monitoring have not been undertaken. Because SEA is largely voluntary, no SEA review package has been developed to determine the efficacy and influence of SEA. The only information available on the outcomes of SEA in South Africa to date is the work undertaken by Retief et al (2004) on the status of SEA practice in the country. Their key findings included:

- Most SEAs included management and monitoring arrangements. In many cases SEMPs, environmental management frameworks and SOERs were specifically included. This highlighted the need for SEA to be used as much more than just an assessment tool. SEA was expected to address the entire decision-making and management process. Moreover, the SEA involved an assessment of the capacity of the resource base but not a traditional impact assessment of proposed activities
- The need to integrate sustainability issues into planning procedures was an important driving force for the implementation of SEA
- The need to inform, and provide a framework for, project level EIA was an important objective for the large majority of SEAs.

The case studies described in Boxes 13.1 and 13.2 reveal that integrative approaches to SEA have a discernible impact on planning documents. When SEA is applied early in the process and is intimately linked to planning, environmental issues become integrated into the formulation of visions, objectives, programmes and implementation plans. However, it is difficult to judge the impact of SEA on environmental quality in South Africa because there is a lack of monitoring and compliance enforcement capacity within government.

Conclusion

The emergence of SEA in South Africa has occurred within broader policy changes in the environmental and planning systems. Apartheid planning, characterized by physical planning and land use control have given way to achieving sustainability, equity and good governance in spatial planning and land development. Concomitantly, environmental management has shifted from the apartheid preoccupation with nature conservation to a focus on environmental rights and promoting environmentally sustainable development. The development of SEA in South Africa coincided with the recognition of a lack of integration of environmental considerations in the planning system. Ironically, although the benefits of SEA have been recognized in national planning policy and legislation, acknowledgement of SEA in national environmental policy has been lacking.

Despite the lack of formal guidance, SEA practice in South Africa has increased steadily since the early 1990s, and has tended to be varied, flexible and responsive to the different decision-making contexts within which it has been applied. Even with increasing use of SEA, and the provision for its application in planning policy and legislation, most SEAs have been undertaken voluntarily and have not been triggered by legal requirements. The flexible nature of SEA has allowed it to flourish in South Africa in the absence of definitive legislation and in spite of the lack of a specific government department promoting its use. The high number of SEAs conducted thus far is surprising, especially considering the voluntary nature of SEA in South Africa. Moreover, SEA has become established despite the fact that institutions at all levels of government are still transforming and have not yet stabilized. It can therefore be expected that SEA practice will increase when government institutions are able to respond to the SEA enabling provisions in planning legislation.

Spatial planning SEAs mostly assessed the capacity of the resource base and included provisions for management and monitoring arrangements such as SEMPs, SOERs and indicators. It appears that there is a growing tendency for SEA practice to follow an integrative approach, rather than an EIA-based procedure. This integrative approach is particularly suited to South Africa's situation as a developing country struggling with human and financial resource constraints. Table 13.2 provides a summary of the South African SEA system. Because South Africa does not have a formal SEA system, the table reflects emerging SEA practice, the requirements of the generic SEA guidelines (DEAT, 2000) and anecdotal evidence.

The challenges in South Africa in linking SEA to planning procedures relate to the specific development context and to the SEA system, as well as to the SEA process and methods. The following key challenges can be identified:

Development context:

- recognizing the imperative of addressing past injustices and providing equitable access to land and natural resources;
- recognizing the need for efficiency because of human and financial resources constraints.

SEA system:

- expanding and refining the legislative basis for SEA;
- preparing clear guidance on the integration of SEA with planning;
- reviewing the SEA system to identify barriers to SEA performance;
- improving professional capacity to apply and implement SEA.

SEA process and methods:

- establishing screening criteria for triggering SEA;
- developing methods to identify thresholds and limits of acceptable change;
- setting minimum requirements for SEA processes and outputs;

Table 13.2 *Evaluation of SEA of land use plans in South Africa*

Criterion	Criterion met	Comment
		SYSTEM CRITERIA
Legal basis	▲	Emerging planning policy and legislation require SEA to be undertaken for provincial and municipal spatial development frameworks
Integration	▲	Level and extent of integration with planning not specified
Guidance	☐	No SEA guidance relating specifically to planning exists
Coverage	▲	Only spatial development frameworks have SEA requirements
Tiering	▲	Not established but examples exist where SEA served as a screening mechanism for EIA
Sustainable development	■	Concept of sustainable development is central to SEA
		PROCESS CRITERIA
Alternatives	■	Consideration of alternatives highlighted as a key process element
Screening	▲	Although screening is included as a key process element no screening criteria exist
Scoping	■	Scoping is considered a key process element
Prediction/evaluation	■	SEA guidance proposes that plans be assessed against sustainability frameworks
Additional impacts	▲	Need to consider cumulative effects in SEA mentioned but no clear guidance provided on how this should be achieved
Report preparation	☐	No guidance exists on SEA report preparation.
Review	■	Proposed that outcomes of SEA be subject to public and authority review
Monitoring	■	Formulation of plan for monitoring and auditing proposed
Mitigation	☐	Guidance document does not propose development of mitigation strategy
Consultation and public participation	■	Consultation and public participation key to SEA
		OUTCOME CRITERIA
Decision making	?	Preliminary research suggests that influence of SEA on decision making varies considerably
Costs and benefits	?	Fact that SEA conducted voluntarily suggests that proponents perceive benefits to outweigh costs

Table 13.2 *Evaluation of SEA of land use plans in South Africa (continued)*

Criterion	Criterion met	Comment
Environmental quality	?	No information exists
System monitoring	☐	South Africa does not have a formal SEA system to monitor

Notes: ■ – Yes
    ▲ – Partially
    ☐ – No
    ? – Don't know

- recognizing that SEA processes need to be flexible in order to respond to the specific context in which SEA is being applied;
- ensuring that SEA is applied early in the planning process;
- recognizing that, where possible, SEA should be intimately integrated with the planning process;
- ensuring that SEA facilitates streamlining as well as integration of EIA with planning authorization processes;
- reviewing the effectiveness of SEA in order to benchmark best practice and facilitate continual improvement.

The key lessons learned from South Africa's experience in applying SEA within the planning system are that:

- SEA should be aligned with nationally and locally defined sustainable development goals
- SEA should form an integral part of the planning process to avoid duplication and enhance effectiveness
- SEA should address the entire planning process by including a management, implementation and monitoring plan
- SEA can function as both an EIA-based and integrative approach
- SEA can contribute to a decision-making framework by establishing limits of acceptable change, thresholds, sustainability criteria and indicators
- SEA should fit the purpose for which it is applied to avoid it becoming an additional burden in an already complex planning process.

Acknowledgements

A special thank you to Kogi Govender for providing information and responding to queries on the uMhlathuze SEA case study. Sincere thanks are also due to Susie Brownlie and Keith Wiseman for providing detailed constructive criticism that improved an earlier draft of this chapter.

Notes

1   *Draft Land Use Bill*, 6 April 2002, Ministry of Agriculture and Land Affairs, Pretoria
2   *Local Government: Municipal Systems Act*, no 32 of 2000, Government Gazette no 21776, Republic of South Africa, Cape Town, www.info.gov.za/documents/index.htm
3   *Local Government: Municipal Planning and Performance Management Regulations*, Government Gazette no 796 of 2001, no 22605, Pretoria, Republic of South Africa, Cape Town
4   *National Environmental Management Act*, no 107 of 1998, Government Gazette no 19519, Republic of South Africa, Cape Town
5   *National Environmental Management Act: Second Amendment Act*, no 8 of 2004, Government Gazette no 25289, Republic of South Africa, Cape Town

References

Aliber, M. and Mokoena, R. (2003) 'The land question in contemporary South Africa', in Daniel, J., Habib, A. and Southall, R. (eds) *State of the Nation: South Africa 2003–2004*, HSRC Press, Cape Town

Annandale, D., Bailey, J., Ouano, E., Evans, W. and King, P. (2001) 'The potential role of strategic environmental assessment in the activities of multi-lateral development banks', *Environmental Impact Assessment Review*, vol 21, pp407–429

Booysen, S. and Erasmus, E. (1998) 'Public policy-making', in Venter, A. (ed) *Government and Politics in the New South Africa*, 2nd edition, van Schaik Publishers, Pretoria

Council for Scientific and Industrial Research (2002) *Strategic Environmental Management Plan for the uMmhlathuze Municipality*, CSIR, Durban

Department of Environmental Affairs and Tourism (2000) *Strategic Environmental Assessment in South Africa*, Guideline document, DEAT, Pretoria

Department of Environmental Affairs and Tourism (2002) *National Framework Document: Strengthening Sustainability in the Integrated Development Planning Process*, DEAT, Pretoria

Department of Land Affairs (1997) *White Paper on South African Land Policy*, DLA, Pretoria

Department of Land Affairs (1999) *Green Paper on Development and Planning*, National Development and Planning Commission, DLA, Pretoria

Department of Land Affairs (2001a) *Guidelines for the Integration of Environmental Planning into Land Reform and Land Development*, DLA, Pretoria

Department of Land Affairs (2001b) *Policy for the Integration of Environmental Planning into the Land Reform Process*, DLA, Pretoria

Department of Provincial and Local Government and German Agency for Technical Co-operation (2001) *IDP Guide Pack, Guide 0: Overview*, DPLG and GTZ, Pretoria

Department of Water Affairs and Forestry (2001) *A Guide to Strategic Environmental Assessment for Water Use in Catchments*, DWAF, Pretoria

Hanekom, S. X., Rowland, R. W. and Bain, E. G. (1987) *Key Aspects of Public Administration*, revised edition, Southern Book Publishing, Pretoria

Khan, F. (2002) 'The roots of environmental racism and the rise of environmental justice in the 1990s', in McDonald, D. A. (ed) *Environmental Justice in South Africa*, University of Cape Town Press, Cape Town

Lahiff, E. (2001) *Land Reform in South Africa: is it Meeting the Challenge?* Policy Brief 1, Programme for Land and Agrarian Studies, School of Government, University of the Western Cape, Cape Town

Lahiff, E. (2003) 'Land policies and practices', in Reed, D. and de Wit, M. (eds) *Towards a Just South Africa: the Political Economy of Natural Resource Wealth*, WWF Macro-economics Program Office and CSIR-Environmentek, Pretoria

Ministry of Agriculture and Land Affairs (2001) *White Paper on Spatial Planning and Land Use Management*, MLA, Pretoria

Reed, D. (2003) 'Historical overview of institutional and political arrangements', in Reed, D. and de Wit, M. (eds), *Towards a Just South Africa: the Political Economy of Natural Resource Wealth*, WWF Macroeconomics Program Office and CSIR-Environmentek, Pretoria

Retief, F. (2003) 'SEA practice in South Africa: experience with a rural infrastructure development programme', in Jones, C., Phylip-Jones, J., Sadler, B., Simmons, S., Sprenger, C., Walmsley, J. and Wood, C. M. (eds) *Environmental Assessment Outlook 2003*, Institute of Environmental Management and Assessment, Lincoln

Retief, F., Rossouw, N., Jones, C. and Jay, S. (2004) 'The status of strategic environmental assessment practice in South Africa', Paper to *International Association for Impact Assessment Conference, Vancouver*, IAIA, Fargo, ND

Rossouw, N., Audouin, M., Lochner, P., Heather-Clark, S. and Wiseman, K. (2000) 'Development of strategic environmental assessment in South Africa', *Impact Assessment and Project Appraisal*, vol 18, pp217–223

Sowman, M., Fuggle, R. and Preston, G. (1995) 'A review of the evolution of environmental evaluation procedures in South Africa', *Environmental Impact Assessment Review*, vol 15, pp45–67

Therivel, R. and Partidário, M. (eds) (1996) *The Practice of Strategic Environmental Assessment*, Earthscan, London

Turner, S. (2001) *Sustainable Development: What's Land Got to Do With It?*, Policy Brief 2, Programme for Land and Agrarian Studies, School of Government, University of the Western Cape, Cape Town

Urban Dynamics and de Villiers Brownlie Associates (2001) *Lower Breede River Sub-Regional Spatial Development Framework*, Overberg District Council, Western Cape Province, Overberg

Wiseman, K. (2000) 'Environmental assessment and planning in South Africa: the SEA connection', in Partidário, M. R. and Clark, R. (eds) *Perspectives on Strategic Environmental Assessment*, Lewis Publisers/CRC Press, Boca Raton, FL

Wood, C. M. (2002) *Environmental Impact Assessment: a Comparative Review*, 2nd edition, Prentice Hall, Harlow

14

Sweden

Tuija Hilding-Rydevik and Monica L. C. Fundingsland

Introduction

In 1971, the Swedish government initiated a national development project, 'Den fysiska riksplaneringen', which aimed to incorporate ecological factors into municipal land use planning. A government proposal concerning the integration of environmental issues into land use planning was issued in the following year. Since 1972, there have been considerable municipal and governmental efforts to incorporate environmental (and more recently sustainable development) issues into municipal land use planning. The government has gradually increased the role of the municipalities in implementing national environmental goals and in promoting sustainable development, notably through Government Bill 2000/01:130[1] and by introducing measurable sustainability indicators. The result is that environmental issues are now established as part of the land use planning agenda at municipal level. Municipalities have quickly become engaged in new developments in the field. This has also been the case with SEA.[2] As a result, therefore, SEA had entered the Swedish land use planning arena by the end of the 1980s through voluntary initiatives in a number of municipalities (Hilding-Rydevik, 1987, 1990; Asplund and Hilding-Rydevik, 1996).

SEA was formally introduced into Swedish land use planning in the early 1990s, first for relatively project-oriented development plans and later for more strategic comprehensive plans. There have not been any extensive studies of SEA practice for the comprehensive plans to date. However, there have been some follow-up studies and evaluations of SEA for the more detailed development plans. The aim of this chapter is to highlight and discuss the experience of SEA of Swedish land use plans, at a time when the legislation has undergone substantial change due to the implementation of the Directive 2001/42/EC ('the SEA Directive') (European Commission (EC), 2001). The situation into which the new SEA legislation has been introduced is one where many environmental officials involved in municipal land use planning experience a battle every day to keep environmental issues on the planning agenda (Asplund and Hilding-Rydevik, 2001). This is despite political and legislative efforts to integrate environmental issues into land use planning, voluntary environmental organizations being in a relatively strong position, and the widespread use of environmental decision aiding tools such as SEA, sustainability indicators and environmental accounting. The question is, therefore, whether new SEA legislation and practice will have any effect on this situation.

Context

Swedish land use planning

> *In principle, there is a planning monopoly in Sweden, and the planning system is therefore basically designed for the municipalities*
>
> Alfredsson and Wiman (1997, p11).

This quote neatly summarizes Swedish land use planning. In Sweden there is no formal spatial planning at either the regional or the national level, and the main responsibility for land use planning lies with the 290 municipalities. These authorities have a high degree of autonomy and a monopoly on planning. They have the right to levy taxes and serve an important role in community planning. Central government seeks to influence spatial planning mainly through legislation and guidance, and through its 21 regional arms, the county administrative boards. These have a predominantly advisory role with respect to land use planning, and ensure that national objectives and guidelines are adhered to at municipality level.

At central government level, the Ministry of Environment and Community Development is responsible for environmental, planning and building issues. The key governmental agencies for land use planning and environmental management are the National Board of Housing, Building and Planning and the Swedish Environmental Protection Agency.

The two main tools for Swedish land use planning are municipal comprehensive plans (MCPs) and detailed development plans (DDPs). These are regulated by the Planning and Building Act 1987[3] (PBA). The other legislation relevant to land use planning is the Environmental Code,[4] introduced in 1999 to bring together formerly discrete environmental laws into consolidated framework legislation.

MCPs cover the entire area of a municipality and provide recommendations for the long-term use of land and the management of the built environment, but are not legally binding documents. In some cases, aspects of the MCP need a more thorough treatment, in which case so called 'detailed' (fördjupad) comprehensive plans (DCPs) are developed, which have the same legal status as MCPs.

DDPs, on the other hand, regulate the land use for specified areas within the municipality and these plans are legally binding. For areas not covered by DDPs, the municipalities may develop area regulations where it is deemed necessary in order to achieve national or local environmental objectives. Area regulations are also legally binding.

Finally, real estate plans may be developed in order to assist with the implementation of DDPs.[5] In addition to land use planning at the municipal level, there is a PBA provision which enables a regional plan to be adopted if there is an evident need to coordinate the plans of several municipalities. There are currently only two regional plans in Sweden, covering the counties of Stockholm and Gothenberg.[6]

SEA in the Swedish land use planning system

The overarching legal provisions concerning the SEA of plans and programmes were incorporated into the Environmental Code in July 2004. The Planning and Building Act specifies the legal requirements for the SEA of Swedish land use plans within the framework of the Environmental Code.

The need to incorporate SEA into the Swedish land use planning system was recognized in 1979 in the first draft of the 1987 PBA (Hilding-Rydevik, 1990). However, it was not introduced as a legal requirement until 1992, when the revised PBA formally stipulated the need for the SEA of DDPs. This requirement was subsequently extended to MCPs in 1996.[7] Both area regulations and regional plans remain exempt from the PBA SEA requirements. SEA requirements also exist in other sectors, including road transport (introduced in 1987) and energy.

In September 2004, approximately 150 municipalities needed to revise their MCPs and thus to undertake SEA to comply with the SEA Directive. Approximately 30–50 DCPs are prepared every year[8] and the Planning and Building Act requires these to include a SEA. Roughly 2000 DDPs are prepared each year, but no estimates exist for how many undergo SEA. However, an evaluation of assessment practice in the Stockholm municipality indicated that roughly 30 per cent of all DDPs had undergone SEA (Skeppström, 1998).

Discussions about the revision of the Planning and Building Act to incorporate SEA requirements may have been the inspiration for the considerable voluntary practice of SEA in Sweden during the late 1980s and early 1990s. A number of municipalities even developed their own regulations and guidelines (Hilding-Rydevik, 1987, 1990; Asplund and Hilding-Rydevik, 1996). Several research projects have been conducted, documenting a number of both positive and negative experiences of the early SEAs. The most obvious effect of the SEAs was that, whereas the analysis of environmental impacts, especially in MCPs, had previously been almost non-existent (Hilding-Rydevik, 1990), environmental impacts were being considered in land use plans. Other positive experiences identified by these SEA studies included:

- greater attention being paid to environmental issues;
- a strengthened environmental perspective within land use planning;

- environmental issues becoming a universal concern rather than being perceived as a sectoral interest (Asplund and Hilding-Rydevik, 1996);
- greater cooperation between different municipal administrations;
- fewer comments were received from the environmental agencies at the later stages of consultation (Johansson, 1992);
- politicians perceived it to be easier to make decisions because SEA increased their knowledge about the content and potential impacts of different plans (Johansson, 1992; Balfors, 1994).

Interestingly, the documentation of the environmental impacts of land use plans demonstrated the need to make economic calculations concerning the impact of proposals equally clear (Balfors, 1994). In Huddinge Municipality, for example, both local politicians and public officials agreed that the potential for SEA results to influence the contents of DDPs was limited, mainly due to the fact that many land use decisions had already been made prior to the DDP (Johansson, 1992). Extending SEA to MCPs was seen as the solution to this, as MCPs offered the possibility of considering more strategic alternatives.

Case study: Greater Stockholm Regional Plan 2000

An indication of more recent experience of Swedish SEA practice can be gained from an examination of the integrated assessment of the Greater Stockholm Regional Plan 2000 (Box 14.1). This plan is interesting for several reasons. Firstly, it attempts to integrate the assessments undertaken for environmental, social and economic issues in order to give them parity with each other. Secondly, it reflects truly strategic planning because it involved choices of great importance to the environmental situation in the Stockholm region. Finally, the case is of particular value in the Swedish context because practical experience of SEA was documented.

SEA system

Legal basis

The Swedish legislative tradition is that of framework laws; that is, legislation does not specify regulatory detail. Instead, the effectiveness of legislation is, to a large extent, determined by its interpretation in guidelines and its subsequent implementation in professional practice. Notwithstanding this, the PBA provision for SEA was far weaker for MCPs than for DDPs prior to the transposition of the SEA Directive into Swedish legislation. In fact, the term environmental impact assessment was not even mentioned in connection with MCPs.[9] Instead, the Planning and Building Act required the plan's proposals and impacts to be clearly stated in the documentation,[10] and that the SEA was to be part of the consultation process prior to the plan being adopted.[11] The scope and extent of the SEA was determined by the municipality in each individual case. However, for major land use changes such as a new road or a housing development, it was assumed that a

Box 14.1 Integrated assessment of Greater Stockholm Regional Plan 2000

The Greater Stockholm Region includes the largest Swedish city, and capital, Stockholm. The region has 1.8 million inhabitants, one fifth of the Swedish population, and has 26 municipalities. Ninety-five per cent of the inhabitants live in the 10 per cent of the region which constitutes the most densely built-up area, and 50 per cent of the region's employment is in the city of Stockholm. The region covers an area of 649,000ha, of which 60 per cent is agricultural land or afforested. There are 25,000 islands in the archipelago and 850 freshwater lakes.

Regional Plan 2000 has a planning horizon of 30 years. It sets out the basic criteria for the use of land and water areas, and provides guidelines for the location of buildings and facilities. The overriding goals for the Greater Stockholm Region are to develop international competitiveness, good living conditions for the whole population, and a long term sustainable environment.

The SEA of Regional Plan 2000 started in 1997 and was finalized in 2002 (Boverket och Naturvårdsverket, 2000c). The Office of Regional Planning and Urban Transportation chose to conduct three separate strategic assessments – environmental, economic and social – and then to integrate these in the final plan in order to contribute to sustainable development goals. One specific aim of the SEA was to facilitate the appraisal of whether various alternatives, measures and planning proposals contributed to meeting targets for regional planning, including general national and regional environmental objectives.

The final integration of the results of the different assessments was achieved through workshops, resulting in a set of recommendations for the development of the Greater Stockholm Region. The workshops indicated that the work undertaken to identify conflicting goals or goal sharing between economic, social and environmental issues was an important matter that ought to be considered during the consultation process.

One of the experiences from the SEA was that the planning process was not sufficiently prepared for the effect of impact assessment. As a result, the expectations of the scope, role and importance of the SEA in the planning process do not appear to have been agreed between the different actors. The extent to which environmental concerns had been taken into account in the adoption of principles, alternatives and plan proposals was unclear.

The positive experiences from the overall impact assessment (including the SEA) included the contribution towards a more defined and transparent planning process, which encompassed analysis, consideration of international development scenarios, and the production of alternative options for the future development of the region. The assessments also contributed to making key strategic issues and alternatives more explicit at an earlier stage in decision making (Boverket och Naturvårdsverket, 2000d).

SEA would be a self-evident part of the MCP (Boverket, 1996). It was also assumed that the SEA would take a broad perspective, and consider social and economic, as well as environmental, aspects.

DDPs were more heavily regulated, and a SEA was required if the plan gave consent to land uses or developments with significant impacts on the environment, human health or natural resource management. It was further stipulated that the SEA must enable an overall appraisal of the impacts of a planned construction, activity or measure to be made.[12] Although DDPs relate more to the project level rather than the plan level, some DDPs include larger developments involving strategic choices with important environmental implications.

The implementation of the SEA Directive in Swedish land use planning legislation has brought about some major changes. Both the Environment Code and the Planning and Building Act have been revised to incorporate the requirements of the SEA Directive. The new SEA requirements include provisions for:

- clear statements about the need to undertake an impact assessment;
- the issues that need to be addressed;
- the types of information that need to be provided in the environmental report;
- the consideration of alternatives;
- the communication of results;
- the relationship to the Espoo Convention and its provisions concerning transboundary impacts;
- the monitoring of impacts.

In terms of detail and clarity, the new Swedish SEA legislation is a giant step forward.

Integration

The previous Swedish land use planning SEA legislation did not stipulate the need to undertake a separate SEA process for MCPs. Instead, SEA practice relied on the well-defined spatial planning process, which included a requirement for impacts to be analysed and presented. There were no explicit legal requirements concerning the integration of SEA and land use planning. However, the legislation has been interpreted to mean that these should be integrated (see, for example, Boverket och Naturvårdsverket, 2000d). The question is to what extent this has been undertaken in practice.

The results from several studies indicated that the level of integration of SEA with comprehensive municipal planning varied. In a pilot study by Bjarnadóttir and Åkerskog (2003), four of the six plans investigated displayed weak links between the presentation of the SEA results and the plan components. Furthermore, it was generally not apparent at which stage in the planning process the SEA had been carried out. A recent evaluation of 104 DDPs indicated that the links between the assessment (which is often a separate report) and the plan were rarely documented (Oscarsson et al, 2003). However, another study provided examples where the integration between the SEA and the planning processes had worked well, such as the drafting of the MCP in Storuman Municipality and of the DCP for the Skavsta area (Boverket och Naturvårdsverket, 2000d).

A two-year, full-scale study of the SEA of MCPs indicated, among other things, that the potential for integrating SEA into the municipal land use planning process was determined at a very early stage in the planning process (Asplund and Hilding-Rydevik, 1996). In one of the cases that was investigated, 33 meetings (including informal preparatory meetings) had been held over a period of 2 years, and most of the basic assumptions had been in place by the seventh meeting. The SEA experts became involved only at the tenth meeting, which proved to be too late (Asplund and Hilding-Rydevik, 1996). Integration of SEA into the Swedish land use planning process poses a major challenge to existing professional and organizational norms and cultures, and it will take time to achieve effective integration of the two.

In general, the integration of environmental issues (not only SEA) into the municipal comprehensive planning context is probably where most conflicts arise. This is where inertia to change in professional practice is manifested, and where improvements are needed in order to support the implementation of sustainable development and make SEA effective in terms of influencing the planning process and plan proposals (Asplund and Hilding-Rydevik, 2001; Dovlén, 2001; Håkansson 2001; Hilding-Rydevik, 2003). With the implementation of the SEA Directive, the integration of environmental issues with plan and programme preparation in order to support sustainable development has become one of the main targets of SEA in Sweden.[13] However, although the SEA legislation has become much clearer, it does not provide any guidance about how to achieve integration in practice.

Guidance

A number of reports and guidelines were prepared in relation to the previous SEA legislation, both general and sector specific. The main documents relating to SEA in land use planning are listed in Box 14.2. Since these guidelines do not have a firm basis in legislation, they tend to be ambitious and idealistic. However, this may be a characteristic of guidelines in general. A national project to investigate the application of environmental objectives to spatial planning was undertaken between 1997 and 2000 (Samhällsplanering med miljömål i Sverige, SAMS). One of the purposes of SAMS was to investigate the use of environmental objectives and indicators in SEA, with a particular focus on MCPs and regional plans (Boverket och Naturvårdsverket, 2000d). The SAMS project led to the publication of a number of reports, many of which have been influential in the discussion of SEA implementation in Sweden (Boverket och Naturvårdsverket, 2000a, 2000b, 2000d and 2001). General guidelines for the new SEA legislation are currently being prepared by the EPA, and guidelines relating specifically to the Planning and Building Act are being prepared by the National Board of Housing, Building and Planning.

Box 14.2 Swedish guidance documents and reports on SEA of land use plans

- *Boken om översiktsplan. Parts 1–3* (Boverket, 1996). Description and interpretation of the PBA and its implementation. Also covers broad SEA requirements
- *Boken om MKB för detaljplan* (Boverket, 2000b). EIA for DDPs
- *Sociala och ekonomiska konsekvenser i översiktsplaneringen* (Boverket, 2000c). Social and economic impacts in municipal comprehensive planning
- *Fysisk planering med strategisk miljöbedömning (SMB) för hållbarhet* (Boverket, 2000a). Land use planning and SEA for sustainability
- *Strategiska miljöbedömningar – ett användbart instrument i miljöarbetet* (Naturvårdsverket, 2000b). General guidelines for how SEA can be applied to different planning contexts. Includes examples of SEA of municipal plans and the regional plan for Stockholm
- *Fysisk planering med strategisk miljöbedömning* (Naturvårdsverket, 2000a). Land use planning and SEA
- *SMB och översiktlig fysisk planering* (Boverket och Naturvårdsverket, 2000d). Ideas and experiences of SEA, based on case studies, examples and expert opinion.

Tiering

There is, in principle, a tiered system for the SEA of Swedish land use plans (see, for example, Boverket, 1996). At the higher tier are the strategic MCPs and at the lower tier the more project oriented DDPs. However, in practice, it is not clear how, or to what extent, the SEAs of MCPs and DDPs have been linked. It has been reported that MCPs do not sufficiently evaluate the different areas and thus do not provide guidance about what DPPs should include (Oscarsson et al, 2003). The 2004 SEA legislation has not introduced any specific requirements concerning tiering, beyond stating that authorities and municipalities undertaking SEAs 'shall aim at co-ordinating' these.[14]

SEA process

There has been considerable variation in MCP SEA practice and, particularly, in the coverage of environmental impacts since the 1995 PBA. This can largely be explained by the fact that the Planning and Building Act did not previously stipulate the process by which the assessment should be undertaken (Bjarnadóttir and Åkerskog, 2003). Under the new legislation, the same SEA regulations apply to both MCPs and DDPs.

Alternatives

There were no explicit requirements in the previous SEA legislation concerning the assessment of alternatives for either MCPs or DDPs. However, the guidelines listed in Box 14.2 clearly describe and encourage good international SEA practice, and this includes the assessment of alternatives. The findings from a pilot study of MCP SEAs (Bjarnadóttir and Åkerskog, 2003) concluded that municipal land use planning was based partly on the development of scenarios but that the consideration of alternatives was not necessarily reflected in the SEA. A study of DDPs indicated that the consideration of alternative designs or locations was often lacking (Persson, 1996; Skeppström, 1998; Oscarsson et al, 2003). The new SEA legislation requires the consideration of the 'do nothing' scenario and of reasonable alternatives in relation to the plan's aims and/or geographical scope.[15]

Screening

The need to undertake the SEA of plans and programmes in Sweden was previously determined by whether a legal requirement existed; in other words screening by specification or list, rather than by evaluating the significance of potential impacts (Lerman, 2003). The Planning and Building Act required all MCPs to be subject to SEA (above) but there were no specific screening procedures. For DDPs, however, SEA was required only when the plan was expected to cause significant environmental impacts on the environment, health, and the management of land, water and other resources. Screening could be undertaken as part of the plan preparation process. The new SEA legislation outlines screening procedures although the government has also provided a list of plans for which SEA will always be required.[16]

Scoping

There were no explicit scoping requirements in the previous SEA legislation relating to MCPs or DDPs. However, Swedish SEA guidelines promoted good assessment practice and emphasized the importance of good scoping procedures. Practice for DDPs indicated that scoping procedures were reported in half of the plans (Oscarsson et al, 2003).

The Planning and Building Act indicated the required scope of the environmental elements of an MCP and stated that the plan had to comply with environmental quality standards and take national interests into consideration. However, the analysis of synergistic and other impacts was not required under the previous legislation. The SEAs of Swedish municipal plans have been criticized for being too broad and, in particular, for the assessment report not always being appropriate to decision making (Emmelin, 1997). Moreover, SEAs tended to cover social and economic as well as environmental impacts, and the type of environmental issues that were addressed varied greatly (Bjarnadóttir and Åkerskog, 2003).

The new SEA legislation has clear requirements for both scoping procedures and the scope of the assessment, including an extensive list of potential impacts and a requirement to consider the relationship between different environmental aspects.[17]

Prediction and evaluation

The pilot study undertaken by Bjarnadóttir and Åkerskog (2003) indicated that the prediction and evaluation methods used for SEA were generally not documented. The study also indicated that the level of detail of the SEA of municipal land use plans tended to correspond to the level of detail of the plan. However, in cases where environmental or sustainable development indices or green accounting were used as a basis for the SEA of the MCP, the methods are sometimes made quite explicit (for example, Helsingborgs kommun, 1997).

The methods used for presenting impacts have often included baseline maps showing the location of proposed development, supported by text. During the early 1990s, matrices with a variety of scales and modes for presenting the significance of environmental impacts were widely used (e.g. happy or gloomy faces, numbers, flowers, '+' or '– –', or qualitative value judgements). However, the significance of impacts was not always analysed.

Report preparation

The reporting of environmental impacts in Swedish land use SEAs has been varied. The Planning and Building Act previously stipulated that the environmental, economic and social impacts of the municipal land use plan should be clearly outlined in the plan. For MCPs, impacts could either be presented in a separate chapter within the draft plan or in a separate report. For DDPs, the environmental impacts had to be clearly reported, along with the justification for the policies included in the final plan. There were clear requirements for making both the proposed plan and the SEA report publicly available prior to the plan being adopted. In the new SEA legislation, the reporting requirements are clearer, and will ensure better consistency in reporting procedures.

Review

The county administrative boards have the formal role of reviewing the MCP, including the SEA report, according to the Planning and Building Act. It appears that the SEA reports for DDPs do not reveal whether the SEAs have been reviewed before being made publicly available along with the DDP (Oscarsson et al, 2003).

Mitigation and monitoring

The previous legislation did not contain any explicit requirements for monitoring or mitigation in relation to MCPs or DDP SEAs, and practice has not been widely reported. However, the evaluation of 11 DDPs from the Stockholm municipality revealed that most of the mitigation measures that had been proposed in the SEAs had been implemented (Skeppström, 1998). The new legislation introduced requirements for the responsible authority to obtain information about the significant environmental impacts of plan or programme implementation[18] and to include mitigation measures in plan SEA reports.[19]

Consultation

Consultation has been an important element of both the Swedish land use planning process and of SEA. Municipalities were required to undertake extensive consultation for both MCPs and DDPs in order to enable the county administrative board, other municipalities, and (for detailed plans) any households that might be affected by the plan, to express their views. Furthermore, the results of such consultation had to be documented in a consultation report. The consultation process not only provided a channel for the expression of public opinion but also improved the basis for decision making, thus serving as a quality control mechanism for the Swedish land use planning system.

In the new legislation, the need to publicise the draft SEA report has been made clearer. New requirements also include the need to make certain information available to the parties that have been consulted during the process. Thus, when the plan is approved, a public statement must be made explaining how environmental issues have been integrated, how the SEA and the consultation responses have been taken into consideration, the reasons for choosing one alternative over the others, and the proposed measures to monitor the significant environmental impacts of the plan.[20]

SEA outcome

The collective evidence from interviews, evaluations and empirical case studies is that SEA has contributed to a number of positive changes to Swedish land use planning. Environmental issues have been given more emphasis, thus allowing environmental impacts to be identified earlier; impacts are being described clearly; cooperation between different actors in the planning process has increased; the planning process has become more transparent; the basis for decisions has become better informed; and environmental knowledge and awareness have increased (Nilsson, 1991; Johansson, 1992; Asplund and Hilding-Rydevik, 1996; Boverket och Naturvårdsverket, 2000d).

Many of these experiences were recorded in the research and development projects that documented early voluntary practice of SEA. However, these represent particular cases where there was a commitment to SEA and to taking the results of SEA into account. It is, however, evident that the 1995 SEA legislation for MCPs exhibited major flaws, and there have also been weaknesses in the implementation of SEA (Käärik, 1999; Åkerskog, 2004; Johannesson, 2004).

The practice of SEA in relation to DDPs is far more positive, probably due to the fact that the legal provisions have been more prescriptive. The Swedish Association of Local Authorities understands that many municipalities undertake SEA during the drafting of DDPs, since the SEA procedure is perceived as providing a good way to incorporate environmental issues into the planning process

(Thune Hedström, 2004). The evaluation of the impacts of DDPs in the Stockholm municipality indicated that 85 per cent of politicians thought that SEA had affected political decisions, and that the role of SEA in relation to DDPs was of great importance (Nolvall, 1998; Skeppström, 1998). This provides some grounds for optimism about the effectiveness of the 2004 SEA legislation.

Conclusion

A summary evaluation of the effectiveness of the current Swedish SEA systems, processes and outcomes is provided in Table 14.1. Environmental issues would be expected to be on current Swedish land use planning agendas even without the existence of SEA requirements. Extensive practice under the well-developed planning and environmental legislation puts great emphasis on environmental issues. However, SEA remains the only tool for effectively promoting the analysis of environmental impacts and alternatives in land use plans. Tools to integrate environmental issues or to promote sustainable development in municipal planning include environmental accounting, environmental and sustainable development indicators, welfare indices, Agenda 21 processes and the implementation of Swedish national environmental targets. Besides being used in SEA, a number of these tools have been used in land use planning since the mid-1990s, mainly in relation to MCPs. Nevertheless, in spite of considerable effort, inertia in integrating environmental issues into Swedish land use planning processes remains.

The environmental sector has become strong in the Swedish municipalities, but when environmental issues are to be integrated with, or weighed against, other issues in the land use planning process, especially economic and technical issues, a number of difficulties arise (Asplund and Hilding-Rydevik, 2001; Dovlén, 2001; Håkansson, 2001; Isaksson, 2004; Storbjörk, 2004). The dominant planning paradigm, and routine professional practice, is often still an obstacle to organizational learning and to the development of planning approaches that promote sustainable development. It remains to be seen to what extent the clearer and more extensive 2004 legislation will contribute, at least partly, to remedying this situation. The interpretation of Swedish framework legislation, forthcoming guidelines and professional practice will determine whether or not the SEA of land use plans proves to be successful and effective. In the Swedish land use planning context and legislative culture, it is crucial to monitor SEA practice in order to develop an understanding of its role and effectiveness in promoting environmental integration and sustainable development. Without this, the SEA legislation and its implementation could become merely symbolic.

Acknowledgements

We are grateful to Ebbe Adolfsson, Swedish Environmental Protection Agency and Robert Johannesson, National Board of Housing, Building and Planning, who reviewed a draft of the text.

Table 14.1 *Evaluation of SEA of land use plans in Sweden*

Criterion	Criterion met	Comments
		SYSTEM CRITERIA
Legal basis	■	Legislation existed but did not regulate practice in detail. New SEA legislation clearer and more detailed
Integration	▲	Previous legislation was interpreted to mean that SEA and land use planning should be integrated. Practice varied. Although new SEA legislation is clearer, it does not provide guidance about how to achieve integration
Guidance	■	General and land use planning SEA guidelines produced previously and currently being prepared for new SEA legislation
Coverage	■	Municipal comprehensive plans (MCPs) and detailed development plans (DDPs) require SEA
Tiering	▲	SEAs of Swedish land use plans should, in principle, be tiered but practice is unclear. New SEA legislation has not introduced any specific regulations concerning tiering, beyond encouraging coordination
Sustainable development	■	SEA in Sweden includes environmental, social and economic aspects.
		PROCESS CRITERIA
Alternatives	▲	No explicit requirement in Planning and Building Act to consider alternatives, but recommended in guidelines. Some examples in practice. New SEA legislation requires consideration of reasonable alternatives and 'zero alternative'
Screening	▲	DDPs require SEA if use of screening procedures outlined in SEA legislation indicates significant environmental impacts likely. Government list of plans always requiring SEAs includes MCPs
Scoping	▲	No previous explicit scoping requirement but recommended in guidelines. Some practice. SEA legislation has clear requirements for both scoping procedures and scope of the assessment
Prediction/ evaluation	▲	Methods not always documented. Impact significance determined qualitatively
Additional impacts	☐	No previous explicit requirement to assess secondary, synergistic or cumulative impacts. SEA legislation now requires this

Table 14.1 *Evaluation of SEA of land use plans in Sweden (continued)*

Criterion	Criterion met	Comments
Report preparation	■	Environmental impacts previously made public within draft plan or in separate report. New SEA legislation makes reporting requirements clearer and should ensure greater consistency in reporting procedures
Review	▲	Impact assessment subject to review
Monitoring	□	No previous explicit monitoring requirement. Practice not widely reported. New SEA legislation introduced requirement for monitoring significant environmental impacts of plan implementation.
Mitigation	▲	No previous explicit requirement to mitigate adverse environmental effects of land use plans. Some practice documented. New SEA legislation introduces clear provisions for mitigation
Consultation and public participation	▲	Consultation, not directly linked to SEA, required for land use plans. Results made public. New SEA legislation makes need to announce draft SEA and other information clearer
		OUTCOME CRITERIA
Decision making	?	Influence of previous SEA system uncertain. Environmental benefits probably greater for DDPs than MCPs. New legislation requires description of modifications to plan to reflect SEA findings
Costs and benefits	■	SEA generally perceived as good way to incorporate environmental issues in planning process.
Environmental quality	?	Unclear
System monitoring	□	No evaluation of outcomes of SEA of land use plans undertaken or required by new SEA legislation

Notes: ■ – Yes
    ▲ – Partially
    □ – No
    ? – Don't know

Notes

1 Government Bill 2000/01:130 (2001) The Swedish Environmental Objectives Interim Targets and Action Strategies, www.regeringen.se/sb/d/108/a/1197 (in Swedish)
2 English information about SEA in Sweden is available from the Nordregio website: www.nordregio.se/EA/sweden.htm
3 Planning and Building Act (1987) Law 1987:10, Updated to include SFS 2003:132, www.riksdagen.se/debatt/ (in Swedish)

4   Environmental Code (1999) Laws 1998: 808, 2005: 356 Directives 1999:109, 2001:25, 2002:37, 2003:61, www.sou.gov.se/miljobalken/ (in Swedish). An English version is available at www.sweden.gov.se/sb/d/2023/a/22847
5   Planning and Building Act (PBA) Ch. 1 § 3
6   www.boverket.se
7   Law 1995: 1197 (came into force 1996)
8   Proposition 2003/04:116 Miljöbedömningar av planer och program, Stockholm
9   PBA Ch. 4
10   PBA Ch. 4 § 1, stipulated by Law 1998:839
11   PBA Ch. 4 § 8
12   PBA Ch. 5 § 18, stipulated by Law 1998:839
13   Environmental Code § 11
14   Environmental Code Ch. 6 § 22
15   Environmental Code Ch. 6 § 12
16   Environmental Code Ch. 6 § 11
17   Environmental Code Ch. 6 § 12
18   Environmental Code Ch. 6 § 18
19   Environmental Code Ch. 6 § 12
20   Environmental Code Ch. 6 § 16

References

Åkerskog, A., Landscape Planning Department, Swedish Agricultural University (2004) Telephone interview, 28 January

Alfredsson, B. and Wiman, J. (1997) 'Planning in Sweden', in *Swedish Planning – Towards Sustainable Development*, Special book edition of *Plan*, Gävle

Asplund, E. and Hilding-Rydevik, T. (1996) *Knowledge, Environment and the Future. Plan Level EIA: Case Studies from Two Municipalities*, Trita-IP FR 96-14, Department of Infrastructure and Planning, Royal Institute of Technology, Stockholm (in Swedish)

Asplund, E. and Hilding-Rydevik, T. (eds) (2001) *Arena for Sustainable Development: Actors and Processes*, Trita-IP FR 01-88, Department for Regional Planning, Royal Institute of Technology, Stockholm (in Swedish)

Balfors, B. (1994) *Environmental Impact Assessment and Municipal Land Use Planning: An Example from Karstorp in Norrköping*, Swedish Council for Building Research, Stockholm (in Swedish)

Bjarnadóttir, H. and Åkerskog, A. (2003) 'Sustainable development and the role of SEA in municipal comprehensive planning in Sweden', in Hilding-Rydevik, T. (ed) *Environmental Assessment of Plans and Programmes: Nordic Experiences in Relation to the Implementation of the EU Directive 2001/42/EC*, Report 2003:4, Nordregio, Stockholm

Boverket (National Board of Housing, Building and Planning) (1996) *Municipal Comprehensive Plans*, Boverket, Karlskrona (in Swedish)

Boverket (National Board of Housing, Building and Planning) (2000a) *EIA for Detailed Development Plans*, Boverket, Karlskrona (in Swedish)

Boverket (National Board of Housing, Building and Planning) (2000b) *Land Use Planning with Strategic Environmental Assessment for Sustainability*, Boverket, Karlskrona (in Swedish)

Boverket (National Board of Housing, Building and Planning) (2000c) *Socio-economic Impacts in Municipal Comprehensive Planning*, Boverket, Karlskrona (in Swedish)

Boverket och Naturvårdsverket (National Board of Housing, Building and Planning and Swedish Environmental Protection Agency) (2000a) *Planning with Environmental Targets! A Guide*, Naturvårdsverket, Stockholm (in Swedish)

Boverket och Naturvårdsverket (National Board of Housing, Building and Planning and Swedish Environmental Protection Agency) (2000b) *Planning with Environmental Targets! An Ideas Catalogue*, Naturvårdsverket, Stockholm (in Swedish)

Boverket och Naturvårdsverket (National Board of Housing, Building and Planning and Swedish Environmental Protection Agency) (2000c) *Planning with Environmental Targets! Strategic Environmental Assessment of the Greater Stockholm Regional Plan 2000*, Naturvårdsverket, Stockholm (in Swedish)

Boverket och Naturvårdsverket (National Board of Housing, Building and Planning and Swedish Environmental Protection Agency) (2000d) *SEA and Strategic Land Use Planning*, Naturvårdsverket, Stockholm (in Swedish)

Boverket och Naturvårdsverket (National Board of Housing, Building and Planning and Swedish Environmental Protection Agency) (2001) *A Discussion of Ideas Concerning SEA in Planning*, Naturvårdsverket, Stockholm (in Swedish)

Dovlén, S (2001) *On the Communication of Professional Environmental Perspectives in Land-Use Planning*, Trita-IP FR 01-96, Department of Infrastructure and Planning, Royal Institute of Technology, Stockholm

Emmelin, L. (1997) 'Planning and impact assessment, the battle of professions', *Miljosekvensen*, vol 2, p97 (in Swedish)

European Commission (2001) 'Directive 2001/42/EC of the European Parliament and of the Council of 27 June 2001 on the assessment of the effects of certain plans and programmes on the environment', *Official Journal of the European Communities*, vol L197, pp30–37, 21 July

Håkansson, M. (2001) *Striving for Sustainability: The Perspective of Professions and Professionals in Local Environmental Work*, Trita-IP FP 01-96, Department of Infrastructure and Planning, Royal Institute of Technology, Stockholm

Helsingborgs kommun (Helsingborg municipality) (1997) *Impacts of Municipal Comprehensive Plans: Environmental, Social and Economic Impacts and Weighting*, Helsingborgs stad, Stadsbyggnadskontoret (Helsingborg Town and Country Planning Office), Helsingborg (in Swedish)

Hilding-Rydevik, T. (1987) *Municipalities, Ecology, Protection of Environment and Natural Resources: a Study of Organisation and the Handling of Environmental Issues*, Report R99, Swedish Council for Building Research, Stockholm (in Swedish)

Hilding-Rydevik, T. (1990) *Environmental Impact Assessment of Projects and Plans in Municipal Comprehensive Planning*, Report R11, Swedish Council for Building Research, Stockholm

Hilding-Rydevik, T. (2003) 'Concluding remarks', in Hilding-Rydevik, T. (ed), *Environmental Assessment of Plans and Programs: Nordic Experiences in Relation to the Implementation of the EU Directive 2001/42/EC*, Report 2003:4, Nordregio, Stockholm

Isaksson, K. (2004) *Sustainability: Weighting, Prioritising, Challenges*, Trita-Infra 04-003, Municipality and the Territory, Urban Planning Unit, Royal Institute of Technology, Stockholm (in Swedish)

Johannesson, R., Boverket (National Board of Housing, Building and Planning) (2004) Telephone interview, 3 February

Johansson, H. (1992) *EIA in Huddinge Municipality: an Evaluation of Environmental Impact Assessments in Land Use Planning*, Huddinge Municipality, Huddinge (in Swedish)

Käärik, A. (1999) 'Report of Swedish experiences of SEA in comprehensive municipal planning and infrastructure in Sweden', in *Tema Nord Miljö*, p539, Copenhagen

Lerman, P. (2003) 'Impact assessment in Swedish planning', in Hilding-Rydevik, T. (ed), *Environmental Assessment of Plans and Programs: Nordic Experiences in Relation to the Implementation of the EU Directive 2001/42/EC*, Report 2003:4, Nordregio, Stockholm

Naturvårdsverket (Swedish Environmental Protection Agency) (2000a) *Land Use Planning with Strategic Environmental Assessment*, Report 620-5041-9, Naturvårdsverket, Stockholm (in Swedish)

Naturvårdsverket (Swedish Environmental Protection Agency) (2000b) *Strategic Environmental Assessment: a Useful Tool for Environmental Management*, Report 5109, Naturvårdsverket, Stockholm (in Swedish)

Nilsson, K. (1991) *Evaluation of Environmental Impact Assessment: Korsta-Petersvik in Sundsvall Municipality*, Miljödelegationen Sundsvall-Timrå, National Board of Housing, Building and Planning, Sundsvall (in Swedish)

Nolvall, L. (1998) *EIA in Stockholm, Evaluation of Environmental Impact Assessments of Stockholm's Detailed Development Plans*, (draft), Department of Human Geography, University of Stockholm, Stockholm (in Swedish)

Oscarsson, A., Olausson, I. and Heiter, Å. (2003) *EIA of Detailed Development Plans – Application and Quality*, EIA Centre, Swedish University of Agricultural Sciences, Uppsala (in Swedish)

Persson, J. (1996) *The Search for EIA: Literature Review of EIA in Land Use Planning*, SACTH 1996:1, Institute for Urban Design and Planning, Chalmers University of Technology, Göteborg (in Swedish)

Skeppström, S. (1998) *EIA Effectiveness in Detailed Development Plans*, Examansarbetsserien 1998:17, Department of Land and Water Resources, Royal Institute of Technology, Stockholm (in Swedish)

Storbjörk, S. (2004) *Prioritising Environmental Issues? Municipal Politicians and the Conditions for Local Environmental Management*, Trita-Infra 04-015, (The Municipality and the Territory), Urban Planning Unit, Kommunen och territoriet Royal Institute of Technology, Stockholm (in Swedish)

Thune Hedström, R (2004) Swedish Association of Local Authorities and Regions, statement at seminar, *Guidance on SEA of Plans and Programmes Seminar*, 18 February, Swedish Environmental Protection Agency, Stockholm

15

United Kingdom

Carys Jones, Mark Baker, Jeremy Carter, Stephen Jay,
Michael Short and Christopher Wood

Introduction

The current development of SEA in relation to land use planning in the UK is being driven primarily by implementation of Directive 2001/42/EC ('the SEA Directive') (European Commission (EC), 2001), which came into force in July 2004. In the UK, this is taking place in a complex and dynamic situation, involving four distinct but related dimensions. These are: the SEA Directive itself; reform of the land use planning system; the existence of devolved administrations with responsibility for planning and the environment; and a legacy of knowledge and experience of the environmental and sustainability appraisal of development plans.

The SEA Directive has led to the introduction of new legislation, guidance and practice on assessing the environmental effects of land use plans, at both regional and local levels. However, the concept of assessing the environmental consequences of land use plans was not unfamiliar to UK planners. Previously, the UK had developed considerable experience in assessing the effects of development plans through environmental appraisal (EA) and the more recent sustainability appraisal (SA). As well as discussing the implementation of the SEA Directive, this chapter also highlights the developing experience of planning authorities, taking the experience of one local planning authority (LPA) as a case study.

Context

Land use planning system

The primary legislation for planning is the Town and Country Planning Act 1990, as amended by the Planning and Compulsory Purchase Act 2004. These acts are given force through secondary legislation and guidance from central government.

The structure of local government in England is single tier in 36 metropolitan areas and 46 non-metropolitan unitary authorities, and two tier in London (32 borough councils) and in 34 county councils and their associated 237 district councils (Cullingworth and Nadin, 2002). Before the development of any land is carried out, planning permission must be sought from the relevant authority, usually the LPA. The authority will make a decision on whether to grant permission, taking account of the development plan for the area concerned. Development plans indicate the way in which a LPA proposes to use land under its control for a specified period (typically ten years). However, the development plan is not prescriptive, and a LPA must also have regard to any other material considerations, such as government policy, when making a decision on development.

In 2004, major reform of the planning system was inaugurated which, amongst other things, moved the emphasis for strategic planning from LPAs to the regional level. Regional planning bodies are now responsible for the preparation of statutory regional spatial strategies, which guide development by establishing broad locations and criteria for development. County councils retain some of their strategic planning role through the preparation of minerals and waste plans, and through working with regional planning bodies on any sub-regional strategies that cover their areas. At the local level, LPAs will now be preparing local development frameworks (LDFs) made up of

- local development plan documents, consisting of:
  - core strategy;
  - proposals map;
  - area action plan;
  - site-specific allocations of land;
- supplementary planning documents;
- statement of community involvement.

In addition, a formal scheme must be drawn up showing the programme for preparing each of the documents. Under this system, the statutory development plan for a local authority area consists of the relevant regional spatial strategy together with its development plan documents. This reform signals the introduction of a broader spatial planning approach, in which a wide set of issues is to be given consideration. It is intended that plan preparation times will be shortened through the guiding influence of regional spatial strategies. The emphasis is also upon the early plan-making stages, involving data collection and consultation, and a more accessible and transparent system is sought through greater community involvement.

SEA legislation and guidance

The implementation of the SEA Directive in the UK is through framework legislation that applies to all plans and programmes subject to the directive. One set of regulations applies solely to England, or to both England and any other part of the UK (*The Environmental Assessment of Plans and Programmes Regulations*

2004).[1] Separate regulations apply to each of Scotland, Wales and Northern Ireland, covering plans and programmes relating solely to these territories. These are all collectively referred to below as 'the Regulations'; they cover all sectors referred to in the SEA Directive, including land use planning, and translate the SEA Directive into UK law with little expansion of its requirements. However, the Scottish Executive has announced its intention to extend the scope of the SEA Directive for plans and programmes relating to Scotland through additional legislation, by which SEA will be required for a wide range of strategies, plans and programmes (Scottish Executive, 2003b). Throughout the UK, however, SEA has applied to the full range of plans and programmes prepared for land use planning, including those still being prepared under the pre-reform planning system, since July 2004.

Guidance on undertaking SEA within planning has been issued by central government (Office of the Deputy Prime Minister (ODPM), 2003c),[2] indicating a five-stage process, with the emphasis on integrating SEA with the plan-making process. The recommended approach to SEA combines the 'baseline-led' approach of the SEA Directive with the 'objectives-led' approach of evolving SA practice in England. Thus, objectives and indicators for SEA (not a requirement of the SEA Directive) are set at the early stages in conjunction with the collection of baseline data. The intention is to use such objectives and indicators to describe, analyse and compare environmental effects. This guidance is designed to assist the carrying out of either SEA or SA. However, under the reformed planning system, a full SA (which is intended to comply with the SEA Directive) will be required for regional spatial strategies and local development frameworks. The SEA guidance for planning authorities is therefore soon to be subsumed by guidance specifically on SA (ODPM, 2004c).

In addition, various supporting guidance material exists to assist authorities in implementing SEA. During the development of the ODPM guidance for planning authorities a series of pilot studies (ODPM, 2003b) was undertaken. These studies analysed the effectiveness and feasibility of the draft guidance and explored various elements of practice required for SEA. At the regional level, the South West Regional Assembly initiated a series of studies (Brooke et al, 2004), with local authorities and regional partners, to consider the implications of the SEA Directive and help the region prepare for its implementation. The ODPM maintains a website on SEA containing links to relevant legislation and guidance.[2]

Environmental and sustainability appraisal of development plans

The implementation of SEA in the UK is set against a background of a 'prototype' form of assessment, environmental appraisal. This was initiated in 1992, when government guidance instructed LPAs to consider the environmental effects of development plans (Department of the Environment (DOE), 1992), and LPAs subsequently developed considerable experience in undertaking EA. The EA process had its roots in policy analysis, with a three-stage approach of describing environmental stock, scoping the plan and appraising the plan. This takes an objectives-led approach, which is rather different in concept to the baseline-led approach of the SEA Directive.

However, EA was gradually replaced by a broader sustainability appraisal, in which social and economic, as well as environmental, impacts of development plan, are assessed. The initial focus for SA was at the regional level, with a recommendation that it be applied to development plans (Department of the Environment, Transport and the Regions (DETR), 2000). Research has confirmed the uptake of SA for development plans (Therivel and Minas, 2002; Short et al, 2004), the development of innovative practice for both EA and SA, such as team approaches and the use of panels to support the process. This shift towards SA is reinforced through ongoing commitment by government, and the specific requirement for the SA of regional spatial strategies and local development frameworks in the reformed planning system.

The application of SA includes meeting the requirements of the SEA Directive, even for plans and programmes not necessarily falling with the remit of the directive. Concerns have, however, been raised about the relationship between SEA and SA, and whether environmental issues will become sidelined in SA (Sheate et al, 2004). In addition, analyses of EA and SA practice to date have indicated some weaknesses, for example, in the consideration of alternatives and the use of baseline information (Short et al, 2004). The challenge is, therefore, to reconcile the specific procedures of the Directive and its clear environmental focus, with the existing weaker and broader appraisal systems that have become embedded in planning practice.

Case study: Sefton Council environmental and sustainability appraisals

Sefton is located in the north west of England, and is one of the five metropolitan districts of Merseyside. It has a population of 290,000 and is one of the largest and most varied metropolitan authority areas in the UK. It includes six separate towns, a coastline of national and international nature conservation importance, and a rural area comprising high quality agricultural land and small villages – all within the Merseyside Green Belt. Sefton also lies within the Mersey Forest.

This case study of Sefton Council highlights the evolving approaches to assessing the environmental effects of development plans, the benefits and weaknesses experienced by the authority, and the progression to SEA. It draws on research recently undertaken on the use of environmental and sustainability appraisal in English land use planning (Short et al, 2004).

Background and approach

The SA of the Sefton Unitary Development Plan First Deposit Draft (Sefton Council, 2002) was a progression of the EA of the development plan in the early 1990s. The SA was based on regional action for sustainability criteria, and previous

EAs. The appraisal was undertaken in house with ongoing discussions between the appraisal group (two planners directly involved in plan preparation, two external to the planning department, and an independent chair from the University of Liverpool) and the policy team. Appraisal occurred at the plan review stage, thus evaluating policies when it was possible to influence them. Assessment was based on scoring and weighting plan policies against a range of sustainability criteria and objectives, leading to an agreed final score.

Influences of the appraisal

The appraisal process focused the development of the plan on sustainability as opposed to environmental issues. Environmental issues were important, but it was not apparent that the environmental content changed to any great degree as a result of the appraisal. Overall, 12 policies were deleted, nine new policies were added and a number were merged together. The new policies addressed environmental risk, and consolidated sustainable development issues. The SA was perceived as worthwhile, as criteria and objectives were developed and embedded in the plan development process.

Although some weaknesses were experienced, these were outweighed by the positive aspects (Box 15.1). Indeed, the appraisal process itself was perceived as important – if not more important – than the outcomes, with the informality and simplicity of approach being key features.

Box 15.1 Strengths and weaknesses of Sefton Sustainability Appraisal

Strengths

- dialogue that developed between the appraisal group and the policy team;
- development of policies;
- timing that allowed policies and appraisal to evolve together;
- overall learning process.

Weaknesses

- potential to get caught up in detail and mechanics of the process, particularly in relation to scoring and weighting;
- short time frame;
- overlap of membership between the appraisal group and the policy team, which made ownership of changes to policies difficult;
- lack of assessment of compatibility of policies; and
- lack of a policy impact matrix.

This pre-SEA Directive approach to SA did not explicitly address the key elements required by the directive. Thus only selected issues were covered: mitigation through changes to policies; integration of appraisal in decision-making; consultation and public participation; and monitoring. Nevertheless, much positive experience for the future in the context of SEA was evident.

Implementing SEA

The first stage was to develop a stepwise screening methodology to consider significance when deciding if SEA was required. New action for sustainability indicators plus specific SEA indicators were developed, with the intention of utilizing common approaches across all the Merseyside authorities to minimize conflicts. In addition, the objective was to prepare indicators and baseline material, following consultation, and utilize these for the next three to four years. Thus, the move to SEA draws on experience of the previous application of EA and SA.

SEA system

The UK's formal SEA process for land use planning is now firmly based upon the provisions of the SEA Directive. Its *legal basis* rests on the regulations referred to above, which mirror the provisions of the directive faithfully, while currently containing no additions that would take the UK beyond its requirements. The vast majority of the plans and programmes subjected to SEA will be those prepared under the planning system; several hundred environmental reports are expected each year (ODPM, 2004a).

The regulations are predicated on the assumption that SEA is integrated with the preparation of land use plans from the commencement of the planning process. The draft guidance on SA, into which SEA is due to be subsumed, is very clear about the desirability of *integration*:

> SA is an integral part of good plan-making and should not be seen as a separate activity. . . . The Government expects . . . Local Planning Authorities . . . to take an integrated approach to achieving these [sustainability] objectives in their plans
>
> ODPM (2004c, p16).

However, pre-regulations practice has not been encouraging, as some EAs and SAs of local and regional plans were commenced too late in the plan-making process to be properly integrated (Curran et al, 1998; Smith and Sheate, 2001; Counsell and Haughton, 2002).

The government has issued general SEA *guidance* for the whole of the UK (ODPM et al, 2004), to be used where no specific sector guidance has been developed. Specific interim SEA guidance for Scottish and English planning authorities preparing land use plans was published earlier (ODPM, 2003c; Scottish Executive, 2003a), although this is due to be replaced by the SA guidance. This recommends five stages:

A   setting the context, establishing the baseline and deciding on the scope;
B   developing and refining options;
C   appraising the effects of the plan;
D   consulting on the plan and SA report;
E   monitoring implementation of the plan.

ODPM (2004c, pp17–19).

Figure 15.1 shows the inter-relationship of these five stages. A number of appendices are also given in the guidance, on topics such as collecting and presenting baseline information.

The *coverage* of the UK SEA system includes all land use plans:

* local plans;
* unitary development plans;
* structure plans;
* minerals and waste local plans;
* regional planning guidance;
* the Spatial Development Strategy for London;
* local development documents;
* regional spatial strategies.

The exceptions are those that determine the use of small areas at local level or are minor modifications to existing plans and where preparation commenced before 21 July 2004 and adoption was prior to 21 July 2006. Pre-regulations practice in the UK demonstrated that virtually all the authorities responsible undertook EAs or SAs, despite their not being mandatory (Therivel and Minas, 2002; Short et al, 2004).

In principle, the UK now has a comprehensive *tiered* environmental assessment system. The EA of government policy has been an avowed intention since the early 1990s (DOE, 1991; DETR, 1998). The regulations apply to the new spatial strategies prepared at the regional level and to district and unitary authority local development documents. Project EIA, of course, has been in place since the implementation of the European EIA Directive (Commission of the European Communities, 1985) in 1988. The tiered SEA system in England can therefore be represented by Figure 15.2.

In reality, few central government departments have undertaken meaningful policy EA but, recently, ODPM has started to undertake formal SEA of its planning guidance (ODPM, 2004b). While the quality of the pre-regulations EA of regional guidance was poor (Smith and Sheate, 2001; Counsell and Haughton, 2002), the practical basis for their assessment, and for that of local development documents, exists.

The objective of the SEA Directive is to promote *sustainable development* (European Commission, 2001, Article 1). It is perhaps ironic that neither the regulations nor the original English SEA guidance (ODPM, 2003c) refers to sustainable development by name. The Scottish guidance specifically spells out sustainable development principles relevant to environmental assessment (Scottish

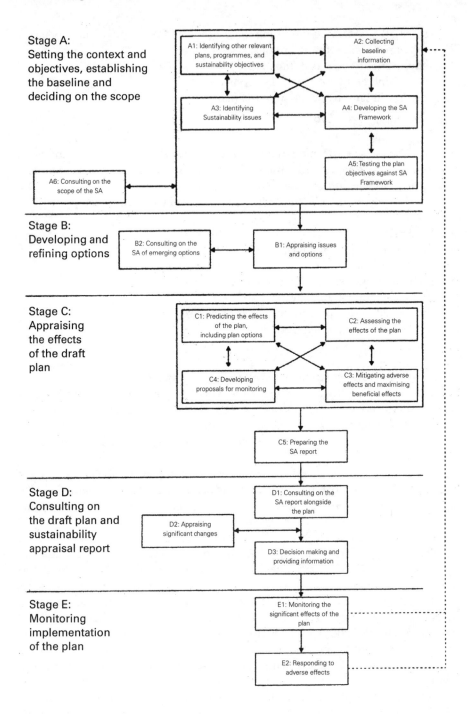

Figure 15.1 *Relationship between UK sustainability appraisal tasks*

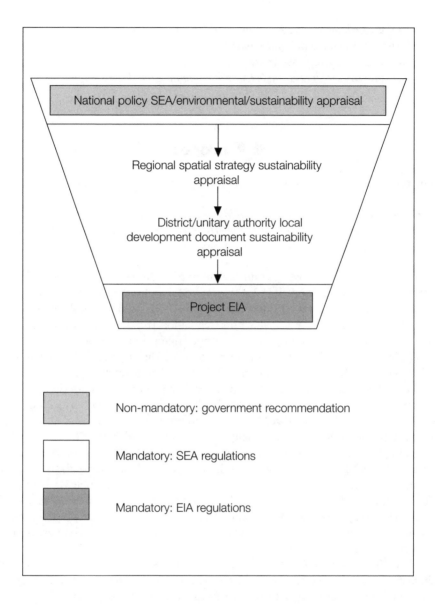

Figure 15.2 *Tiering of environmental assessment in the UK*

Executive, 2003a, para 16), and the generic UK SEA guidance contains a chapter on SEA and sustainable development. The draft SA guidance states clearly that the 'purpose of SA is to promote sustainable development through better integration of sustainability considerations into the preparation and adoption of plans' (ODPM, 2004c, p16). Achieving sustainable development is taken to mean meeting four objectives, no one of which is more important than another, at the same time:

- *social progress which recognizes the needs of everyone;*
- *effective protection of the environment;*
- *prudent use of natural resources;*
- *maintenance of high and stable levels of economic growth and employment.*

ODPM (2004c, p23).

SEA process

The regulations contain three requirements relating to *alternatives*. Thus:

> *the report shall identify, describe and evaluate the likely significant effects on the environment of . . . reasonable alternatives*
>
> Regulation 12 (2).[3]

Secondly, the report must contain 'an outline of the reasons for selecting the alternatives dealt with' (Schedule 2, paragraph 8). Finally, the LPA's final statement must include 'the reasons for choosing the plan . . . as adopted, in the light of the other reasonable alternatives dealt with' (Regulation 16(4)(e)). The draft guidance contains an annex on identifying and comparing options in which it proposes a hierarchy of alternatives (need or demand → mode or process → location → timing and detailed implementation) (ODPM, 2004c, Annex 10).

However, pre-regulations practice gives few grounds for confidence about the treatment of alternatives (Sheate et al, 2004). A recent analysis of 25 EA/SA reports indicated that only three treated the environmental impacts of alternatives adequately and another three partially (Jones et al, submitted).

Screening is unlikely to be a major activity in the UK. The regulations specify criteria (Schedule 1) to determine whether a plan should be assessed, and require authorities to seek the views of the consultation bodies (Regulation 9(2)). However, the draft guidance makes it clear that all new and modified regional spatial strategies and local development documents require a SA, into which SEA is to be integrated. Small area planning documents, including local development schemes, do not require SA (ODPM, 2004c).

The Environment Agency, the Countryside Agency, English Nature and English Heritage must be consulted by planning authorities 'when deciding on the scope and level of detail of the information that must be included in the [environmental] report' (Regulation 12(5)). The draft guidance suggests that this consultation should be based on a *scoping* report that includes:

- plan objectives;
- other relevant plans, programmes and objectives;
- baseline information;
- social, environmental and economic issues identified;
- the framework for the SA;
- the alternatives to be considered;

- any other proposed methodologies;
- proposed structure and level of detail of report.

ODPM (2004c, Annex 7).

It is not mandatory to consult the public on the scope of the report. Pre-regulations practice has not emphasized scoping, although there have been informal approaches to the consultation bodies for guidance on the content of reports.

The regulations require *prediction and evaluation* of impacts. The environmental report must 'identify, describe and evaluate the likely significant effects on the environment of . . . implementing the plan' (Regulation 12(2)). The draft guidance suggests that the potential effects of the preferred options 'should be quantified where possible, or a subjective judgement made where this is not possible, with reference to the baseline situation' (ODPM, 2004c, p59).

Once the changes to the sustainability baseline have been identified, they should be described 'in terms of their magnitude, their geographical scale, the time period over which they will occur', and so on. The significance of these effects should then be assessed in terms of 'scale and permanence and the nature and sensitivity of the receptor' (ODPM, 2004c, p59, see also Annex 8) and compared with the baseline data and with the targets prepared earlier in the process. To date, the predictions and assessments in most EA/SA reports have been presented in tables that indicate that, for example, an air pollution effect may be worse under scenario A than under scenario B.

The regulations require the likely significant *additional impacts* of land use plans to be assessed. Thus, 'short, medium and long-term effects, permanent and temporary effects, positive and negative effects, and secondary, cumulative and synergistic effects' (Schedule 2, para 6) must be described in the environmental report. The draft English guidance contains an annex on secondary, cumulative and synergistic effects, which states:

> *Many sustainability problems result from the accumulation of multiple small and often indirect effects, rather than a few large and obvious ones. Examples include loss of tranquillity, changes in the landscape, and climate change'*

ODPM (2004c, p134).

There is, however, little evidence from pre-regulations practice that these types of effects have been dealt with well in England.

Report preparation is a crucial requirement of the regulations. The environmental report must include descriptions of, inter alia, the environmental characteristics of the area, existing environmental problems, environmental protection objectives, predicted effects, mitigation measures, reasons for selecting alternatives and monitoring arrangements (Schedule 2). Unsurprisingly, the extant guidance has focused on the provision of this information (ODPM, 2003c; Scottish Executive, 2003a; ODPM, 2004c; ODPM et al, 2004; see also Therivel, 2004). The draft SA guidance suggests that a SA report should include:

1 summary and outline;
2 appraisal methodology;
3 background;
4 sustainability objectives, baseline and context;
5 plan issues and options;
6 plan policies
7 implementation.

ODPM (2004c, Annex 7).

Pre-regulations practice has not been encouraging. Of 25 EA/SA reports analysed by Jones et al (submitted) only 5 met the requirement to identify and describe the likely significant effects of implementing the plan (prediction and evaluation above); 14 did so partly; and 6 did not meet this requirement. Four out of 25 reports met the requirement to evaluate these significant effects; 12 did so partially; and 9 did not meet it.

Environmental reports are made available for *review*. The consultation bodies and the public consultees (affected parties) must be notified about the availability of the draft plan and its accompanying environmental report, and be given sufficient time to express their views (Regulation 13(2),(3)). If significant changes are made to the preferred options in the light of public participation, these changes must be assessed and the environmental report modified (ODPM, 2004c, p61). It appears that pre-regulations environmental reports were regarded as providing sufficient information for decision making, despite the fact that their quality was often poor (Lee et al, 1999). Only 2 of the 25 LPA EA/SAs analysed by Jones et al (submitted) involved a review of the entire appraisal process. Ten LPAs just reviewed the appraisal report and 13 did not meet the requirement at all.

The significant environmental effects of the implementation of land use plans must be monitored by the responsible authority to identify unforeseen adverse effects and take appropriate action (Regulation 17). The environmental report must describe the measures envisaged concerning *monitoring* (Schedule 2). The draft SA guidance contains an annex on monitoring, which suggests that a series of questions should be addressed in the report:

1 What needs to be monitored?
2 What sort of information is required?
3 What are the existing sources of monitoring information?
4 Are there any gaps in the existing information, and how can these be filled?
5 What should be done if adverse effects are found?
6 Who is responsible for the various monitoring activities, when should these be carried out, and what is the appropriate format for presenting the monitoring results?

ODPM (2004c, Annex 11)

The LPA must include 'the measures that are to be taken to monitor the significant environmental effect of the implementation of the plan' in its final statement

(Regulation 16(4)(f)). Of the 25 EA/SAs analysed by Jones et al (submitted), 2 LPAs monitored all the anticipated plan impacts, 13 monitored some of the plan impacts and10 did not monitor impacts at all.

The *mitigation* 'measures envisaged to prevent, reduce and, as fully as possible, offset any significant adverse effects on the environment of implementing the plan' must be specified in environmental reports (Regulations, Schedule 2, para 7). The draft guidance stresses the importance of avoiding adverse effects and maximizing beneficial effects. It suggests that mitigation measures may involve changes to the plan, such as adding, deleting or refining policies and proposals or bringing forward new alternatives (ODPM, 2004c, p60). Other proposals include: refining options (to increase positive effects and minimize adverse effects); technical implementation measures; tiering to EIA; changes to other plans; and contingency arrangements for dealing with possible adverse effects.

The regulations contain several requirements relating to *consultation and public participation*. They require reference to the consultation bodies at the screening, scoping and review stages of the SEA process and public participation at the review stage. Transboundary consultations, which are likely to be relatively rare in the UK, are channelled through central government. The LPA must prepare a final statement which includes an explanation of:

- how the environmental report has been taken into account;
- how the opinions of the consultation bodies, of the public consultees, of the public generally, and of any transboundary consultations have been taken into account

Regulation 16(4).

Although the regulations do not require consultation with the public until the environmental report is finalized, the draft guidance indicates that the public 'must' be consulted on the SA of the issues and options (before the final decision is made) (ODPM, 2004c, p28). No advice on methods is proffered.

Pre-regulations practice is once again discouraging. Of the 25 EA/SA processes studied by Jones et al (submitted), only 10 LPAs consulted both key environmental organizations and public groups or individuals. A further six LPAs met this requirement partly and nine did not meet it at all.

SEA outcome

The aim of SEA is to influence land use plan *decision making*. It is for this reason that the regulations require the competent authority to state, once the decision on the plan has been made:

- how environmental considerations were integrated into the plan;
- how the environmental report was taken into account;
- how the results of consultations were taken into account;

- the reasons for choosing the alternative adopted;
- proposals for monitoring environmental effects of plan implementation

Regulation 16(4).

There is scope for increasing this influence since Short et al (2004) reported that more than two-thirds of LPAs believed that pre-regulations EA/SA had little or no influence on development plan objectives and policies, and nearly two-thirds believed that their plan would have developed in the same manner without any appraisal having been undertaken. Jones et al's (submitted) reported that only 11 of 25 LPAs took the environmental report fully into account during decision making. Eight partially met the requirement to do this and six did not meet it at all. However, 13 of the 25 LPAs showed evidence of change to development plans as a result of appraisal, often in the fine tuning of policies and proposals. Six of the 25 LPAs prepared the requisite final statement, 8 met this requirement partially and 11 did not prepare a statement.

It is notoriously difficult to obtain information about the *costs and benefits* of EIA (Wood, 2002). SEA is no different. Short et al (2004) showed that pre-regulations EA/SAs cost an average of £9,000 (3 per cent of the total cost) and took an average of 35 days to complete (less than 0.5 per cent of the time spent on the plan). Therivel and Minas (2002) reported similar results, but ODPM (2004a) estimated that post-regulations land use plan SEAs might cost £10–50,000 and require 50–60 person days.

ODPM (2004a, p3) suggested that the total cost of UK compliance with the SEA Directive might be £25–40 million per annum. Despite its lack of significant influence on plan content (partially explained by lack of legal force and synchronicity), 87 per cent of LPAs believed the overall appraisal process to be worthwhile because of the additional knowledge about sustainable development and the environment gained, the fine tuning of policy, site related benefits and improved liaison with consultees (Short et al, 2004; see also Therivel and Minas, 2002). Jones et al (submitted) also reported that SEA was generally regarded positively – that is, that its benefits probably outweighed its costs.

As in the case of EIA (Wood, 2002), evidence that SEA has led to any improvement in *environmental quality* generally is likely to remain theoretical or anecdotal. In the UK, as elsewhere, it is extremely difficult to distinguish the effect of SEA from that of an array of other anticipatory environmental management measures. Short et al (2004) reported that perhaps 10 per cent of pre-regulations EA/SAs had generated some site-related benefits.

The SEA Directive contains a provision for SEA *system monitoring* – the European Commission must prepare a five year review on its application and effectiveness by July 2006 (EC, 2001, Article 12, para 3). Unsurprisingly, this provision has not been transposed into the regulations. However, if the record of government sponsored and other research into UK EIA is any guide (Wood, 2002), ad hoc monitoring of the UK SEA system will be rigorous. The various studies of pre-regulations EA/SA practice (Smith and Sheate, 2001; Counsell and Haughton, 2002; Therivel and Minas 2002; Short et al, 2004; Jones et al, submitted) indicate that an appropriate foundation has been laid.

Conclusion

Table 15.1 provides a summary of the UK SEA system as it stands following the implementation of the SEA Directive, which has provided the model for the regulations and guidance that now apply to planning, and has greatly raised the profile of SEA for local planners. Unsurprisingly, therefore, the strengths and weaknesses of the SEA system now in place in the UK closely reflect those of the SEA Directive, especially since the UK government has not formally sought to go beyond the dictates of that directive. So, for example, the regulations' limited provisions for consultation during scoping mirror exactly those of the SEA Directive. Similarly, the regulations' emphasis on measuring likely significant effects upon the environment illustrates the SEA Directive's own unmistakable EIA pedigree.

However, on closer inspection, a more complex picture emerges of the SEA system evolving within land use planning in the UK than that of simple, direct transposition of European legislation. This becomes evident when government guidance, as opposed to legislation, for SEA in land use planning is considered. Here, there are signs of other influences on the shape that SEA is now taking within planning. Firstly, pre-regulations SEA practice continues to be influential. For example, environmental objectives, rather than just baseline information, are recommended as a basis for assessing the likely effects of a plan (ODPM, 2003c). This is clearly inherited from the policy based approach to the SEA of land use plans that evolved throughout the 1990s, under the name of EA. In other respects, too, the experience and practice that planning authorities in the UK developed prior to the regulations, as illustrated by the Sefton case study above, is now being incorporated into the formal SEA system via official guidance.

Secondly, there has been a concerted shift towards SA, as a comprehensive method of capturing and assessing not only the environmental, but also the explicitly economic and social, implications of plans (ODPM, 2004c). This reflects not just the natural evolution that has been taking place of EA at a local level, but also broader governmental objectives being pursued through the language of sustainable development. This has raised questions about whether environmental issues are being marginalized, and whether SEA's objectives can be properly achieved if they are subsumed into broader SA (Royal Commission on Environmental Pollution, 2002). Interestingly, it is here that the influence of devolution on the development of SEA for planning can best be seen: the Scottish Executive has not followed the UK government down the road of SA, but has stated its preference for SEA as a stand-alone exercise (Scottish Executive, 2003b). Future comparative studies of SEA practice either side of the Scotland–England border may well prove informative on the relative merits of the two approaches.

Finally, reform of the UK planning system itself has provided an opportunity for SEA to be further developed. Although the new regime of plan making is complex, and may prove difficult to coordinate with SEA/SA requirements, the over-riding characteristic of the proposed place of assessment within this new system is that of complete integration with plan preparation (ODPM, 2003a). This suggests that the wealth of experience of assessing environmental effects at

Table 15.1 *Evaluation of SEA of land use plans in the UK*

Criterion	Criterion met	Comments
	SYSTEM CRITERIA	
Legal basis	■	Regulations specifically implement European SEA Directive. SEA mainly integrated into town and country planning system
Integration	▲	Guidance states SEA should be started when plan first considered, although not fully practised pre-regulations
Guidance	■	Interim SEA guidance issued 2003, to be replaced by sustainability appraisal guidance
Coverage	■	Comprehensive coverage of impacts (as defined in SEA Directive) of significant land use plans
Tiering	▲	SEA not mandatory at higher policy level; tiering for regional spatial strategy SEA, local development document SEA and project EIA
Sustainable development	▲	Some, but not all, guidance stresses sustainable development as objective of SEA although regulations make no mention
	PROCESS CRITERIA	
Alternatives	■	Impacts of reasonable alternatives must be identified, described, evaluated, and choice of alternative explained
Screening	■	Plans requiring SEA specified in guidance
Scoping	▲	Consultation bodies, but not public, must be consulted about scope and level of detail of information in environmental report
Prediction/ evaluation	▲	Impacts of plans must be identified, described and evaluated but assessment against environmental criteria not compulsory
Additional impacts	■	Likely significant effects of land use plans include secondary, cumulative synergistic and long term effects
Report preparation	■	Environmental report must include baseline, predicted impacts, preferred alternative, incorporation of environmental considerations, mitigation, monitoring
Review	■	Consultation bodies and public consultees must be invited to express opinion on plan and environmental report

Table 15.1 *Evaluation of SEA of land use plans in the UK (continued)*

Criterion	Criterion met	Comments
Monitoring	▲	SEA reports must describe measures for monitoring significant effects of plan implementation, although not fully practised pre-regulations
Mitigation	■	Mitigation measures to prevent, reduce and offset significant environmental effects of plan implementation must be described in environmental report
Consultation and public participation	■	Consultation bodies consulted on screening, scoping and report. Public consulted on report. Opinions must be taken into account in decision
		OUTCOME CRITERIA
Decision making	▲	Too early to evaluate. Environmental/ sustainability appraisal (EA/SA) led to minor modifications to some land use plans
Costs and benefits	▲	Too early to evaluate. EA/SA generally regarded positively, partly due to indirect benefits
Environmental quality	?	Too early to evaluate. Pre-regulation EA/SA processes generated very minor 'on the ground' benefits
System monitoring	?	No provision for system monitoring. Some monitoring studies of EA/SA

Notes: ■ – Yes
    ▲ – Partially
    ☐ – No
    ? – Don't know

more strategic levels within UK land use planning is now being drawn upon to advantage.

Notes

1   Statutory Instrument SI 2004, No 1668
2   All ODPM documents referenced below are available from www.odpm.gov.uk
3   Quotes from, and specific references to, the regulations refer to SI 2004, no 1668 (those applying to England, or to England along with another part of the UK)

References

Brooke, C., James, E., Jones, R. and Therivel, R. (2004) 'Implementing the strategic environmental assessment (SEA) Directive in the south west of England', *European Environment*, vol 14, pp38–152

Commission of the European Communities (1985) 'Council Directive of 27 June 1985 on the assessment of the effects of certain public and private projects on the environment', *Official Journal of the European Communities*, vol L175, pp40–48, 5 July

Counsell, D. and Haughton, G. (2002) 'Sustainability appraisal – delivering more sustainable regional planning guidance?', *Town and Country Planning*, vol 71, pp14–17

Cullingworth, J. B. and Nadin, V. (2002) *Town & Country Planning in the UK*, 13th edition, Routledge, London

Curran, J. M., Wood, C. M. and Hilton, M. (1998) 'Environmental appraisal of UK development plans: current practice and future directions', *Environment and Planning B*, vol 25, pp411–433

Department of the Environment (1991) *Policy Appraisal and the Environment: a Guide for Government Departments*, DoE, London

Department of the Environment (1992) *Planning Policy Guidance Note 12: Development Plans and Regional Planning Guidance*, HMSO, London

Department of the Environment, Transport and the Regions (1998) *Policy Appraisal and the Environment: Policy Guidance*, DETR, London

Department of the Environment, Transport and the Regions (2000) *Planning Policy Guidance Note 11: Regional Planning*, The Stationery Office, London

European Commission (2001) 'Directive 2001/42/EC of the European Parliament and of the Council of 27 June 2001 on the assessment of the effects of certain plans and programmes on the environment', *Official Journal of the European Communities*, vol L197, pp30–37, 21 July

Jones, C., Short., M., Baker, M., Carter, J. and Wood, C. M. submitted 'The use of environmental and sustainability appraisal in English land use plan-making', submitted to *Journal of Environmental Planning and Management*

Lee, N., Colley., R., Bonde, J. and Simpson, J. (1999) *Reviewing the Quality of Environmental Statements and Environmental Appraisals*, Occasional Paper 55, School of Environment and Development (Planning and Landscape), University of Manchester, Manchester

Office of the Deputy Prime Minister (2003a) *Creating Local Development Frameworks*, Consultation Paper, ODPM, London

Office of the Deputy Prime Minister (2003b) *SEA Directive: Guidance for Planning Authorities: Pilot Studies*, ODPM, London

Office of the Deputy Prime Minister (2003c) *The Strategic Environmental Assessment Directive: Guidance for Planning Authorities*, ODPM, London

Office of the Deputy Prime Minister (2004a) *Full Regulatory Impact Assessment on Regulations*, ODPM, London

Office of the Deputy Prime Minister (2004b) *Strategic Environmental Assessment Environmental Report, Consultation on Planning Policy Statement 10: Planning for Sustainable Waste Management*, ODPM, London

Office of the Deputy Prime Minister (2004c) *Sustainability Appraisal of Regional Spatial Strategies and Local Development Frameworks*, Consultation Paper, ODPM, London

Office of the Deputy Prime Minister, Scottish Executive, Welsh Assembly Government and Northern Ireland Department of the Environment (2004) *A Draft Practical Guide to the Strategic Environmental Assessment Directive*, ODPM, London

Royal Commission on Environmental Pollution (2002) *Twenty-third Report: Environmental Planning*, Cm 5459, The Stationery Office, London

Scottish Executive (2003a) *Environmental Assessment of Development Plans: Interim Planning Advice*, Scottish Executive, Edinburgh

Scottish Executive (2003b) *Strategic Environmental Assessment*, Consultation Paper, Paper 2003/31, Scottish Executive, Edinburgh

Sefton Council (2002) *Report on the Sustainability Appraisal of the First Deposit Draft*, July, SC, Liverpool

Sheate, W. R., Byron, H. and Smith, S. (2004) 'Implementing the SEA Directive: sectoral challenges and opportunities for the UK and EU', *European Environment*, vol 14, pp73–93

Short, M., Jones, C., Carter, J., Baker, M. and Wood, C. M. (2004) 'Current practice in the strategic environmental assessment of development plans in England', *Regional Studies*, vol 38, pp177–190

Smith, S. P. and Sheate, W. R. (2001) 'Sustainability appraisal of English regional plans: incorporating the requirements of the EU strategic environmental assessment directive', *Impact Assessment and Project Appraisal*, vol 19, pp263–276

Therivel, R. (2004) *Strategic Environmental Assessment in Action*, Earthscan, London

Therivel, R. and Minas, P. (2002) 'Ensuring effective sustainability appraisal', *Impact Assessment and Project Appraisal*, vol 29, pp81–91

Wood, C. M. (2002) *Environmental Impact Assessment: a Comparative Review*, 2nd edition, Prentice Hall, Harlow

16

United States

Ron Bass

Introduction

The requirement to prepare strategic environmental assessments, known as programmatic environmental impact statements (PEISs) under the National Environmental Policy Act (NEPA), pre-dated similar mandates in other parts of the world. The reason for the early application of EIA to policies, plans and programmes (PPPs) was that no distinction was made in NEPA and its implementing regulations between project level EIA and plan level EIA. Since the early 1970s, federal agencies have been preparing PEISs on land use plans, as well as on other types of policy level and programme level decisions. Thus, there is a considerable track record of SEA preparation, particularly by the federal agencies responsible for most federal land use planning and management: the US Forest Service (USFS), the US Bureau of Land Management (BLM), the National Park Service (NPS), and the US Fish and Wildlife Service (USFWS). Together, these agencies are responsible for managing more than 260 million hectares of federal land in the US. Most of the plans they prepare are subject to NEPA and have PEISs that either accompany them or are fully integrated into them during their preparation (Bass and Herson, 1999).

The US has a federal system of government, with a national government and 50 separate state governments. Subject to certain restrictions in the US Constitution, states are free to adopt their own legislation regulating the environment. Each state, therefore, has a different approach to land use planning, and only 16 states have chosen to adopt state legislation modelled upon NEPA, known as 'little NEPAs'. Thus, since NEPA only applies to *federal* actions, most states have no requirement for the EIA of either projects or plans. California is a notable exception (Bass et al, 1999).

This chapter reviews, compares and contrasts the preparation of PEISs as they apply to federal agency land use plans. It does not address state level EIA requirements.

Context

NEPA applies to all agencies of the federal government and requires that an environmental impact statement (EIS) be prepared for major federal actions that significantly affect the environment. The term 'federal action' has been broadly interpreted to include land use plans, as well as other types of PPPs (Bass et al, 2001).

While NEPA applies to all federal agencies, only a small number are involved in land use planning. Approximately one-third of the geographical area of the US is under the authority of, and is managed by, the federal government, most of it in the western states. Although other federal agencies (for example, the US Departments of Defense and Energy) also control and manage federal land, the most extensive federal land holdings are under the jurisdiction of four key land and resource management agencies:

- USFS (81 million hectares of national forests and grasslands);
- BLM (109 million hectares of resource management districts and national monuments);
- NPS (34 million hectares of national parks and historic sites);
- USFWS (36 million hectares of national wildlife refuges).

Figure 16.1 shows the federal land under the jurisdiction of these agencies.

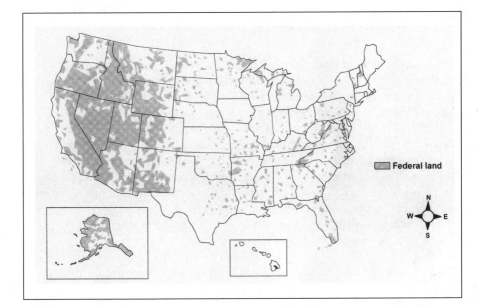

Source: Compiled from agency maps

Figure 16.1 *Federal lands in the US*

The roles, responsibilities and land management activities of each agency differ due to the nature of the land they are managing, and their planning activities derive from different federal laws, regulations and other mandates. However, each of these agencies is legally required to prepare comprehensive land management plans for the areas under their jurisdiction. Fortunately, the land planning processes of the four agencies and their integration with NEPA are similar. Thus, for illustrative purposes, this chapter focuses on the NPS. Table 16.1 summarizes the general planning framework of the NPS, which provides the basis for the case study.

Table 16.1 *Framework for National Park Service land use planning and resource management*

Area managed (approx)	Type and number of planning units	Primary planning law	Planning regulations	Planning web site document and key guidance
34 million hectares	National Parks (54) Historic Sites (73) Other units (109)	National Park Service Organic Act 16 US Code 1 et seq	'Management Policies to Guide the Management of the National Park System – Chapter 2'	http://planning.nps. gov/tools.cfm Director's Order 2 (NPS, 1998a), National Park Planning Guidance (NPS, 1998b)

Source: http://planning.nps.gov/tools.cfm

All the federal land management agencies typically include 'elements' (such as subject areas) in their plans that relate to the activities that would occur on the land, to the resources present on the land, and to other plan issues. Table 16.2 lists elements that may be found in federal land use plans.

The USFS and the BLM are multiple use agencies whose legislative mandates allow a very broad range of activities, including extractive ones such as timber harvesting, energy development and mining, as well as motorized recreation. However, the NPS and the USFWS manage their lands more for environmental protection purposes. Thus, their plans do not typically include extractive development or intensive motorized recreation.

Generally, a federal land use plan contains goals, objectives and proposed actions relating to each of the plan elements:

- Goals – broad statements that describe the general direction for the land in the future. Typically, goals are not measurable
- Objectives – more specific statements as to the desired future condition for each activity or resource. Typically, objectives are measurable
- Proposed actions – description of the specific activities that the agency will undertake and/or facilities it will develop to achieve the objectives.

Table 16.2 *Elements frequently included in US federal land use plans*

Environmental resources

- air quality;
- soils;
- water resources;
- cultural resources (for example, historical and archaeological);
- Native American resources;
- biological resources including endangered species;
- wilderness areas;
- wild and scenic rivers;
- other unique areas (such as national monuments, areas of critical environmental concern);
- scenic and visual resources.

Proposed activities

- habitat protection and restoration;
- non-motorized recreation (e.g. hiking, fishing, camping);
- motorized recreation (such as off-highway vehicles, snowmobiles);
- transportation and utility corridors;
- timber harvesting;
- mining;
- energy development (including oil, gas, coal).

Other plan issues

- economic impacts;
- social equity;
- land exchanges (with private landowners).

Note: These terms and their meaning many differ slightly from agency to agency.

SEA system

NEPA became effective in 1970 and was the first EIA (and SEA) law in the world. NEPA requires federal agencies to prepare EISs for any 'major federal action significantly affecting the quality of the human environment'.[1] The Council on Environmental Quality (CEQ, 1978) regulations implementing NEPA define 'major federal action' to include PPPs prepared by federal agencies.[2]

The environmental review process established for NEPA by CEQ involves three phases, as shown in Figure 16.2.

In applying this three-phase process to federal land use and resource management plans, most federal agencies determine that an EIS is necessary. This is because of the comprehensive nature of land use plans and the fact that most plans, even those designed to protect environmental resources, will result in

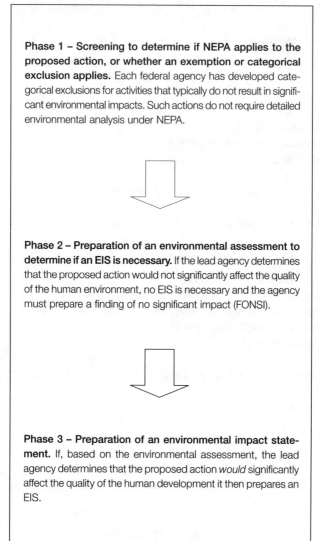

Phase 1 – Screening to determine if NEPA applies to the proposed action, or whether an exemption or categorical exclusion applies. Each federal agency has developed categorical exclusions for activities that typically do not result in significant environmental impacts. Such actions do not require detailed environmental analysis under NEPA.

Phase 2 – Preparation of an environmental assessment to determine if an EIS is necessary. If the lead agency determines that the proposed action would not significantly affect the quality of the human environment, no EIS is necessary and the agency must prepare a finding of no significant impact (FONSI).

Phase 3 – Preparation of an environmental impact statement. If, based on the environmental assessment, the lead agency determines that the proposed action *would* significantly affect the quality of the human development it then prepares an EIS.

Source: Bass et al (2001, p23)

Figure 16.2 *Three phases of NEPA*

some significant impacts that cannot be mitigated. Additionally, some of the land management agency regulations specifically require them to prepare an EIS for a land management plan.

By contrast, for most project level federal actions, lead agencies rarely prepare EISs. Rather, most federal agencies prepare environmental assessments that generally conclude that there will be no significant impacts and thus prepare 'findings of no significant impact' (FONSIs). In total, federal agencies prepare about 500 EISs and more than 50,000 environmental assessments/FONSIs annually (Bass et al, 2001; Wood, 2002). EISs prepared for federal land use plans, and other types of strategic actions, represent more than 25 per cent of all EISs prepared under NEPA (Environmental Protection Agency (EPA) online).

The NEPA regulations set forth the procedural and content requirements for EISs, which are the same for project-level and plan-level activities. Although NEPA's procedural requirements are the same for PEISs prepared for land use plans and project-level EISs prepared for individual actions, in practice there are considerable differences in the scale of analysis, the methods of evaluation and the nature of the impacts being evaluated. A PEIS is typically focused on a broad geographical area and emphasizes cumulative impacts. Thus, PEISs tend to be far more general than project-specific EISs (Bass et al, 1999). Table 16.3 summarizes some of these differences.

All federal land management agencies have fully integrated NEPA into their land use planning processes. Many of the steps that are conducted as a regular part of their land use planning are derived from NEPA and from the CEQ (1978) NEPA regulations, as well as from their own NEPA procedures. Table 16.4 shows the main steps in the NPS's planning process with the key NEPA steps highlighted. As Table 16.4 reveals, the requirements of NEPA are fully integrated into the NPS's planning requirements, as they are into those of other federal land management agencies. There are minor but important differences in the respective agencies' planning laws, regulations, and guidance documents (BLM, 2000; USFWS, 2000; USFS, online a).

In addition to the NEPA regulations issued by CEQ (1978), each federal land management agency has developed its own regulations and/or manuals that

Table 16.3 *Differences between programmatic and project US NEPA documents*

NEPA requirement	Programmatic documents	Project documents
Tier	First-tier	Second-tier
Proposed action	Entire plan including goals, objectives, actions, and maps	Specific proposed activity or facility
Alternatives	Built into plan; typically have different objectives	Differing ways to meet same objective
Affected environment	Broad geographical area	Individual site and surroundings
Main impact focus	Cumulative effects	Direct and indirect effects
Mitigation measures	Conceptual and built-into plan	Specific and typically added to a proposed action

Table 16.4 *Integration of NEPA principles and concepts into the US National Park Service planning process*

NEPA requirement	National Park Service general management plans
Scoping	Step 1: Reconfirm park purpose and significance
	Step 2: Acknowledge special mandates and commitments
	Step 3: Acknowledge service-wide laws and policies
	Step 4: Identify the need for management actions and prescriptions
Description of affected environment	Step 5: Analyse resources
Writing 'statement of purpose and need'	Step 6: Write purpose and need
Developing a range of reasonable alternatives	Step 7: Describe the range of potential management actions
	Step 8: Define alternatives
	Step 9: Develop and map management zones for each alternative
Assessment of environmental impacts	Step 10: Describe the environmental impacts of the alternatives
	Step 11: Estimate costs of the alternatives
	Step 12 Select appropriate management strategies and tactics
Draft EIS	Step 13 Issue draft plan and draft EIS
Public and interagency review of EIS	Step 14 Review and consultation
Final EIS	Step 15: Select a preferred alternative
Record of decision	Step 16 Develop implementation plan
Monitoring	Step 17 Monitor effectiveness of actions

Source: NPS (1998a)

establish specific approaches, methods, and rules for preparing NEPA documents, including PEISs. Guidance differs from agency to agency, but typically includes agency-specific NEPA regulations NEPA handbooks, NEPA memoranda from agency legal staff and related documents (see, for example, NPS's web site[3]).

CEQ (1997) has issued a NEPA guidance document entitled *Considering Cumulative Effects,* which is particularly useful in the preparation of PEISs for land use plans. That report spells out an 11-step approach to the assessment of cumulative impacts and provides examples of how federal agencies have addressed cumulative impacts from a variety of different types of federal action, including land use plans. The Environmental Protection Agency (1999) has also issued guidance on the treatment of cumulative impacts in EISs.

While the above discussion summarizes the key laws and regulations governing PEIS preparation for federal agency land use plans, they are not the only federal laws that apply to planning. Rather, there are dozens of other laws that affect how each element of a land use plan is prepared. The goals, objectives and proposed actions relating to each plan element must comply with all applicable laws and regulatory standards related to the relevant resource. For example, if a plan designates an area that allows cattle grazing, it must address whether the grazing will affect water resources regulated by the Clean Water Act. Table 16.5 lists the major laws that must be integrated with the application of NEPA.

For each plan element and environmental impact topic, the federal agency staff preparing the plan must be familiar with the applicable laws governing that subject, as well as with the consultation and integration requirements of each. Additionally, at each step of the planning process, the lead agency should consult with the applicable regulatory agency and ensure that the other laws have been properly integrated into the plan. This concept of step-by-step integration is illustrated in Figure 16.3 using the BLM planning process as an example.

In evaluating the environmental consequences in a land use plan EIS, a federal land management agency must consider 'the relationship between short-term uses of man's environment and the maintenance and enhancement of long-term

Table 16.5 *Environmental laws integrated with US NEPA and federal land use planning processes*

Land use plan elements and impact areas	Applicable law
Air quality	Clean Air Act
Soils	Watershed Protection and Flood Prevention Act
Agricultural land	Farmland Protection Policy Act
Water resources	Clean Water Act
Historical and archaeological resources	National Historic Preservation Act Archaeological Resource Protection Act
Biological resources, including endangered species	Endangered Species Act Fish and Wildlife Coordination Act
Wilderness areas	Wilderness Act
Wild and scenic rivers	Wild and Scenic Rivers Act
Social equity	Executive Order 12898: *Federal Actions to Address Environmental Justice in Low Income and Minority Populations*
Native American resources	Native American Grave Protection and Repatriation Act Native American Religious Freedom Act
Unique resource areas such as national monuments	Antiquities Act
Timber harvesting	National Forest Management Act
Grazing	Taylor Grazing Act
Mining	General Mining Act

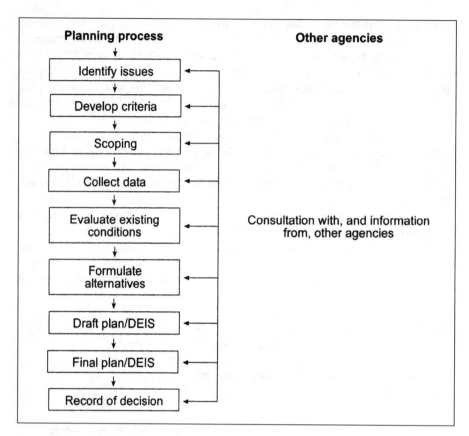

Source: Bass et al (2001, p6)

Figure 16.3 *Integration of US NEPA requirements with Federal Planning processes*

productivity'.[4] Although this language was included in NEPA long before 'sustainability' became a widely known public policy, it generally corresponds to today's notion of sustainable development.

One of the advantages of preparing a PEIS on a land management plan is the role it plays in subsequent decision-making. NEPA provides for a multi-level approach to agency planning, known as tiering. Tiering refers to the process whereby an agency evaluates more general matters in broad-scale EISs (known as the first tier) and later prepares narrow-scale EISs or environmental assessments which incorporate by reference the general discussions from the first document and concentrate solely on the issues specific to the individual proposal (Bass et al, 1999).[5] Tiering is a tool that is useful for streamlining the environmental review of individual projects and is widely used by federal land management agencies. Figure 16.4 demonstrates the concept of tiering.

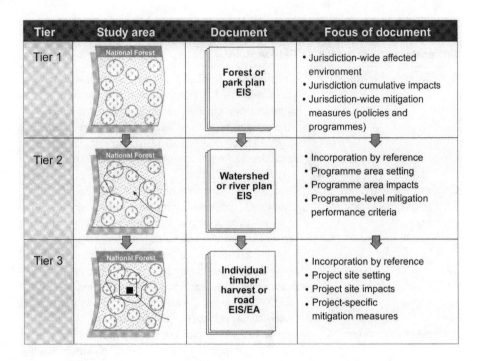

Tier	Study area	Document	Focus of document
Tier 1	National Forest	Forest or park plan EIS	• Jurisdiction-wide affected environment • Jurisdiction cumulative impacts • Jurisdiction-wide mitigation measures (policies and programmes)
Tier 2	National Forest	Watershed or river plan EIS	• Incorporation by reference • Programme area setting • Programme area impacts • Programme-level mitigation performance criteria
Tier 3	National Forest	Individual timber harvest or road EIS/EA	• Incorporation by reference • Project site setting • Project site impacts • Project-specific mitigation measures

Source: modified from Bass et al (2001, p124)

Figure 16.4 *Tiering in US environmental impact assessment*

SEA process

NEPA requires that a PEIS include the following subjects:[6]

- cover sheet (for example, a one-page summary of the EIS);
- summary (of the plan, the alternatives, and the impacts);
- table of contents;
- statement of purpose and need (for example, the goals of the plan);
- alternatives;
- affected environment;
- environmental impacts;
- mitigation measures (typically the actions built into the plan);
- list of agencies and organizations consulted;
- appendices and index.

These are the same legal requirements as for project EISs. Over the past few years, however, federal land management agencies have developed new approaches to planning and PEIS preparation that are different from those typically found in project level EISs. Some of the latest trends are summarized in Table 16.6.

Table 16.6 *Current trends in PEIS preparation for US land use plans*

Current area of emphasis	Explanation
Collaborative planning	Collaboration implies more cooperation with stakeholders – for example, resource industry organizations, environmental groups, community associations, recreational user groups, and so on. Collaboration includes establishment of advisory committees, frequent meetings in local communities, task forces, and so on
Cooperation with state and local governments and tribal organizations	Federal land management agencies increasingly cooperate with other levels of government to ensure federal land management plans reflect their views. Cooperation includes joint federal/state planning activities – for example, joint studies, joint public meetings, sharing of staff. May also include granting of 'cooperating agency' status under NEPA (CEQ, 2000) whereby non-federal agencies are co-opted to participate in PEIS preparation
Adaptive management	Systematic process for continually monitoring, evaluating, improving natural resource management policies and practices by learning from on-the-ground outcomes of operational programmes. Based on recognition that predictions about future of natural resources made in land use plans are often not able to describe accurately all conditions that might occur once plan implemented
Integration of laws	In addition to complying with its own planning law and NEPA, federal agency preparing land use plan has to comply with other federal and state laws. 'Integration' involves use of planning process to achieve compliance with various laws and inclusion of results of analysis requirements in single document. Agencies often enter into programmatic agreements with other resource management agencies setting forth how requirements of various laws will be met during planning process
Legal defensibility; emphasis on a well-documented administrative record	Under the US legal system, land use plan decisions are made in accordance with agency planning laws and with Administrative Procedures Act (APA).[7] APA applies to all federal agencies, prescribes legal standards that plans and EISs must meet to be documented and supported by an 'administrative record'. APA sets forth legal standards by which courts will review adequacy of administrative

Table 16.6 *Current trends in PEIS preparation for land use plans (continued)*

Current area of emphasis	Explanation
	records. Agencies currently paying greater attention to development of adequate administrative records to ensure legal defensibility of planning decisions
Planning models and prototypes	Over time, planning (particularly NEPA requirements relating to planning) has become complicated and slow. Some federal agencies now finding ways to streamline their preparation and review of land use plans and related EISs. Recognizing need for consistency from plan to plan, federal agencies developing models and prototypes for plan preparation and how plan should look. USFS has developed prototype planning process recommended for all national forests (USFS, online b)
Environmental justice	Under Presidential Executive Order 12898 and its implementing procedures, every federal agency involved in preparing land use plan PEISs must determine whether plan would result in impacts to low-income or minority persons to greater extent than to general population. In practice, compliance with Executive Order requires disaggregation of land use plan environmental impacts by income and racial status
Promoting economic development	Under Bush administration, federal agency land use plans focusing more on economic development. Policy emphasis includes more energy and fuel development, increased timber harvesting, and other activities intended to foster economic growth in local communities surrounding federal land

Many of these trends have been proposed to improve the planning and NEPA processes. However, some critics allege that many changes are designed to weaken environmental protection. The Council on Environmental Quality (2003) recently released an evaluation of NEPA in which it recommends numerous other improvements, many of which would benefit the practice of PEIS preparation (below).

Case study: NPS Yosemite Valley Plan and EIS

Yosemite National Park is a world-renowned natural resource area. The Yosemite Valley Plan and EIS, prepared by NPS, was selected as a case study because it provides a good example of a PEIS prepared by a federal land management agency and illustrates the integration between planning and EIA.[8] Unfortunately, the popularity of Yosemite with both US and international visitors, and its proximity to major metropolitan areas in California, has brought overcrowding and significant impacts to the park's unique natural resources. In response, NPS decided to prepare a management plan for the Yosemite Valley, the most frequently visited area of the park. Perhaps the most unique feature of the planning process and the PEIS was the high degree of scoping, public outreach and public review employed during its preparation.

Framework for plan and EIS

The primary planning document designed to guide NPS in protecting and managing Yosemite National Park is the 1980 *General Management Plan*. This long-range plan for the entire park outlined five broad goals:

1   reclaim priceless natural beauty;
2   reduce traffic congestion;
3   allow natural processes to prevail;
4   reduce crowding;
5   promote visitor understanding and enjoyment.

The Yosemite Valley Plan, which is tiered from the General Management Plan, is intended to help in achieving these goals and, in the process, to restore Yosemite Valley's natural processes. The EIS prepared for the Yosemite Valley Plan was a supplement to the EIS prepared for the General Management Plan, a common practice under NEPA.

The Final Yosemite Valley Plan/Supplemental Environmental Impact Statement (SEIS), a combined and fully integrated document, is a consolidation of several planning activities over the last two decades. It is a comprehensive document that presents and analyses four action alternatives and a 'no action' alternative for managing natural and cultural resources, facilities and visitor experiences in Yosemite Valley. The Final Yosemite Valley Plan/SEIS was prepared in compliance with the CEQ (1978) NEPA regulations, as well as the NPS's NEPA procedures. As with all final EISs, it was preceded by a draft EIS that was released for public comment and review in March 2000.

Importance of public participation

Public participation in the Yosemite Valley planning process was imperative in ensuring that NPS understood and considered the issues and concerns of a broad spectrum of interest groups and park visitors. During the preparation of the draft and final Yosemite Valley Plan/SEIS, public participation enabled NPS to:

•   analyse and incorporate comments from previous planning activities;
•   define the range of issues to be addressed;

- provide opportunities for the public to obtain the knowledge necessary to make informed comments;
- collect public, Native American and agency comments on the draft Yosemite Valley Plan/SEIS;
- produce the best possible plan.

Over 6000 public comments from previous Yosemite Valley planning activities over the last nine years were used in developing the draft Yosemite Valley Plan/SEIS alternatives. Additionally, during the public comment period on the draft Yosemite Valley Plan/SEIS, NPS held 14 formal public meetings throughout California. In addition, public meetings were also held in Seattle, Denver, Chicago and Washington. Yosemite National Park staff received over 10,000 public comments during this period.

Numerous other public involvement activities were conducted by NPS throughout the Yosemite Valley planning period, including:

- *Planning Update* newsletters to a mailing list of over 10,000 names;
- 63 open house sessions at the Yosemite Valley Visitor Center;
- 26 ranger-led interpretative walks discussing the *Yosemite Valley Plan*;
- ten wayside exhibits located near areas that could be affected by implementation of the plan;
- informational inserts in the park newspaper.

The thousands of comments received by NPS indicated what many liked about the draft Yosemite Valley Plan/SEIS and what concerned some people. While considering public comments, scientific data, the 1980 General Management Plan goals and applicable laws and policies, NPS carefully reviewed the draft plan and made some revisions that were incorporated into the final plan. Many concerns emerged as the plan progressed. As a result of the extensive public involvement process, the final plan SEIS contained goals and objectives for the future of the plan as well as more than 250 specific proposed actions to improve the Yosemite Valley.

SEA outcome

In April 2002, CEQ organized a task force to evaluate NEPA's effectiveness and make recommendations to modernize NEPA. The task force consisted of representatives from the nine federal agencies that prepare the lion's share of NEPA documents (CEQ, 2003). In the first detailed evaluation of NEPA for more than seven years, the task force recommended major improvements in the implementation of NEPA, focusing on six specific areas of NEPA practice, one of which was programmatic analysis and tiering.

To determine prevailing attitudes about NEPA, the task force issued a notice in the *Federal Register,* the official US government publication, to solicit comments on 'ways to improve and modernize NEPA analyses and documentation, and to foster improved coordination among all levels of government and the public' (CEQ, 2002, p45510). The task force conducted interviews with many federal agency NEPA liaison staff, who are typically the senior officials with responsibility for NEPA oversight and implementation in each federal agency. Additionally, to broaden the opinions it received about NEPA, the task force spoke with state and local governments, tribal organizations, interest groups and the public about the law's implementation and established a web site to seek input from NEPA practitioners.

Despite CEQ's efforts to focus the evaluation, the task force received more than 650 comments covering the gamut of NEPA implementation topics. Nevertheless, in keeping with its original intent, the task force report grouped recommendations under the six areas of practice but included a further set of recommendations for the additional matters considered. *Modernizing NEPA Implementation* was released in September 2003 (CEQ, 2003) and CEQ conducted four regional round tables in 2003 to explain its recommendations and to seek additional comments from interested persons.

The task force recognized the value of programmatic NEPA analyses and the use of tiering but acknowledged that there were current limitations. It suggested that CEQ should promote consistent, clear, cost-effective, programmatic NEPA analyses, documents and tiering that met agency and stakeholder needs (CEQ, 2003). Specifically, with regard to programmatic documents, the task force identified the need for additional guidance that:

- emphasizes the importance of collaboration as federal agencies expand the use and scope of programmatic NEPA analyses;
- recommends that the first tier document should include an initial section that explains the relationship between the programmatic analysis and its PEIS, and future tiered analyses and their documentation, and describes how stakeholders will be involved;
- emphasizes that programmatic documents should explain where and when deferred issues that were raised by the public and/or regulatory agencies will be addressed and should describe the proposed temporal and spatial scales that will be used when analysing those issues;
- develops criteria for agencies to use when evaluating whether a programmatic document has become outdated and articulates a general life expectancy for the different programmatic documents.

It is too soon to determine whether the task force report will result in additional guidance from CEQ, or whether agencies will implement the recommended improvements themselves.

Conclusion

As this chapter reveals, the concepts of SEA are generally well integrated into land use planning at the federal level under NEPA and the four major land management agencies are very familiar with the process of preparing PEISs. Since the enactment of NEPA more than 35 years ago, federal agencies have prepared hundreds of plan level environmental documents; Table 16.7 summarizes their collective experience. Despite the considerable experience of the four federal land management agencies, further guidance is still needed on how to prepare PEISs and how to integrate them into federal land use planning. Nevertheless, the wealth of land use plan SEA practice in the US can provide valuable lessons for SEA practice in other jurisdictions, especially those in which SEA is a relatively new concept.

Table 16.7 *Evaluation of SEA of land use plans in the US*

Criterion	Criterion met	Comments
		SYSTEM CRITERIA
Legal basis	■	CEQ NEPA regulations together with individual agency NEPA and planning regulations provide strong legal framework for assessing impacts of federal land use plans
Integration	▲	Integration between NEPA and federal land use planning highly developed under the programmes of federal land management agencies – to point that they are considered a single process
Guidance	▲	No standardized guidance or methodology for preparing PEISs or approach to evaluation of environmental impacts, which frustrates agency staff who implement NEPA at strategic level
Coverage	■	Due to broad definition of 'proposed action', NEPA documents must be prepared for every type and size of federal land use plan, not just comprehensive resource management plans
Tiering	▲	While tiering is well-established practice, it is misunderstood and sometimes misused by, for example, using out-of-date documents
Sustainable development	□	While sustainable development is a major policy issue anticipated by NEPA, it has never been an important component of EIA, and is seldom referred to specifically in PEISs
		PROCESS CRITERIA
Alternatives	▲	Planning processes established by regulations of each federal land management agency require development of alternatives, reinforcing NEPA

Table 16.7 *Evaluation of SEA of land use plans in the US (continued)*

Criterion	Criterion met	Comments
		requirements for consideration of alternatives in PEISs
Screening	■	Screening is typically not an issue because agencies recognize need for PEISs for most land use plans
Scoping	■	NEPA provides good framework for scoping (CEQ, 1981). In addition, each federal land management agency has included scoping as integral part of its planning regulations and process
Prediction/ evaluation	▲	Considerable uncertainty as to whether quantitative or qualitative methods should be used, despite CEQ's guidance on cumulative impacts (CEQ, 1997)
Additional impacts	□	No requirement for this in NEPA and little evidence in practice
Report preparation	■	Most agencies have considerable experience in report preparation. Some employ experienced private consultants to assist in preparing PEISs
Review	■	Review of PEISs for federal land use plans well established. Most agencies distribute documents widely to other agencies and public
Monitoring	▲	NEPA requires that 'record of decision' includes a monitoring programme. Federal land management agency planning regulations require monitoring but practice very uneven
Mitigation	▲	Many mitigation measures to solve environmental problems built into plans early in process because of good integration between federal land use planning and NEPA, but implementation varies greatly
Consultation and public participation	■	Both consultation and public participation are integral to the use of PEISs
		OUTCOME CRITERIA
Decision making	▲	NEPA primarily procedural. Federal agencies may approve plans despite their resulting in significant environmental impacts
Costs and benefits	□	No systematic data collected on cost of PEISs. Research on benefits has not separated programmatic and project level NEPA documents.
Environmental quality	▲	While many examples of environmental quality being improved through plan level EIA exist, overall results have been mixed

Table 16.7 *Evaluation of SEA of land use plans in the US (continued)*

Criterion	Criterion met	Comments
System monitoring	☐	CEQ responsible for system monitoring, but staffing and funding shortages led to discontinuance (after 30 years) of CEQ's annual report summarizing NEPA trends. CEQ undertook several effectiveness studies of EIA but none focused on SEA exclusively

Notes: ■ – Yes
　　　▲ – Partially
　　　☐ – No
　　　? – Don't know

Notes

1　40 Code of Federal Regulations (CFR) 1500 et seq
2　40 CFR 1508.18
3　http://planning.nps.gov/document/do12handbook%2Epdf%2Epdf
4　40 CFR 1502.16
5　40 CFR 1502.20
6　40 CFR 1502.10
7　5 USC 500 et seq
8　The Yosemite Valley Plan/PEIS case study is taken from the Yosemite National Park planning website http://www.nps.gov/yose/planning/yvp/

References

Bass, R. and Herson, A. (1999) 'Environmental impact assessment of land use plans: experience under the National Environmental Policy Act and the California Environmental Quality Act', in Petts, J. (ed) *Handbook of Environmental Assessment*, volume 2, Blackwell, Oxford

Bass, R. E., Herson, A. I. and Bogdan, K. M. (1999) *CEQA Deskbook: a Step-by-Step Guide on How to Comply with the California Environmental Quality Act*, 2nd edition, Solano Press, Point Arena, CA

Bass, R. E., Herson, A. I. and Bogdan, K. M. (2001) *The NEPA Book: a Step-by-Step Guide on How to Comply with the National Environmental Policy Act*, 2nd edition, Solano Press, Point Arena, CA

Bureau of Land Management (2000) *Land Use Planning Handbook*, USBLM, Washington, DC

Council on Environmental Quality (1978) 'Regulations for implementing the procedural provisions of the National Environmental Quality Act', *40 Code of Federal Regulations*, 1500–1508

Council on Environmental Quality (1981) *Memorandum for General Counsels, NEPA Liaisons and Participants in Scoping*, CEQ, Executive Office of the President, Washington, DC

Council on Environmental Quality (1997) *Considering Cumulative Effects under the National Environmental Policy Act*, CEQ, Executive Office of the President, Washington, DC

Council on Environmental Quality (2000) *Identifying Non-Federal Agencies in Implementing the Procedural Requirements of NEPA*, CEQ, Executive Office of the President, Washington, DC

Council on Environmental Quality (2002) 'National Environmental Policy Act Task Force notice and request for comments', *Federal Register*, vol 67, pp45510–45512, 9 July

Council on Environmental Quality (2003) *Modernizing NEPA Implementation: Report of the NEPA Task Force*, CEQ, Executive Office of the President, Washington, DC

Environmental Protection Agency (1999) *Consideration of Cumulative Impacts in EPA Review of NEPA Documents*, Office of Compliance and Enforcement, USEPA, Washington, DC

Environmental Protection Agency (online) *NEPA Document Data Base*, Office of Compliance and Enforcement, USEPA, Washington, DC, www.epa.gov/compliance/nepa/index.html

Fish and Wildlife Service (2000) 'National Wildlife Refuge System planning policy', *Federal Register*, vol 65, pp33891-33919, 25 May

National Park Service (1998a) *Director's Order 2: Park Planning*, NPS, Washington, DC

National Park Service (1998b) *National Park Planning Guidance*, NPS, Washington, DC

US Forest Service (online a) *National Forest Management Act Planning*, USFS, Washington, DC www.fs.fed.us/emc/nfma/

US Forest Service (online b) *National Forest Management Act, Land and Resource Management Plan Prototype*, USFS, Washington, DC, http://maps.fs.fed.us/fp/r2/arnf/

Wood, C. M. (2002) *Environmental Impact Assessment: a Comparative Review*, 2nd edition, Prentice Hall, Harlow

17

World Bank

Jean-Roger Mercier and Kulsum Ahmed[1]

Introduction

The World Bank lends financial support and provides technical assistance to developing countries and those in economic transition. The World Bank is made up of two organizations, the International Bank for Reconstruction and Development (IBRD), which was established in 1945 and has as its clients middle-income country governments, and the International Development Association (IDA), which was established in 1960 and which provides credits to poorer client country[2] governments at concessionary rates.[3] Currently, the World Bank has 184 member countries[4] and assists its client countries (about 100 countries with nearly 5 billion inhabitants) in reducing poverty[5] and supporting environmentally and socially sustainable development.[6] The basic focus of World Bank assistance to any given country is determined by a country assistance strategy (the priority activities and reforms that comprise the mutually agreed programme in the country that will be supported by the Bank) to reduce poverty in a sustainable manner. This priority setting is supported by country specific analytical work as well as by 16 Bank-wide sectoral strategies, including the Bank's *Environment Strategy*, approved by the Board of Directors in July 2001 (World Bank, 2001). Lending by IDA and IBRD over the last three years has averaged a total of about US$20 billion per annum. During 2003–2004, two-thirds of this lending went to investment and one-third to macroeconomic and sectoral adjustment.

The Environment Strategy states that strategic environmental assessment is part of a systematic approach to ensuring that environmental matters are considered early in the development planning process:

> *Strategic – sectoral, regional, and policy-focused environmental* assessments
> *(SEAs) will be used more systematically as analytical tools through a structured*
> *learning program involving clients and partners for addressing complex cross-*
> *sectoral environmental issues and for integrating [the] environment at early*
> *stages in sectoral decision-making and planning process[es]*

> World Bank (2001, p23).

An associated strategy paper provides details about the importance of SEA for policy, plan and programme (PPP) analysis (Kjörven and Lindhjem, 2002). SEAs of World Bank activities have been conducted in several different contexts: for example, in response to the Bank's operational policy for environmental assessment; in the context of technical assistance to client countries, etc. In the summer of 2004, an earlier operational directive on adjustment lending was converted into a policy on development policy lending (World Bank 2004a). This, too, has important implications for the development of SEA in Bank operations. These instruments are described in subsequent sections in this chapter, along with examples of SEAs.

There is no Bank requirement for SEAs in the context of land use planning in client countries. However, SEAs, or more specifically, regional environmental assessments (REAs), have been carried out in the context of compliance with Bank policies and as part of the Bank's technical assistance to clients. For the purposes of this chapter, REAs and other forms of resource planning related SEAs have been chosen as being most relevant to the SEA of land use plans.

Policy context

After reviewing international experience and its own practice in SEA, the World Bank assigned the following purpose to SEA: a participatory approach for upstreaming environmental and social issues to influence development planning, decision making and implementation processes at the strategic level. Operationally, there are three main forms of SEA: sectoral EA; regional EA; and other types of SEA. These tools are used and developed along with other specialized tools: country environmental analysis (CEA, see below), poverty and social impact analysis (PSIA),[7] and social analysis (SA).[8] Synergies are actively sought between these tools, whenever relevant for the borrowers.

The option of using sectoral and regional environmental assessments in World Bank operations was first introduced in 1989, with the adoption of an operational directive on environmental assessment (OD 4.01). This was the forerunner of the current Bank procedure and operational policy (OP) on *Environmental Assessment* (World Bank, 1999a, 1999b). The OP states that:

> *EA is a process whose breadth, depth, and type of analysis depend on the nature,*
> *scale, and potential environmental impact of the proposed project. . .The borrower*
> *is responsible for carrying out the EA. . . Depending on the project, a range of*

instruments can be used to satisfy the Bank's EA requirement: environmental impact assessment (EIA), regional or sectoral EA

World Bank (1999b, pp1–2).

Within this framework, several REAs and many sectoral EAs have been carried out. An early review of the experience with sectoral EA was undertaken in 1993. The update of the *Environmental Assessment Sourcebook* on sectoral EA (World Bank, 1993) lists the advantages of sectoral EA, reviews its main application under OD 4.01, describes application case studies, and concludes by discussing the main challenges to sectoral EA. These include timing and status, costs, use of appropriate terms of reference and of consultants, adjustment to circumstances and ensuring specificity and follow-up.

A review of regional EA, published in 1996 as an update to the EA Sourcebook (World Bank, 1996), presents the rationale for, and the advantages of, REA. It describes the purpose of REA as 'to improve investment decisions by bringing environmental opportunities and constraints into development planning at the regional level' (World Bank, 1996, p1) and goes on to analyse the limited experience of REA in World Bank operations. The update recommends an REA process in the application of OD 4.01 which includes:

the design stage essentially consist[ing] of determining the scope of the REA (scoping), preparation of TOR [terms of reference] and selection of the REA team. The execution stage involves the preparation of the REA. What makes the REA process different from other EA processes is that the regional/spatial perspective needs to be present throughout, and that the scope poses some particular challenges in design and execution

World Bank (1996, p4).

A more recent impetus for the application of SEA took place in August 2004, when the Board of Directors approved a new operational policy and a Bank procedure (OP/BP 8.60) on development policy lending (DPL) (World Bank, 2004a, 2004b). Development policy loans provide quick disbursement, to countries with external financing needs, to support structural reforms in a sector or the economy as a whole. They support the policy and institutional changes needed to create an environment conducive to sustained and equitable growth. The new policy applies uniformly to all development policy lending, replacing the previous different types of lending (for example, structural adjustment loans, sectoral adjustment loans, among others). The framework for the policy is summarized in Box 17.1.

The policy provides uniform treatment of environmental, social and poverty aspects. Under this policy, for each loan, the Bank is required to determine whether specific country policies supported by the operation are likely to have significant effects on the country's environment and natural resources. For policies with likely significant effects, the documentation for the operation that is submitted to the Bank's Board is required to assess the borrower's systems for reducing adverse

Box 17.1 Treatment of poverty/social, environmental and fiduciary aspects in World Bank development policy lending

The policy framework includes the following elements:

- *Uniform operational policy* All development policy loans are covered by the same operational policy (previously different types of development policy loans were subject to different policies)
- *Analytic underpinnings* A DPL operation draws on relevant analytical work undertaken by the Bank, the country and third parties. For each development policy operation proposed for Bank financing, the Bank prepares a programme document that describes and appraises the operation. The programme documentation describes the main pieces of analytical work used in preparing the operation and shows how they are linked to the proposed DPL operation
- *Consultation* The Bank advises borrowing countries to consult with, and engage the participation of, key stakeholders in the country in the process of formulating the country's development strategies. Bank staff describe in the programme document the country's arrangements for consultation and participation relevant to the operation, and the outcomes of the participatory process adopted in formulating the country's development strategy. Relevant analytic work conducted by the Bank, particularly on poverty and social impacts and on environmental aspects, is made available to the public as part of the consultation process in line with the Bank's disclosure policy
- *Disclosure* The programme document is available to the public after the operation has been approved by the Executive Directors. In addition, the letter of development policy (in which the borrowing government details the measures that will be taken to implement the policy and the institutional reforms to be undertaken) is available to the public after the Executive Directors approve the operation, unless they decide otherwise
- *Results monitoring and risk management* The borrower is responsible for managing operational risks affecting the development effectiveness of the development policy operation. The Bank independently identifies the financial and non-financial risks (including environmental risks) associated with the programme and ensures that the operation contains appropriate mitigation measures and monitorable indicators to track high probability risks.

effects and enhancing positive effects associated with the specific policies being supported. The policy also emphasizes upstream analytical work as a source of information for the analysis of environmental effects, as well as for the institutional analysis. If there are gaps in analytical work or shortcomings in the borrower's systems, then the programme documentation should describe how such gaps or shortcomings would be addressed before or during programme implementation, as appropriate.

Although a number of – not necessarily perfect – tools can be used to analyse the environmental implications of policy reforms, two broadly accepted and structured analytical tools in the environmental and natural resource area are CEA and SEA. A CEA identifies a country's priorities and challenges, and systematically evaluates the environmental implications of key policies and the country's institutional capacity to address them. A SEA, on the other hand, looks at the environmental implications of specific sectoral reforms, thereby helping to ensure that the environmental consequences of PPPs are identified before adoption, that feasible alternatives are properly considered, and that all stakeholders are fully involved in the decision-making process.

Following the adoption of OP/BP 8.60 (World Bank, 2004a, 2004b), it is expected that the use of SEA as a tool will increase. Examples of sectors in which SEA is expected to grow, and which are closely linked with land use planning, include agriculture and rural development, transportation, and water, sanitation and flood protection. SEAs for these sectors are expected to be conducted across all the six operational regions of the Bank, with a likely concentration in Latin America and the Caribbean, Sub-Saharan Africa, and Europe and Central Asia regions, since there is typically a higher percentage of development policy loans in these regions. The Bank is developing guidance, analysis of good practice, and training and capacity building activities to respond to this increasing demand.

Case studies

The previous section laid out the Bank policy context under which SEAs have been conducted. Another context in which the Bank has supported SEA in client countries has been through non-lending technical assistance activities or as activities financed as part of a technical assistance loan. In this section, examples of SEAs that have been conducted under these different contexts are described.

SEAs are prepared by Bank borrowers in the context of loans and credits that build domestic capacity for environmental assessment. For instance, Ghana chose to conduct a SEA of coastal zone management within the framework of an environmental management capacity building project in the late 1990s. This SEA stream is not subject to any systematic monitoring by the Bank but is probably quite limited in number and in scope.

Specific efforts have been targeted at capacity building in client countries. Country SEA capacity has been (and is being) built using a wide variety of approaches and instruments, including grant funding for training sessions, either through regular World Bank units or through the dedicated World Bank Institute, dedicated technical assistance grants or loans/credits, or dedicated components of investment (mostly in infrastructure) or adjustment (especially environmental sector) lending. In particular, this capacity has been used to help integrate general environmental and sustainability concerns into plans (for example, assistance with the application of the recent EIA law in China, which recommends the EA of certain plans) or into water basin management, a critical form of spatial resource use planning.

An example of a REA conducted in response to OD 4.01 was for a flood protection project in Argentina. The REA update to the EA Sourcebook recommends the Argentina Flood Protection EA (Ministerio del Interior, 1995) as best practice because it:

> *helped design four key project components to help improve the environmental and economic benefits of the project. These included (a) a component to strengthen EA procedures in key institutions within the seven provinces; (b) technical assistance for urban environmental management; (c) environmental education and awareness programmes in communities benefiting from protection works; and (d) support to protection and management initiatives for wetlands and other ecosystems. . . . perhaps the most important contribution of the REA was its direct contribution to screening potential investments under the project and assessing the cumulative impacts of selected sub-projects.*

World Bank (1996, p4).

Nile River Basin

The Nile River Basin transboundary environmental analysis is a particularly interesting application of REA. It formed part of a non-lending activity that was intended to help the ten Nile Basin riparian countries cooperate in achieving the common goal of improved sustainable resource management. Box 17.2 describes this REA in greater detail.

SEA system

Because of the critical importance of SEA worldwide and its potential application to Bank business, the Bank embarked upon a structured learning programme which included a sub-programme designed to learn from past SEAs when it adopted its environmental strategy in 2001. This helped to identify elements of good practice in a sample of 25 SEAs and similar instruments utilized over the past ten years. The criteria employed to evaluate these practices are presented in Table 17.1. These criteria build on, and expand, the SEA performance criteria published by the International Association for Impact Assessment (IAIA) in 2002. Some of the SEAs used in this learning sub-programme illustrate key aspects of SEA that are relevant more broadly, including the application of SEA to land use plans. The complete review was expected to be disseminated during 2005 on the Bank's website.

A critical element that SEA addresses is tiering. This process takes place when a SEA, by design, helps to pave the way for better and easier project level EAs. In the case of the Poland Hard Coal Sector Adjustment Loan, the SEA included the screening of over 100 potential mining sites to determine whether or not future projects should be subjected to micro-level or to programmatic-level environmental assessments. The government also used the SEA outcome extensively to harmonize

Box 17.2 Nile River Basin Transboundary Environmental Analysis

The Nile River Basin is a unique environment that has played a significant role in world history. Today, it provides a home and subsistence for about 160 million people, many of them among the world's poorest.

A transboundary environmental analysis (TEA) was undertaken as part of the Nile Basin Initiative (NBI) that was launched formally in February 1999 as a cooperative effort of the Nile riparian countries. The TEA aimed to identify priority transboundary environmental issues to be tackled and defined elements of an agenda for environmental action.

The TEA report describes the key environmental issues and threats (land degradation, wetlands, lake degradation and biodiversity loss, water quality degradation, and natural disasters and refugees). The root causes of these threats can be found in widespread poverty, inappropriate macro- and sectoral policies, inadequate regulatory systems, institutional constraints, including the need for improved land use planning, limited awareness and information, population growth, climatic vulnerability and urbanization.

The elements of the agenda for environmental action prepared in response to this analysis have been grouped into six components: political commitment, outreach activities, preventive measures, curative measures, resources management programmes and monitoring of environmental changes. An initial set of activities that were high on a common agenda for action on a regional level were implemented through the first transboundary environment project – the largest component of a broad basin-wide programme of the NBI aimed at creating trust, capacity and an enabling environment for sustainable cooperative investments in the Nile Basin. Financial support for the TEA process came from the Global Environment Facility (GEF), the United Nations Development Programme (UNDP) and the World Bank.

Among the recent related activities under the NBI umbrella is the preparation of a sectoral and strategic social and environmental assessment of power options in the six countries forming the Nile Equatorial Lakes region. The first phase, which is ongoing, covers three countries of the Nile Equatorial Lakes Sub-Basin: Rwanda, Burundi and Western Tanzania. The objective of the SEA is to evaluate power generation options, including their potential for benefit sharing on various levels; identify the best options for meeting electricity demands taking into account economic, financial, technical, environmental, social and political considerations; and allow for informed and transparent decision making in the selection of power investments (interconnection and/or increased investment in the individual grids; potential of demand-side management; trade-offs to be considered in the selection of large infrastructure for energy production, including development of hydropower facilities).

Source: Global Environment Facility et al (2001)

Table 17.1 *World Bank criteria for assessing SEA good practice*

A good quality SEA process is	Criteria
I Integrated	1.1 Addresses the interrelationships of biophysical, social and economic aspects 1.2 Is tiered to policies in relevant sectors and (transboundary) regions and, where appropriate, to project EIA and decision making
2 Sustainability led	2.1 Facilitates identification of development options and alternative proposals that are more sustainable[9]
3 Focused	3.1 Provides sufficient, reliable and usable information for development planning and decision making 3.2 Concentrates on key issues of sustainable development, including key trade offs between the stakeholders 3.3 Is customized to the characteristics of the decision-making process 3.4 Is cost- and time-effective
4 Accountable	4.1 Is the responsibility of the leading agencies for the strategic decision to be made 4.2 Is carried out with professionalism, rigour, fairness, impartiality and balance 4.3 Is subject to independent checks and verification 4.4 Documents and justifies how sustainability issues were taken into account in decision making
5 Participative	5.1 Informs and involves interested and affected public and government bodies throughout the decision making process 5.2 Explicitly addresses their inputs and concerns in documentation and decision making 5.3 Helps to achieve consensus between the stakeholders 5.4 Has clear, easily understood information requirements and ensures sufficient access to all relevant information
6 Iterative	6.1 Ensures availability of the assessment results early enough to influence the decision-making process and inspire future planning 6.2 Provides sufficient information on the actual impacts of implementing a strategic decision to judge whether this decision should be amended and to provide a basis for future decisions
7 Influential	7.1 Has made an impact on the finally adopted strategic decision and its implementation

Table 17.1 *World Bank criteria for assessing SEA good practice (continued)*

A good quality SEA process is	Criteria
	7.2 Influences the overall attitude and institutional structure of the government bodies towards environmental and social sustainability issues 7.3 Makes the government bodies want to be involved in a similar process, should the opportunity arise

Note: The precise wording of some criteria is not suitable for situations in which the SEA was not integrated into a specific strategic decision making process. In these cases the 'spirit' of the criteria was applied.
Source: IAIA (2002[10], modified by the deletion of IAIA's 1.1 and the addition of part of 3.2 and the whole of 5.3 and 7)

its environmental and mining legislation with European laws and regulations (Spolka Restrukturyzacji Kopaln, 2004).

Sustainability concerns are central to the SEA approach. In the case of the Nepal Power Development Project (Ministry of Water Resources and Ministry of Population and Environment, 1997), the most sustainable projects were selected from 138 available medium-scale (10–300MW) hydropower sites through a screening and ranking process. This was done by incorporating environmental and social criteria at two stages of the process: coarse screening (in which 44 projects were retained) and final ranking of the 24 most suitable sites.

SEA process

Analysis of *alternatives* is where SEA is perhaps expected to make the greatest difference and, to some extent, compensate for some of the shortcomings of project level EIA. The Energy Environment Review for Egypt (Environmental Resources Management, 2003) focused on identifying win–win solutions at a national level for the energy sector and prioritizing among policies by systematically screening potential policies and retaining only those that gave good environmental value for money.

Following preparation, SEA requires a process of *review* by national authorities. This review is a major quality enhancement mechanism. In many countries, even if SEA is required or strongly recommended by national laws, regulations or guidelines, lack of proper and competent review may be its Achilles' heel. A good practice example is the Water Sector Adjustment Loan for Indonesia (Government of Indonesia, 1999), where the SEA preparation was carried out under the auspices of the government's Inter-agency Task Force on Water Sector Policy Reform. This task force operated under the joint chairmanship of the National Development Planning Agency and the Public Works Ministry and included representatives of the Ministries of Home Affairs, Public Works, Mining and Energy, Forestry, and

Agriculture, as well as of the two existing river basin organizations, of two provincial public works departments, of the Indonesian Institute of Sciences research organization and of two NGOs.

Monitoring of the actual effects of a plan, programme or policy and implementing the appropriate mitigation measures as effects appear, whatever the quality and relevance of the SEA preparatory stage, is key to the success of SEA. Although experience in this field is limited and has not been analysed or reported upon in a systematic way, the example of the Mumbai Urban Transport Project (Mumbai Metropolitan Region Development Authority, 2001) reflects an important step in this direction. In this example, the monitoring plan, at a sectoral level, addressed environmental quality, resettlement issues and traffic movement. Parameters were defined, a list of recommended sites and of suggested sampling duration and frequency was provided, and responsibility for implementation was defined.

Stakeholder *consultation*, combined with disclosure of the key documents of a SEA process, is considered by many to be a central feature of SEA. For many decision makers this is a crucial aspect, which helps to increase the public support for the outcome of the SEA. In the Gujarat Highways Project (ND Lea International, 1996), government bodies, national and local NGOs, people affected by the project, and national and local experts were very extensively involved throughout the decision-making process, starting at the earliest stages of the sectoral EA preparation. A community consultation programme was designed by the Roads and Buildings Department and by the other government bodies including the Social Welfare, Revenue and Forest departments.

SEA outcome

Influence on *decision making* by public officials is the most obvious outcome of an effective SEA. Though measures and the magnitude of this influence are often very difficult to establish, especially for integrated SEA processes, there is a growing caseload of SEAs that appear to have influenced decision or policy making to one degree or another.

In the Bali Urban Infrastructure Project (DHV Consultants, 1996), the SEA not only impacted on the implementation process and decision making between critical alternatives but also framed the environmental management plan for the relevant sectors. The main focus of the project is tourism, and although its impact on environmental degradation is substantial, building the inter-linkages is not easy. In the process of carrying out the SEA, training was provided to the project management team, to the Ministry of Public Works and to the Ministry of Infrastructure. The trained staff managed to give good feedback on how to link several aspects together. Those managing urban infrastructure projects in other islands used the outcomes of the Bali infrastructure SEA in their own projects and applied the lessons learned.

Although the *benefits* of SEA cannot always be definitively measured, or at least are not measured with a reasonably uniform yard stick, it is easier to estimate the *costs* of SEA preparation and relate them to the SEA's impact on decision making. Anecdotal evidence from some of the SEAs and similar instruments that have been reviewed during the World Bank's funding activities show costs of SEA preparation of US$70,000–250,000 and durations from one month to two years or more. Better coordination and reporting between governments and donor agencies will be needed to establish more statistically significant SEA costs and benefits.

Conclusion

Table 17.2 summarizes the performance of the World Bank SEA system against the effectiveness criteria.

Table 17.2 *Evaluation of SEA of land use plans in the World Bank*

Criterion	Criterion met	Comments
World Bank does not have a formal SEA system, so this table reflects emerging SEA practice relating principally to investment lending (OP/BP 4.01)		
SYSTEM CRITERIA		
Legal basis	▲	Bank requires borrower to prepare sectoral or regional EA for sectoral or regional investment lending. No legal requirement for EA of development policy lending
Integration	▲	Integration of SEA done during preparation of land use related lending activities (typically 3–24 months before implementation of activity)
Guidance	▲	Guidance on conducting regional EA exists. No specific guidance on land use planning
Coverage	■	SEA applies if land use planning part of investment project
Tiering	▲	Tiering occurs if borrower engaged in series of 'telescopic' activities, from policy reform to discrete investments. Otherwise, does not occur
Sustainable development	■	SEA system designed to facilitate delivery of sustainable development
PROCESS CRITERIA		
Alternatives	▲	Good practice exists but not universal
Screening	■	Takes place if land use planning part of lending package
Scoping	▲	Good practice exists but not universal.

Table 17.2 *Evaluation of SEA of land use plans in the World Bank (continued)*

Criterion	Criterion met	Comments
Prediction/ evaluation	▲	Good practice exists but not universal
Additional impacts	▲	Good practice exists but not universal
Report preparation	■	SEA reports always prepared and made publicly available
Review	■	Information subjected to public consultation, disclosure in country concerned and worldwide, also to World Bank internal undisclosed review
Monitoring	▲	Strongly recommended by Bank. Not always implemented
Mitigation	■	Mitigation measures always proposed in SEA reports. Implementation varies
Consultation and public participation	■	Information subjected to public consultation, disclosure in country concerned and worldwide, also to World Bank internal undisclosed review
	OUTCOME CRITERIA	
Decision making	□	Has happened in past but not routinely. Influence on decision making at core of present and future efforts to make SEA more effective
Costs and benefits	?	Insufficient information available to evaluate
Environmental quality	▲	Examples exist but not universal
System monitoring	■	World Bank SEA system has been reviewed, leading to changes

Notes: ■ – Yes
　　　▲ – Partially
　　　□ – No
　　　? – Don't know

The ongoing SEA work programme at the World Bank builds on past efforts and is intended to start some new key initiatives, internally as well as externally.[11] On the internal front, the Bank intends to:

1　finalize the review of Bank experience with SEA in a systematic manner in order to continue to learn from good practice and disseminate these lessons;
2　raise the awareness of managers and lead technical specialists about the benefits of SEA for better and more sustainable positive development impacts;
3　provide technical support to staff and clients for the preparation and development of SEAs, in response to Bank policies;

4 encourage new and innovative approaches to SEA that apply the lessons learned from previous SEA experience to new SEAs, including SEAs of land use plans.

Externally, in partnership with other international organizations, the World Bank's development strategy is focused on knowledge sharing and resource mobilization with a view to:

1 participating in the aid agencies' efforts to harmonize approaches to environmental assessments[12];
2 participating in the development of technical guidance on SEA;
3 identifying and making better use of regional and local SEA expertise;
4 participating in larger capacity enhancement and awareness building efforts for the benefit of the Bank's client countries.

Target 9 of Millennium Development Goal (MDG) 7 on environmental sustainability requires countries to 'integrate the principles of sustainable development into country policies and programmes, and reverse the losses of environmental resources.'[13] SEA is clearly a key tool for countries to address this MDG target, not least in helping to assure the sustainability of land use plans.

Notes

1 The views expressed in this chapter are those of the authors and should not be attributed to the World Bank
2 Countries eligible for IDA financing are those that had a per capita income of less than $875 in 2002
3 Other organizations that are part of the World Bank Group include the International Finance Corporation, which lends to the private sector in developing countries; the Multilateral Investment Guarantee Agency, which guarantees investments in client countries; and the International Centre for Settlement of International Disputes which facilitates the settlement of investment disputes between governments and foreign investors
4 See www.worldbank.org for a general introduction to the World Bank, its mission and activities
5 See www.worldbank.org/poverty
6 See www.worldbank.org/sustainabledevelopment
7 See www.worldbank.org/psia
8 See www.worldbank.org/socialanalysis
9 That is, that contribute to the overall sustainable development strategy as laid down in the Rio 1992 Declaration (United Nations Conference on the Environment and Development, 1992) and defined in the specific policies or values of a country
10 See www.iaia.org
11 The Bank will continue to share progress on these internal and external efforts through a combination of events and tools, including the Bank's SEA website: www.worldbank.org/sea
12 See www.aidharmonization.org
13 See www.developmentgoals.org

14   All World Bank related documents referenced below, except those noted, are available
from www.worldbank.org (mostly under 'documents and reports')

References

DHV Consultants (1996) *Bali Urban Infrastructure Programme – Umbrella Environmental Assessment*, Government of Bali, Denpasar

Environmental Resources Management (2003) *Energy-Environment Review*, World Bank/ Egyptian Environmental Affairs Agency[14], Cairo

Global Environment Facility, United Nations Development Programme and World Bank (2001) *Nile River Basin Transboundary Environmental Analysis*, Nile Basin Initiative, Environment Department, WB, Washington, DC

Government of Indonesia (1999) *Water Sector Adjustment Loan: Sectoral Environmental Assessment*, Inter-Agency Task Force on Water Sector Policy Reform, GOI, Jakarta

Kjörven, O. and Lindhjem, H. (2002) *Strategic Environmental Assessment in World Bank Operations*, Environment Strategy Paper 4, Environment Department, World Bank, Washington, DC

Ministerio del Interior (1995) *Flood Protection Project: Regional Environmental Assessment*, Final report, Sub-unidad Central de Coordinación para la Emergencia, MDI, Buenos Aires (in Spanish)[14]

Ministry of Water Resources and Ministry of Population and Environment (1997) *Power Development Project: Sectoral Environmental Assessment*, MWR, His Majesty's Government of Nepal, Katmandu

Mumbai Metropolitan Region Development Authority (2001) *Mumbai Urban Transport Project: Consolidated Environmental Assessment*, MMRDA, Mumbai

ND Lea International (1996) *Gujarat State Highways Project: Sectoral Environmental Assessment*, Roads and Buildings Department, Government of Gujarat, Gandhinagar

Spolka Restrukturyzacji Kopaln (2004) *Hard Coal Mine Closure Environmental Assessment*, SRK, Katowice

United Nations Conference on Environment and Development (1992) *Rio Declaration on Environment and Development: Programme of Action for Sustainable Development*, United Nations, New York

World Bank (1993) *Sectoral Environmental Assessment*, Environmental Assessment Sourcebook Update 4, Environment Department, WB, Washington, DC

World Bank (1996) *Regional Environmental Assessment*, Environmental Assessment Sourcebook Update 15, Environment Department, WB, Washington, DC

World Bank (1999a) *Environmental Assessment*, Bank Procedure 4.01, Operational Manual, WB, Washington, DC

World Bank (1999b) *Environmental Assessment*, Operational Policy 4.01, Operational Manual, WB, Washington, DC

World Bank (2001) *Making Sustainable Commitments: an Environment Strategy for the World Bank*, Environment Department, WB, Washington, DC

World Bank (2004a) *Development Policy Lending*, Bank Procedure 8.60, Operational Manual, WB, Washington, DC

World Bank (2004b) *Development Policy Lending*, Operational Policy 8.60, Operational Manual, WB, Washington, DC

Conclusion

Carys Jones, Mark Baker, Jeremy Carter, Stephen Jay, Michael Short and Christopher Wood

Introduction

This concluding chapter follows the same structure as Chapters 4–17. It commences with a brief discussion of the differing contexts for the SEA of land use plans in the 13 countries and the World Bank covered in this book. The various case studies presented in the different chapters are then reviewed. The evaluation of the SEA of land use plans is split into three sections. An evaluation table drawing together all 14 jurisdictions is presented, which enables comparisons to be drawn between aspects of the SEA systems and, to a lesser extent, between countries.

The evaluation commences with a review of the SEA system criteria followed by a discussion of SEA process criteria, and concludes by discussing the outcome or effectiveness of the SEA of land use plans. Finally, likely future developments in the SEA of land use plans are outlined.

Context

The 13 countries, plus the World Bank, selected for inclusion within this international evaluation of SEA systems together cover a wide range of different land use planning and SEA traditions and experiences. SEA originated within the *US* 35 years ago. A requirement to prepare a SEA report was introduced under the National Environmental Policy Act 1969 which made no distinction between project-based EIA and plan-based assessments. As a result, there is a considerable track record of SEA practice, with hundreds of plan level environmental documents prepared since the 1970s.

A non-mandatory federal SEA system was established in *Canada* in 1990, and subsequently strengthened in 1999 and 2004, within a complex land use and resource planning federal, provincial, territorial and municipal governmental context.

In *New Zealand*, environmental assessment has been intertwined with the statutory planning framework, although not in a formal sense as a prescribed mandatory requirement. The Resource Management Act 1991 provides for plan and policy-based environmental assessment (EA) but the assessment of the environmental effects of projects has a much stronger profile as it is mandatory rather than discretionary.

The high-density living environment in *Hong Kong* has led to a planning system based around three spatial tiers of plan making – territorial, sub-regional and district/local – with an overall framework set by the Territorial Development Strategy (TDS). Although EA has been employed in various plan making activities since the early 1990s, the TDS was subject to the first formal application of SEA in Hong Kong.

The political and historical (apartheid) context has given the *South African* land use planning system distinct characteristics. Although some EAs date from the 1970s and EIA requirements were introduced by 1997, recent developments have seen the introduction of new forms of integrated development planning, which include requirements relating to SEA.

The context for SEA within many developing countries has been through the policies and requirements of the *World Bank*. Although there is no mandatory World Bank requirement for the SEA of land use plans in its client countries, SEAs, regional EAs, sectoral EAs and other types of SEA have been carried out in compliance with recently strengthened Bank policies.

As explained in Chapter 1, European countries were required to implement the requirements set out in the European SEA Directive by July 2004. This has given an enormous boost to current developments in SEA procedures and practice, and led to a coalescence of SEA systems operating within European countries. However, past SEA experience and individual land use planning contexts are often very different. *Denmark* has a longstanding land use planning system involving strategy and plan-making activities at the regional, municipal and local levels. SEA has been a voluntary part of this system since 1997, becoming a formal requirement in 2004.

Similarly, voluntary SEA has been a characteristic of the *Swedish* land use planning system since the late 1980s. These voluntary initiatives have been undertaken at the municipal level, which dominates the Swedish land use planning system.

In *Germany*, there has been extensive SEA-type experience in the complex multi-tier land use planning system through the highly developed system of landscape plans that operate at a variety of spatial scales and are equivalent to SEAs.

Portugal's land use planning system also operates at regional, national and local scales. The non-standard approach to plan making makes the implementation of SEA requirements very challenging, as SEA has not yet been applied to the generally weak strategic decision-making processes.

There have been immense upheavals in the laws and institutional frameworks that constitute the two-tier land use planning system in *Hungary*. SEA has not been a specific requirement of the current plan-making process, which essentially operates through counties and municipalities, and as a result the only formal SEA carried out to date relates to the Regional Operational Programme of the National Development Plan.

The land use planning system in *Ireland* is based on the provisions of the Planning and Development Act 2000, and involves a hierarchy of plans and programmes that could feasibly undergo SEA. There was no formal procedure for, and little experience of, SEA within the planning process prior to the implementation of the SEA Directive.

Sustainability appraisal (SA) (intended to meet the requirements of the SEA Directive) is being undertaken at all levels of plan making, from the regional to the local, in the complex *UK* (English) planning system, which is currently being reformed. SEA-type environmental appraisals of plans have been undertaken since the early 1990s although, like SA, these have generally taken the form of 'objectives-led' approaches rather than the 'baseline-led' approach advocated in the SEA Directive.

The *Netherlands* has a long tradition of land use planning at three major tiers of government – national, provincial and municipal. While there has been no formal tradition of the SEA of large-scale land use plans, SEA trials have been run and small scale land use plan SEAs have been undertaken.

As more SEAs are undertaken in the 13 countries and the World Bank, they may expose the complications, illogicalities and duplications in many land use planning systems such as those in Germany and in the UK. There may well also be pressure to strengthen the SEA of the national policies that influence land use planning in these countries. Furthermore, it is likely that they will seek to encourage the extension and strengthening of both SEA and land use planning in the countries that receive aid from them, as the World Bank intends to do in collaboration with other aid agencies (see also Therivel, 2004, p209).

Case studies

The case studies presented in Chapters 4–17 examine a broad range of assessment experiences and outline how SEA can be practically implemented in land use planning. The diversity of case studies illustrates an interesting cross section of the main issues influencing implementation of SEA legislation and guidance. The examples from Hungary, The Netherlands, South Africa, Sweden, the UK and the World Bank illustrate, in different ways, how the general principles of SEA can be implemented in diverse contexts. The cases from Denmark, Hong Kong and the US illustrate the place of best practice examples in SEA and land use planning, thereby assisting understanding of where strengths lie in practice.

The importance of public participation in the SEA and land use planning processes is exemplified in the New Zealand and Canada cases, particularly in relation to the involvement of native peoples in decision making. The role of public hearings as part of the SEA process in Canada is also of particular interest. In New Zealand, an informal approach to SEA and land use planning provides a comparison with those countries where SEA is far more formalized. The Irish pilot SEA indicates how practical use of SEA is being introduced into land use planning in Ireland. The German case study offers an interesting and informative view of how the monitoring element of SEA practice can be addressed. Finally, in Portugal, the paucity of SEA experiences in land use planning meant that no suitable example could be described (hence the presentation of the guidance preparation practice case study).

The case studies reflect the cultural, legislative and institutional contexts of each jurisdiction covered in this book, and the flexibility of the applicability of SEA to land use planning. Most of the examples selected seek to show how SEA can be introduced into land use planning to improve the consideration of environmental concerns in decision making. Inevitably, since no formal SEA system was in place in many of the jurisdictions when the case studies were undertaken, many weaknesses in the SEA of land use plans are revealed. It is likely that, if the case studies were to be selected a few years later, many of these weaknesses will have been addressed as a result of the improved practice necessitated by formal SEA requirements.

SEA systems

The overall evaluation of the 13 countries and the World Bank against the 20 criteria is shown in Table 18.1. System criteria refer to the pre-conditions for SEA, and indicate the extent to which an adequate framework is in place for effective SEA to be carried out. It can be seen that these system inputs to the SEA of land use plans perform less well than do process inputs, but better than SEA outcomes (effectiveness outputs).

A *legal basis* for the SEA of land use planning can ensure that SEA is applied to a full range of plans, and is practised to certain standards. The US was the first to have strict legal requirements for SEA (for federal land use plans, required under the National Environmental Policy Act). All eight European Union (EU) countries now have, or are in the process of establishing, a strong legal basis for SEA, as they implement the SEA Directive. They are doing so in different ways, in line with their legal traditions, but are generally bringing into force legislation that implements the SEA Directive to the letter, rather than going beyond its requirements.

Elsewhere, legal provisions for the SEA of land use planning are partial or weak – for example, New Zealand's Resource Management Act implies that certain elements of SEA should be carried out for planning activities, but does not formally require SEA. Although it can be argued that SEA has benefited from the flexibility that a lack of codification permits (Therivel and Partidário, 1996), there does appear to be some correlation between a strong legal basis and the completeness of the ensuing process (Table 18.1).

Table 18.1 *Evaluation of SEA of land use plans*

Criterion	Canada	Denmark	Germany	Hong Kong	Hungary	Ireland	The Netherlands	New Zealand	Portugal	South Africa	Sweden	United Kingdom	United States	World Bank
SYSTEM CRITERIA														
Legal basis	□	■	■	▲	■	■	■	▲	□	▲	■	■	■	▲
Integration	■	■	■	■	▲	■	▲	■	▲	▲	▲	▲	▲	▲
Guidance	■	▲	▲	■	▲	▲	▲	▲	■	□	■	■	■	■
Coverage	▲	■	■	▲	■	■	■	▲	■	▲	■	■	▲	■
Tiering	□	■	▲	■	□	■	▲	▲	~	▲	▲	▲	▲	▲
Sustainable development	■	■	▲	■	□	■	□	▲	~	■	▲	▲	□	■
PROCESS CRITERIA														
Alternatives	▲	■	■	■	■	■	■	■	▲	■	▲	■	■	■
Screening	■	■	■	■	■	■	▲	▲	▲	■	▲	■	▲	▲
Scoping	▲	■	▲	■	■	■	~	▲	▲	■	▲	■	■	▲
Prediction/evaluation	▲	■	■	▲	■	■	■	▲	▲	■	▲	▲	■	▲
Additional impacts	▲	■	▲	■	▲	▲	■	▲	▲	▲	□	■	□	▲
Report preparation	■	■	■	■	■	■	■	▲	▲	□	■	■	■	■
Review	□	■	▲	■	■	▲	▲	■	▲	■	▲	▲	■	■
Monitoring	▲	▲	■	■	■	■	■	▲	▲	■	□	▲	▲	▲
Mitigation	■	■	■	■	■	▲	▲	■	~	□	▲	■	▲	■
Consultation and public participation	▲	■	■	▲	■	■	■	■	▲	■	▲	■	■	■
OUTCOME CRITERIA														
Decision making	□	■	■	■	~	~	~	▲	~	~	~	▲	▲	□
Costs and benefits	■	■	■	▲	~	~	~	~	~	~	■	▲	□	~
Environmental quality	□	~	▲	▲	~	~	▲	~	~	~	~	~	▲	▲
System monitoring	■	▲	▲	▲	~	~	■	▲	~	□	□	~	□	■

Notes: ■ – Yes
▲ – Partially
□ – No
~ – Don't know
Country performance comparisons should be made with great caution since they rely on different authors' uncalibrated judgements

The degree of *integration* of SEA with plan making is likely to determine the extent to which a plan will be shaped by the findings of SEA. All the SEA systems evaluated stipulate or recommend integration, to a greater or lesser extent. For example, Canadian guidance states that the early integration of environmental considerations into policy and plan development is a key SEA principle. Similarly, some EU countries, such as Ireland, are implementing the SEA Directive in a way that ensures the full integration of SEA with plan preparation. Where this criterion is only partially met, integration may be recommended but not necessarily carried out (for example, Portugal), or conversely, sometimes practised even when not required (for example, Sweden). Overall, there is a growing recognition of the importance of integration to good practice SEA (Fischer, 2001), although this is not yet being translated into regulatory requirements.

Most of the 14 systems have some form of SEA *guidance* in place or forthcoming, geared either fully or partly to land use planning. In EU countries, this is largely in response to the SEA Directive; for instance, the UK is developing elaborate guidance to assist planning authorities in carrying out SA that meets the directive's requirements. Elsewhere, guidance tends to be limited (for example, the US) or not specific to planning (for instance, South Africa). In Hong Kong, however, a case-by-case approach is taken, with a study brief being issued by the Environmental Protection Department for each SEA. The value of guidance, particularly at capacity building stages (Partidário, 1996), is thus largely being recognized.

A SEA system should be comprehensive in its *coverage* of both land use plans and of the environmental effects considered. The EU countries now meet this criterion fully, by virtue of the requirements of the SEA Directive; all land use plans above certain thresholds are subject to SEA, generally from the regional level downwards, and should be assessed for a wide range of possible impacts. This may represent a totally new assessment of plans (as in Portugal) or an expansion of coverage (for example, in The Netherlands). In Hungary, however, some retraction of coverage seems likely.

The SEA Directive is therefore having the effect of standardization of coverage within the EU. In most countries, it will also lead to more detailed assessment than formerly was the case (for instance, in Sweden). Elsewhere, this criterion is also met, either fully or partially. In the US, for example, programmatic EISs are prepared for most federal land use plans, whereas the SEA of some land use plans in Canada depends on whether or not circumstances warrant.

Tiering indicates the extent to which SEA is organized hierarchically, with one level of assessment informing the next level down (through to project level EIA). The extent to which the SEA systems evaluated meet this criterion varies considerably and depends largely on the extent to which land use plans are tiered. In Hong Kong, for example, clearly defined levels of planning strategies and plans provide a strong basis for a parallel system of SEA. Similarly, in Ireland, SEA is being fitted to a hierarchical planning system (although with the absence of policy level SEA). However, where the organization of land use planning is more complex (e.g. in Germany), practice departs from the ideal, and tiering is compromised (Noble, 2000).

Furthermore, potential linkages are not always formalized, especially between SEA and EIA (e.g. in Canada). Nonetheless, tiering may occur opportunistically even if no strict system is in place; for instance, SEAs carried out by the World Bank have provided the basis for subsequent project level assessments.

The concept of *sustainable development* is increasingly providing a set of fundamental goals to which SEA should contribute. However, the SEA systems vary in the extent to which they are placed in this context. Some are set explicitly in a sustainable development framework, most notably South Africa, where sustainability objectives are central to planning legislation and to SEA. Some EU countries also echo the SEA Directive's objective of promoting sustainable development in their legislation (for example, Denmark), although not all make reference to this (for instance, Hungary). Even where it is not directly referred to, however, the underlying themes of sustainable development may be implied (e.g. in the US – see Chapter 1). Much depends here on the prominence of the notion of sustainable development in the land use plans assessed (Briassoulis, 1999).

The overall picture that emerges for system criteria is therefore one in which firmer legal and administrative foundations are being laid down for the SEA of land use plans. This is generally occurring in parallel with the expanding agenda of sustainable development, especially where planning has itself been explicitly linked to its achievement. In addition, stronger and more formal links are being forged between SEA and the planning systems covered in this book, through the more comprehensive coverage of plans being assessed, and through the integration of SEA processes with plan making, insofar as planning structures and procedures allow (Eggenberger and Partidário, 2000).

SEA processes

SEA systems shape the processes for undertaking the SEA of land use plans. The performance of SEA process elements (inputs) against the evaluation criteria is stronger than that of either SEA system inputs or outcomes (outputs) (Table 18.1). Part of the rationale for SEA, and a major perceived benefit of the process, is the consideration of *alternatives*. This is covered, either fully or partially, in all 14 SEA systems. The implementation of the SEA Directive between them will require both consideration of alternatives and provision of reasons for choices.

However, SEA practice is limited with performance often being weak. In Hong Kong and New Zealand there is some evidence that alternatives have been addressed, with instances of good practice for some World Bank-funded schemes. The extent to which SEA should influence the choice of a preferred action, and the level of assessment to be applied to each alternative (Noble, 2000), is yet to be fully resolved.

Screening to identify land use plans to be subject to SEA does not appear to be a significant issue in the SEA process, with the majority of the systems containing clear specifications in their legislation and/or guidance, including those transposing the requirements of the SEA Directive. The recognition that most plans require SEA renders screening a relatively minor element of the US system. In New

Zealand, screening is part of plan preparation, and is included for World Bank schemes if land use planning is part of a lending package. A range of approaches is evident (Therivel, 2004), including criteria and thresholds (the most popular approach), lists (The Netherlands and Sweden), and case-by-case evaluation (Denmark). In the South African system, screening is regarded as a key element but criteria are lacking. Overall, practice appears to work reasonably well.

There is clear recognition of the importance (Therivel and Brown, 1999) of *scoping*, which is now an integral part of SEA in the US. In Hong Kong, scoping has a sustainable development focus and occurs as part of the baseline study, whereas in New Zealand, scoping is part of plan preparation. Consultation clearly plays a role, with Hungary, Ireland and the UK specifying input from environmental authorities. Only Denmark emphasizes a distinct role for the public in scoping. Overall, there is no evidence of specific techniques or approaches being recommended. Practice includes broad coverage of potential impacts in Sweden and some (but not universal) good examples from World Bank assessments.

The *prediction/evaluation* of likely effects is an integral part of SEA involving either evaluation of changes from a baseline, or testing proposals against environmental objectives (Partidário, 1996; Sheate, 2001). While the EU member states need to comply with the baseline-led approach of the SEA Directive, there is experience of a variety of other approaches, including the use of standards (such as for air and water modelling in Hungary) and matrices (in Ireland, Sweden and the UK). Most member states intend to combine the required baseline approach with a variety of policy appraisal tools (also utilized in South Africa) such as objectives, criteria, indices, scenarios and options. Overall, the prediction of impacts in SEA remains somewhat undeveloped.

Their poor coverage in project level EIA has led to *additional impacts* (secondary, synergistic or cumulative) long being regarded as best considered through SEA (Wood and Djeddour, 1992). Indeed, SEA legislation such as the European SEA Directive makes specific reference to such impacts. However, the coverage of these additional impacts in legislation is partial. In addition, overall practice is not encouraging. The World Bank cites good practice in coverage of these impacts but this is not universal. It is disappointing that, notwithstanding the professed aim of SEA to deal with such impacts, this criterion had a relatively low level of compliance compared with the other process criteria.

Documentation of the SEA process and its findings during *report preparation* (Verheem and Tonk, 2000) to record the process and aid transparency is apparent in most systems, with such reports usually being publicly available. The SEA Directive requires EU member states to include specific elements in SEA reports, with some already being part of routine practice. Even where a separate report is not yet a legislative requirement, the associated land use plan often includes many of the relevant elements. Portuguese guidance indicates a more intricate approach with a report at each of four key, distinct methodological stages.

A clear and transparent *review* stage (Verheem and Tonk, 2000), with publicly available findings, is evident or proposed for all the systems evaluated. Approaches vary, with implied review in Ireland through the requirement for quality control, internal checks in Canada, earlier public participation fulfilling the review function in Denmark, and review being part of the wider planning context in New Zealand. The option of independent review exists in The Netherlands. The integration of review with plan assessment is recommended in Portugal to avoid overload of resources. Existing review practice tends to vary considerably.

The 14 jurisdictions demonstrate commitment to *monitoring* as a check on the achievement of plan objectives, on the success of mitigation measures, and on the verification of predictions (Therivel and Brown, 1999). Nevertheless, existing practice is variable with some systems having little (e.g. Sweden) or no (as in Hungary) experience of monitoring for land use plans. However, there is experience of monitoring through the planning process (e.g. in Germany) and other environmental monitoring regimes (as in Ireland), which provides a basis for SEA monitoring. In The Netherlands, it is recognized that monitoring may be most appropriate through subsequent projects. However, the difficulty of ensuring compliance is highlighted, as is the lack of follow-up of progress (for instance, in Canada).

The concept of *mitigation* through enhancement of environmental benefits and reduction of negative effects (Therivel and Brown, 1999) is broadly recognized in the 14 SEA processes. Examples of good practice exist (as in Canada), with only South Africa lacking any requirement to develop mitigation strategies. Mitigation can take various forms, such as the minimization of impacts on subsequent development sites in Germany. The integration of land use planning and SEA in the US allows early mitigation to influence plans, and mitigation is always proposed in World Bank SEA reports. However, practice in all the 14 systems varies.

There is widespread recognition of the key importance of early and wide *consultation and public participation* (CPP) (Curran et al, 1998). There is clearly a high level of commitment to this element of the SEA process in the systems evaluated. Nevertheless, systems differ as to when CPP is required and whether environmental authorities and/or the public are involved. Thus, New Zealand includes CPP during plan development and when changes to the plan are considered, Ireland focuses on screening and scoping, and the UK involves environmental authorities in screening and scoping and the public only when the report has been prepared. The transboundary implications of CPP are highlighted by Hungary and Ireland. Despite the perceived importance of CPP, practice is variable in the 14 SEA systems, with both good and bad examples evident.

The commitment to SEA process elements is encouraging in a climate of rapid change. However, despite strong commitment to the principles of the SEA process, wider practical experience is relatively limited. Even in systems where the concept of SEA has existed for some time, several process elements have yet to be developed in full. Unsurprisingly, few systems possess methodological and technical guidance on undertaking the process elements of SEA. The weaker elements, particularly treatment of additional impacts, and even CPP, will need particular focus to achieve practical success.

SEA outcomes

Outcome criteria relate to the impact of undertaking the SEA process. They concern the effect of SEA on the preparation of land use plans, and beyond that, on such critical issues as environmental quality. Unsurprisingly, since SEA outcomes measure outputs, or the effectiveness of the SEA of land use plans (Thissen, 2000), the performance of the 13 countries and the World Bank against these evaluation criteria is weaker than for the process quality determinants (whether system or process inputs) (Table 18.1).

The effect of SEA procedures on *decision making* is a key outcome criterion. As Sadler and Verheem (1996) noted, SEA can be viewed as a decision-aiding tool. Despite the fact that, in theory, SEA can help to improve the quality of decisions, the experience of the countries referred to within this book indicate that this may not always happen in practice. In over one-third of the countries, the influence of SEA on decision making is currently unknown, principally because the outcomes of SEA procedures have yet to be evaluated. Furthermore, in Ireland and Portugal, for example, the SEA systems are not yet sufficiently advanced to be expected to influence decision-making procedures.

Nevertheless, in some SEA systems, notably Hong Kong and Denmark, there is evidence of beneficial influences of SEA on land use planning decisions. Moreover, in other cases, including Hungary and the UK, it seems that SEA may have a partial influence on the outcome of land use planning decisions informed by SEA.

This book has provided an indication of the *costs and benefits* associated with the SEA of land use plans. In over one-third of the countries explored, including Sweden, Hong Kong and Canada, the benefits of SEA are believed to have outweighed any costs associated with the process, which usually relate to time and financial expense. Examples of benefits experienced as a result of undertaking SEA during land use plan preparation include raising awareness of negative environmental impacts, allowing them to be minimized, the generation of consensus between different stakeholder groups and the strengthening of planning procedures from an environmental perspective.

Despite these positive findings, however, it is apparent that no definitive judgement about the effectiveness of the SEA process, or whether the costs of SEA are outweighed by the benefits of the process, can yet be made in the majority of countries. Even where there is insufficient information to decide on this issue, there is generally optimism about the potential of the SEA process to create benefits in the future. Moreover, as Wood (2002) suggested, the spread of SEA across the globe (often in the absence of any formal legislative requirements) indicates that the benefits of the process are perceived to outweigh any associated costs.

SEA has the potential to improve *environmental quality*. As Sadler (2001, p26) noted:

> *SEA is a process to systematically analyse and document the environmental effects and consequences of proposed strategic actions.*

As environmental issues must be considered as part of any transparent, accountable and holistic decision-making system, SEA can make a crucial contribution to improving environmental quality. Despite the potential of SEA in this respect, only in Hong Kong is it claimed that SEA has improved environmental quality by protecting key natural habitats and introducing environmental considerations into other policy areas. However, in the majority of the 14 systems, the influence of SEA on environmental quality is thought to be, at best, partial. Furthermore, it is often stated – for reasons that include a lack of information and the influence of other variables aside from SEA – that it is not yet possible to determine the influence of SEA on environmental quality.

Only through SEA *system monitoring* will it be possible to determine whether the theoretical benefits of undertaking SEA, including strengthening decision making and improving environmental quality, are more than aspirational goals. Monitoring should help to determine more clearly the costs and benefits associated with the SEA of land use plans, and to secure the resources to develop SEA in the future. The review of SEA reports and their outcomes on a countrywide basis can help to determine the effectiveness of the SEA process.

It is revealing that system monitoring procedures exist in only three of the SEA systems explored in this book, namely Canada, The Netherlands and the World Bank. In the case of Canada, the review undertaken by the government was critical of SEA practice and its influence on public sector policy making. Although a sobering picture of the Canadian SEA system was revealed, the system monitoring procedures have nevertheless provided an opportunity to improve the effectiveness of the system. Similarly, the last review of the World Bank SEA system resulted in changes to the procedures employed. Experience suggests, therefore, that where system monitoring procedures do exist, they have the potential to influence SEA procedures beneficially.

Future developments in SEA

It is clear from Table 18.1 that Denmark and Hong Kong appear to have the strongest SEA of land use plans, whereas Portugal and South Africa have the weakest. However, as explained in Chapter 1, tabular country comparisons should be treated with greater caution than country criteria performance comparisons. Many desirable future developments were discussed or implied in Chapters 4–17. However, only those future developments that were specifically mentioned in the conclusions to those chapters are reported in this final section.

Perhaps the most obvious future development in the SEA of land use plans is the clarification and strengthening of its institutional and *legal basis*. This was mentioned in relation to Canada, Germany, Hungary, The Netherlands, Portugal and South Africa, although the point was made in relation to New Zealand that legislation is not essential provided the will to undertake SEA exists. The early and complete *integration* of SEA with land use planning appears to be an inexorable trend if the aspirations expressed in relation to Denmark, Hong Kong, The Netherlands, New Zealand, South Africa, Sweden, the UK and the US are any guide. Better *guidance* on procedural and methodological aspects of SEA remains an overt priority in Canada, South Africa, the US (notwithstanding the wealth of its experience) and the World Bank.

While extending the *coverage* of SEA to national and state plans was mentioned specifically in relation to Germany, extending the coverage of SEA to economic and social factors was thought to be important in Portugal, and the resolution of the SEA/sustainability appraisal dichotomy was seen as being an issue in the UK. *Tiering*, both in regard to the SEA of related plans and policies and to the EIA of projects, was regarded as a critical issue in Hong Kong, Ireland, Portugal, South Africa and the World Bank. The associated goals of communication, flexibility and harmonization were stressed by Ireland and Portugal, South Africa and the World Bank respectively. The alignment of SEA with *sustainable development* goals was emphasized explicitly only in relation to South Africa and implicitly only in relation to Sweden.

Better treatment of appropriate *alternatives* in SEA was emphasized in relation to Denmark and The Netherlands. The need for better *screening*, especially of land use plans for small areas, was mentioned in relation to Hungary, Ireland and South Africa. The need to ensure that there was appropriate public participation in *scoping* in Irish SEA was highlighted, reflecting the positive Danish experience of early CPP. Several points were made about further developments in *prediction/evaluation* in SEA. Improved data-gathering was important in Canada and Hong Kong, the need to define environmental objectives, indicators and thresholds was stressed in Ireland and South Africa, and the need to encourage new and innovative approaches to SEA was noted in South Africa.

It is interesting that the need to improve the poorly handled treatment of *additional impacts* in SEA was not mentioned at all (Table 18.1). It was observed that there was a need to strengthen the documentation of the SEA process during *report preparation* in Canada. The need for a reputable *review* body in The Netherlands, and for independent third party reviewers in Portugal, was stressed. Improved *monitoring* of SEAs was regarded as crucial in relation to Hong Kong (if SEA was not to become a paper exercise), Ireland and South Africa. No future developments in *mitigation* in SEA were mentioned. Apart from the advantages of improving public participation in scoping (above), the need for *consultation and public participation* at the different SEA stages to be handled carefully was emphasized in relation to Hong Kong and Portugal.

The need for SEA to be properly taken into account in existing *decision-making* processes was, perhaps surprisingly, only mentioned in relation to Hong Kong. The necessity to ensure that the *costs and benefits* of SEA were properly balanced was emphasized in South Africa (where it was necessary to be efficient and to avoid complexity) and in Sweden and at the World Bank (where it was felt that the advantages of undertaking SEA needed to be publicized).

No future developments in improving *environmental quality* through SEA were mentioned although, as with striving for sustainable development and many other criteria, this is implicit throughout. The need for SEA *system monitoring* to learn from experience, fill implementation gaps and disseminate good practice was emphasized in relation to Canada, South Africa, Sweden and the World Bank.

The importance of *expertise* in the future development of SEA was emphasized in relation to several jurisdictions. In Denmark, the need for SEA to be undertaken by planners, rather than by environmental experts, was stressed whereas suitable technical oversight was sought in Hong Kong. The need to build appropriate SEA capacity was considered to be crucial in Portugal, South Africa and the World Bank (where identifying and making better use of local SEA expertise was a goal). The necessity to train SEA practitioners is apparent.

Interestingly, *research* into SEA procedures and methodologies was only mentioned twice. In Sweden, the need for comparative studies to learn from the experience of other countries was considered to be desirable. In the UK, comparative research on English and Scottish SEA experience was recommended to ascertain the respective merits of SEA and SA approaches.

The burgeoning practice of SEA will drive both methodological and procedural research over the coming years, and another set of case studies similar to those reported in this book undertaken in the future would undoubtedly reveal numerous interesting developments.

It appears that, while the potential of SEA to reduce the negative and enhance the positive environmental impacts associated with the implementation of land use plans remains, many of the constraints upon the development of SEA tabulated in Chapter 2 continue to apply. While some of the opportunities listed in Chapter 2 are beginning to be grasped, many are unachieved. Hopefully, the inevitable improvements to SEA practice in the future will be accompanied by the realization of the opportunities of SEA. Then SEA will start to deliver its promise (Chapter 1) to improve the environment, to raise environmental awareness and to help to achieve sustainable development goals.

References

Briassoulis, H. (1999) 'Who plans whose sustainability? Alternative roles for planners', *Journal of Environmental Planning and Management*, vol 42, pp889–902

Curran, J. M., Wood, C. M. and Hilton, M. (1998) 'Environmental appraisal of UK development plans: current practice and future directions', *Environment and Planning B: Planning and Design*, vol 25, pp411–433

Eggenberger, M. and Partidário, M. (2000) 'Development of a framework to assist the integration of environmental, social and economic issues in spatial planning', *Impact Assessment and Project Appraisal*, vol 18, pp201–207

Fischer, T. B. (2001) 'Practice of environmental assessment for transport and land-use policies, plans and programmes', *Impact Assessment and Project Appraisal*, vol 19, pp41–51

Noble, B. (2000) 'Strategic environmental assessment: what is it? and what makes it strategic?' *Journal of Environmental Assessment Policy and Management*, vol 2, pp203–224

Partidário, M. (1996) 'Strategic environmental assessment: key issues emerging from recent practice', *Environmental Impact Assessment Review*, vol 16, pp31–55

Sadler, B. (2001) 'A framework approach to strategic environmental assessment: aims, principles and elements of good practice', in Dusik, J. (ed) *Proceedings of International*

Workshop on Public Participation and Health Aspects in Strategic Environmental Assessment, Regional Environmental Center for Central and Eastern Europe, Szentendre

Sadler, B. and Verheem, R. (1996) *Strategic Environmental Assessment: Status, Challenges and Future Directions*, Publication Number 53, Ministry of Housing, Spatial Planning and the Environment, The Hague

Sheate, W. (2001) 'The rise of strategic assessment tools', *Journal of Environmental Assessment Policy and Management*, vol 3 pp iii–x

Therivel, R. (2004) *Strategic Environmental Assessment in Action*, Earthscan, London

Therivel, R. and Brown, A. L. (1999) 'Methods of strategic environmental assessment', in Petts, J. (ed) *Handbook of Environmental Impact Assessment*, Volume 1, Blackwell, Oxford

Therivel, R. and Partidário, M. (eds) (1996) *The Practice of Strategic Environmental Assessment*, Earthscan, London

Thissen, W. A. H. (2000) 'Criteria for evaluation of SEA', in Partidário, M. and Clark, R. (eds) *Perspectives on Strategic Environmental Assessment*, Lewis Publishers/CRC Press, Boca Raton, FL

Verheem, R. and Tonk, J. (2000) 'Strategic environmental assessment: one concept, multiple forms', *Impact Assessment and Project Appraisal*, vol 18, pp177–182

Wood, C. M. (2002) *Environmental Impact Assessment: a Comparative Review*, 2nd edition, Prentice Hall, Harlow

Wood, C. M. and Djeddour, M. (1992) 'Strategic environmental assessment: EA of policies, plans and programmes' *Impact Assessment Bulletin*, vol 10, pp3–22

Index

Page numbers in *italics* refer to Figures, Tables and Boxes.
The acronym SEA is used for 'strategic environmental assessment' throughout the index.